DISCARD

CHRISTIAN COMMUNICATION

A Bibliographical Survey

Compiled by
Paul A. Soukup

Bibliographies and Indexes in Religious Studies, Number 14
G. E. Gorman, Advisory Editor

GREENWOOD PRESS
New York • Westport, Connecticut • London

Library of Congress Cataloging-in-Publication Data

Soukup, Paul A.
   Christian communication : a bibliographical survey / compiled by
Paul A. Soukup.
      p.   cm.—(Bibliographies and indexes in religious studies,
   ISSN 0742-6836 ; no. 14)
   Includes indexes.
   ISBN 0-313-25673-X (lib. bdg. : alk. paper)
      1. Communication—Religious aspects—Christianity—Bibliography.
   2. Communication—Bibliography.   I. Title.   II. Series.
   Z5633.R45S66   1989
   [BV4319]
   016.3022′0242—dc20   89-12076

British Library Cataloguing in Publication Data is available.

Library of Congress Catalog Card Number: 89-12076
ISBN: 0-313-25673-X
ISSN: 0742-6836

First published in 1989

Greenwood Press, Inc.
88 Post Road West, Westport, Connecticut 06881

Printed in the United States of America

The paper used in this book complies with the
Permanent Paper Standard issued by the National
Information Standards Organization (Z39.48-1984).

10 9 8 7 6 5 4 3 2 1

Contents

Foreword

As part of the Greenwood Press series entitled Bibliographies and Indexes in Religious Studies, we have developed a subsidiary series of bibliographic surveys dealing with a broad range of topics in religion and theology. The purpose of these surveys is to cover both general disciplines and discrete subjects of interest to the scholarly community which have not received detailed treatment in recent years. Each work is meant to stand as a self-contained unit and consists of a substantial introduction to the subject viewed through the literature plus an annotated guide to serial and mono-graph literature which the author believes is important to an adequate understanding of the topic. The first part of each volume, the introductory essay or survey chapter, discusses the development of the subject in terms of key concepts and seminal or controversial works; the annotated biblio-graphy which follows this analysis is intended to substantiate and extend the introductory remarks by surveying a widely representative sample of literature from all traditions and viewpoints related to the topic.

Within this broad framework the Advisory Editor has two aims in mind: first, to cover all traditions, Western and non-Western, which might fit the most generous definition of "religion"; second, to devise a series of subject-oriented volumes which, within a given discipline, would range from the general to the specific in order to provide a thorough survey of all areas and segments of a subject. It is with this framework in mind that Dr. Paul Soukup, S. J., of Santa Clara University has prepared his bibliographical study of Christian communication.

When first considering this topic and discussing it outside the small cir-cle of Christian communicators, there were regularly two reactions that say much about the raison d'etre for Dr. Soukup's study. First, colleagues who teach in the general area of media and communication studies tend to ask, "What is *Christian* about communication?" Second, many professionals within the Christian tradition seem to feel that Christian communication refers primarily to the "electronic" church as exemplified by Praise the Lord, Jimmy Swaggert *et al.* Of course there are those that take a some-what broader view and include homiletics and interpersonal communication as important components of the Christian life; but on the whole those who should know better, either by virtue of training or religious commitment, appear strikingly naive with regard to the full significance, the genuine vulnerability and broad influence of Christian communication, both inside and outside the churches. Part of the problem, and one at which Dr. Soukup hints in his opening chapter, is the lack of substantive, systematic study of this interdisciplinary area and the concomitant failure of the church to have developed a theology of communication. And this in turn may be a manifestation of the interdisciplinary complexity of Christian communication, a field encompassing not only communication theory and rhetoric but also interpersonal communication, mass media, cultural and visual arts, and a host of theological subdisciplines—evangelization, social ethics, liturgy, catechesis, etc.

The complexities to which we are alluding should become strikingly apparent if one recognizes that communication, from the Latin *communicare* ("to share"), has the same root as communion, from the Latin *communio* ("general participation"); both are from *communis* ("common"). Accordingly, one may say that the various types of communion which are central to Christian doctrine and practice are clearly communication-based. At the risk of wandering into the realm of symbol and metaphor, it should be possible to recognize aspects of communication within the several communion relationships that typify semitic religions, whether these are referred to as vertical and horizontal or, more descriptively, as God-man, man-man, man-community. In the case of vertical communion/communication, for instance, a particular Judaeo-Christian heritage is a specific arrangement of symbols and stories designed to re-create and preserve a God-man experience. Most typically, the symbols and stories which exemplify the communication between God and man eventually are systematized into creeds, the purposes of which are to define and codify the meaning and faith content of the communication/communion experience. Much, perhaps even most, theological language in this context is an effort to communicate the sense of "unity with the other" and the experience of grace that comes with communion. Andrew Greeley clinically but clearly summarizes the essence of vertical communion: "often the experience of goodness involves a feeling that one has been the object of communication. Often, also, it is felt that it is possible to communicate back to the other."[1] If vertical communion possess such a clear communication component, how much more is this the case in man-man and man-community relationships, whether in secular or sacred settings. Much of the literature on social responsibility and ethics, on liturgy and ritual and on doctrine and catechesis deals with aspects of horizontal—and indeed vertical—communion/communication. The horizontal consequences of Christian communion and communication have been succinctly stated by John Paul II, although not in this specific

---

[1] Andrew Greeley, *Religion: A Secular Theory* (New York: Free Press, 1982) 108.

context: "bringing people together in fraternal unity, especially the poor; serving them, sharing with them the bread of the earth and the bread of love; building up with them a more just world ..."[2]

Given these intricacies and the broad scope of the discipline, Dr. Soukup has tackled a field that is perversely indeterminate; this has been made all the more difficult by his intentionally inclusive understanding of Christian communication—it refers to "any communication used by the Christian churches and to a quality or style of communication consistent with Christian ethics or practices." Homiletics, probably the one genuinely well developed aspect of the subject because of evangelical Protestant concentration on this as a key to Christian formation, is not treated; it may well form a separate title in this series. In his introductory chapter Father Soukup provides a brief but broadly indicative outline of the history and issues of Christian communication, as well as a clear summary of the various approaches to its study. This I believe is an excellent starting point for anyone new to the field, as its wide coverage is matched by a most accessible style and presentation. The range of references in this survey suggests that Dr. Soukup is immensely well-read in his field, and this is borne out by the bibliography which constitutes the bulk of the work. In its comprehensiveness, depth, and detail this analysis of literature on Christian communication far exceeds anything attempted to date by any organization or scholar. Accordingly, it should guide students firmly through the maze of available literature, and it should also help scholars to broaden their competence in the several areas which constitute this discipline. If Paul Soukup's work fulfills these aims, it will more than repay its progenitor for the efforts involved. Beyond that one hopes that its admirable treatment may serve as the bibliographical starting point for a fully developed theology of communication.

G. E. Gorman
Advisory Editor
Riverina-Murray Institute of Higher Education
Wagga Wagga NSW Australia

---

[2] Dermot A. Lane, *Foundations for a Social Theology: Praxis, Process and Salvation* (Dublin: Gill and Macmillan, 1984) 153. John Paul was making these comments in the context of the 42nd International Eucharistic Congress and the re-emerging relationship between the eucharist and social justice. For Christians these desired effects of the eucharist can be taken as a model for the role of communication/communion in all horizontal relationships.

Preface

This book attempts to provide an introductory guide to the study of Christian communication by surveying and annotating a fairly representative cross section of literature. It differs from other bibliographic guides (for example, Hill [65], Adams [52], Soukup [70]) primarily in this: it does not limit its scope to any one area of communication—television or dance or theory, for example. Rather, this book includes all the general categories of communication studies: language, interpersonal communication, and the variety of media, both large and small. Similarly, it does not limit the definition of "Christian communication." In this volume, Christian communication refers both to any communication used by the Christian churches and to a quality or style of communication consistent with Christian ethics or practices. The only material deliberately excluded is that on homiletics, since several recent bibliographies more than adequately cover it (Achtemeier and Aycock [51], Toohey and Thompson [75], Litfin and Robinson [69]).

This introduction contains an outline of the book and a rationale for the materials included in each section of the bibliography. The first chapter provides a more detailed introduction to the general areas of Christian communication. That chapter sketches the historical background, notes some fundamental issues, and suggests some ways of approaching those issues. The bibliographic chapters come next, followed by a name index and a title index.

Arrangement

The initial bibliographies for this collection came from several sources. A computer search of the U. S. Library of Congress collection provided the first set of materials. Search terms for that and for subsequent searches included such items as "Christian," "religious," "Catholic," "Protestant," "Lutheran," "Baptist," etc., and "communication," "press," "film," "radio," "television," "small group," "interpersonal," and so forth. The Dialog Information Service provided the means to search through other computerized database collections including Books in Print, British Books in Print, Dissertation Abstracts International, the Religion Index, and ERIC (Educational Resources Information Clearinghouse). Manual searches of the collections at the Graduate Theological Union, the Centre for the Study of Communication and Culture, and the Billy Graham Center provided additional titles. Finally, references in dissertations and other books listed in the bibliography located still more titles.

Each item in this bibliographic guide has been personally checked. Because of this process, this collection remains incomplete. Libraries and inter-library loan services could not locate some items; foreign language materials and some dissertations proved particularly hard to track down. Painful as this choice is, especially as I look over hundreds of bibliographic possibilities left out, I have not included items that I or a co-worker could not review. I have also chosen to omit items that did not seem clearly relevant to the general topic of Christian communication or that did not advance the discussion in some way. For example, many religious publications have editorialized about the need for better means of religious communication; by and large references to these editorials do not appear here. News magazines and the religious press have also carried much in the way of news reporting about the communication efforts of the church; unless an article had historical interest, I omitted it.[3]

The arrangement of the materials follows a fairly straightforward order, based on the general academic division of communication studies. First comes a list of resources for the study of Christian communication: periodicals which address specific aspects of religious communication or which consistently run articles of interest; bibliographic guides to the material (these also appear in the subject areas); directories of personnel working in Christian communication; and directories or catalogues of materials.

There follows, in chapter 3, a listing of materials dealing with communication theory or communication in general. While some items might refer to a particular medium of communication, this section contains information that cuts across several media or that addresses theoretical questions or issues. The following topics appear in this chapter: communication theory and theology; Church documents, policy statements and commentaries; ethics and the social responsibility of communication; Christian critiques of communication; and media education.

Historical materials come next. These divide fairly cleanly into histories and historical source material (for example, Augustine's work on the theory of Christian rhetoric [355]) and biographies of individuals working on Christian communication projects. The biographies tend to a common ha-

---

[3]I would however ask any reader who knows of materials that he or she feels should be included in this bibliography to please let me know of them. Readers can write to me at the Communication Department; Santa Clara University; Santa Clara, CA   95053; U. S. A.

giographic style: for each subject they narrate the birth and early family surroundings, a rebellious youth, a conversion, marriage and/or ministerial preparation, missionary call, appeal of communication ministry, and success over obstacles.

For completeness, material on rhetoric forms the fifth chapter. This consists primarily of references to existing bibliographies on homiletics which more than adequately cover that material, and some general material on religious language. This latter category provides a link with important developments of a communicative theology as well as with a foundational debate about the very nature of language and its religious possibilities. After this material on language and flowing from it come sections on narrative theology and religious literature. Finally the chapter concludes with material on orality and on writing.

Interpersonal communication usually refers to various kinds of unmediated communication or to communication that occurs between two individuals or within a small group. Thus, chapter 6 includes material dealing with one-on-one communication or dialogue, witnessing (that is, personal testimony about one's faith), small group communication and conflict in church settings, and—an exception to the non-mediated rule—the telephone.

The largest section of the bibliography encompasses mass communication. Mass communication media address large undifferentiated groups and by definition involve technological assistance. Chapter 7 has nine subsections: mass communication in general, religious journalism and the religious press, religious public relations, religious film, religious broadcasting in general, Christian radio, Christian television, studies of the audience for religious broadcasting, and religious uses of cable distribution systems. Individual works tend to take one of several approaches to their topic: a how-to manual explaining to a newcomer how to set up a ministry in radio, for example; an evaluation study, exploring why a given medium or communication product qualifies as Christian; or an in-depth study exploring the uses and effectiveness of a particular medium for the spread of the Gospel or the work of the church.

The next chapter cuts across clear definitional boundaries. Intercultural communication clearly relates to mass media since the mass communication setting must respond to audience needs in other cultures. At the same time intercultural communication also refers to interpersonal communication between members of different cultures. For this reason, the materials that address these questions appear in this separate section.

Finally, the last chapter, chapter 9, collects material that deals with mediated communication which does not necessarily address a mass audience. This includes religious art; religious drama; religious dance; music; sound media; comic books; computers; video; and new communication technologies. While some of these areas such as religious art, music or drama might well have separate bibliographies devoted just to them, they deserve inclusion here because they raise questions of particular relevance to the study of communication. Debates about religious art or sacred dance, for example, extend back for centuries and provide a wealth of theoretical material in defining what forms a "Christian medium" of expression. Much recent study of Christian communication has ignored this material and struggles to answer questions for which literary or dramatic critics have already developed tools and methods.

*   *

Acknowledgements

Many people and organizations have helped in making this annotated bibliography possible. I would like to thank the Bannan Foundation for funding the overall project and Santa Clara University for supporting my work through a reduction of my class teaching schedule. Rüdiger Funiok, SJ, and Reinhold Iblacker, SJ, and their graduate assistants of the Institut für Kommunication und Media in Munich proved invaluable in tracking down and annotating many of the German language entries. Paul Duffy, S. J., of Xavier College in Melbourne, provided similar assistance for many of the materials originating in Australia. Jean Bianchi of the Centre Recherche et Communication in Lyon generously sent me French language materials. My own student assistants—especially Christine van Dijk, who became interested enough to devote two summers to the project, but also Mala Matacin, Ron White, and Jim Sette—spent countless hours checking library card catalogs, running down books, and keeping the working database current. Finally, the library staffs at Santa Clara University, the Graduate Theological Union in Berkeley, the Centre for the Study of Communication and Culture in London, and the Billy Graham Center at Wheaton College, Wheaton, Illinois provided wonderful working environments and lots of books. My heartfelt thanks to all.

Chapter 1

History, Issues, Approaches

"Christian communication" poses a problem. Well-meaning people ask what it is, while others see the answer so clearly and so urgently that the question itself sounds foolish to them. The relatively few scholars who study Christian communication have difficulty convincing their colleagues that, rather than representing an ideology, it forms an area worth attention. Church leaders faced with budget decisions want to know how to choose worthwhile communication programs and projects. Highly visible media ministries generate satisfaction or anxiety, depending on one's perspective.

Despite an historically close association of communication with Christian religious beliefs and practices, Christians and Christian churches have shown a great deal of ambivalence about communication. For every individual who rushes to embrace a given communicative style or medium, at least one other limits or condemns it. Each new medium encounters similar resistance and generates its own particular misgivings. In our own day, for example, the high costs associated with radio and television and their primary use as entertainment media make church leaders hesitate to begin a media ministry while the possibility of reaching millions compels their attention. Often those who do use the electronic media proceed as individuals or come from Christian traditions which place more emphasis on evangelistic preaching and less on ecclesial structure.

The ambivalence arises from several sources, including the cost-benefit uncertainty already mentioned. Part of the ambivalence stems from a lack of clarity about the term, "communication," itself. Define it too broadly as in Watzlawick's dictum, "one cannot *not* communicate," and absolutely every Christian word or action becomes Christian communication. This seems too pat. Part of the ambivalence arises from an unclear relationship between church and society. The communication industry today presents one of the most public faces of society. On the one hand the church seeks a place in that industry's output; on the other hand, the church sees a need to criticize the industry and its values (Boyd [299]). How can it do both? Part of the ambivalence comes from the situation of the Christian churches themselves. Differences in interpretation of the Bible and differences in church structure and governance lead directly to different judgments about the communication appropriate for Christian life and mission.

All of these factors lead to a growing sense that whatever it is, "Christian communication" deserves serious systematic study. That kind of study would begin to fulfill at least four needs. First, it would clarify the definition of Christian communication by allowing scholars to debate their terms and situate their own studies in a larger context. The very discussion would stimulate further work and reflection. A dialogue that includes practitioners as well as scholars would move things forward even more rapidly and would promote other kinds of scholarly progress. As things now stand, few people writing in this area seem to know of others with similar interests; many write in church publications that do not include citations. Consequently, writer after writer re-invents terms and categories while the general area of Christian communication fails to develop any critical reflection. Even doctoral and master's degree candidates appear unable to find resources beyond a few well-known books. Second, systematic study of Christian communication would re-introduce into general communication studies a consistent body of material with a long historical tradition. Many of the debates about representation, mediation, and narrative have already appeared in theological circles in relation to communication and religious practice. This forms a huge unknown resource for contemporary scholarship. Third, this study would respond to the often-repeated calls of church leaders and church communicators for a "theology of communication," or at least for a theological reflection on communication. The difficulty here lies not so much in the work completed, but in its lack of discussion. Finally, just as mass communication cuts across all demographic lines, the study of Christian communication cuts across ecclesial divisions. In this, it offers a starting point for ecumenical endeavors and discussions and provides yet another common contact for Christians of different traditions.

The remainder of this chapter situates the bibliography within a larger framework of study for Christian communication. The next section provides a brief history of Christian communication and its study. A section outlining some key issues for further study follows. A third section presents several different approaches to the study of Christian communication, many of them suggested by the literature reviewed here.

History

Christian communication has a history that goes back to the beginnings of Christianity. The crowds marvelled at Jesus because, unlike the scribes, he spoke with authority. He also spoke in parables, using images of daily life—farming, weddings, housecleaning. He spoke like one of them but he spoke convincingly of the kingdom of God. Not quite a generation later, Paul wrote that faith comes through hearing and Paul himself never hesitated to proclaim the crucified and risen Jesus, "in season and out of season." The Christian community passed on the tradition of Jesus, orally and then in writing (Kelber [563]), making use of the various communication media available. Within three generations, Christians maintained not only an oral and written tradition, but also utilized music, art, and images (Murray [1164]) to proclaim, sustain, and pass on their faith.

Debates about the appropriate use of communication techniques and technology run deep in the Christian tradition. Throughout that tradition, reflection tends to follow practice. In other words, people make use of various means of communication first; only later comes a theoretical judgment about that practice. Rarely—but occasionally nonetheless—does a church council or hierarchical authority decide whether or not to allow the continued use of a particular medium or device.

No less an early figure than Tertullian (c. 230) questioned the use of pagan literature, art and philosophy (including its rhetoric) in Christian teaching [1133, page 40]. At the same time, in their polemics against paganism, others (foreshadowing the iconoclastic debates) questioned whether images had any place in worship (Athenagoras [1136], Justin Martyr [1156]). Despite these objections both literary and artistic decoration continued in Christian circles (Murray [1164]). Again, at the end of the fourth century, Jerome (340-420) raised his voice against pagan literature and its embellishments, banishing them from the repertoire of Christian preachers and writers.[1] However, writing a few years later, Augustine (354-430) argued that Christian teaching and doctrine deserved the same decorations and rhetorical defenses as did pagan literature and pagan religious teachings [355]. Augustine's position, which has enjoyed continued success even to this day, argues that the techniques of communication are themselves neutral, able to support truth or falsity, and able to accomplish good or bad. Therefore, the church should use them for good.[2]

Western Christianity, following Augustine, has had fewer problems with decoration and imagery in worship and preaching than has Eastern Chris-

---

[1] Jerome. Epistle 22.29.6 *The Letters of St. Jerome.* Trans. Charles Christopher Mierow. *Ancient Christian Writers: The Works of the Fathers in Translation* 33. Ed. Johannes Quasten and Walter J. Burghardt. Westminster, MD: The Newman Press; London: Longmans, Green, and Co., 1963. 165.

[2] For further discussion on this point, see Murphy [404].

tianity. From the East in the eighth and ninth centuries came the clearest—
and most extended—debate about communication and Christianity. Arguing from the prohibitions of the Old Testament, from an essentialist view
of images (that is, that the image shares the essence of what it represents),
and from a quasi-Monophysite Christology, the iconoclasts rejected any
use of images. On the other hand, iconophiles supported the use of images
with arguments based on their communicative usefulness (to teach the unlettered) and on their symbolic (rather than essential) nature (Alexander
[1133]). John of Damascus extends his support of images by comparing
their function to that of the Gospel: both call the Christian to worship;
both serve communication [387]. The debate about images runs deep in
Christian theology because it focuses other issues ranging from Christology
to the role of the saints to philosophic theories of representation.[3] Where
the issue finds resolution in a purely functional way as in Western Christianity (images serve a useful purpose in leading people to God), theology
merely defers examining the significance of representation, an examination
which occurs in conjunction with a different communicative practice.

The Reformation followed within 75 years of the invention of printing
from movable type; it soon brought that new communication technology
into its disputes. Not only did religious controversialists use the press to
publish their treatises and to attack their opponents; not only did rival
religious groups publish their own Biblical translations (Chrisman [365]),
but the printing press itself sharpened attention on the mediational or
representational role of the church. The case of the catechism illustrates
this. Both Protestants and Catholics urged an educational reform as well
as a spiritual renewal. The catechism, a short printed compendium of
Christian teaching that could be studied and easily memorized, formed an
important communication strategy in this reform.

Protestant catechisms owes their origin to Martin Luther who authored
both the short and the long versions. Luther's catechisms went through
many editions within a few years and, along with a rise in literacy and the
spread of Biblical translations [415], fostered a kind of unmediated religion.
Now, for the first time, a Christian could have access to the Scriptures and
to the doctrines of faith without need for a priest or community as an
intermediary. Perhaps fortuitously (for Luther left no comment on this
point), this particular communication strategy reinforces the Protestant
emphasis on salvation by faith alone.[4]

The Council of Trent mandated a Catholic catechism, several versions
of which the Jesuit scholar Peter Canisius prepared as a response to the
Lutheran catechisms. The Catholic catechism was similar in form to the

---

[3] For a different perspective on this point, see Miles [1162].

[4] Elizabeth L. Eisenstein, *The Printing Press as an Agent of Change: Communications and Cultural Transformations in Early-Modern Europe* (Cambridge: Cambridge
University Press, 1979) 349-350.

Protestant: its question and answer format; its rehearsal of the doctrines of faith, beginning with the simplest; its printed format. However, the most notable difference occurs not with its form but with its audience: the Catholic catechism of the Counter-Reformation was addressed not to the laity but to priests. The priests in turn taught the catechism, usually by recitation and memorization. Thus Catholics learned the truths of faith within the context of community where the spoken word held priority and where the Church retained full interpretive authority. Printed catechisms were not widely available to laity in France, for example, until almost 100 years after Trent.[5]

The Catholic Church also chose another communicative strategy—a negative one—for dealing with the Protestant challenge. As religious books, catechisms, and scriptural translations became widely available, the Church tried to limit the circulation of those which did not meet its theological criteria through a process of prior censorship. Unacceptable books found a place on the Index of Forbidden Books, and, through the cooperation of secular authorities, church officials did not allow them to be printed or sold in Catholic areas.

At the same time that the Christian churches adapted their communication to the printing press, they also returned to the earlier debates about the proper use of physical, rhetorical, and musical decoration in worship and in Christian life. Zwingli and others opted to abandon the use of images and music; Luther fostered music and retained images as long as they did not become idols [398]; the Roman Church continued to embellish its liturgy and life with all manner of communicative support. In the Reformation debates, one could almost arrange the churches along a continuum according to the degree to which each accepted communicative mediation in Christian life.

While the Christian churches continued to make use of all manner of communication technology, the process of reflection on these practices tended to seek to improve the practice rather than to judge it. With the Protestant emphasis on preaching, for example, there came a new flowering of rhetoric in the 17th and 18th centuries. Catholic schools saw similar revivals but characteristically also included developments in music, drama, and dance, as befit their liturgical tradition (Rock [1257], Kennedy [391]).

After commercial printers developed the newspaper as a communication form, the churches quickly took them up. In England religious societies published periodicals and tracts, aimed especially at the working class, as early as the 1780's.[6] In the United States, religious tracts appeared

---

[5] Eisenstein 350.

[6] Peter Roger Mountjoy, "The Working-Class Press and Working-Class Conservatism," *Newspaper History: From the 17th Century to the Present Day*, eds. George Boyce, James Curran, and Pauline Wingate (London: Constable; Beverly Hills, CA: Sage Publications, 1978) 265-280. For a listing of the early Baptist publications, see

almost as early, contributing to the development of a mass press (Nord [406]). Similarly, religious newspapers appeared along the eastern seaboard from the beginning of the 19th century (Stroupe [73]). Differing little in form from their secular counterparts, religious papers highlighted news of church and ethnic group but often also included impassioned attacks on other churches. For example, in the 1840's several papers—Catholic and Protestant—carried a lively debate by their editors regarding the patriotism, political interests, and religious beliefs of newly arrived (mostly Irish) Catholics (Foik [372]). The religious press in general served as popular adjuncts to the churches in fostering of group identity. In addition, in hierarchical churches like the Catholic Church, the papers also helped governing bodies instruct and admonish their adherents. For example, the decree of the Third Council of Baltimore urged support for Catholic papers to facilitate Catholic teaching [267]. Many Protestant churches used the newspapers not only to reach their own members but also to evangelize others, seeing in the newspaper another means of outreach to non-believers (Barrett [357], Norton [407], Stroupe [73]). Although this evangelical use, particularly among fundamentalist groups has not disappeared, today the religious or denominational press in North America serve largely to inform church members of news and to foster learning and faith (Marty and Deedy [751]). Book publishing constitutes yet another strong aspect of the religious press in the United States. Many denominations sponsor publishing houses which issue general circulation works as well as catechetical and denominational books (Hostetler [384], Mitchell [754], Noling [756]).

As one might expect from cultural and political differences, the European religious press follows somewhat different lines from the North American. Often journals shared an affiliation with both church and state and the religious press provided information intended to inform political opinion as well as to teach religious attitudes (FISC [733], Hemels [742], Mehnert [403]). While recognized by the churches, the rights of the press remained circumscribed by the rights of truth.[7] Today the European religious press follows two different models. On the one hand, some papers—those associated with Christian Democratic parties, for example—still retain some political connections; other independent religious papers like the *Tablet* in Britain offer political comment as well as religious news; finally, others run by churches—*Civiltà Cattolica* for example—comment on political news with an eye to influencing public opinion. On the other hand many religious papers, usually those associated with dioceses or particular churches, follow a more American model and report news of church events and issues. The European religious press in general remains very much attuned to issues of ethics and information rights (Jorgenson [283]).

Taylor [74].

[7]For two Catholic views on this point, see Leo XIII [241] and Pius XII [763].

In other parts of the world a Christian press followed the church missionaries and grew along with literacy (Prelot [764], Catholic Media Council [725]). Almost every religious group published Chinese language papers in China before the revolution; Lowenthal lists hundreds of such papers [396]. Other parts of Asia also boast a flourishing Christian press despite contemporary debates regarding form and function (Thomas [781], Zachariah [787]). The African church presses date back to the 19th century and serve every part of that continent (Eilers [732]). Many might find the extent of Christian publishing in the Third World surprising. Eilers lists about 300 Catholic publications and publishing houses in Africa alone [83]. His directories of church press, radio, and television in Africa and Asia run to over 1600 pages, combined [84,85].

Interestingly enough, significantly less conflict occurs about the appropriateness of the press, books, newspapers, and magazines to Christian life than about almost any other communication technology. Certainly, different churches approach the press differently (for example, the Catholic Bishops in the United States condemned the misinformation spread about the Catholic Church [266]) but, after the 19th century, no one questioned whether printing should have a role in the Church.

One cannot say the same thing about film. Except for some instructional films suited for Sunday school classes, almost no one set out to produce religiously oriented films for general distribution. One attempt at this—by a Catholic affiliated film club in Belgium—ended unsuccessfully in the 1930's (Lefeber [871]).

Instead the churches tried to influence the film industry to produce morally acceptable films. In this religious organizations took two complementary approaches: they protested against objectionable films and they cooperated with and promoted acceptable films. The Catholic Legion of Decency, started in the 1930's in the United States attracted significant ecumenical support and had a measurable influence on Hollywood.[8] The Legion rested on three pillars. First, the Hollywood Production Code spelled out moral guidelines for film plots and detailed norms for acceptable images. Studios voluntarily subscribed to the Code which Martin Quigley and the Rev. Daniel Lord, S. J.—a film critic and one-time adviser to Cecil B. DeMille—authored [437]. Second, the publication of film ratings (from "unobjectionable for all" through "partly objectionable" to "condemned") in churches and in the religious press publicized a moral evaluation of films. These ratings followed the Production Code as well as other church guidelines. Third, church members voluntarily agreed to abide by the ratings and avoid films with objectionable treatments (Phelan [289]). Faced with the possibility of a massive consumer boycott, the studios generally accepted the Code. The concept of the Legion also found considerable theoretical

---

[8] Robert Sklar, *Movie-Made America* (New York: Vintage Press, 1975) 173-174.

support in official church documents such as Pius XI's encyclical, *Vigilanti Cura* [251].

Cooperation with Hollywood led to some church-oriented films but few of any lasting merit (Campbell and Pitts [82]). The more profoundly religious films have come from individual directors, working freely on religious themes or questions.[9] More recently some Evangelical groups have begun producing films—usually for non-theatrical showing although increasingly some do aim for theatrical releases. While the Catholic Church has dropped the Legion of Decency in favor of a more general film reviewing service, the Evangelical churches have increased their suspicion of major film releases, judging many of them anti-Christian (Henderson-Hart [862]).

Another church-sponsored response to film introduced an approach to communication which still exists today—media education. Through the establishment of film clubs and study circles, churches sought to improve the quality of films not so much by consumer boycotts but by improving the taste of the audiences. Despite some early attempts to use film in church study groups in the United States (Smith [883]), this approach by and large began in Europe and proved more successful there (Lefeber [871], Amgwerd [330]). However, media education, directed more towards television and newer communication media, has taken root in the United States, particularly through the efforts of the Media Action Research Center (Logan and Moody [344]).[10]

The 1920's and 1930's saw the beginning of a philosophical development that has had a significant, but indirect, effect on religious communication. During this time, philosophers exploring the status of language and meaning questioned whether religious language actually had any referent. Logical positivists, followed by the linguistic analysis school, attacked the status of religious discourse on several grounds: religious statements had no concrete referent; religious statements could not be verified; religious statements could not be falsified; and religious statements had no cognitive content.[11] In his introduction to the various positions—pro and con—Tilley [518] arranges the philosophers of religious language into four groups: the narrow empiricists, who look for concrete reference for language; the cognitivists, who hold that religious language has analogical meaning; the non-cognitivists, who find religious language meaningful in an emotive way, for example; and the personal empiricists, who place religious meaning as a referent to personal experience. Others who fall outside of these groups have found a solution in the later work of Ludwig Wittgenstein, with its concept of different "language games" for different realms

---

[9] For some discussion, see Bamberger [835], Bedoulle [837], Desser [850], and May and Bird [879].

[10] For additional material on media education around the world, see Pungente [347].

[11] For essays representative of the different positions, see the collection edited by Charlesworth [468].

of experience and meaning. High [490] and Hordern [491] summarize this position.

Even though this issue of religious language lies a bit out of what many consider the normal realm of communication, it does prompt serious thinking about a condition for the possibility of any Christian communication. Over the years, the examination of religious language has shed light on what might constitute the "religious" in communication. Scholars have found that they do have a tradition to support this reflection: Wilder [523] looks back to early Christian rhetoric and Boyle [361] to Erasmus for models. Burke [465] proposes a rhetorical approach, grounded in the nature of language, while Bochenski [462] relies on logic. Others give more general, introductory treatments (Christian [469], Hick [489], Ping [506]).

The most recent development in this area comes from the re-discovery of narrative by theology. Moving away from an absolute reliance on philosophical theology to ground their discourse, a number of theologians have turned to the "logic" and rhetoric of the story as a means to convey Christian truth. Theoretical work here comes from Crossan [526] and Dunne [545], who show stories at work in the Christian tradition. Navone [534] provides a good overview of the work of the leading contributors to this movement.

Turning again to the period of the 1920's and 1930's, churches, especially in the United States with its fairly free approach to licensing, quickly took to radio. Some of the first radio broadcasts featured church services; soon thereafter independent churches and ministers utilized radio to reach people in their homes (Rodgers [989]). Often they explained their ministry in terms of fulfilling the Great Commission that they preach the Gospel to all nations (Mt. 24:14). One can note several distinct approaches with regards to radio and the churches. First, different denominations used the radio for preaching: the "pulpit of the air" provided the individual minister or denomination with a wider audience. As technical sophistication increased, these radio addresses reached other parts of the country through syndication or through network broadcasting (Miller [978]).[12] Second, non-church groups sponsored general religious radio programming: as network programming grew, the radio networks used representative bodies—Protestant, Catholic, and Jewish—to manage religious sustaining time (that is, free) programming. The program material became "generically" religious: sermons or religious music broadly enough based to attract a wide audience and polite enough not to offend listeners. One difficulty in this plan, however, lay in the fact that large religious groups, especially the Baptist and evangelical churches, found themselves excluded from the networks (Saunders [412]). Third, some religious organizations

---

[12] For the sometimes gripping narrative accounts of these efforts, see, for example, any of the various biographies of religious broadcasting pioneers: Bloom [939], Epp [428], Fuller [434], Pepple [447].

or representatives planned specialized programming for particular groups or purposes. These ranged from children's educational and Bible study programs to the personal attacks of the Rev. Bob Shuler to the overtly political broadcasts of Father Coughlin (Aikman [419], Marcus [440]).

A fourth church-based approach to radio involves advocacy. More and more religious organizations have taken up such advocacy with governmental and regulatory bodies in order to influence the structure and programming of radio. In the United States the National Council of Churches had led the way in this regard, defending the rights of minorities, for example, to challenge the licenses of unrepresentative or discriminatory stations (Jennings [385]). In Latin America and Asia, the churches have begun to work towards a new communication policy in various countries (Lee [286], UNDA [293]). Fifth, religious radio follows a different model altogether when it appears as programming on government sponsored stations. Most European countries provided for religious programming as part of the of the basic radio service. The BBC gives a good example of this approach with both the majority religion as well as minority religions represented in sermons, services, and songs (Dinwiddie [947], Falconer [678,430], Wolfe [417]). Sixth, groups of missionaries, usually American, pioneered missionary radio by setting up short wave radio stations throughout the world to preach the Gospel. Extraordinary examples of these efforts are HCJB in Quito, Ecuador (Neely [444]), RVOG in Addis Ababa (Frames [953]), and the Far East Broadcasting Company (Ledyard [965]). A similar effort by the Catholic Church has resulted in Vatican Radio (Pius XII [254]) and Radio Veritas in the Philippines.

In many respects the advent of television has added little to the situation developed by the churches in regard to radio. This fact stems from the initial economic and political development of television: when it came to television, most countries simply continued policies and practices first enunciated in dealing with radio. Televised religious services and homilies, advocacy in regard to television, specialized television programming—in all of this churches continued the course first taken with radio.

The most dramatic change, however, appeared in the United States with the spread of cable delivery systems and their need for additional program materials. Cable television involves the distribution of the television signal, not by broadcasting to a home antenna but by wire brought directly into the home to the television set. Originally developed as a means to supply a better signal in marginal reception areas, cable has grown through FCC deregulation into a major distribution system with about 50% of U. S. homes now wired. Because broadcast interference poses no problem with cable, a single cable system can supply an average of 48 channels to each home. Cable operators usually provide all the local broadcast stations plus a range of other services: local access programs from city councils, schools, and churches; premium services—sporting events and unedited films; "superstations"—programming from satellite distributed remote stations.

Television ministries quickly moved to cable, particularly in those places where broadcast stations denied them air time. Because cable operators needed to fill empty channels, many offered religious programmers free cable access. Some ministries specialized in cable distribution, providing worship services or preaching at first. Later, various television ministries which combined their preaching and church services with "religious entertainment" shows (discussions, celebrity interviews, witnessing, singing, and so forth) began to appear with some frequency. These ministries grew in number and influence as they combined direct mail fund raising (to pay for their production costs) and a political agenda with their preaching (Elvy [1017], Frankl [1022], Hadden and Swann [378]). For the most part, Baptist, evangelical, and Pentecostal churches dominate the television ministries in the United States. Having been excluded from network radio and television, these groups had already developed program formats and funding (necessary to purchase time on the stations) which prepared them to compete in the newly deregulated television and cable marketplace in the United States (Hadden and Shupe [377]).

With the introduction of radio and television, more and more churches began a process of reflection upon communication as a form of ministry. The very availability of what most people perceived as powerful media for teaching and social influence made the churches review their own priorities for communication and outreach. Many of the early debates recognized the fact that these media had negative as well as positive qualities (Carnell [301]). At the same time most church documents encourage the greater use of the mass media for evangelization and education (Vatican II [268], Pontifical Commission [257], Dunnam [674], Gill [232], Jones [239]). Religious communication professionals, theologians, and church bodies began work to develop a "theology of communication" as a means of grounding their practice (Hamelink [122], Soukup [70]).[13]

Church drama and religious drama form another development, begun in the 1930's and flowering in the 1950's. Led by the work of several British playwrights, including T. S. Eliot, Charles Williams, and Christopher Fry, Christian drama experienced a revival both in church performances and on the commercial stage (Speaight [1229]). Previous to this renewal churches had used drama mainly to illustrate scriptural events. With Eliot's *Murder in the Cathedral* (produced originally as a chancel drama), a new approach to church drama dawned. Later, with the commercial success of the play, Eliot and others began writing drama with religious themes for the commercial stage. Through the 1940's and 1950's directors and critics argued that drama could and should become an integral part in the life of the church

---

[13] For a more detailed discussion on this point, see below, page 21.

(Browne [1192], Eastman [1201]). Many churches began to make greater
use of chancel plays as a part of worship as well as to encourage drama
groups for biblical study and aesthetic appreciation (Ehrensperger [1202]).
Spurred by this renewed interest, several collections of plays and guides
to church drama appeared, mostly in the 1960's (Weales [1234], Bachman
and Browne [1187], Burbridge and Watts [1193]). With the greater experience of drama came an increase in historical and theoretical studies which
helped to situate drama in the church and in theology (Haughton [191],
Lynch [1215], McCabe [1216]).

The 1950's also witnessed the beginnings of a slow growth of academic
interest in religious communication. While never large in number or scope,
these studies began to evaluate the effectiveness of broadcast religion and
to analyze its audiences. The studies themselves fall into three general
types: audience effects studies, audience uses and gratifications studies,
and content analyses.

The first examine the effect of a given show upon members of the audience. For the most part the studies of religious broadcasting in the United
States indicate that older, less educated, rural women who already belong
to an evangelical church form the largest part of the audience for evangelical programs. The research also indicates a smaller audience than the
electronic church claims for itself. The programs tend primarily to confirm
the belief of their viewers (Parker [1091], Horsfield [1038], Hoover [1036]).

The second group of studies examines the ways audience members use
religious programming. Some find in it a kind of "spiritual viewing," akin
to an earlier generation's spiritual reading. Some watch or listen to religious
shows in a kind of ritual manner—as an expression of their own religiosity.
Others watch religious programming out of dissatisfaction with commercial
television fare (Abelman [1075]). Still others tune in to the broadcasts for
instrumental reasons: to find out news of the church or to hear a sermon
(Abelman [1076]).

Third, content analysis studies measure the kinds and amounts of different elements which make up a given program or set of programs. These
studies have measured, for example, how many minutes of prayer, song,
preaching, and fund raising occur on the average in a program. For example, Abelman calculated that 75% of programming is overtly religious and
that solicitations for funds average $190 per hour [999].

The rise of the television evangelists and their growing political impact
has spurred many other studies, particularly those measuring audience size,
determining whether broadcast religion harmed local churches, or investi-
gating personality and demographic characteristics of viewers (Abelman
and Neuendorf [1000], Robinson [1094]).

The Christian churches have also explored other ways of communicating the Gospel, keeping in the public eye, and facilitating organizational
management. These efforts have included the whole range of small media

(cassettes, slide projectors, puppets, comic strips, and so forth), particularly in local congregation, religious education and missionary settings (Cousineau [618], Jensen and Jensen [624], Lowe [693], Sarno [634]). The Christian churches have made use of public relations techniques to reach the world beyond church doors (Austin [790], Carty [797], Greif [808]) and newsletters to stay in touch with the local congregation (Knight [810]). This area has generated the greatest number of "how-to" books, willing to teach basic publication skills for every church. Even computers have joined the repertoire of communication tools (Bedell [1278], Clemens [1281], Foltz [1283]). Finally, the churches have quickly adapted to new communication technologies, notably videotex (described in Ouellet [1298]).

This brief historical survey gives just a sense of the scope of Christian communication. Today, more and more people use the various means of communication in the service of the Gospel; increasing numbers also reflect on their use. Thankfully much of this reflection finds an outlet and an audience through conference proceedings and specialized periodicals.[14]

Issues

Because of its inherent importance to human life, communication exists in a paradoxical situation. On the one hand, people take it for granted, at least until it fails, and spend little time explicitly reflecting on the nature of communication. On the other hand, communication demands reflection precisely because it plays such an essential role in any human activity; moreover, it must itself become the tool of its own analysis. The study of Christian communication participates in this paradox but brings its own resources to it. However, many of the issues raised by discussion of Christian communication remain unresolved—the discussion has not progressed that far yet. This section outlines some key issues under four headings: foundational issues, strategic issues, audience issues, and analytical issues. Those listed here do not exhaust the range of possible issues; however, they have caught my interest, either of themselves or because someone has stated the problem well.

Foundational Issues

Foundational issues refer to those issues which cut across all discussion—attempts to explain why communication might be inherently religious, for example. They provide a methodology for the study of Christian communication or a definition of its practice. Four of these issues appear in the literature.

---

[14] See the section on periodicals for many representative titles. Conference proceedings appear in the subject areas of the bibliography.

The first, and perhaps the most basic, foundational issue has to do with the theoretical starting point from which one examines Christian communication. What set of tools and methods should one use? Different people choose different methods and these, of course, lead to varying results.

The most popular tool for analyzing the religious use of communication comes directly from the study of theology. "Is there a 'theology of communication'?" people ask. The general response involves trying to apply criteria from theology to communication, usually to support a judgment about some communication product or strategy. Because so many branches of theology exist, this method soon breaks down into competing specializations. This issue has generated so much discussion in so many different areas that I will treat it more extensively in a separate section, "On a Theology of Communication," beginning on page 21.

Another tool for analyzing Christian communication comes from a general cultural theory, and more specifically from that proposed by the late Canadian scholar Marshall McLuhan. McLuhan's work has caught the imagination of Christian communicators around the world, providing, in fact, one of the few widely cited bodies of work. McLuhan argues that the technology of communication (its medium—speech, writing, printing, and now electronics) influences the content of communication. As radio and television use increase, he suggests, they create a new "language" or style of communication, one that relies less on logic and exposition and more on imagery and emotion. While some use his work polemically, claiming that the church must respond to a "new communication age" characterized by the new audio-visual language, others make his analysis the basis for a cultural study that would find its spiritual force in communication (Babin [611], Mann [197]). The chief fault in this approach lies in its failure to define or adequately describe the audio-visual language, differentiating it from ordinary language. While many claim a special language for film and television, it remains unclear whether this "language" refers to a grammatical code (in the manner of linguistics) or to a rhetoric of sound and image. Another problem comes with the uncritical acceptance of McLuhan's ideas—ideas which he himself characterizes as "probes" or unproven suggestions. As a cultural critic, McLuhan often suggests several readings of a given situation; as a writer, he tends to employ catchy aphorisms ("The medium is the message"). While some of his ideas ring true and have occasioned some scholarly follow-up, many remain untested. Those wishing to follow McLuhan in the area of Christian communication would do well to carefully examine their data and then to argue their own position without relying too much on McLuhan's work as a kind of proof-text. (Ong [204] provides a good example of the careful development of ideas similar to McLuhan's.)

Other cultural commentaries independent of McLuhan do exist. Like the work of many critics, these tend to react to situations rather than to explain them but they often possess a certain persuasive power. Some examine the cultural world of television soap operas, advertising, and drama, noting how these differ from the Christian world view (Fore [308], Marty [696]). Others use the Bible's imagery and accounts as an avenue into a deeper understanding of our own day (Chappuis [180]).

A third tool used in the analysis of Christian communication has its roots in critical theory. Modelling itself in some ways on the critique of the culture (or communication) industries attempted by the neo-Marxist Frankfurt School, this group, grounding itself in Christian principles, examines and measures communication. Some, following Tillich, have placed the theoretical foundation in a theology of culture (Palmer [1168]); others, notably von Balthasar, examine art and beauty as the basic theological categories with which to approach contemporary life ([165]). Peukert [206], Copray [105] and Bartholomäus [169] use the work of Jürgen Habermas as a point of departure. Habermas, a contemporary leader of the Frankfurt School, has analyzed communication as a central construct in a system which seeks human liberation. Finally, Ellul provides yet another measured grounding for a critical appraisal of communication, based on his own reading of culture in the light of the Scriptures [306].

A growing body of work on Christian communication takes its methodology from that of the social sciences. Careful data collection and statistical evaluation provide the ultimate touchstone for the validity of one's conclusions regarding any Christian communication. The North American origins of this method appears clearly in the sponsors or academic backgrounds of these studies. Surveys measure audience size, interests or other characteristics;[15] intensive interviews evaluate the motivation of viewers and the impact of programs (Hoover [1036]). A weakness of this approach as a grounding methodology lies in its unquestioned assumption of its own relevance as a universal method.

A fifth method has deeper historical roots, since it draws on the study of literature. For over 40 years theologically-motivated literary critics have explored the ways in which drama, poetry, and prose fiction reveal the Absolute or lead people to an experience of God. Methods vary. Some look exclusively at the "content" of a work (plot, characters, setting), noting Christian themes or Christian characters (Stewart [555], Ziolkowski [559]). Others examine the form and function of literature, finding in each an avenue to the transcendent (Detweiler [1142], Wilder [220]). Still others pose more theoretical issues, as does Lynch [550], for example, when he asks how the secular images faith. Coupled with the rediscovery of narrative in theology, this method offers students of communication a well-grounded and long-discussed theoretical body of information that one can fairly easily carry over from writing or performance to other mediated communication.

---

[15] See Gallup [736] and Horsfield [1038] for reviews.

Some good examples of methods applied to literary texts, which could well apply to other media, include the work of Wilder [558], Lynch [549], and TeSelle [557]. This latter work contains an excellent critique of the methodology.

These five different tools (theology, cultural studies, critical studies, social studies, literary criticism) provide at least five different theoretical starting points for the study of Christian communication. The resolution of this methodological issue will have profound consequences; lack of attention to it explains the dramatically different results and evaluations currently given to church communication projects and policies[16]

A second foundational issue has less to do with the method of study and more to do with the evaluation of a given means of communication as Christian. What makes something Christian? The adjective applies first of all to individual members of the Christian churches; can it apply as well to activities or technologies? Another way of putting the question asks whether there exist any "marks" of Christian communication, just as there exist "marks" of the church—that it is "one, holy, catholic, and apostolic." Ideally, one might derive such characteristics from the method of study; for example, a theology of communication would hallow certain practices. But the same difficulty that arose before applies here as well: who chooses which theological ground to use?

An historical example will more clearly illustrate both the importance and the problematic nature of this issue. During the iconoclastic-iconophile debates of the eighth and ninth centuries, the iconoclasts often used as arguments against icons statements first used by the early church against the pagan idols; iconophiles, in their defense, slightly modified the pagan arguments that justified statues and paintings as only symbolic and not as essential representations (Alexander [1133]). In 500 years the criteria for what counted as legitimate "Christian art" had noticeably shifted. Political considerations further complicate this picture, for the Roman emperors in Constantinople actively took part in the debates. In a similar way the use of the printing press in the 16th and 17th centuries involved defenses of printing (Boyle [361]) as well as the well-known Index of Forbidden Books. The church position remained fluid for years, and political as well as theological factors worked toward defining a "Christian use" of the printing press.

A third foundational issue comes from the nature of communication. Given the inescapable character of communication, does "Christian communication" refer to a specific set of actions or functions or ministries, or does it apply to all church activity? This issue often shows up (usually around budget time) in church planning offices: does a communication of-

---

[16] See for example Hadden's critique of a major study in the *Review of Religious Research* [1031].

fice deal with specific items—a broadcast ministry, for example—or does it work with every church office, helping them with public relations, with group processes, with in-house matters? Does a communication office lead the way in issues of justice regarding governmental communication policies, or does that task belong to an office of social concern? Church policy statements reflect this shift in the understanding of communication. For example, the United States Catholic Conference's recent instructions on communication [221,264] move from a specific use of media to a more general consideration of the effects of media on society. The statements of the World Council of Churches also show this same movement [271,272]. This particular debate reflects a somewhat recent shift in the whole notion of communication, probably associated with a closer academic scrutiny of communication. At one time communication (as Christian communication within it) was wholly practical—the work of a journalist, for example, typified communication. Today, however, the wider scope of Christian communication finds support in a cultural preoccupation with communication.

One way or another, this particular debate emerges almost everywhere people have to make choices about communication. In this volume, I have chosen to define communication broadly and to include both theoretical and practical materials; that makes sense for an aid to research. Whether it does in general practice remains an unresolved and foundational issue.

A fourth foundational issue extends far beyond the scope of Christian communication but influences it nonetheless. The church's relationship with the media of communication has to do with the church's place in society. The church no longer leads society as it did at one time; instead, the communication industries take the place of the church as a source of information and influence.[17] How, then, should the church relate to the means of communication? Should it solely take the role of a critic? Should it work with or through the media? Are there other options? Each Christian tradition—Catholic, Orthodox, Anglican, Protestant, Evangelical, etc.—in each country attempts to respond to these questions. Some look to past models; others call for a creative solution. For example, Bacquet [161] and Gritti [1028] sketch some of these attempts in France.

How one works out these foundational issues will greatly influence every aspect of one's Christian communication. The choice of research tool, the measure of "Christian," the definition of communication, and the view of the relation between church and society all cut across every other question and manner of dealing with communication and religion.

---

[17]On this point, see George Gerbner and Kathleen Connolly, "Television as New Religion," *New Catholic World*, 221.1322 (March-April, 1978): 52-56; and Taylor [1068].

Strategic Issues

Strategic issues of Christian communication deal with pragmatic decisions about which media to use, how to use those media, and how to set that use in motion. For the most part, practitioners draw these questions much more narrowly than do the academics. Without becoming too specific, though, we can identify several issues that a broad range of Christian communicators must face.

One issue that appears many times, but especially in evangelical and fundamentalist writings, has to do with the urgency of the task of Christian communication. For the first time in human history, we possess the technology to fulfill the Great Commission (Mt. 24:14) that the disciples proclaim the Gospel to every nation, indeed to every human being (Gjelsten [1304]). This urgency fairly demands the use of the most sophisticated of the mass media: satellites, radio, television. A certain pragmatic value attaches to this approach—use the media that do the job and do not worry about any unintended consequences. Others would proceed more cautiously, noting the ill effects of television, the one-way nature of broadcasting, and the re-shaping of the Christian message by the means of its communication (Bachman [295], Fore [1020], Girardet [1024]). The resultant worry caused by this deadlock has led Marty in an introduction to a study of Christian communication projects [693] to question the "grimness" of Christian communicators.

A second clearly strategic issue concerns cooperation among Christian churches in communication ventures. The costs and the technical demands have at times forced ecumenical cooperation, often with great success and fruitfulness. For whatever reason, this seems more apparent with regards to missionary communication in Africa—in the case of the Radio Voice of the Gospel, for example (Aske [938], Lungren [970]) or of the work of the Catholic Media Council (as evidenced in its ecumenical media directories, for example [85]). The World Association for Christian Communication sponsors similar ecumenical projects around the world; its newsletter and journal provide abundant examples of these [2,35]. New possibilities for cooperation continually present themselves; the 1988 debate in the United States about the Vision Interfaith Satellite Network (VISN) dramatizes one possibility among many for inter-church cooperation in communication (UNDA [1111]).

Finally, a third strategic issue touches a particular nerve among United States Christian broadcasters and academic researchers. Television evangelists and others associated with the National Religious Broadcasters (Armstrong [888]) refer to themselves and their work as the "Electric Church," while the National Council of Churches and many researchers use the term, the "Electronic Church" ([1031]). The differing terminology reflects a much deeper disagreement in the use of the electronic mass media; to some, the former term indicates an acceptance of the strategies of the fundamentalist NRB, while the latter term reflects the opposition of the NCC to paid religious broadcasting and on-air fund raising. The disagreement has long historical roots as well, dating back to the rivalry between the groups for Protestant programming on the early radio networks (Saunders [412]). In this study, I have opted to use the more common academic label, "electronic church," but without any prejudice to the National Religious Broadcasters or their strategies for Christian communication.

Audience Issues

The two issues that occur here come from my own reflection on reading many of the research studies and theoretical pieces about Christian mass communication. First of all, Christian writers tend to assume a "powerful effects" model of the media. That is, they judge that the media have irresistible and clear effects on people, virtually ignoring the research data developed at least since the 1960's that hold that the media have only limited effects and that individuals use a particular medium to satisfy a particular need, often in ways not envisioned by the message creator. The powerful effects model works as an implicit presumption when people fear that the television evangelists will keep people out of their local churches. It lies behind the worry that the media have changed people's attitudes to the church or to religion in general. Such claims also abound, particularly in critical reviews of the mass media, reviews which hold that a given media content will corrupt or otherwise influence its viewers. None of these cases consider alternative causes or correlation effects. A key area for further reflection occurs here with the need to clarify the nature of the audience and its power vis-a-vis the media and its messages.

The "powerful effects" thinking implies a weak audience. This pairing seems also to underlie some of the calls for media education. Here the educators appear to constitute a kind of informed elite who can deliver individuals from the risks of media exposure. This second audience issue raises two questions. Has the media educators' implicit presumption led them to read the evidence of media effects erroneously? This would seriously jeopardize their endeavors. Their lack of clarity with regard to the effects of the media needs careful attention. Second, with what attitudes do educators approach students in media education courses? Where an elitism creeps in, the tradition of dialogic communication suffers.[18]

---

[18] For more discussion of the dialogic tradition, see Cotterell [581], DeWire [582,583], and Visser 'T Hooft [269].

Analytical Issues

Individuals concerned with Christian communication attempt to apply a Christian moral code to their own communication, to communication in general, and to society's regulation of communication. Each of these applications demands an analysis of the situation. Several larger issues characterize these analytic endeavors.

The first such issue resembles the more general one of determining the "marks" of a truly Christian communication. Many communicators and churches simply take the communication of Jesus as their model [257]. Christian communication generally chooses a dialogic model (Soukup [70, pages 50-56]) and uses it as an ideal, even when the technology or circumstances force a mass communication strategy. How can the attributes of interpersonal communication (dialogue, caring, attention) apply to a mediated, mass communication? For some creative suggestions, see Brooks [174] and Morris [201].

Another set of issues enters the picture when religious communicators attempt a critique of society's communication patterns. Drawing upon the Christian tradition for inspiration, they have focused on a number of areas in which public communication and commercial communication fail. These include issues of justice, equality, and power; issues of exploitation and manipulation; issues of violence and sexuality; and issues of truth and honesty (Fore [308], Boyd [299]). Churches have formed a consistent body of critics of films and television particularly, calling their producers, writers, and artists to a higher standard. Ethics in journalism forms a related area where the churches call professionals to higher standards; this theme seems to draw more attention in Europe than in the United States (Boventer [275], Guissard [279]).

Finally, religious communicators, led largely by the Film and Broadcast Commission of the National Council of Churches, has offered a consistent critique of U. S. government policies regarding the regulation of communication (Report of the NCC Study Commission [936]). This and other critiques touch upon access to communication, concentration of ownership, community responsibility, and regulation of content (for example, of pornography) (Fore [1020], Jennings [385]).

In a more global context, the churches have also taken up the cause of the New World Information and Communication Order, lobbying governments to support the United Nations efforts in this regard (Lee [286], UNDA [293], Christian Conference of Asia [276]). The NWICO emerged from the efforts of a group of Third World nations who protested what they regarded as the control of news and information by the dominant countries. For example, five wire services (Associated Press, United Press International, Reuters, Agence France Presse, and TASS) control most international news coverage; consequently, news of the superpowers dominates and Third World countries appear only in times of natural disaster or political instability. Similarly, powerful commercial interests control the other media—telephones, television production, computers, and so forth. The NWICO demands led to a UNESCO investigation into the status of communication around the world; its recommendations and final report have yet to be fully accepted and implemented.[19]   Much of the report details issues of communication in various countries; some concrete suggestions move toward establishing more local control over communication. The MacBride Report acknowledges the role churches have played in some areas of communication reform. Other church-related efforts have examined communication themes with international dimensions first noted by the religious groups themselves: the right to communicate (Mole [243]) and the right to information (Jorgenson [283], Celam-Decos [336]).

These dozen issues illustrate some of the recurrent themes in the discussions of Christian communication. Some seemingly have no solution and will provide material for fruitful debate for years to come; others have already gathered a certain consensus in religious circles and have the possibility of moving to a successful solution. Like the realm of communication itself, the issues combine highly theoretical questions with practical consequences. Before turning to an overview of the approaches to the study of Christian communication, I will sketch out in a bit more detail an area that has appeared in several different places in the preceding set of issues: a theology of communication.

On a Theology of Communication

Of all of the issues that Christians discover in studying communication, the desire to have a theology of communication stands out. Theological reflection on practice has long characterized the Christian life: the rich tradition of a "faith seeking understanding" has led to an enormous philosophical and theological description of almost every aspect of life. Christians place events and practices from birth to death under the light of faith. The growing importance of communication for society called the Church's attention to the religious status of this part of life. Once taken for granted, communication comes under scrutiny now from the perspectives of both philosophical and scriptural theology.

One type of such theological reflection begins with a philosophical investigation into the process of communication. The word, "communication," shares an etymological heritage with "communion" and "community"; the process of communication validates this common link by its potential to bring about communion and community. These terms carry great the-

---

[19] The report, known as the MacBride report after its chairman, is published by UN-ESCO: Sean MacBride et al., *Many Voices, One World: Communication and Society Today and Tomorrow* (New York: Unipub, 1980).

ological weight, since both describe the fruits or marks of God's Spirit. Therefore, because communication has the potential to effect both, communication itself must have at least an indirect religious character (Gabel [186]).

Other attempts to develop a theology of communication begin from a kind of theological commentary on the process of communication. A favorite technique in this approach has the theologian gloss a Biblical text which illustrates a relevant aspect. For example, Chappuis [180] provides an extended commentary on the meeting of Jesus with the Samaritan woman—their conversation provides a model of all communication. Badejo [162] develops a different model for Christian communication through a commentary on Mark 7:31-37—the healing of the deaf mute.

Another approach follows Scripture less closely. Instead of examining a particular text, it looks for Biblical models of attentive communication. The ultimate warrant for these models comes not from any improved communication but from the approval of the Scriptural examples. Webber [219] develops the consequences for communication from the Biblical teaching on Creation, the Fall, and the Incarnation. Jørgensen [195] and Kraft [130] look only at the Incarnation in sketching an ideal of Christian communication. In a similar way, Aske [159] examines the life of Jesus. All of them see the perfection of communication in entering the life of another without privilege or power.

More explicitly theological approaches start with particular doctrinal reflections rather than with the Scriptures. Ramsdell [144] suggests that the nature of the Church leads to specific obligations for its communication. In a widely known article Dulles [184] similarly reasons from the nature of the Church. In his phrase, "the Church is communication."

Church documents [257,271,272,221] tend to follow more analytic approaches that combine Scriptural warrants with theological conclusions. In all of these, though, a certain core of images or models emerges. The *Trinitarian* model for communication aims for perfect communion as its goal with love the chief attribute of the process. The *Christological* model takes Jesus for the "perfect communicator" and all communication finds its measure in him. The *ecclesiological* model of communication, as we have seen, asks whether a particular instance or style of communication builds community. The *Incarnational* approach sees identification or inculturation as the essential of a Christian communication. The *sacramental* model uses the general philosophical and theological category of representation to judge one's communication.[20]

The general attempt at a theology of communication has its difficulties, however. First of all, it lacks unity: each specific theological approach

---

[20] Although the terminology here comes primarily from the Catholic document, "Communio et Progressio," [257] most other Christian traditions use similar categories. For a comparison, see Hamelink [122], Soukup [70], and Ellul [306].

will evaluate communication differently. Each Scriptural text grounds a slightly different approach to communication. Second, it lacks expertise: theologians tend not to know the area of communication and communication scholars or practitioners tend not to know the area of theology. This leads to an unfortunately superficial discussion. Third, it lacks consistency: different national and cultural backgrounds treat the same questions and resources in different ways; few scholars continue to work in the area for more than a few years; everyone seems to start from scratch.

This section, while too brief to review all of the material on theology and communication, at least introduces some of the terms, methods, and models. Soukup [70] gives a much more detailed look at the variety and liveliness of this discussion.

Approaches to Study

Because Christian communication encompasses so much, it should not surprise anyone that people have developed many different approaches to describing and studying it. Without wanting to cut off discussion and development of these approaches too soon, in this section I will describe only six ways of looking at Christian communication. The six, defined either topically or by methodology, are historical, religious, instrumental, functional, relational, and academic approaches.

The historical approach to the study of Christian communication takes its method from historiography. While I know of no general histories, sketching in more detail the impressionistic history suggested in an earlier section of this introduction, several have written solid histories of various aspects of Christian communication. Some examples include Allen [350] on Catholic social doctrine and American television; Armstrong [888] and Hadden and Swann [378], giving two perspectives on the television evangelists in the United States; Bauer [358], Glässgen [375], and Vogt [1071], all writing on broadcasting by the Catholic Church in Germany; Gosselin and Cabriès [376], describing Protestant religious broadcasting in France; Hemels and Schmolke [742] on the Catholic press in the Netherlands; Jennings [385], writing on the public communication policy actions of various religious bodies in the United States; Lungren [970], on the Radio Voice of the Gospel in Africa; Mehnert [403], on the Evangelical press in Germany; Spoletini [261] on Catholic communication efforts in Latin America; Wolfe [417] on the BBC and the churches; and Yum [418] on Methodist Church communication in Korea. More work remains here: comprehensive histories as well as the opportunity to interview still-living pioneers of electronic religious communication.

The religious approach to the study of Christian communication resembles the historical in its method but focuses more closely on the ways in which different religious traditions utilize communication media. One can distinguish Christian approaches by their theological "bias": Catholics with their emphasis on church structure and sacrament; Protestants with their faithfulness to the Word; the Orthodox with their esteem for icons; and so forth. Some have begun this kind of study, for example, Purdy [1170], Nichols [1165], and Spanos [1228] examine the workings of sacrament as a grounding for Christian communication. Murphy [404], Wilder [523], TeSelle [557], and Ellul [306] take very different approaches to the Word. Trubetskoi [1178], Ouspensky [1167], and Frary [1148] examine the communicative impact of icons in the Orthodox tradition. In addition to these, others have looked at the communication policies of specific denominations: Baragli at the official Catholic documents [223]; Uranga at the Catholic Church in Latin America [227]; and Hamelink at the World Council of Churches [122].

The instrumental approach forms the most common and probably the easiest approach for quick reference. Here, people divide Christian communication among the different media or instruments it uses: conversation, preaching, telephone, publishing, film, radio, television, and so on. This makes for a fairly straightforward method of exposition, even if it does not allow a great deal of refined analysis beyond the characteristics of one medium. Since this book follows that organization, I will offer no specific examples here, but refer the reader to the section listings.

Swann [828] proposes a functional method of analyzing religious communication. He notes that church use of communication falls under one of three headings, according to the purpose of the communication: evangelism, nurture of believers, and public relations or communication in general. This strikes me as a sound way to examine the varieties of religious communication; however, I would add a fourth function, at least. Evangelism describes communication directed outside of the church while nurture of believers describes a parallel communication directed to the church. Where public relations relates the church in a purely informational way to groups outside its members, I would add a parallel communicative function to characterize informational communication within the church. Thus, four functions for religious communication emerge: *evangelism* and *nurture* describe **faith** communication outside and within the church; *public relations* and *information* describe **news** communication outside and within the church.

Other additions drawn from audience uses and gratifications studies might further refine these four major functions. One might study the needs *evangelism* meets for the consumers of this kind of material. For example, considering only televised religious programming, do people seek these programs out to satisfy a need for "safely" hearing the Gospel or to remind them of the revival meetings of their youth? Does the *nurture* provided by the programs replace other religious activities or substitute for watching commercial television fare? Do non-members of the electronic church watch it for *information* about key figures or for a kind of cynical entertainment? Do members watch in order to keep up with new developments within the church? Several studies and summaries suggest that all these varied activities might motivate different viewers (Abelman [999,1001,1075], Hoover [1036], Horsfield [1038]). This functional approach to the whole question of religious communication provides a kind of neutral view—one that ties in well with sociological studies of other aspects of contemporary society.

A relational approach to the study of Christian communication focuses on how the church relates to society. Various communication models might explain the actions of a church in relation to itself and to the world (Granfield [1285], Gritti [121]). This kind of study looks less at actual media use than at advocacy issues that put the churches in the forefront of debates about the New World Information and Communication Order, for example [293]. Other ways to relate church and society on communication topics include the right to information or communication (Jorgenson [283], Mole [243], and Gabel [735]) and the enforcement of the public's ownership of the airwaves (Jennings [385]).

Finally, the academic (for want of a better term) approach aims at the arrangement of materials with the greatest analytical power. For example, I have proposed elsewhere [70] a six by four matrix to aid in sorting out the literature dealing with theology and communication. Six analogues for communication (linguistic, aesthetic, cultural, dialogic, mechanical, and theological) intersect with four basic themes (religious self-understanding, Christian attitudes toward communication, pastoral uses of communication, and ethics or advocacy) to form a structure that allows one to differentiate the sometimes confusing and overlapping writings on theology and communication. In another place [210], I suggest that a similar model could benefit from a correlation with Niebhur's five types of Christian culture.

Although these six general approaches to the study of Christian communication cover most of the material, there may well exist other, better, ways to sift through the key issues. Perhaps these can serve as starting points for now.

Chapter 2

Resources

This chapter includes resource materials for the study of Christian communication: periodicals which specifically address the topic or which carry significant articles; bibliographies; directories of personnel or organizations engaged in Christian communication projects; and catalogues of materials.

Periodicals

[1] *ACCF Journal.*

"An occasional publication of the Asian Christian Communications Fellowship, this journal publishes theme issues on various aspects of Christian communication, usually as it relates to the situation in Asia. Subscriptions: ACCF; Serangoon Garden; P. O. Box 461; Singapore 9155. $14 (Asia) $19 (outside Asia).

[2] *Action: World Association for Christian Communication Newsletter.*

This general newsletter about Christian communication of every kind appears 10 times a year and features many short articles and notes about people working in communication, particularly in missionary areas. Its regular features include listings of courses, conferences, newsletters and resources. Subscriptions: $10 per year: *Action;* 357 Kennington Lane; London SE11 5QY; England. 8 pages.

[3] *ADRIS Newsletter.*

"The newsletter of the Association for the Development of Religious Information Services," this publication is devoted to the goal of promoting coordination and cooperation among bibliographic and information services and systems that deal with or touch upon religion. Each issue contains a calendar, announcements, book notices, and so forth. Subscriptions: ADRIS;

Department of Theology; Fordham University; Bronx, NY 10458; USA. $5 per year, plus $2 foreign postage.

[4] *Asia Region Newsletter.* World Association for Christian Communication.

The quarterly newsletter of the Asia Region of the World Association for Christian Communication, this eight page publication carries conference notes, informal communications, and contributed features. Apply to Agustine Loorthusamy (AR-WACC Secretary): Asian Social Institute; 1518 Leon Guinto Street; Malate, Manila; Philippines.

[5] *The Beam.* International Magazine of Christian Radio and Television.

This magazine is published monthly by the Radio and Television Commission of the Southern Baptist Convention. Box 12223; Fort Worth, TX 76116; USA.

[6] *Boletín Informativo MCS.*

This is a bimonthly publication which carries articles and discussion of mass media issues for the Catholic Church in Latin America. Subscriptions: UNDA-AL; Carrera 15, no. 10-41; Apartado 8009; Bogotá, 1, D.E., Colombia; or, SERPAL; Am Kieferwald 21; D-8000 Munich 45; West Germany.

[7] *Boletín UCLAP.*

This bulletin, a quarterly newsletter, is published by the Unión Católica Latinoamericana de Prensa, an affiliate of International Catholic Press Union (UCIP). Subscriptions: UCLAP; Rua Frei Luis 100; Casilla 90023; 25600 Petropolis, RJ; Brazil.

[8] *Catholic Action.*

Published monthly by the National Catholic Welfare Council (the predecessor of the United States Catholic Conference), in the 1940's, it carried a regular feature "The Catholic Radio Bureau" which reported news items and editorial comments about broadcasting efforts by the Catholic Church.

[9] *The Christian Broadcaster.*

A quarterly journal published by the World Committee for Christian Broadcasting; 475 Riverside Drive; New York, NY 10027; USA.

[10] *Christian Communication Spectrum.*

The newsletter of the Billy Graham Program in Communications, this quarterly is available from Wheaton College; Wheaton, Illinois; USA.

[11] *Communicatio Socialis: Zeitschrift fur Publizistik in Kirche und Welt.*

This quarterly, founded in 1967, publishes general articles on religious communication. Subscriptions DM 38 per year from Verlag Ferdinand Schoningh; Juhenplatz 1-3; D-4790 Paderborn; West Germany.

[12] *Communicatio Socialis Yearbook: Journal of Christian Communication in the Third World.*

This yearbook "proposes to provide a forum for ideas, sharing of experiences, and evaluation of performances mailny for the Christian communicators in Africa, Asia, Oceania and Latin America." Each volume of approximately 300 pages contains articles, documentation, a chronicle of events, reports and book reviews. Available from Satprakashan Sanchar Kendra; Sat pracher Press; Indoere; M. P. 452 001; India.

[13] *communication humaine aujourd'hui.*

A newsletter published every other month by the Centre National de Press Catholique in Paris, this features news and short articles, usually focused on a particular theme. Subscriptions are 110 F per year, from Centre National de Press Catholique; 19, rue de l'Amiral-d'Estaing; 75116 Paris; France.

[14] *Communication.*

This general newsletter has been published since 1969 and is available from Catholic Communications Centre; 74 Greenwich Road; Greenwich 2065; NSW Australia.

[15] *Communication: Crec-Avex.*

This quarterly newsletter chronicles the work of the communication training center, Crec-Avex, in Lyon, France. Crec-Avex; B. P. 70; 69132 Ecully Cedex; France.

[16] *The FCP Newsletter.*

The newsletter of the the Fellowship of Christian Puppeteers, this periodical comes out four times a year and features news, ideas, costume designs, play scripts, and so forth. The newsletter is included in FCP membership ($10/year in the US; slightly more for foreign subscriptions). Office of the FCP Secretary; 13461 Appalachian Way; San Diego, CA 92129; USA.

[17] *Homiletic.* A Review of Publications in Religious Communication.

This semi-annual review (published in June and December) is sponsored by the Academy of Homiletics and by the Religious Speech Communication Association. Each number carries two or three articles, usually addressing some topic in homiletics; the bulk of the issue, though, gives reviews of materials on preaching, sermons, the history of preaching, Biblical interpretation, theology, worship, communication theology, art and media, human sciences and culture, and dissertations. Subscription information: *Homiletic;* Lutheran Theological Seminary; 61 West Confederate Avenue; Gettysburg, PA 17325. 1988 subscription cost: $7.00.

[18] *Information Bulletin of the Catholic Media Council.*

This bulletin, published twice a year, carries articles and reports on the activities of the Catholic Media Council in West Germany. Subscriptions: Catholic Media Council; Bendelstrasse 7; P. O. Box 1912; D-5100 Aachen; West Germany.

[19] *Informations.*

This newsletter is published three times a year by the International Catholic Press Union. Available from: UCIP Geneve; 37-39 rue de Vermont; B. P. 197; Ch-1211 Geneva 20; Switzerland.

[20] *Intercom.*

This "pastoral and liturgical magazine published by the Catholic Communications Institute of Ireland" is geared to priests and religious. It carries a variety of articles on pastoral topics and communication. Subscriptions are available only with membership in the Institute ($15 per year). Apply to Membership Secretary; 7/8 Lr Abbey Street; Dublin 1; Ireland.

[21] *Interlit.*

This is published 4 times a year by the David C. Cook Foundation, a nonprofit institution dedicated to international Christian education. David C. Cook Foundation; Elgin, IL 60120; USA.

[22] *International Christian Broadcasters Bulletin.*

This monthly notice and guide comes from the information service of International Christian Broadcasters, Inc. 101 North Cascade Avenue; Colorado Springs, CO 80902; USA.

[23] *JESCOM International.*

This newsletter of and for Jesuits working in communication around the world appears four times a year. It features news of individuals and programs and usually a thematic presentation. Recent themes include religious communication work by regions of the world and a survey of communication studies programs around the world. Available from the Jesuit Center for Social Communication; C. P. 6139; 00195 Rome, Italy. No subscription price listed.

[24] *JESCOMEA Feedback.*

This quarterly newsletter from the Communications Secretariat of the Jesuit Conference of East Asia reports on the activities of Jesuits working in communications ministry in East Asia. Copies are available from the Jesuit Conference of East Asia; P. O. Box 4132; Manila, Philippines 2802.

[25] *The Journal of Communication and Religion.*

Formerly *Religious Communication Today,* the journal of the Religious Speech Communication Association, this semi-annual contains articles and resources (book reviews, bibliographies, and so forth). It "welcomes articles on any aspect of religious speech communication" from any recognized research approach. Subscriptions are $6.00; *Journal of Communication and Religion;* c/o Dr. Franklin Karnes; Manhattan Christian College; Manhattan, KN 66502.

[26] *Kirche und Film: Ein Informationsdienst.*

This monthly publication on film is available from Gemeinschaftswerk der Evangelischen Publizistik; Friedrichstrasse 2-6; 6000 Frankfurt a. M; West Germany.

[27] *Kirche und Rundfunk: Informationsdienst fur Horfunk und Fernsehen.*

This general information digest on radio and television is published every other week. Available from Gemeinschaftswerk der Evangelischen Publizistik; Friedrichstrasse 2-6; 6000 Frankfurt a. M.; West Germany.

[28] *Literature and Belief.*

This yearly monograph series, published by the Center for the Study of Christian Values in Literature at Brigham Young University, offers a variety of articles that "focus on the moral/religious aspects of high quality literature," or those that "project a critical theory of literary analysis based on moral/religious considerations." Subscriptions: *Literature and Belief;* A-279 Jesse Knight Building; Brigham Young University; Provo, UT 84602; USA.

[29] *Lumen Vitae.*

This "international review of religious education" deals occasionally with religious communication, particularly as it touches on evangelization and catechetics. Published quarterly at Brussels; subscription rates vary according to country; $22 per year. *Lumen Vitae;* 186, rue Washington; 1050 Brussels; Belgium.

[30] *Lumière et vie.*

This periodical features mainly Roman Catholic catechetics but issues special numbers on communication from time to time. It is published five times a year and is available from *Lumière et vie;* 2, place Gaillton; 69002 Lyon; France.

[31] *Mass Media Newsletter.*

Published twice monthly by Mass Media Ministries, Inc., (P. O. Box 180; Mystic CT 06355; USA) from 1973 to 1981, this newsletter provided capsule reviews and articles on media materials for Christian uses.

[32] *MCS.*

This monthly bulletin, published by the Roman Catholic Comisión Episcopal de Medios de Comunicación Social, carries short articles and notices dealing with religious communication. Subscriptions: Boletin del Secretariado Nacional; ANASTRO; 1-28033 Madrid; Spain.

[33] *Media and Values.*

This Canadian monthly supplies news on the media, new techniques on communication, and reflection on media products. Free. Available from *Media and Values;* P. O. Box 5300; Sydney, N. S. B1P 6L2; Canada.

[34] *Media&Values: A Quarterly Resource for Media Awareness.*

Published quarterly by the Media Action Research Center, *Media&Values* promotes the study of the impact of television on viewers; it also provides a resource for the study of media in society. Directed by a board consisting of representatives of 14 religious groups, the publication typically publishes a theme issue with articles, short perspectives, and a reflection/action section. The usual issue runs 24 pages. Subscriptions: $14.00 per year, 1962 South Shenandoah; Los Angeles, CA 90034; USA.

[35] *Media Development.*

The World Association for Christian Communication publishes this, its official journal, four times a year. Edited in London, each issue follows a particular theme; in addition each number also has a "forum" section for debate about other issues and a book review section. Typical journal issues run 48 pages. Subscriptions: $25.00 per year. 357 Kennington Lane; London SE11 5QY; England.

[36] *Medium: Zeitschrift fur Horfunk, Fernsehen, Film, Bild, Ton.*

This monthly publishes theme issues on various aspects of communication and includes religious issues. 60 DM per year. Gemeinschaftswerk der Evangelischen Publizistik; Friedrichstrasse 2-6; 6000 Frankfurt a .M.; West Germany.

The same publisher also issues *Medien Dokumentation* at irregular intervals on various topics.

[37] *Multimedia International.*

This periodical devoted to issues of group media or small group communication has published two series. The first, running from 1973 to 1975 issued bimonthly monographs on a variety of topics associated with religious communication. The second series, from 1976, issues an annual or yearbook which collects essays around a common theme. Some recent themese include the committed Christian in secular communication, communication in religious congregations, group media, and communication training. Available from Multimedia International; CP 6139; 00100, Rome; Italy.

[38] *OCIC Info.*

This is the bimonthly newsletter of the Organisation catholique internationale du cinéma; it deals with items on the cinema and audiovisual communication. Available for $10 per year from OCIC; Rue de l'Orme, 8; B-1040 Brussels; Belgium.

[39] *OCS Nouvelles.*

This newsletter of the Canadian Catholic office of communication is published 8-10 times per year and is available from l'Office des communications sociales; 4005, rue de Bellechasse; Montreal, Quebec; Canada.

[40] *Proclaim.*

Published 10 times a year by the Department of Communication, United States Catholic Conference, this newsletter for Catholic communicators features reports on the Catholic Communication Campaign projects, media resources (usually program notices), reports on regulatory actions by the FCC or the U. S. courts, and an update on network programs dealing with religious themes. The four page newletter can be obtained from the Department of Communication, United States Catholic Conference; 1011 First Avenue, Suite 1300; New York, NY 10022; USA.

[41] *Religion and Life.* Ralph Rolls, ed.

Published by the British Broadcasting Corporation twice yearly at the request of the School Broadcasting Council, this magazine provides a program guide to religious radio specials as well as discussion guides for each program. 35 Marylebone High Street; London W1M 4AA; England.

[42] *Religious Broadcasting.*

The official publication of the National Religious Broadcasters, an evangelical organization, this monthly magazine carries a variety of articles and trade information about Christian communication. Subscriptions are $18 per year, from *Religious Broadcasting;* Box 1174; Dover, New Jersey 07801; USA.

[43] *Religious Education.*

The Journal of the Religious Education Association and the Association of Professors and Researchers in Religious Education, *Religious Education* publishes occasional articles dealing with communication as well as special editions devoted to the theme. See particularly 82.2 (Spring 1987) for the full text of the report of the National Council of Churches Study Commission on Theology, Education and the Electronic Media, including essays by individual commissioners and and annotated bibliography. Subscriptions come with membership in the association ($35/year): 409 Prospect Street; New Haven, CN 06511-2177; USA.

[44] *Religious Theatre.*

This semi-annual publication carries plays, reviews, and news notes. Florida Presbyterian College; St. Petersburg FL 33733; USA.

[45] *Sacred Dance Guild Journal.*

This magazine is published three times a year and carries information about dance and religion as well as some choreographed dances. The journal comes with membership in the Sacred Dance Guild. For information, write Sally Alderice; R.D.#2; Valatie, NY 12184; USA. $16/year.

[46] *Sonolux Information: A Group Media Journal.*

This quarterly, published by Sonolux, an international Catholic group media service, provides theme issues on various aspects of religious communication using group media. It is available from SONOLUX; Pettenkoferstrasse, 26; 8000 Munich 2; West Germany.

[47] *UMCom, United Methodist Communications: The Communicator.*

"A newsletter for church communication leaders," this publication comes out 10 times a year from the Office of Public Relations; United Methodist Communications; 810 Twelfth Avenue, South; Nashville, TN 37203; USA.

[48] *UNDA-AL: Comunicación, estudios y documentos.*

This magazine, published by the Asociación Católica Latinoamericana para la Radio y la Televisión carries general articles on church communication in Latin America. For subscription information, contact UNDA-AL; Cochabamba 2567, 4, "29"; 1252-Buenos Aires; Argentina.

[49] *Visions—The Video Newsletter.*

This is a monthly newsletter providing information regarding video productions, including a theological analysis of current programs, reports on new developments, reviews of new resources, and case studies. $18.00 from Wesley Foundation Books and Video; 211 N. School Steet; Normal, IL 61761; USA.

[50] *The Wide World of UNDA.*

The monthly newsletter of the International Catholic Association for Radio and Television, this 12 page publication features news of the organization around the world, a feature presentation on some aspect of religious communication, updates on technology, and other notices. Subscriptions: $9.00 in Europe; $13.00 outside of Europe. UNDA; rue de l'Orme, 12; B-1040 Brussels; Belgium.

Bibliographies

[51] Achtemeier, Elizabeth and Martha Aycock. *Bibliography on Preaching, 1975-1985.* N.p.: Union Theological Seminary in Virginia, 1986.

This listing of titles on preaching treats recent publications under the categories of books, periodical articles, essays, and theses. It divides each category into the following headings: the preacher, history and sociology of preaching, theology and hermeneutics of preaching, evangelism, sermon development, effective preaching, sermon forms, lectionary preaching, preaching from specific texts and/or themes, electronic media, preaching and the ministry, preaching and worship/music, sermon collections, and children's sermons. The authors annotate few entries. 61 pages.

[52] Adams, Doug. *Bibliography of Christian and Jewish Religious Dancing.* N.p.: privately printed, n.d.

An annotated bibliography on dance in worship, including references to and summaries of early Christian texts. 76 pages.

[53] Amani, Leo Masawe. *Religious Symbolism: A Selected Bibliography.* London: Centre for the Study of Communication and Culture, 1980.

This bibliography of over 400 entries, first prepared for a conference on religious symbolism and intercultural communication, presents a first look at much material on religious symbolism. The presentation follows these divisions: (1) symbolism in general, philosophical perspectives, anthropological perspectives, myth, psychological perspectives; (2) religious symbolism in general, philosophical perspectives, anthropological and sociological perspectives, psychological perspectives; and (3) Christian symbolism, theological perspectives, Scriptural perspectives, liturgical uses, Christian art, mysticism. Many of the entries have annotations. 63 pages.

[54] Ames, Charlotte, ed. *Directory of Roman Catholic Newspapers on Microfilm: United States.* Notre Dame, IN: Cushwa Center for the Study of American Catholicism, University of Notre Dame, 1982.

This list, arranged geographically, provides an index to Roman Catholic newspapers available in microform. It includes the dates available and OCLC numbering information. 69 pages.

[55] Baragli, Enrico. "Verso una Teologia degli Strumenti di Comunicazione Sociale?" *La Civiltà Cattolica* 121.2 (1970): 141-150.

In this review essay, Baragli summarizes the writings of over a dozen Italian, French, Spanish, Belgian, and Canadian authors on the question of whether there can be a theology of mass communication. In summary he notes that the theological reflection on communication is too recent to be well developed, that the means of communication are too diverse to come under one heading, and that other questions enter into the discussion. Examples of these latter questions include the nature of the theological imagination, the nature of society, and the nature of instrumentality. 10 pages.

[56] R. R. Bowker Company. *Religious Books, 1867-1982.* 4 vols. New York: R. R. Bowker Company, 1983.

This bibliographic guide, prepared by the research staff of the R. R. Bowker Company, provides listings of all religious publications contained in the Bowker records as well as in the Library of Congress records. Three volumes contain the materials arranged according to the Library of Congress subject headings; a fourth volume provides an author/title index. Each entry lists the title, author, publisher, place and date of publication, a general contents note, and both the Library of Congress and Dewey classification numbers.

[57] R. R. Bowker Company. *Religious and Inspirational Books & Serials in Print 1985.* New York: R. R. Bowker Company, 1985.

This annual of publishers' listings of religious communication of all kinds includes publishers' addresses for books and serials. The material is arranged alphabetically. 1648 pages.

[58] Brunkow, Robert deV., ed. *Religion and Society in North America: An Annotated Bibliography.* Clio Bibliography Series 12. Santa Barbara, CA; Oxford: Clio, 1983.

This bibliography has one section devoted to "modes of religious expression and representation" and includes there materials on architecture, the arts, music, radio and television, religious literature, and secular literature. The section is limited to 23 pages and omits much (for example, there are only four entries under radio and television); however, the material on architecture and literature seem complete. 515 pages.

[59] Burr, Nelson R. *A Critical Bibliography of Religion in America.* Religion in American Life 4. Princeton, New Jersey: Princeton University Press, 1961.

This volume of the Religion in American Life series (Vol. 4, parts 3-5) contains bibliographic essays on religion and the arts, architecture, and music in America and on religion and literature (including a brief section on the religious press) in America. 1219 pages.

[60] Christians, Clifford G. and Robert S. Fortner. "The Media Gospel." *Journal of Communication* 31.2 (Spring 1981): 190-199.

This review essay examines television evangelism and tries to balance both critical and supportive works. Choosing the internal validity of each book as a criteria for evaluation, the authors look at works by Armstrong, Engel, Muggeridge, and Owens. A helpful quality of this essay is its introduction grounding the books for review in terms of a common Christian tradition which shares the elements of God-centeredness, human sanctity as a species, and a fellowship of the road. 10 pages.

[61] Cook, John W. "Theology and the Arts: Sources and Resources." *Theology Today*, 34.1 (April 1977): 45-51.

This brief bibliographic essay lists materials dealing with theology and the arts, including painting, iconography, biblical illustration, and architecture. 7 pages.

[62] Dick, Donald. "Religious Broadcasting: 1920-1965, A Bibliography." *Journal of Broadcasting* 9.3 (Summer 1965): 249-279; 10.2 (Spring 1966): 163-180; 10.3 (Summer 1966): 257-276.

This bibliographic guide presents an exhaustive list of over 1300 items dealing with religious broadcasting. "All materials which seemed to have relevance are listed. No attempt was made to evaluate materials listed." The listings are divided into the following classes: (1) sources of bibliographic information; (2) unpublished theses and dissertations; (3) books, documents, and pamphlets; (4) unpublished, mimeographed, and miscellaneous materials; (5) periodicals; and (6) articles in periodicals. This collection does provide a marvelous resource for future work but many of the entries, particularly among the periodical articles, need evaluation. 67 pages.

[63] Ferré, John P. "Religious Perspectives on Commercial Television in the United States." *Critical Studies in Mass Communication* 2 (1985): 290-295.

This review essay examines the works of 32 individuals who have criticized television in the United States from the perspective of religion. It briefly notes each individual, sometimes with biographical data, and recounts the substance of the critique. Early figures tended to be more optimistic than later ones. This essay provides a good reference and a good starting point for further work. 6 pages.

[64] Herzog, Wilhelm. *Church and Communication in Developing Countries: A Bibliography.* München: Verlag Ferdinand Schöningh, 1973.

This book contains a listing of 351 unannotated titles (book and journal article) dealing with religious communication in the Third World. The titles are crossed indexed according to geographical location, media, and general subject area. 67 pages.

[65] Hill, George H. and Lenwood Davis. *Religious Broadcasting, 1920-1983: A Selectively Annotated Bibliography.* New York: Garland Publishing, Inc. 1984.

Intended for the "seasoned researcher as well as for the student doing his first term paper," this bibliography provides an introduction to work in religious radio and television, listing 1644 books, dissertations, and articles. Each book and most of the dissertation entries carry an annotation; the article listings merely show the basic bibliographical data. Book topics reviewed include religious broadcasting in general, biography, public relations and journalism; article topic headings include broadcasting, Catholic, Controversy, General, Lutheran, Networks, overseas, personalities, radio, television, and an addendum of miscellaneous titles. The article entries tend to reflect pieces run in popular magazines rather than those in scholarly journals. A name and program index conclude the volume. 243 pages.

[66] *Intercom 1981.*

This periodical carries an ongoing series of bibliographic articles, indexing books and articles on religious communication in Brazil. Portuguese. *Intercom 1981;* Rua Augusta, 555; Sobreloja; San Paulo, SP, cep 01305; Brazil.

[67] Johnson, Albert. *Best Church Plays: A Bibliography of Religious Drama.* Philadelphia: Pilgrim Press, 1968.

This annotated bibliography provides a 149 page listing of plays suitable for church use and supplies 10 different indices, categorizing plays as Biblical, Christmas, Easter, Missionary, Historical, and so forth. The annotation includes number in cast, running time, setting, and brief summary. In addition an appendix contains the addresses of publishers, authors, and agents. 180 pages.

[68] Lippy, Charles H., ed. *Religious Periodicals of the United States: Academic and Scholarly Journals.* New York: Greenwood Press, 1986.

This general guide to academic and scholarly religious periodicals surveys 100+ periodicals, giving a profile and history of each as well as sources for further information and a publication history. Arranged alphabetically, the book also includes a chronological capsule, an index by sponsoring organization, and a name index. 609 pages.

[69] Litfin, A. Duane and Haddon W. Robinson, eds. *Recent Homiletical Thought: An Annotated Bibliography, Vol. 2, 1966-1979.* Grand Rapids, MI: Baker Book House, 1983.

This continuation of the Toohey and Thompson work follows the same divisions as the first volume and annotates 1898 recent titles in homiletics as well as providing a list of periodicals which treat homiletics. The editors note that this more recent collection brings forward a new generation of authors; that a large quantity of applied "research" comes from D. Min. programs but that it seldom goes beyond the initial study; that dialogue preaching seems to have died out; and that most authors have an overwhelming expectation of the preacher. 249 pages.

[70] Soukup, Paul A. *Communication and Theology: Introduction and Review of the Literature.* London: World Association for Christian Communication, 1983.

Written as an extended review essay, this book situates 238 works on theology and communication in terms of their model of the communication process and of their basic question. The materials fit into a six by four grid. Communication models include linguistic, aesthetic, cultural, interpersonal, mechanical, and theological; basic questions deal with religious self- understanding, Christian attitudes toward communication, pastoral uses of communication, and ethics or advocacy. The book also contains the outlines of a theological study program for communication and two bibliographies—the books reviewed and a more inclusive one arranged by subject matter. 114 pages.

[71] Soukup, Paul A. "Theology and Communication." *Critical Studies in Mass Communication* 2 (1985): 295-299.

This review essays notes 36 works that attempt to bridge the distance between the discipline of theology and the general area of communication studies. Soukup divides the material into three areas: those which move from theology to communication, those which move from communication to theology, and those which present a critique of communicative practice. 5 pages.

[72] Stroup, George W., III. "A Bibliographical Critique." *Theology Today* 22 (1975): 133-143.

In this review of the literature on narrative theology, the author divides the material into three categories: "(1) narrative as 'religious' autobiography and biography, (2) narrative as a formal quality of human experience, and (3) narrative as the primary genre in Christian Scripture." He concludes the essay with a brief investigation of the value of narrative for theology. 11 pages.

[73] Stroupe, Henry Smith. *The Religious Press in the South Atlantic States, 1802-1865: An Annotated Bibliography with Historical Introduction and Notes.* Durham, North Carolina: Duke University Press, 1956.

This bibliographical work lists those newspapers and magazines in the South (Virginia, the Carolinas, Georgia, Florida, and West Virginia) which assigned more than half their space to religious questions. After a thorough and readable historical introduction to the various denominations in the South in the first half of the nineteenth century, the book provides a bibliography of 159 religious publications and includes title, place of publication, date of first and last issues, periodicity, format, circulation, editor, publisher or proprietor, the denominational affiliation, and a general indication of content. The volume closes with chronological, denominational and geographical indices. 172 pages.

[74] Taylor, Rosemary. "English Baptist Periodicals, 1790-1865." *The Baptist Quarterly* 27 (1977): 50-82.

This bibliography provides a guide for historical research into the publications of the Baptists in England between the years 1790 and 1865. The former date saw the opening number of the *Baptist Annual Register,* the first Baptist periodical in Britain; the latter, the first issue of the *Sword and the Trowel,* "the first magazine devoted to the interests of a single Baptist church." The works in this bibliography appear chronologically by year and include title, numbering, dates, imprints, editor, size and price, an annotation describing the publication, and an indication of the locations in which extant copies may be found. The bibliography lists 97 entries and includes an index of editors and an index of titles. 33 pages.

[75] Toohey, William and William D. Thompson, eds. *Recent Homiletical Thought: A Bibliography, 1935-1965.* Nashville: Abingdon Press, 1967.

This collection, representative rather than complete, provides annotations of 2137 works on homiletics and preaching. Materials, coded as Protestant or Catholic in orientation, fall into three major headings: books, articles, and dissertations and theses. Each major section follows these headings: general works, preaching and theology, topics of preaching, the preacher, the congregation, the setting, the sermon, delivery, history, and bibliography. 303 pages.

[76] Troxell, Kay. *Resources in Sacred Dance: Annotated Bibliography.* Peterborough, NH: Sacred Dance Guild, 1986.

An updating of Wolbers' bibliography [78], this annotated list provides material on books, booklets, pamphlets, articles and other publications as well as non-print materials dealing with sacred dance. 40 pages.

[77] Walsh, Michael J., et al. *Religious Bibliographies in Serial Literature: A Guide.* Westport, CN: Greenwood Press, 1981.

This volume, the result of a cooperative project of the Association of British Theological and Philosophical Libraries, introduces and describes existing indexing and abstracting services in religious, theological, and religio-philosophical literature. Designed for library staffs and for researchers in religious studies and theology, the book aims to serve as a bibliographic help. For its 178 entries this guide provides the following information: title, subtitle, bibliographic data, publishing history, a description of the physical arrangement of the book, a description of its coverage, a comment describing its value, the publisher's address, and the International Standard Serial Number. The volume also contains subject and title indices. 216 pages.

[78] Wolbers, Mary Jane. *Resources in Sacred Dance.* East Stroudsbury, PA: n.p., 1964.

This listing provides a guide to books, periodical literature, and unpublished manuscripts dealing with dance. It also offers some other suggested resources in sacred dance, noting the use of dance in worship and religious education. 22 pages.

Many works on Christian communication—not themselves bibliographic in nature—also include bibliographies as a guide to further study. For bibliographies of materials on writing, see [566], [570], and [573]. For further reading on mass media and the churches, see [720], [759], [803], [826], [1101], and [1106]. For materials on other media (art, drama, dance, comics, and so forth), see [1135], [1153], [1155], [1182], [1188], [1197], [1203], [1213], [1214], [1250], [1253], [1277], and [1294].

Directories

[79] Anderson, Robert and Gail North. *Gospel Music Encyclopedia.* New York: Sterling Publishing Co., 1979.

This encyclopedia provides an alphabetical and photographic listing of active Gospel music performers, a guide to Gospel awards, and a sampler of Christian music. 320 pages.

[80] Armstrong, Ben, ed. *The Directory of Religious Broadcasting.* Morristown, NJ: National Religious Broadcasters, 1982.

A comprehensive directory of religious broadcasting in the United States, this volume contains listings of radio stations by state; a guide to religious programming; listings for shortwave and foreign stations; listings for television broadcast and cable stations; and listings for film, music, and publishing companies engaged in religious communication. Each listing contains name, address, and telephone number as well as some basic descriptive information. 468 pages.

[81] Associated Church Press. *The Associated Church Press Directory.* Geneva, IL: The Associated Church Press.

This annual publication lists member publications, addresses, telephone numbers, editor's names, staff members, circulation and other statistics, and advertising rates. The Associated Church Press is a professional organization supporting the work of those engaged in religious publication and journalism. The Associated Church Press; P. O. Box 306; Geneva, IL 60134-0306; USA.

[82] Campbell, Richard H. Michael R. Pitts. *The Bible on Film: A Checklist, 1897-1980.* Metuchen, N.J.: The Scarecrow Press, 1981.

This index of "every [theatrical release] film, either motion picture or television program, based on the Bible" provides a reference list arranged chronologically and by Old and New Testament. Citations include title, release year, country of origin, release company, running time, production credits and cast, as well a a capsule review. 214 pages.

[83] Eilers, Franz-Josef and Wilhelm Herzog. *Catholic Press Directory: Africa/Asia.* München: Verlag Ferdinand Schöningh, 1975.

This reference work gives a listing of Roman Catholic newspapers and periodicals alphabetically by country in Africa and Asia. Each listing consists of the publication title, address, periodicity, language, page size, number of pages, printing method, publisher, editor, printer, year founded, circulation, area of circulation, and readership characteristics. In addition the book provides an overview of each country (population, area, ethnic growth, languages, religions, media availability, and leading press and religious institutions). Where available church communication office information is also given. 318 pages.

[84] Eilers, Franz-Josef, Marcel Vanhengel, Wasil A. Müller, Hans Florin, and Knud Jørgensen, eds. *Christian Communication Directory Africa.* Paderborn: Ferdinand Schöningh; London: WACC; Geneva: Lutheran World Federation, 1980.

This directory lists Christian communication institutions in Africa, according to information provided by each institute. The material, arranged by country, is further subdivided according to nine categories: Church communication centers, news and information services, publishing houses, printing presses, periodicals, radio/TV stations, radio/TV production houses, AV/film centers, and research and training centers. Each listing indicates the institution name, director, address, legal status, personnel, foundation date, church affiliation, objectives and activities and other specific information such as readership or special equipment. The directory lists the following countries: Algeria, Angola, Benin, Botswana, Burundi, Cameroon, Central African Republic, Congo, Egypt, Ethiopia, Gabon, Ghana, Guinea,

Ivory Coast, Kenya, Lesotho, Liberia, Madagascar, Malawi, Mali, Mauritius Island, Morocco, Mozambique, Niger, Nigeria, Reunion, Rhodesia, Rwanda, Senegal, Seychelles, Sierre Leone, Somalia, South Africa, South West Africa/Namibia, Sudan, Swaziland, Tanzania, Tchad, Togo, Transkei, Tunisia, Uganda, Upper Volta, Zaire, and Zambia. 544 pages.

[85] Eilers, Franz-Josef, Marcel Vanhengel, Wasil A. Müller, Hans Florin, and Marc Chambron, eds. *Christian Communication Directory ASIA*. Paderborn: Ferdinand Schöningh; Aachen: Catholic Media Council; London: WACC; Geneva: Lutheran World Federation, 1982.

This guide attempts "to list all Christian media institutions" in Asia as part of an ongoing project to compile similar guides for Africa, Oceania, and Latin America. The classification follows nine categories: Church communication centers, news and information services, publishing houses, printing presses, periodicals, radio/TV stations, radio/TV production houses, AV/Film centers, and research and training institutes. Organized by country, the directory includes as much of the following information as provided by the institutes: the institution name, director, address, church affiliation, foundation date, personnel, objectives, and activities. Other information (for example, equipment, publisher, and so forth) is given where relevant. The guide lists these countries: Asia (continental), Bangladesh, Burma, Hong Kong, India (by state), Indonesia, Japan, Korea (South), Macau, Malaysia, Nepal, Pakistan, Philippines, Singapore, Sri Lanka, Taiwan, Thailand, and Vietnam. A name index completes the volume. 1036 pages.

[86] Grayken, Mary, ed. *Interfaith Media Directory*. Washington, D. C.: Interfaith Conference of Metropolitan Washington, 1983.

This directory covers media resources available to the Christian, Jewish, and Islamic communities in the Washington area, listing religious newspapers, newsletters, locally produced radio programs, network television programs, and local cable television programs. The first section lists media resources according to denomination; the second, newspapers; the third and fourth, radio and television. Each entry lists the sponsoring group, its address, the type of media, editors or producers, contents, deadlines, and circulation or distribution.

[87] International Christian Broadcasters. *World Directory of Religious Radio and Television Broadcasting*. South Pasadena, CA: William Carey Library, 1973.

This directory arranges its survey of Christian broadcasting stations by continent and by country within each continent. A map and an brief overview of church-related broadcasting activities begin each region's material. For each country, the directory lists the city, the station name, call letters, ownership, power, wavelength, and frequency. In addition, for each station, the directory indicates types of programming (Christian, non-Christian, Protestant, Catholic), cost per 15 minute segment, and station type (cultural, religious, or commercial). A listing of studios preparing Christian materials and the status of Christian broadcasting complete each country's entry in the directory. This volume also includes a directory of international Christian radio stations and a general index. 808 pages.

[88] Lutheran World Federation. *Lutheran Communication Directory, 1981-1982.* Geneva: Lutheran World Federation, 1981.

This directory lists communication contacts and regional activities for the Lutheran Church around the world. Each entry includes institution name, address, director, types of communication activity (e. g., publications, radio, television, etc.), and brief descriptions. More recent editions may be available from the Department of Communication; Lutheran World Federation; 150, route de Ferney; 1211 Geneva 20; Switzerland. 96 pages.

[89] National Religious Broadcasters. *The Directory of Religious Broadcasting.* Morristown, NJ: National Religious Broadcasters.

This annual provides listings of broadcasters, services, stations, suppliers, programs, and so forth, that would be of interest to those engaged in religious broadcasting. It is available for $49.95 from National Religious Broadcasters; Box 1926; Morristown, NJ 07960; USA.

Catalogues

[90] Dalglish, William A., ed. *Media for Christian Formation.* Dayton, OH: Geo. P. Pflaum, 1969.

This book is a guide to audio-visual resources for Christian education, based not on denominational source but on quality of the product. Listing books, films, filmstrips, posters, records, slides, and tape recordings, it gives a brief description of each, an indication of appropriate grade level (pre-school through adult), and a judgment of merit. In addition to the evaluations, the book has a listing by title, a subject listing, and guides to libraries and to other sources of the materials. Though dated now, it does give a good indication of resources and may suggest ideas for others interested in the production of Christian communication materials. 393 pages.

[91] Fabun, Don, ed. *A Media Sourcebook.* Berkeley: Pacific School of Religion, 1973.

This mimeographed set of reprinted essays, how-to guides, and catalogues provides resource material on film, photography, cable television, broadcasting, music, church and the media, and a variety of other communicative areas. Each section ends with a bibliography. While some material is dated, other suggestions still have validity and value. 202 pages.

[92] Mathieson, Moira B., ed. *UNDA-USA 1983 Catalogue of Catholic Television and Radio Productions*. Washington, D. C.: UNDA-USA, 1983.

This catalogue of programs produced by Catholic agencies lists them first by the themes of family, parish, spirituality, education, social concerns, etc. This listing as well as the title listing is keyed to the longer program listings in which each production appears under its producer, whether that be a diocese or a syndicator. Each item contains a brief summary, a note on the format, the availability of the program for rental or sale, the production date, and a brief evaluation. In addition the catalogue contains information on the communication offices of each Catholic diocese in the United States. 352 pages.

[93] National Video Clearinghouse. *The Video Tape/Disc Guide: Religious Programs*. Elgin, IL: David C. Cook Publishing Co.; Syosset, NY: The National Video Clearinghouse, Inc., 1981.

This catalogue lists over 1350 video titles available from a variety of distributors. The materials fall into the following headings: business, children, fine arts, general interest/education, health/science, instruction, entertainment, and recreation. Title, subject, running time, format, release year, awards, producer, availability, and a brief synopsis are given for each entry. In addition to the entries, the book gives indices and a guide to wholesalers and distributors. Finally, several brief essays on the use of video in the church or church classroom introduce the material. 178 pages.

Chapter 3

Communication Theory

This chapter contains general materials on communication and the Christian Churches. The first section lists items that cut across categories or that address issues of communication theory and research. The next section presents material on theology and communication; for more bibliographical references to this material, see [70] and [210]. The third section contains Church statements on communication or communication policy as well as commentaries on those statements. The next section lists materials dealing with communication ethics, particularly from the Christian tradition. Section five lists some general critiques of communication—either of public or commercial communication or of the Churches' communication. Finally, the last section presents material dealing with media education.

Theory

[94] Abbey, Merrill R. *Man, Media and the Message.* 1960. New York: Friendship Press, 1970.

Designed as a brief introduction to communication and as a handbook of National Council of Churches thought and practice in the area of communication, this book sketches the impact of communication media on the world and argues that Christian communication emerges from a theology of reconciliation, witness, and gift. The book contains both general communication theory and examples of church communication ranging from mission work to television and radio to film to printed texts. 159 pages.

[95] Adams, Henry Babcock. "Revelation in the Light of Communication Theory: A Dialogue of Perception and Response." *Encounter* 25 (1964): 470-475.

Using concepts from semantics and information theory—levels of meaning and feedback—Adams suggests that we can know God's will. The former guides our interpretation of Scripture and the current demands of morality, while the latter allows us to check our understanding. 6 pages.

[96] Adams, Jay E. *Communicating with 20th Century Man.* Phillipsburg, NJ: Presbyterian and Reformed Publishing Co., 1979.

This short booklet, written from an evangelical point of view, argues that the Church's problems of communication stem from a de-emphasis upon the sovereignty of God, that people are searching for answers that the Bible can give, and that what is needed is to balance the form and substance of the message, something that liberal Protestantism and Roman Catholicism have failed to do. 36 pages.

[97] Allmen, J. J. von, G. Bavaud, et al. *Communion et communication: Structures d'unité et modèles de communication de l'Evangile.* Geneva: Labor et Fides, 1978.

These papers represent the ongoing discussions of the theological faculties of the universities of Fribourg, Geneva, Lausanne and Neuchatel on the topic of communication and ecclesial communion. This ecumenical group explores the possibility of rapport among the churches on the basis of the communication of the Gospel, examining the question from the perspectives of historical and pastoral theology. 148 pages.

[98] Atkinson, John. *The Media: A Christian View.* London: Epworth Press, 1979.

Defining the mass media as television, radio, the press, the cinema, and the stage, this book provides a general introduction to these media in Britain. Chapters deal with the nature of each, with the business and production aspects of each, with owners and advertisers, with minorities, and with controverted issues such as obscenity and violence in the media. The only specifically religious material deals with religious broadcasting and with the Methodist Church positions on some of the issues of sexuality, language, and violence. A final chapter gives an overview of local communities and communication—local radio, for example. 158 pages.

[99] Babin, Pierre. "Impact de l'audio-visuel sur la vie des chrétiens." *INTER* 16.16 (October 15, 1982): 2-9.

In this essay Babin defines what he means by the audio-visual civilization—sound, word, and image mediated electronically. He notes several areas in which the communication created by these new media have had an impact on contemporary life: destabilizing all structures, creating a closer world community, reviving religious feeling, establishing an alternative leadership, promoting a new learning, and so forth. 8 pages.

[100] Bahr, Hans-Eckehard. *Verkündigung als Information.* Hamburg: Furche-Verlag, 1968.

Bahr considers the proclamation of faith as an element of the process of information. He follows the trend of the 60's to apply aspects of cybernetics to preaching and evangelization. While valuable, the treatment remains elementary and somewhat dated. 144 pages.

[101] Biernatzki, W. E. *Catholic Communication Research: Topics and a Rationale.* London: Research Facilitator Unit [Centre for the Study of Communication and Culture], 1978.

This booklet suggests 40 research topics for religious communication, giving a brief explanation of each together with comments from various scholars. The topics themselves fall under seven headings: (1) faith, morals, and the secular media; (2) media structures; (3) media processes and effects; (4) religious uses of the media; (5) education through and for the media; (6) the theology and philosophy of the media; and (7) communication theory and research methodology. The list might serve as "suggestions for topics for term papers, theses and even dissertations" as well as ideas for major research studies. The booklet also contains a discussion of the nature and types of Christian communication. 36 pages.

[102] Bouldin, Don. *Ears to Hear, Eyes to See.* Nashville, TN: Broadman Press, 1987.

Bouldin points out how extensive the use of media has been in spreading God's word. Communication, he says, is part of the Christian life. Jesus, "the Master Communicator," provides a model for Christian communication: he appealed to human emotions and used every available method to communicate God's message. Christian communicators must understand their audience as well as their message because different things appeal to different individuals. Media are important because "not every person can be reached with the same instrument." Bouldin ends by encouraging everyone to become an instrument through which others can learn of God's love. 176 pages.

[103] Brooks, Peter. *Communicating Conviction.* London: Epworth Press, 1983.

This well-crafted book is designed as an introduction to methods of communicating the Christian faith. After a preliminary chapter of cultural analysis, the author presents excellent overviews on words, stories, pictures, dialogue and communication theory. 155 pages.

[104] Christians, Clifford G. "A Cultural View of Mass Communications: Some Explorations for Christians." *Christian Scholar's Review* 7 (1977): 3-22.

Joining other communication scholars in rejecting the stimulus response, scientistic, and positivistic strains in communication research as problematic, Christians opts for the cultural approach redefined with Christian overtones. Every cultural approach posits the importance of values; by emphasizing the moral aspect of being human, communication research will examine symbols and meanings as constitutive of community. But these symbols take their meaning against the background of the God who communicates and within the limits of creation. Christians argues for a stronger contribution of Christian men and women to communication research through the articulation of their biblical vision of human being. 20 pages.

[105] Copray, Norbert. *Kommunikation und Offenbarung.* Düsseldorf: Patmos, 1984.

This volume presents an analysis of the theses of Jürgen Habermas and offers a rather comprehensive study of their implications and that of the theory of action on Fundamental Theology. 346 pages.

[106] Craddock, Fred B. *Overhearing the Gospel.* Nashville, TN: Abingdon, 1978.

Asking, "How does one person communicate the Christian faith to another?" Craddock turns to Kierkegaard's theory of indirect communication. Taking his cue from Kierkegaard and commenting on the quotation, "There is no lack of information in a Christian land; something else is lacking, and this is something which the one man cannot directly communicate to the other," he examines the listener, the speaker, and the message and develops the proposal that the Christian communicator (or homilist) evoke the experience of the other and allow them to overhear the message that they might make of it what they will. 144 pages.

[107] Cummings, H. Wayland and Charles Somervill. *Overcoming Communication Barriers in the Church.* Valley Forge, PA: Judson Press, 1981.

A basic introduction to the study of communication, this volume applies communication theory to church settings in a comprehensive and helpful fashion. Within a social science framework, it presents material on intrapersonal, interpersonal, group, and organizational communication as well as brief comments on the mass media. Final chapters focus on ways of assessing communication effectiveness through checklists of appropriate behaviors. 175 pages.

[108] Dayan, Daniel, Elihu Katz, and Paul Kerns. "Armchair Pilgrimages: The Trips of John Paul II and their Television Public: An Anthropological View." *On Film* 13 (Fall 1984): 25-34.

Using Victor Turner's theory of liminality, the authors analyze televised papal pilgrimages as "anti-structural" events which allow home viewers to participate in a pilgrimage. Further, the authors persuasively argue that the papal travel is enacted less as a pilgrimage than as a medieval "adventus." The overall value of the article lies in its suggestion of descriptive categories for dealing with televised religious events. 10 pages.

[109] Dennett, Herbert. *Christian Communications in a Changing World.* London: Victory Press, 1968.

This guide to evangelism from the evangelical perspective works both as a reference to the then current [1968] Christian communication efforts and as a textbook for the beginner in the field. It provides broadly introductory chapters on language, audience, writing, literature, broadcasting, church outreach, and intra-church communication. 118 pages.

[110] Departmento de Comunicación Social, Consejo Episcopal Latino-americano. "Evangelización: Perspectiva del comunicador social." *Boletín informativo MCS* 80 (1978): 3-12.

This essay describes the kinds of communication best suited to evan-gelization—that which can produce a real and renewing effect in people and society. While mass communication has the advantages of practicality, economy, grand effects, and access to homes, it does not have the peda-gogical requirements for evangelizing. These are better met by dialogue, personal relationships, and participation. 10 pages.

[111] Devasundaram, Alexander. "The Cathedral as a Centre of Commu-nication." *Indian Journal of Theology* 24.1 (January-March 1975): 16-20.

Based on a study of an Indian Cathedral, this article argues that cathedrals should be the focal point of several type of communication: between church and world; between church and congregation; between church and other churches; and between various elements in the congregation. While raising some interesting issues, the article is too much a case study to be of general use. 5 pages.

[112] Dillistone, F. W. *Christianity and Communication.* New York: Charles Scribner's Sons., 1956.

With a concern for missionary work, this short book examines communica-tion from a Christian perspective and asks how to bridge the gap between two cultures, two ages, or even two people. Image and word characterize the chief means of human communication (sight and sound); these also characterize Christian communication in which Jesus is both the Word of God and the Image of God. Beside the Biblical and an historical section, Dillistone, the Anglican Dean of Liverpool, provides a study of the essen-tial Christian message, the qualities of the missionary, and the effective techniques of communication. 156 pages.

[113] Dillistone, F. W. "Christian Doctrine and its Communication." *Expository Times* 69 (1957-1958): 196-198.

In this address to the Principals of Anglican Theological Colleges, Dillistone calls for a change in the teaching of theology. Noting that communication exists in dialectical relation with community, he argues that the contemporary minister must be able to relate to the world and must be able to communicate credibly. To do this requires a shift of emphasis in theological education from the study of the media of a past age to that of the principles and practices of communication today. 3 pages.

[114] Du Passage, Henri. "Mécanique et Prière." *Études* 208 (juillet-août-septembre 1931): 513-525.

Responding to a parody by Georges Duhamel proposing a church whose rites would come to the people mediated by radio, records, film, and television, Du Passage notes that the life of the church must involve interaction among the people and that the sacraments require presence. Even preaching, perhaps more skilled on radio or film, still demands the active attention of the hearers, something which radio or film does not promote. 13 pages.

[115] Düsterfeld, Peter. "Soziale Kommunikation in einer pluralen Gesellschaft: Warum Kirche kein 'Anbieter' ist." *Telekommunikation in einer demokratischen Gesellschaft.* Ed. Zentralstelle Medien der Deutschen Bischofskonferenz und Katholische Akademie Stuttgart. Bonn: Hohenheimer Medientage, 1984. 25-35.

The church should not go into the marketplace of ideas, offering faith as one option. Instead it should strive for a "profile" that presents it as different from the others. 11 pages.

[116] Eilers, Franz-Josef. "Towards a Training Strategy for Church Communication." *Communicatio Socialis* 12 (1979): 356-360.

Communication training should take into account the local, national, and regional needs of the Church. Once these needs are determined the training itself should occur in three steps: selection of candidates based on ability (perhaps determined through workshops); initial training and work experience; and finally further training. Those trained should be employed in communication and the training should fit clearly defined aims for service in the local church. 5 pages.

[117] Eilers, Franz-Josef. "Communications as a Regular Feature of Theology Training." *DIWA—Studies in Philosophy and Theology* Tagaytay City, Philippines: Graduate School, Divine Word Seminary, n.d.

This paper argues the importance of communication in human life, in culture, in modern life, and in the Church and then sketches ideas for three kinds of communication training for seminarians: general training, seminary courses, and specialized courses.

[118] Engel, James F. *How Can I Get Them to Listen? A Handbook on Communication Strategy and Research.* Grand Rapids, MI: Zondervan Publishing House, 1977.

A companion volume to Engel and Norton's *What's Gone Wrong with the Harvest,* this book is an introduction to the communication research techniques of audience analysis and effectiveness measurement. With examples drawn from Christian broadcasting and from studies done at Wheaton College, this book provides an adequate general introduction to the subject. 185 pages.

[119] Engel, James F. *Contemporary Christian Communications: Its Theory and Practice.* Nashville: Thomas Nelson Publishers, 1979.

This general guide to communication theory addresses the problems of evangelization, conversion, and spiritual growth. Well-written and detailed, the book covers the nature of the audience, models of communication, persuasion and attitude theory, media choice, religious behavior and freedom, and culture. 344 pages.

[120] Engel, James F. and Wilbert Norton. *What's Gone Wrong With the Harvest: A Communication Strategy for the Church and World Evangelism.* Grand Rapids, MI: Zondervan Publishing House, 1980.

The writers, from the Wheaton College Graduate faculty, take a "communications" perspective on evangelism in the local church and in the missions, urging that Christians shift from message-centered to audience-centered communication. Placing their argument within the context of a case study, they demonstrate how churches can build on people's experience, basic human needs, and communication planning 171 pages.

[121] Gritti, Jules. "Modèles de communication en regard de l'Eglise." *Nouvelle Revue Théologique* 97 (1975): 51-64.

Applying various models of communication (Lasswell's, the two- step flow, the functional, and the dependency) to the internal communication of the Catholic Church, Gritti shows how each of them aptly describe the communication at various points in the Church since the 19th century. Taking the lead from the Second Vatican Council and from *Communio et Progressio,* he argues that the interdependency model better represents the "People of God" theology than does any other model. 14 pages.

[122] Hamelink, Cees. *Perspectives for Public Communication: A Study of the Churches' Participation in Public Communication.* Baarn, Holland: Ten Have, 1975.

This study argues for a different approach to communication by the Christian churches—that the churches "contest those processes of public communication which are an expression of social structures which incapacitate people to manage their own minds." The work begins with an insightful analysis of four official church documents on communication (from the Lutheran Church, from the World Council of Churches, and from the Roman Catholic Church), noting their arguments and theological motives. Then it moves to an alternative analysis of public communication, one informed by dialogic thinking and ideology criticism. From this latter perspective comes the recommendation for an alternative church response. 174 pages.

[123] Jackson, B. F., Jr., ed. *Communication—Learning for Churchmen.* Vol 1. of *Communication for Churchmen.* Nashville: Abingdon Press, 1968.

This introductory volume to the Communication for Churchmen series combines general information on communication with specific material on print and audiovisual resources. William Fore begins with an essay on communication in general, reviewing topics such as the nature and process of communication, communication technology, education and communication, and a theological view of communication. In this latter section he argues that communication finds its proper theological context in the doctrine of revelation and that the church forms a channel of revelation; its guidelines should include the word, the tradition, the community of memory, and the goal of increasing love of God and neighbor. Dangers to Christian communication include intellectualization, aestheticism, institutionalism, literalism, allegorization, and manipulation.

Howard M. Ham provides an overview of learning theory as a background to effective communication. Benjamin Jackson, the series editor, contributes an essay on printed resources (from textbooks to magazines and newspapers) for church use. Finally, James C. Campbell examines audiovisuals, defining the term, suggesting ways for their use in churches, and providing guidelines in choosing media and training users.

The work is thorough and scholarly and stands the test of time well. 303 pages.

[124] Jackson, B. F. Jr., ed. *Television-Radio-Film for Churchmen.* Vol. 2 of *Communication for Churchmen.* Nashville: Abingdon Press, 1969.

This second volume of the Communication for Churchmen series contains three essays. Peter A. H. Meggs writes about television and the church, giving some general background on television and then reviewing the variety of Christian broadcasting. He also sketches new possibilities for church involvement with television, including advocacy and legal work. Everett C. Parker, in his treatment on radio, begins with advocacy and public service issues and then considers radio programming. He reviews the history of religious broadcasting in the United States and provides some information on program types as the industry changes. Finally, John M. Culkin suggests that commercial film offers a good teaching tool for churches. Grounding his understanding of film in the work of McLuhan, he offers a method of teaching film, illustrating it with a case study of *La Strada*.

This book continues the tradition of thorough scholarship found in volume 1; similarly, despite its age, it presents solid and valuable information for a general introduction to communication. 317 pages.

[125] Jackson, B. F., Jr., ed. *Audiovisual Facilities and Equipment for Churchmen.* Vol. 3 of *Communication for Churchmen.* Nashville: Abingdon Press, 1970.

This third volume of the Communication for Churchmen series presents the most technical information of the series. James E. Alexander begins with an essay on sound in the church, a primer on sound amplification, microphones, acoustics, and telephone systems. Edward A. George offers a similar introduction to audiovisual equipment, discussing the merits of various kinds of audio and projection equipment and suggesting criteria for evaluating the equipment. Finally, Donald P. Ely draws out guidelines for building specialized communication rooms or classrooms equipped for communication. Each of the essays is thorough and well-prepared; however, the technical nature of the discussion, at least in the first two, make them largely outdated now because of the rapid developments in communication technology. One might benefit from the general principles. 313 pages.

[126] Kappenberg, Barbara. *Kommunikationstheorie und Kirche: Grundlagen einer kommunikationstheoretischen Ekklesiologie.* Frankfurt am Main: Peter D. Lang, 1981.

This book, more about communication theory than the Church, attempts to apply the categories and models of communication (from sender-message-receiver to communicative competence) to the Church. There is little ecclesiology except as illustration of the communication theory's applicability. 288 pages.

[127] König, Franz. "Kirche und Kommunikation." *Communicatio Socialis* 1 (1968): 6-20.

In this brief essay, Cardinal König of Vienna sketches out a positive approach to communication, drawing on the work of the Second Vatican Council. 15 pages.

[128] Kraemer, Hendrik. *The Communication of the Christian Faith.* London: Lutterworth Press, 1957.

This book, based on the author's Laidlaw Lectures at Knox College, Toronto, explores communication and evangelism from a variety of perspectives: biblical, historical, and cultural. The biblical material shows God as a God who speaks, who has created the human race for communication; divine communication (revelation or prayer) establishes human community—on the contrary, sin destroys communication. The history of the Church illustrates how Christians have veered from "communication between" people to "communication of" doctrine, an occurrence influenced by the Church's relations with the state. The cultural analysis highlights a breakdown in communication with the possibility of restoration arising from both indirect communication (allowing the Church to be what it is) and direct communication (proclaiming the Gospel through kerygma, diakonia, and koinonia). 128 pages.

[129] Kraft, Charles H. "The Incarnation, Cross-Cultural Communication, and Communication Theory." *Evangelical Missions Quarterly* 9 (Fall 1973): 277-284.

Four principles ground Kraft's theory of communication: (1) both sender and receiver must have the same frame of reference; (2) the greater the predictability of information, the less impact it will have; (3) the greater the specificity of the message, the greater the impact; and (4) what the receiver discovers has greater import than what is predigested. 8 pages.

[130] Kraft, Charles H. *Communicating the Gospel God's Way*. Pasadena, CA: William Carey Library, 1979. [Originally published in the *Ashland Theological Bulletin* 12.1 (Spring 1979).]

The Bible provides not only the message for our communicating the Gospel, but also the method. God communicates with us to be understood and to evoke a response; to do this, God chooses the incarnation. This model of communication has 10 characteristics: it has impact; it takes the initiative; it chooses the receptor's frame of reference; it is personal; it interacts; it surprises; it takes on specific form; it invites personal discovery; it invites self-identification; and it evokes commitment. Such Biblically-based communication demands credibility of the communicator since the message and messenger reinforce each other. 60 pages.

[131] Kraft, Charles H. *Communication Theory for Christian Witness*. Nashville, TN: Abingdon Press, 1983.

Addressed to "Evangelical Christians who are committed to communicating God's good news," this book draws on Biblical material and classical American communication theory (general semantics, proxemics, message-receiver models, etc.) to present an overview of communication for the Christian. Since the Christian message is personal insofar as God is the message, all Christian communication should attend to its interpersonal quality. From this starting point, other aspects of communication emerge:

the receiver, meaning, media, context, source credibility, and change. Well-written with many examples, the book encourages a greater understanding of communication by those engaged in Christian witness. 255 pages.

[132] Kuhns, William. "Religious Education in the Age of Electronics." *Catholic High School Quarterly Bulletin* 26.4 (January 1969): 17-19.

Following McLuhan, Kuhns argues that the electronic media have created a new environment for religious communication and teaching. He suggests three characteristics for the present situation: (1) "coexpressionism"— modern communication, unlike print, addresses more than one sense at a time; (2) sensitivity to the meanings and importance of environments; and (3) personal meaning drawn from mediated experience. Each characteristic means that religious communication must become less analytic and more experiential. 3 pages.

[133] Lonsdale, David and Philip Sheldrake, eds. "Communications, Media and Spirituality." *The Way* Supplement 57 (Autumn 1986): 3-100.

This theme issue examines "how developing communications techniques can be helpful to spirituality as well as how a new spirituality is needed to express a new cultural language." The essays treat a variety of subjects: new communications in the Church (Robert A. White); the iconography of communications (Dafydd Miles Board); Christian discernment (James McDonnell); the spirituality of media people (Pierre Babin); communications apostolates (John E. O'Brien); the charism of religious orders and media work (John Orme Mills); communication and theology (Paul A. Soukup); and audio-visuals and Ignatian spirituality (William Hewett). 98 pages.

[134] Mathews, W. R. "Understanding and Communication." *Church Quarterly Review* 158 (1957): 435-441.

In this Founder's Day Meeting address to the Society for the Promotion of Christian Knowledge, Mathews notes that effective communication requires a clear understanding of one's subject. Religion, like many other areas, encounters problems in communication because of confusion about its subject; however, one should not lose hope because Christianity, though it involves ideas, primarily is a way of life. Christian love survives even when theology is dimmed. 7 pages.

[135] McDonnell, Thomas P. "Marshall McLuhan—The Man Who Infuriates the Critics." *U. S. Catholic* 31.11 (March 1966): 27-32.

An interview with McLuhan, this piece situates his work within communication studies and then interrogates McLuhan regarding the significance of his observations for the Church. Church communication, liturgy, *Inter Mirifica,* and film ratings make up most of the content covered. Though a bit dated in its concerns, the interview does offer a good introduction to McLuhan. 6 pages.

[136] McKenzie, Leon. *Decision Making in Your Parish: Effective Ways to Consult the Local Church.* Mystic, CT: Twenty-Third Publications, 1980.

Arguing that "parish surveys can assist leaders in making informed decisions, and in devising strategies for the implementation of decisions," this book describes in some detail mail survey techniques. Chapters cover the basics of surveys, including designing the instrument, choosing the sampling frame, determining the sample size, random selection, cover letters and mailing, dealing with non-response, organizing and interpreting the data, and use of surveys in pastoral ministry. The overall thrust of the volume is that leadership communication improves through wider consultation at the parish level. The book also includes an annotated bibliography of resources. 152 pages.

[137] Meundel, Hans-Dittmar. "Indirect Communication and Christian Education." Diss. Graduate Theological Union [Berkeley, CA]. 1986.

Through a careful reading of various texts of Martin Luther, the author establishes "the true nature of Christian communication" as an indirect communication. He then applies this standard to various aspects of Christian communication, particularly education, examining the works of George Albert Coe and Randolph Crump Miller.

[138] Michalson, Carl. "Communicating the Gospel." *Theology Today* 14.3 (October 1957): 321-334.

One should start a theory of Christian communication by examining the nature of the message—the Gospel, which demands proclamation rather than debate, active living rather than statements about the nature of the church. Other characteristics of the Gospel that define its communication include that it demands a response; that it is the same across generations, having a once-for-all character; and that it is official news, not subject to the whim of the minister. 14 pages.

[139] Parker, Everett C. "Christian Communication and Secular Man." *The Ecumenical Review* 18 (1966): 331-344.

Recognizing the dangers inherent in mass communication (the creation a mass audience, the promotion of false values, the commodification of life), Parker nevertheless urges churches to use mass communication in the service of the Gospel. However, he doubts the value of an advertising approach and instead proposes that the churches deal with the larger issues of our time: the rejection of God, war and peace, urbanization, education, science and technology, industry, racial justice, and food for the world. To lead this, ministers must be trained in the modern methods of communication, churches need to relate to the larger community where decisions are made, and church people should seek responsible positions in the public sector in order to engage in decision making. 14 pages.

[140] Paul, Robert S. "The Communication of the Christian Gospel." *Encounter* 18 (1957): 424-434.

Distinguishing three levels of communication (command, instruction, and encounter), Paul places the perfection of Christian communication on the last level. To truly communicate the Gospel the Church must recognize the autonomy of the individual and must seek to speak to people of this age. The content of this Christian communication must be the good news of God's action in history—which is the Good News of Jesus. This must grip us before any study of communication or technique will benefit us. 11 pages.

[141] Phillips, Donald E. *Karl Barth's Philosophy of Communication.* Hildesheim and New York: Gerg Olms Verlag, 1981.

This dissertation-type study presents a close reading of Barth's *Church Dogmatics* in order to tease out from it an implicit philosophy of communication. Topics include the criticism of world views; concepts of "people," world community, and universal language; an experimental view of language; concepts of knowledge, experience, language, and ecumenical communication. The thesis is that the "primary architectonic principle governing Barth's thought is a movement toward complete fidelity to the object of inquiry as determining the nature of scientific activity, rationality, and discourse." Specific communication concepts include reference, participation in communication, mutual transparency, mutual speech and hearing, and mutual assistance in the act of being. 404 pages.

[142] Pieterse, Hendrik J. C. "Singing the Lord's Song in a Strange Land: Ministry and the Communication of the Gospel." *Theology Today* 42.1 (April 1985): 84-87.

Formed by his experience of ministry in South Africa, Pieterse proposes a view of practical theology which carries with it a theory of communication which is simultaneously a theological theory. The models for this communication are the Incarnation, the Word-event of God's address, and a sense of religious communication as God's action, in which the minister is a victim of the Gospel, rather than the shepherd or the model Christian. 4 pages.

[143] Quant, Trevor. "Random Harvest or Resolute Pursuit? Toward a Strategy for the Church in Relation to the Mass Media." *Journal of Christian Education* 11 (June-December 1968): 36-50.

Since the Church cannot avoid communication, it should take care about its unintended communication. Next it should recognize that personal communication has more influence than mass means of dissemination of information. To effectively use the mass media, the church should have a clear sense of mission, seek communication rather than self-promotion, and use the media for preparation of the audience for the personal contact follow-up. A strategy might then include programs to interest people and a group of committed Christians who would share viewing with non- church people and then enter into discussion (the Methodist class meeting approach). 15 pages.

[144] Ramsdell, Edward T. "Communication from a Christian Perspective." *Religious Education* 50 (1955): 335-339.

After noting that communication problems often result from differences in perspective, perception, and evaluation, Ramsdell argues that Christian communication requires four things, theologically, of the Church: repeated clarification of the meaning of the Gospel; a recognition of the truth common to all which the Gospel presupposes; the exhibiting of the Gospel in its cultural and existential relevance; and a recognition that all communication must become self-communication. 5 pages.

[145] Read, David H. C. *The Communication of the Gospel.* London: SCM Press, Ltd., 1952.

In these, the Warrack Lectures for 1951, Read examines the state of Christian communication. He notes a breakdown in communication, stemming from one of two modern heresies: (1) the tendency to believe that the problem of communication is largely one of technique; and (2) the tendency to ignore the audience and its needs in favor of the message. He continues his analysis with an examination of the media world of our era and then proposes concrete steps for the Church's proclamation. 96 pages.

[146] Reese, James M. *Experiencing the Good News: The New Testament as Communication.* Wilmington, DL: Michael Glazier, Inc., 1984.

This well-crafted introductory text applies the findings from textual communication theories (linguistics, speech-acts, semiotics, reader-response, etc.) to Biblical interpretation. Each short chapter presents a summary of the theory and illustrates it with reference to the Biblical text, concluding with a bibliography. The second part of the book examines religious language and imagination, with special attention to the work of Amos Wilder and to the problem of Biblical inspiration. 203 pages.

[147] Roulet, Philippe, ed. "L'évangile dans une culture de l'image." *Les Cahiers Protestants* n.s. 1 (Février 1985): 1-64.

This theme issue of *Les Cahiers Protestants* publishes the papers and some discussion of a conference on the image and the Gospel. Papers approach the subject theoretically (often influenced by Jacques Ellul [306]), but also practically through commentaries on film and art. The authors include André Dumas ("Paroles et images"); Denis Müller ("Récit et image"); Marc Faessler ("L'image entre l'idole et l'icône"); Jean-Marc Chappuis

("Archétypes, stéréotypes, prototypes, figures du spectacle du monde");
Jean Philippe Rappe ("Image télévisée"); Luc Joly ("L'image porteuse de
sens"); and Bernard Rordorf ("L'art, dépassement de l'image"). 64 pages.

[148] Rowe, Trevor. *The Communication Process.* London: Epworth Press,
1978.

This rather general introduction to communication and persuasion focuses
on public speaking; a last chapter turns to Christian communication, which
the author claims functions more in the way of art than in the way of
abstract theology. 136 pages.

[149] Schillaci, Anthony. "Celebrating Change: Communications and The-
ology." *Projections: Shaping an American Theology for the Future.* Ed.
Thomas F. O'Meara and Donald M. Weisser. Garden City, NY: Doubleday
& Company, Inc., 1970. 166-202.

A reflection on communication and its influence upon society provides a
necessary grounding for any future theology. Communications improvements have so shifted the nature of the world that theologians need a new
vocabulary and a new set of analogies before they can address that world.
This essay gives a three-fold look at this new world: the environment for
theological reflection, the role of change brought about by communication,
and the manner of influencing or controlling communication through the
arts. Schillaci argues his thesis through appeals to various films which either
illustrate or prove his points. 37 pages.

[150] Scragg, Walter R. L. *The Media, the Message, and Man: Communicating God's Love.* Nashville, TN: Southern Publishing Association, 1972.

Combining mission stories from various Adventist groups around the world
with Scriptural material on communication and with reflections from communication studies, Scragg gives a series of meditations on Christian communication. He considers the life of the communicator, the receiver, the
content (God's love), Christ as model of communication, prayer, words,
the media environment, and the church and communication technology.
153 pages.

[151] Sellers, James E. *The Outsider and the Word of God: A Study in
Christian Communication.* New York: Abingdon Press, 1961.

Sellers describes the situation of the contemporary church as one in which
the church must primarily address outsiders—people who may be "Christians by osmosis" (living in a Christian culture but ignorant of the teachings
of the church) or people who are "Christians with a roving eye" (Christians
whose values are largely determined by the secular world). The church needs
to find a way to communicate with these people in her midst. Where the
mass media may play a legitimate role in this communication, the church

must carefully think this through in order to "avoid what David Read [145] calls the two main heresies of Christian communication: overemphasis on content and overemphasis on method. With this background, Sellers considers the situation of the outsider and looks for past models of reaching them. Borrowing the "point of contact" approach from the second century apologists, he suggests that it would provide a useful start. He then examines each of the media, asking whether the church can talk about religion directly or indirectly through them. While somewhat optimistic, he poses many questions and thoughtful reflections about the nature of Christian communication and the nature of its message. 240 pages.

[152] Slate, Carl Philip. "Communication Theory and Evangelization: Contributions to the Communication of Religious Innovations in the Euroamerican Culture Area." Diss: Fuller Theological Seminary, 1976.

After examining persuasion theory and available studies, Slate concludes that mass media sources alone account for few conversions and that speaker-audience settings similarly succeed only where small group or personal contact accompanies them. Based on this he proposes a network model in which the converted individual is incorporated into a local church where s/he finds both individual and group credibility. His suggested strategy for evangelizing Western society involves training local church members in the use of small groups and face-to-face communication. Empirical tests of church groups in four western countries supports this hypothesis. 233 pages.

[153] Spencer, A. E. C. W. "The Catholic Church and Communication." *The Clergy Review* 51 (1966): 916-923.

The Catholic Church faces a crisis because cultural change (dependent on communication and conflict control) has forced it to change its dominant patterns of communication. Despite the centrality of communication to Christian theology and Christian life, the Church had limited communication by a hierarchical control and a stress on secrecy. As the Church opens its communication structures, it will have to resolve the problems the authoritarian system deferred for years. 8 pages.

[154] Stowe, Everett M. *Communicating Reality Through Symbols.* Philadelphia: Westminster Press, 1966.

The ability to transform images into meaning, Stowe states, is a product of the human mind. This book discusses the symbol in relation to man, reality and communication. This book forms part of the Westminster Christian Communication series. 158 pages.

[155] Taylor, John V. *Change of Address.* London: Hodder and Stoughton, 1968.

This collection of the author's essays from the *C. M. S. [Church Missionary Society] Newsletter* focuses on the communication of the Gospel. Taylor asks, "How to communicate a Gospel that will make Christ real to thoroughly modern minds?" Essays describe a variety of ventures and methods, report testimonies to the success (and failure) of missions, and suggest new ways of reaching people beyond the parish. 160 pages.

[156] Watson, Tom, Jr. "Religious Broadcasting and the Communication Process." *Religious Broadcasting* 6.1 (February-March 1974): 16-19.

Christian broadcasters should attend to the lessons of communication theory and evaluate their work according to the measures of desirability, flexibility, intelligibility, credibility, and applicability. 3 pages.

[157] White, Robert A. "The Word and the Electronic Media." *The Way* 20.1 (1980): 24-35.

This essay argues that the media determine both the "communicable moment" and the patterns of thought today. The task for the Christian imagination is to express the central aspects of Christianity within these constraints. White discusses several aspects of the Christian imagination: its language (symbol), its source (faith), its function (union with God), its context (ritual), and its logic (paradox). He also situates this imagination in a brief survey of Christian communication throughout history. 12 pages.

Theology

[158] Antoncich, Ricardo. "Reflexión de la fe y medios de comunicación." *Boletín Informativo MCS* 73 (1977): 49-54.

This essay examines how the communications media—print, electronic media, and group media—can contribute to the theological reflection on faith, whether that be logical, existential, or historical. Antoncich favors the group media because it more clearly elicits an individual response. 6 pages.

[159] Aske, Sigurd. "The Christian Communicator." *Religious Broadcasting* 6.4 (October-November 1974): 8-9.

Jesus Christ alone deserves the title, "Christian communicator" and provides a model in his personal communication—the message does not matter as much as the life of the communicator. The Christian communicator must resist the efforts of the church to make him/her a public relations officer and must instead represent Jesus. Some examples of good Christian communication are found in Luther because he was in touch with the people, the city, and the culture; and in Bishop Hans Lilje who advocated staying close to the Bible and staying simple. 2 pages.

[160] Bachman, John W. "Theology and Communication: Towards a Theological and Theoretical Context for the Role of the Church in Dealing with Modern Media of Communication." *WACC Journal* 23.2 (1976): 14-18.

This essay begins with communication and seeks out theological principles which might correlate with practice. Bachman rejects the transmission model as too authoritarian. He favors those media which reflect incarnation and reconciliation. At the same time he reminds the reader not to lose sight of the reality of sin: media cannot be purely neutral. Finally, multimedia approaches reflect the variety of creation and should be used. 5 pages.

[161] Bacquet, Alexis. *Medias et christianisme.* Paris: Le Centurion, 1984.

After reviewing the basic Catholic Church documents on communication (including that of the French bishops in 1980) and some basic concepts of communication study, the author discusses ways in which the media and Christianity interact, interrogating and criticizing one another. Christianity and the Church take on the roles of faith, hope and active love within the understanding of the media and give witness to the values of service, otherness, truth-seeking, and freedom. 173 pages.

[162] Badejo, E. Victor. "Christian Communication." *Lutheran World* 19 (1972): 99-104.

Commenting on the text from St. Mark's Gospel of the healing of the deaf and dumb man, Badejo notes this act of Jesus as a model for Christian communication. One must respect the dignity of the audience; one must act as well as speak; one must speak to the audience at their level. Christians must also make their good deeds known and follow them and their communication with additional good deeds. 6 pages.

[163] Balthasar, Hans Urs von. *Word and Revelation: Essays in Theology I.* Trans. A. V. Littledale and Alexander Dru. New York: Herder and Herder, 1964.

This work explores the theological nature of "the Word" in Scripture, Tradition, history, and human life. The sections on the implications of the Word, on God speaking as a human, and on the Word and silence hold particular interest for anyone seeking a conceptual model of communication in a Christian context. While never specifically addressing the question of communication media, this study does sketch out a foundation on which such a question would make sense. 191 pages.

[164] Balthasar, Hans Urs von. "Theology and Aesthetic." *Communio* 8 (1981): 63-71.

In this address on the acceptance of an honorary doctorate at The Catholic University of America, von Balthasar summarizes his theological aesthetic, noting the analogical relationship of art and goodness. Like a masterwork emerging from the tradition, Jesus uniquely emerges from the Old Testament revelation, a move only appreciated by the eyes of faith. 9 pages.

[165] Balthasar, Hans Urs von. *The Glory of the Lord: A Theological Aesthetics. I: Seeing the Form.* Trans. Erasmo Leiva-Merikakis. Ed. Joseph Fessio and John Riches. San Francisco: Ignatius Press; New York: Crossroad, 1982.

This first volume of von Balthasar's extended application of aesthetic categories to theology, he works out in detail a hermeneutic based on the third transcendental category. He wishes "to complement the vision of the true and the good with that of the beautiful." This volume situates a theological aesthetics in both the Protestant and Catholic traditions, examines the experience of faith (particularly as mediated), and then examines the form of revelation. This theological exploration suggests a ground for a different approach to a theology of communication, one that would begin with its form. 691 pages.

[166] Balz, Heinrich. *Theologische Modelle der Kommunikation: Bastian–Kraemer–Nida.* Gutersloh, West Germany: Gutersloher Verlagshaus Mohn, 1978.

This is an explication and comparison of three theological models of communication, as found in the writings of Hans-Dieter Bastian, Hendrik Kraemer, and Eugene Nida. All three have developed a theory of Christian communication for the missions, but each stresses a different aspect: Bastian, systems theory; Kraemer, communication among people; and Nida, the Bible and culture. 156 pages.

[167] Barclay, William. *Meditations on Communicating the Gospel.* Nashville, TN: The Upper Room, 1971. [Originally published as *Communicating the Gospel.* Stirling, Scotland: Drummond Press, 1968.]

The first of the Laird Lectures, these three meditations examine the scriptural manner of presenting the Gospel and then apply that to the contemporary era. To fully communicate the Gospel in our own day, Barclay claims, we must read it as literature to get its sense of story; we must approach it linguistically to properly understand its language; we must know it historically to appreciate its background; we must attend to it psychologically to discern its motives; and we must read it with devotion to know Jesus Christ whom we wish to communicate to others. 64 pages.

[168] Barth, Karl. *Church Dogmatics.* Eds., G. W. Bromiley and T. F. Torrance. 4 vols. Edinburgh: T. & T. Clark, 1936-1970.

Barth's primary discussion of Christian communication comes in chapter 4 of volume 1, part 2, in which he discusses "the proclamation of the Church." Here he looks at the mission of the church as one of proclaiming God and as a task for which humans are incapable. Rather, "if there is proclamation, if the attempt does not fail, it is just at the point where success is achieved that it can and will be understood, not as a human success, but as a divine victory concealed in human failure ...." Christian communication is a human activity, but one unlike any other human activity in that it also involves "the self-proclamation of the Word of God."

[169] Bartholomäus, Wolfgang. "Communication in the Church: Aspects of a Theological Theme." *Communication in the Church.* Trans. John Griffiths. Eds. Gregory Baum and Andrew Greeley. Concilium 111. New York: Seabury Press, 1978. 95-110.

Arguing that, as a dimension of the Church, communication falls under the area of investigation of theology, Bartholomäus notes that communicating in the Church (interpersonal communication) and the communication of the Church (organizational communication) must take on the characteristic of freedom. Given its theological status, the Church must support and facilitate non-dominative communication; moreover it must offer a critical (non-ideological) interpretation of the world and of faith to contemporary men and women. 16 pages.

[170] Bernard, Charles A. *Théologie Symbolique.* Paris: Téqui, 1978.

This detailed examination of "the language of symbols" in theology looks at how Christianity has used symbols in its preaching, writing, liturgy, and communication. After a more general introduction to symbols and their use, Bernard looks at specific Christian symbols (liberation, pilgrimage, light and darkness, the figure of Christ) and at Christian sacramental or action symbols (baptism and eucharist). 400 pages.

[171] Bourgeois, Henri. "Théologie et médias." *Lumière et vie* 30.155 (octobre-novembre-décembre 1981): 101-116.

Asking what theology might have to say about the media and their contemporary functions, Bourgeois responds by surveying criticisms of the media, reporting theologians' comments about word and image, and offering his own comments on these areas. He notes how the media have changed contemporary life, weakening some forms of society and strengthening others. Offering a distinction among the image, the imaginary, and fantasy, he responds as well to Ellul's critique of the impact of the media. 16 pages.

[172] Bourgeois, Henri. "Les medias: un objet théologique?" *Bulletin des Facultés Catholiques de Lyon* n.s. 77 (juillet/septembre 1985): 27-34.

Reporting on a 1985 conference which brought to Annecy theologians, communication scholars, and communication practitioners, Bourgeois notes three main themes: defining communication, approaches to communication study, and Christianity and communication. In the last category comes a division of Christian attitudes to communication—naive acceptance, instrumental use, ethical reflection or critique, and industry reform. Theologians themselves wrestle with a methodology for studying communication; some value historical studies of past Christian communication while others suggest a study of religious language, a cultural studies approach, or a cultural critique of communication. While limited to the report format, this essay does suggest several good directions for further study. 8 pages.

[173] Brooks, R. T. "Christian Communication." *Congregational Quarterly* 36 (1958): 25-35.

Christian communication does not involve indoctrination or manipulation. Instead, Brooks gives it these priorities: Christian communication as (1) a relationship between God and man; (2) a relationship between people; (3) the transmission of ideas; and (4) an exercise in language. In each section Brooks points out the distinctive in Christian communication must be rooted in love. "Our words do not have to bridge the gap between heaven and earth. That has been done by the action of the Word and the Spirit of God ... The Church's task ... is to take the material of everyday experience, and hold it up in such away that God can make it a channel of divine grace." 11 pages.

[174] Brooks, R. T. *Person to Person.* London: The Epworth Press, 1964.

This fine discussion of the theory and practice of Christian communication, first prepared as the ninth A. S. Peake Memorial lecture, argues that Christian communication has three marks: it finds people in the context of their own world; it finds them at the deepest levels of their personal existence; and it brings with it a consciousness of wonder, truth, and love which is evidence of the Holy Spirit. To do this we must recognize that the primary form of Christian faith occurs in daily living not only in theological reflection. Christian communication then involves a personal relationship, even in broadcasting; the communication arises out of love and the very "communication of truth is an act of communion with God." Finally, the content of the Christian communication consists of interpreting or drawing "connecting lines between the Biblical manifestations of grace and the everyday ones." This both affirms the goodness and joy in the world and the need for a loving response to it, including self-denial that others might benefit. 84 pages.

[175] Brož, Luděk. "The Task of Communication: The Gospel Today." *Communio Viatorum* 22 (1979): 145-152.

The Holy Spirit, not communication, represents the framework and structure of the Church; communication is a manifestation of that framework. Prayer, humility, contemporaneity, objectivity, and humaneness characterize that communication; moreover, Christian communication shares this characteristic with the God of revelation: it does not persist in itself but reaches to others. Communication then is an angelic ministry engaged in by all Christians—angelic in that the message overshadows the messenger. Since scriptural terms for communication always imply working together, Christian communication should also respect the "hermeneutic rights of others" and move towards dialogue rather than teaching. 8 pages.

[176] Buechner, Frederick. *Telling the Truth: The Gospel as Tragedy, Comedy, and Fairy Tale.* San Francisco: Harper & Row, 1977.

A delightfully written, entertaining, and challenging book, this volume addresses homilists and other Christian communicators about the nature of the Gospel and its truth. The telling of the Gospel puts a frame around the way things are for only in such silence can the truth emerge. Alternately, the Gospel is tragic (revealing sin and emptiness); the Gospel is high comedy (in which we share the laughter of Abraham, Sarah, and God at the Good News); and the Gospel is a fairy tale (in which good and evil battle and in which the disguised world is revealed for what it is). 100 pages.

[177] Cacucci, Francesco. *Teologia dell'immagine: Prospettive attuali.* Roma: Centro dello Spettacolo e della Comunicazione sociale; Bari: Il Edizione Riveduta, 1971.

This study, based on the author's dissertation for the Gregorian University in Rome, examines how the divine image in Christ and in human beings forms a basis for the contemporary communication of the Gospel. After an historical introduction, Cacucci does a careful reading of the relevant texts of Thomas Aquinas (mostly from the *Summa Contra Gentiles,* part three) to set the stage for his own discussion of the divine image in creation. The second part of the study offers a theology of the image drawn from Thomistic and from contemporary sources. The third part applies the material to contemporary communication, particularly to preaching and to film. 287 pages.

[178] Chappuis, Jean-Marc. *Information du monde et prédication de l'Evangile.* Genève: Labor et Fides, 1969.

Although this book has much to do with preaching, its comments on the nature of the Church and its relation to information give it a broader relevance to all of Christian communication. Chappuis, a member of the Protestant faculty of theology at the University of Geneva till his death in 1987, argues eight theses in the book. (1) The Church must preach the Gospel to the world, reaching out to non-believers and to non-practicing believers, in a public manner through a thematic preaching. (2) The thematic preaching consists of an evangelical demythologizing of the information which constitutes the world. (3) Information has both social and personal importance as well as theological significance—found in its ability to serve others by a proclamation of the truth. (4) The Church is simultaneously a sender, a subject, and a receiver of information. As such, it has a specific responsibility to apply its proper competence (theology) to help determine the significance of information. (5) The homiletic task of the Church lies in demythologizing the information of the world, to interpret it in the light of the Gospel. (6) This homiletic work comes from the grace of God present in the Church. (7) The preaching of the Gospel takes the form of a evangelical commentary on human affairs. (8) The commentary obtains not in the order of information, nor in the order of publicity, nor in the order of public relations, but in the order of witness to Christ. The volume concludes with appendices containing more detailed examinations of the material of each chapter in the light of other currents of contemporary thought. 231 pages.

[179] Chappuis, Jean-Marc. "Christology as Basis for Communication Studies." *Media Development* 28.4 (1981).

Chappuis argues that Christology rather than ecclesiology should form the starting point for an examination of communication. Ecclesiology splits the Church from the world; Christology unites the two. Similarly, communication constitutes community and requires a community.

[180] Chappuis, Jean-Marc. *Jesus et la Samaritaine: La Géométrie variable de la communication.* Geneva: Labor et Fides, 1982.

This short meditation and pastoral reflection examines the encounter between Jesus and the woman at the well from ten different communication aspects, including blocked communication, daily talk, verbal communication, dialogue, poetry, existential communication, the manifestation of God, and Christian witness. It provides a rich source of Christian reflection and prayer for the communicator. 64 pages.

[181] Colle, Raymond. *Le processus de communication de la revelation: Approche théologique à partir de cadres sociologique et philosophique.* Diss. Université Catholique de Louvain, Faculté de Théologie, 1969.

This thesis discusses the theological issues of revelation, Scripture and the Church in the language of communication study, particularly in terms of interpersonal communication, communication codes, and network analysis. While the attempt is interesting in itself, it doesn't seem to add anything to the theological or communicative discussion. 123 pages.

[182] Crowe, Frederick E. *Theology of the Christian Word: A Study in History.* New York: Paulist Press, 1978.

This book traces the history of the concept of "the Word" through seven chronological stages from the first century to the twentieth. Differing Christian experience and reflection have given rise to different questions about the Word and have led to various theories about it. This study provides a

70 CHRISTIAN COMMUNICATION

kind of foundational history for any subsequent reflection on the basis of Christian theories of communication. 174 pages.

[183] Desrosiers, Yvon. "Essai de théologie des moyens de communication sociale." *Cahiers d'études et de recherches* 1 (1965): 1-17.

The theology of communication is an instance of the theological reflection on created reality; communication must then be viewed in terms of its contribution to the kingdom of God. Communication builds unity among people and becomes a basis for charity. Beyond this, a reflection on communication connects to reflection on leisure, on art, on the role of the image in belief, and on the role of information and public opinion. 17 pages.

[184] Dulles, Avery. "The Church Is Communication." *Multimedia International* 1 (1972).

Dulles argues that the Church, which seeks community, is constituted by communication. Jesus communicates as the self-expression of the Father; the Church communicates the divine life to its members; and the Church communicates the good news of the Gospel to all people. This communication occurs across the whole range of media: teaching, drama, action, writing, speaking, art, architecture, and so forth. Dulles then examines several different theological starting points (seminary theology, Biblical-kerygmatic theology, radical secular theology), noting how each leads to a particular view of communication.

[185] Esposito, R. Francisco. *La teologia de la publicistica según el pensamiento de S. Alberione.* Barcelona: Ediciones Paulinas, 1980.

Santiago Alberione (d. 1971) founded the Paulinas, a group of religious communities devoted to the press and to evangelization through the mass media. This commentary on his writings is divided into five parts: the concept of preaching today through the mass media; their kerygmatic dimension; the asceticism necessary to work with the media; the missionary aspect of this work; and various methodological questions. 279 pages.

[186] Gabel, Émile. "Communications Media." *Sacramentum Mundi.* Ed. Karl Rahner. 6 vols. New York: Herder and Herder, 1968-70. 1: 387-391.

This entry in the theological encyclopedia summarizes the immediate post-Vatican II Roman Catholic position on communication. After briefly noting the recent development in this area, Gabel suggests three theological themes that inform reflection on communication. (1) "Anything that creates, facilitates, or improves communication" causes people to share in the goodness of God who blesses humanity. Therefore communication is semi-religious by its nature. (2) In God's actions, we find the foundation of a professional ethics of communications. (3) Since communication forms a leisure time occupation, a theology of leisure must inform reflection on communication. This times allows us to realize the self; it reinforces free will by giving us a choice of things to do. 5 pages.

[187] Ganoczy, Alexandre. *An Introduction to Catholic Sacramental Theology.* Trans. William Thomas and Anthony Sherman. New York: Paulist Press, 1984. [Original: *Einführung in die katholische Sakramentenlehre from Die Theologie: Einführungen in Gegenstaned, Methoden und Ergebnisse ihrer Disziplinen und Nachbarwissenschaften.* Darmstadt: Wissenschaftliche Buchgesellschaft, 1979]

In this treatment of sacramental theology, Ganoczy examines the sacraments from several perspectives: historical development, fundamental questions in Catholic teaching, a contemporary (Vatican II) understanding, and one drawn from communication theory. He uses the Augustinian theory of sign and symbol as a reference and then works with a model of interpersonal communication since sacraments represent moments of God's ongoing communication with the human race. The discussion is sketchy but suggestive and well worth reading. 192 pages.

[188] Gavin, Carney, Charles Pfeiffer, William Ruede, and Gayle Uebelhor, eds. *The Word: Readings in Theology.* New York: P. J. Kennedy & Sons, 1964.

A collection of essays by various European Catholic theologians dealing with aspects of the Word of God, this book presents a theology of the Word. More specifically, essays examine revelation, Scripture, preaching, and the effects of God's Word on human beings. Though somewhat dated, the essays do present some valuable reflections and historical studies, particularly of the patristic use of the Word. Contributors include Karl Rahner, Rene Latourelle, Edward Schillebeeckx, and Otto Semmelroth. 301 pages.

[189] Gilbert, Richard R. *Theological Implications for Broadcasting.* New York: Division of Radio and Television, United Presbyterian Church in the U. S. A., 1966.

Reprinted from *Amplify*, the house organ of the Division of Radio and Television, this reflection on broadcasting chooses three theological guidelines to appraise the Gospel and the media used. The guidelines fit the pattern of concentric circles: the application of grace in all the world; the understanding of grace in all of life, and—at the center—the experience of grace in every life. Christianity must use radio and TV because those media form the place where most of the people spend most of their leisure. To do this effectively, communicators must work with theologians—the former medium- and audience-centered and the latter, message centered—despite disagreements and the false starts of "liberal theology." 28 pages.

[190] Harned, David Baily. *Theology and the Arts.* Philadelphia: The Westminster Press, 1966.

This survey of the relationship of theology to the arts begins with the assumptions that the two areas do share common ground and that the Christian Gospel must relate to the contemporary situation. With this in mind, it examines three options for a "theology of art": creation, cross, and consummation. The first appears most clearly in the Roman Catholic tradition and finds expression in the work of Jacques Maritain. The second finds its spokesman in Paul Tillich and contemporary Protestant theology. The third appears in the Orthodox theology of Nicolas Berdyaev. For each position Harned summarizes the relevant theology and illustrates its response to art through the analysis of specific works of literature, painting, or music. 204 pages.

[191] Haughton, Rosemary. *The Drama of Salvation.* New York: The Seabury Press, 1975.

This marvelous study examines the doctrine of salvation from the perspective of drama—it explores "the human experience of God's saving action" through the application of dramatic criticism. At the same time, it posits a basis for Christian drama insofar as the experience of salvation can be seen as worked out in human life. Different chapters explore the raw material, the play, the role, the actors and audience, and the denouement. Each section provides good insight into both Christian living and dramatic action. 148 pages.

[192] Hemmerle, Klaus. "Kommunikation der Kirche—Kirche der Kommunikation." *Communicatio Socialis* 10 (July- September 1977): 253-257.

Basing his argument on the fact that unlimited communication will mark the communion of saints, Hemmerle notes the consequences of this for Christian communication. (1) Christian witness should use the media of communication. (2) The Church cannot ignore interpersonal communication. (3) The Church should encourage dialogue. (4) Individuals have a right to non-communication, to respectful silence. (5) The content of Christian communication is ultimately God. 5 pages.

[193] Hendricks, William. "The Theology of the Electronic Church." *Review and Expositor* 81 (1984): 59-75.

Hendricks summarizes the theology of the electronic church in 12 headings: (1) The intrinsic authority of the Bible. (2) What He's done for others, He'll do for you. (3) Trials dark on every side. (4) It took a miracle. (5) For sinners such as I. (6) Praise the Lord. (7) Are there no foes for me to face? (8) Heaven came down and glory filled my soul. (9) What a friend we have in Jesus. (10) Sweet, sweet Spirit. (11) Physicalist eschatology. (12) The family of God. He criticizes this theology as having a poor sense of authority, Biblical or otherwise; as muddling the notion of experience;

as ignoring the complexity of the doctrine of Providence; as simplifying salvation; and as ignoring ritual. 17 pages.

[194] Heredia, Jaime. *Teología de los instrumentos de comunicación social y magisterio romano.* Diss. Pontifical Gregorian University, Rome, 1978.

This dissertation is primarily a commentary on *Communio et Progressio,* situating the document in the theology of Vatican II and of the authors whose thought helped shaped the post-conciliar theology. Three theological models appear in the document: a Trinitarian one, one based on the Incarnation, and one which sees Jesus Christ as the Perfect Communicator. From these several moral-pastoral applications are developed: a moral theology that sees things in a longer temporal framework; one that is less individualistic; and one that focuses on the human person.

[195] Jørgensen, Knud. "Models of Communication in the New Testament." *Missiology* 4 (1976): 465-484.

Incarnation forms the mode of New Testament communication: the Lord empties himself or (in the language of communication theory) enters our frame of reference. Specifically, this occurs in three ways: Incarnation as dialogue, Incarnation as identification, and Incarnation in another culture— the Logos. We continue the Incarnation in our day through kerygma, didache, and parable; however, the emphasis must fall not on the technique (often a danger for Christian communicators) but on first personally getting the message. 20 pages.

[196] Lafon, Guy. "Communication and Revelation." *Lumen Vitae* 36 (1981): 359-371.

This essay attempts to express revelation and the theological understanding of revelation in the terms of communication theory. Lafon notes the logical, historical, and cultural difficulties of trying to examine revelation; he then begin with an analysis of interhuman communication. This has a profoundly religious dimension since it opens on to the divine and leads ultimately to reconciliation and love. 13 pages.

[197] Mann, Peter. *Through Words and Images.* New York: CTNA [Catholic Telecommunications Network of America], 1983.

This book by a Catholic diocesan producer examines the implications of the communications revolution for society and explores the Church's response to it. After a philosophical description of the "communications age," Mann looks at the Church response under six headings: (1) the Church as communicator, (2) the Church as storyteller, (3) the Church as healer, (4) the Church as liberator, (5) the Church as celebrator, and (6) the Church as artist. 64 pages.

[198] Marsh, Spencer. *God, Man, and Archie Bunker*. New York: Harper & Row Publishers, 1975.

This work of popular theology uses the television program "All in the Family" as a starting point from which to address issues of God, goodness, creation, forgiveness, death, the Bible, the Church, and religiosity. 105 pages.

[199] McCoy, Charles S. "Christian Faith and Communication: Theological Reflections." *The Christian Scholar* 50.1 (Spring 1967): 32-39.

Inquiring into the possibility of communicating the Gospel, McCoy isolates two approaches: ecclesiastical and Christological. He rejects the former because it posits the Church against the world, with the Gospel somehow "owned" by the Church. Instead he holds to a Gospel which challenges the Church as well as the world, a Gospel rooted in the Lordship of Christ. This perspective makes communication central to human life (for the world is created and redeemed and sustained by the One Word of God), and roots that communication in a community of interpretation. 8 pages.

[200] Montgomery, John Warwick. "Mass Communication and Scriptural Proclamation." *The Evangelical Quarterly* 49.1 (January-March 1977): 3-29.

Christianity needs the mass media of communication and the mass media in turn need Christianity. Following Schramm's source-message-receiver model, Montgomery draws a parallel to divine communication and notes that the Trinitarian and Incarnational models reinforce this secular one. On the other hand, the mass media need Christianity to redeem them from their loss of rational and relational communication. 27 pages.

[201] Morris, Colin. "Love at a Distance—the Spiritual Challenges of Religious Broadcasting." *Media Development* 33.4 (1986): 40-41.

Since Christian communication must involve love, every mediated form of communication falls short since it can accommodate neither self-disclosure nor a free response. Broadcasting implies on the one hand a new Gnosticism, denying the enfleshment of communication, and on the other hand a rejection of the Cross, imputing a quest for power. This is the challenge facing the religious broadcaster: to cling to the Christian tradition and not to lose hope. 2 pages.

[202] Navone, John J. *Communicating Christ*. Slough, England: St. Paul Publications, 1976.

This book explores the on-going communication of Christ to the world, through various aspects of Christian living: openness, friendship, self-transformation in Christ, contemporary communication, and so on. The strongest chapter, in terms of its specific applicability to communication and in terms of its use of the analogy of communication, is the one dealing with re-enacting the Gospel truth. In it the author explores several ways of re-enactment (writing, action, representation, etc.) and examines their social and religious utility. 239 pages.

[203] O'Keefe, J. *Can Television Cope with Theology: Hill Street Blues v. James Bond?* Durham, England: NEICE [North of England Institute for Christian Education], 1985.

Television and the mass media in general pose several problem areas for theology: the choice between commodity and person; the question of evangelization through the media (where the media may well present bad theology through good television); and the question of evangelizing the media (in those places where they themselves stand in need of conversion). Television already is doing theology by directing the way people reflect on life, either to a closed world (James Bond) or to an open one (Hill Street). 8 pages.

[204] Ong, Walter J. "Communications Media and the State of Theology." *Cross Currents* 19 (1969): 462-480.

The data gained from the study of oral cultures provides material for a judgment about theology, especially as it shifts away from basic oral and written forms towards multi-media forms. Ong expects theology to become less formulaic and more historical; to become more "objective" (that is, manipulated by computer technology); to become more original; and to rapidly expand its subject matter. 19 pages.

[205] Ong, Walter J. "Technology Outside Us and Inside Us." *Communio: International Catholic Review* 5 (Summer 1978): 100-121.

Arguing from the interiorization of our human technologies, Ong suggests that theology might more fruitfully reflect on its own dependence on technology, particularly communication technology. 22 pages.

[206] Peukert, Helmut. *Science, Action, and Fundamental Theology: Toward a Theology of Communicative Action.* Trans. James Bohman. Cambridge, MA: The MIT Press, 1984.

After introducing both political theology and fundamental theology, Peukert reviews the work of Jürgen Habermas in developing a theory of communicative action. He then adapts this work to theology, noting how the philosophical enterprise of finding a ground for communication comes to its completion in theology. This book gives a sound but sweeping overview of the philosophy of science, the neo-Marxist critique of method, and the theological response. Less a work of apologetics than one of theological exploration, it charts out a course which moves from theology to communication and back again to theology. 330 pages.

[207] Rahner, Hugo. *Eine Theologie der Verkündigung*. Darmstadt: Wissentschaftliche Buchgesellschaft, 1970.

In this work, Rahner attempts to develop the theological basis for Christian proclamation. 202 pages.

[208] Selby, Peter. "The Content of Christian Communication." *The Modern Churchman* 20.4 (1977): 151-160.

This essay examines the relationship between media and message, noting that the Christian message differs from all others since it posits moral choices—even about its media. Any attempt to separate Christian media and message leads to a kind of "kernel theology"—a theology which accepts that religion remains unaffected by the world and that the world can remain unaffected by religion. Selby, writing from an Anglican perspective, challenges this view, urging the "total-life" quality of the Gospel. 10 pages.

[209] Sleeth, Ronald E. "Theology vs. Communication Theories." *Religion in Life* 32 (Autumn 1963) 547-552.

Theologians criticize communication theory from a variety of perspectives: Barth opposes communication theory because God's Word needs no help; Tillich seems to embrace communication theory in his method of correlation but he too warns lest communication become the answer to the human situation. Other theologians choose one of several attitudes to communication: ignore it; oppose it because it elevates the human at the expense of the divine; value it because human communication is a shadow of the divine; suspect it because of its instrumental use; fear it because of the possibility of manipulation; and take concern with it because it can all to easily substitute a new doctrine of man for that of theology. 6 pages.

[210] Soukup, Paul A. "Interweaving Theology and Communication." *Media Development* 32.1 (January 1985): 30-33; also published as "The Integration of Theology and Communication as Fields of Study." *Reflections on a Theology of Telecommunications: Image, Model, and Word*. Ed. Elmer C. Lange. Dayton: Center for Religious Telecommunications, University of Dayton, 1985. 21-27.

This essay sketches out a method for aligning various approaches to the study of communication with various theological models. Beginning with H. Richard Niebuhr's five relations between Christ and culture and with Dulles's models of the Church, Soukup suggests that, for example, a mass media approach correlates with an institutional model of the Church in a world in which the Christian understanding finds room for both Christ and culture. 4 pages.

[211] Sullivan, John. "Theology and Communications." *The Month* 34 (1965): 218-226.

Beginning with Husserl's phenomenology of communication (communication supposes the simultaneous, conscious and reciprocal presence of two persons who desire mutual comprehension) as the basis for society, Sullivan argues that the nature of modern communication does not threaten society but the abuse of its techniques does. Theology, as a reflection on faith carried out by all Christians but especially by theologians, must seek communication in order to complete its enterprise. As such it must seek dialogue and mutual understanding and avoid the dangers of propaganda, treating people as a mass audience, inadequate expression, and false consensus. 9 pages.

[212] Taylor, G. Aiken. "What Shall We Communicate?" *Christianity Today* 3.17 (May 25, 1959): 14-17.

Due to the influence of various theories of communication, theology has incorporated the notions that communication is demonstration (of attitudes, love), and an identification of the messenger with the message and with the audience. However, this theology depends too much on a rationalistic philosophy of communication, neglects the power of God proclaimed through preaching the Word of God, and fails to lead to the regeneration of the sinner in Christ. 4 pages.

[213] Teiner, Ulrich. *Hoffnungslos gestört? Probleme religiöser Kommunikation.* Düsseldorf: Patmos, 1971.

This transcription of an interview with Hans-Dieter Bastian covers various topics dealing with Christian communication, including functions of communication, the role of the Church, tradition, the church and the mass media, a theology of communication, and practical strategies for religious communication. 72 pages.

[214] TeSelle, Sallie McFague. *Speaking in Parables: A Study in Metaphor and Theology.* Philadelphia: Fortress Press, 1975.

This book explores the conditions for and the possibilities of a theology intermediate between parables and systematics. The first part provides a theoretical underpinning through a lucid discussion of the theological tradition, of the nature of metaphor, and of the forms of parable. The second part examines poems, stories and autobiographies as means of religious expression. Throughout TeSelle argues that metaphors and parables form ways of knowing, not merely ways of communicating something already known. 186 pages.

[215] Thomas, T. K. "Education for Christian Communication: Towards a Theological Framework." *WACC Journal* 22.4 (1975): 12-16.

After advocating a middle position regarding communication between that of *Inter Mirifica* and the Uppsala statement of the World Council of

Churches, Thomas focuses on communication with a Christian purpose. Such communication creates community and fosters interpersonal meetings; such communication has the development of peoples as its goal. 5 pages.

[216] Thomas, T. K. "Theology of Communication—Not a Common Cliche: Towards a Theological Framework, Part II." *WACC Journal* 23.1 (1976): 40-43.

Noting that Christian communication must be distinctive rather than divisive, Thomas rejects the term, "theology of communication," for three reasons: (1) semantic confusion; (2) the a posteriori nature of theology; and (3) the need for a total frame of reference. This total frame of reference should include the communicating God of the Bible, the Word made flesh, the mission of the Church, and the involvement of people. 4 pages.

[217] Thomas, T. K. "Communication—The Task of the Church: Towards a Theological Framework, Part III." *WACC Journal* 23.2 (1976): 22-24.

The last essay of Thomas's series on theology and communication, this article discusses three ways in which people have dealt with communication in theological language: (1) the model of the Word made flesh—the Incarnation; (2) the model of the Church—an ecclesiology; and (3) the model of involvement or inculturation. 3 pages.

[218] Van den Heuvel, Albert H. "Christian Perspectives in Communication." *WACC Journal* 22.4 (1975): 1-4.

The sole unique element in Christian communication is Christ himself and it is Christ who must be communicated. Today, this calls for compassion but also for honesty and confrontation in our internal and external communication. 4 pages.

[219] Webber, Robert E. *God Still Speaks: A Biblical View of Christian Communication.* Nashville, TN: Thomas Nelson Publishers, 1980.

Much of this volume is a restatement of Christian doctrine with its communicative aspects highlighted: creation, the Fall, the Incarnation, and so forth. Some of the theological models of communication include God's communication in the Trinity, in history, in Word, in vision, and in the Incarnation. The book is intelligent and thorough, with many examples and Biblical references, but remains an introductory work. 221 pages.

[220] Wilder, Amos N. *Theology and Modern Literature.* Cambridge, MA: Harvard University Press, 1958.

Although this book (and the lectures upon which it is based) primarily explore the conversation between literary criticism and theology, Wilder touches upon the larger theme of Christian communication in two ways.

First, literature and the arts imply communication, and "the church is learning that it cannot ignore such expressions of the society in which it lives" (p. 51). Second, any Christian artistic judgment rests upon a theological foundation; Wilder presents a masterful analysis of Catholic and Protestant theological grounds for art, noting their strengths, weaknesses, similarities, and differences. This analysis and the historical material in the earlier chapters makes this book an important resources for those interested in a theological approach to communication. 145 pages.

Church Documents and Commentaries

[221] Administrative Board of the United States Catholic Conference. *In the Sight of All: Communications—a Vision All Can Share.* Washington, D. C.: United States Catholic Conference, 1986.

This instruction from the episcopal board of directors of the United States Catholic Conference outlines a communication policy for the bishops of the United States and for Catholic communications offices. Choosing a dialogic model of communication (the communication of the Church should be "a public dialogue of faith"), the board applies this model to the style of Church communication, to a shared ministry of communication, to choices of media and allocation of resources, to media education, and to public policy issues. 47 pages.

[222] Baragli, Enrico, ed. *Cinema cattolico: documenti della S. Sede sul cinema.* 2nd ed. Rome: Studio Romano della comunicazione sociale, 1965.

This volume publishes in one collection 130 papal statements on the cinema from Pius X in 1912 to John XXIII in 1963. Texts appear chronologically in Italian or in their original language with an Italian translation. The volume also has a systematic index to the various aspects of film and a subject index, arranged alphabetically. It forms a rather complete reference work for Catholic thought on the cinema to 1963. 437 pages.

[223] Baragli, Enrico, ed. *Comunicazione, comunione e Chiesa.* Roma: Studio Romano della comunicazione sociale, 1973.

This wonderful resource collection of 842 Catholic Church documents on communication (in Latin or, in the case of papal addresses, in the national language, and in Italian) is divided into four "epochs": oral and manuscript communication; printed communication; social communication (the press, cinema, radio, and television); and electronic communication. Relevant church documents are given for each time period. 1448 pages.

[224] Boullet, Michel. *Le Choc des Medias.* Paris: Desclée, 1985.

Part of a series on the heritage of the second Vatican Council, this volume provides a commentary on *Inter Mirifica* and the response to it in the French Church. The book is excellent for its look at the communications work and organizations of the church in France and for its extended discussion of special questions such as a theology of the communicating Church, a spirituality of communication, and the relations among culture, the media, and the Church. 298 pages.

[225] Central Committee, World Council of Churches. *Nairobi to Vancouver, 1975-1983: Report of the Central Committee to the Sixth Assembly of the World Council of Churches*. Geneva: World Council of Churches, 1983.

This report of the Central Committee of the World Council of Churches contains a short section (pages 26-33) detailing the work of the communication department. The report also reviews and evaluates the programs sponsored by that department. 264 pages.

[226] Congregation for Catholic Education. *Guide to the Training of Future Priests concerning the Instruments of Social Communication*. Rome: Tipografia Poliglotta Vaticana, 1986.

Intended as a general guide to be applied to local circumstance, this instruction mandates three levels of communication training in Catholic seminaries: (1) of receivers, (2) of pastors who will both use the media and guide others in its use, and (3) of specialists (teachers of communication and communication practitioners). The guide also contains a collection of Church documents which address communication and a glossary of terms. 55 pages.

[227] Consejo Episcopal Latinoamericano, Departamento de Comunicación Social (DECOS-CELAM). *Evangelización y comunicación social en America Latina: Problemas y perspectivas actuales*. Bogotá: Ediciones Paulinas, 1979.

In 1978 the bishops of Latin America issued an excellent statement on communication, the Church, and the Latin American situation. This book contains that document as well as a superb essay by Washington Uranga describing the development of Catholic church teaching on communication and a report on the regional meetings which led up to the 1978 meeting. 111 pages.

[228] Cousineau, Jacques. "Eglise et mass media." *Cahiers d'études et de recherches* 16 (1973): 1-45.

In keeping with its subtitle, "L'évolution des attitudes sur les communications sociales chez les hautes autorités de l'Eglise catholique," this monograph examines Church documents from Pius XI's *Vigilanti Cura* (1936) [251] to the 1971 pastoral instruction, *Communio et Progressio* [257] with an eye to noting changes and developments in the Catholic teaching about the mass media. For each document examined, Cousineau traces the historical background and highlights significant parts of the text. In addition to the two documents already mentioned, he also considers two allocutions of Pius XII on the ideal film (1955) [252,253], that pope's 1957 encyclical, *Miranda Prorsus*, [255] and Vatican II's *Inter Mirifica* [268] and *Gaudium et Spes*. He concludes that two major changes occur—one in terms of content, with the Church more open and less immediately critical of the media; and one in terms of method, with the Church more likely to consult before issuing a major statement. 45 pages.

[229] Daughters of St. Paul. *Mass Means of Communication*. Boston: St. Paul Editions, 1967.

This volume reprints four Catholic documents on mass communication: Vatican II's Decree on the Media of Social Communication [268], Paul VI's *In Fructibus*, Pius XI's *Vigilanti Cura*, [251], and Pius XII's *Miranda Prorsus* [255]. In addition, the Conciliar statement also appears as captions to a photo essay on communication in the first two-thirds of the book. 202 pages.

[230] Eilers, Franz-Josef, ed. *Kirche und Publizistik: Dreizehn Kommentare zur Pastoralinstruktion "Communio et Progressio" mit deutschen Originaltext*. München: Schöningh, 1972.

This collection of commentaries on the Vatican document, "Communio et Progressio" provides a variety of viewpoints on the relationship of church and media in a post-conciliar world. 198 pages.

[231] Gemeinsame Synode der Bistümer in der Bundesrepublik Deutschland. "Kirche und gesellschaftliche Kommunikation." *Arbeitspapiere der Sachkommission*. Vol. 2. Freiburg/Bresgau: Herder, 1977. 215-246.

This working paper of the German Catholic Synod reviews various approaches to communication and the Church, taking a post-conciliar approach. 32 pages.

[232] Gill, David, ed. *Gathered for Life: Official Report, VI Assembly, World Council of Churches, Vancouver, Canada, 1983*. Geneva: World Council of Churches; Grand Rapids: Wm. B. Eerdmans, 1983.

Section 3.8 of the official report presents the statement, "Communicating Credibly," the WCC's Assembly report on communication. The statement stresses communication which serves people, dialogue, and a communication modelled on Jesus; on this basis, the Assembly calls for a scrutiny of mass media practices, calling the churches to relate to the media "in a manner which is pastoral, evangelical and prophetic." The statement also contains a checklist for credibility, urging the examination of intention, content, style, dialogue, appropriateness, mystery, and value reversal. 363 pages.

[233] Hamerski, Werner. "Reden Pius XII: zu Fragen der Publizistik." *Publizistik* 1963: 611-631.

This essay reviews and summarizes the speeches of Pius XII about communication. 21 pages.

[234] Höller, Karl. "Kommentar zu einem Kommentar über 'Inter mirifica.'" *Communicatio Socialis* 2 (1969): 25-32.

This essay gives a positive reading of the various commentaries on *Inter Mirifica* [268], the document of Vatican II on the means of social communication. 8 pages.

[235] Huter, Alois. "Die Pastoralinstruktion 'Communio et Progressio' und das neuechristliche Bild vom Menschen." *Communicatio Socialis* 5 (1972): 97-108.

Huter provides a positive commentary to the statement of the Pontifical Commission on Social Communication, *Communio et Progressio* [257]. 11 pages.

[236] John Paul II. "Address to the Executive Council of UNESCO, on Culture, Education, and Science." *Origins* 10.4 (June 2, 1980).

In this address the pope calls for an awareness of the need for the preservation of national cultures, particularly in the light of mass- mediated culture. He also asks for a respect for human dignity in media products and for the defense of the right to communicate—the right of access to information and to the means of communication.

[237] John XXIII. *"Pacem in Terris."* 1963. *The Papal Encyclicals.* Ed. Claudia Carlen. 5 vols. Wilmington, NC: McGrath Publishing Co., 1981. 5: 107-129.

In a section in which the pope discusses the dignity of the human person, he includes among the rights derived from the natural law "the right to freedom in searching for truth and in expressing and communicating his opinions, and in pursuit of art, within the limits laid down by the moral order and the common good; ... he has the right to be informed truthfully about public events" (# 12). In this and in the relations among nations truth forms the basis for judging the success or failure of the modern media of communication. 23 pages.

[238] Johnson, David Enderton, ed. *Uppsala to Nairobi, 1968-1975: Report of the Central Committee to the Fifth Assembly of the World Council of Churches.* New York: Friendship Press, 1975.

This report to the World Council of Churches General Assembly contains a short section (pages 210-223) on the communication department and its world-wide projects and planning. It describes the department as having three functions: as spokesman for the WCC, as strategist for the WCC public pronouncements, and as reflector of the mass media. Working primarily as a press office, the communication department also spreads news of the WCC through periodical and book publishing, through a radio service, and through its translation services. 256 pages.

[239] Jones, Penry. "The Churches and the Media of Mass Communications." *The Ecumenical Review* 20 (October 1968): 435-444.

This address to the fourth Assembly of the World Council of Churches presents and comments on the statement on communication later ratified at that meeting (the Uppsala statement [272]). Jones notes that communication media are not neutral and that the churches must speak out, noting that these media affect themselves as much as the world. Further, the churches must proclaim the Gospel in a matter appropriate to the setting and the medium, taking into account especially the narrative quality of the television medium. He urges acceptance of the document in the hope that the churches can take seriously the media and lead them to serve the "truly human." 10 pages.

[240] Kerr, Nicholas, ed. *Australian Catholic Bishops' Statements Since Vatican II*. Sydney: St. Paul Publications, 1985.

This volume contains two statements dealing with communication and children. The first, issued in 1972, "The Need for Mass Media Education," calls for media education. A more recent follow-up, "Children and Television," (1979) echoes that call.

[241] Leo XIII. "*Libertas,* Encyclical on the Nature of Human Liberty." 1888. *The Papal Encyclicals.* Ed. Claudia Carlen. 5 vols. Wilmington, NC: McGrath Publishing Company, 1981. 2: 169-181.

Within the context of his discussion of human liberty (and of the condemnation of liberals), Leo XIII briefly examines liberty of speech and liberty of the press. While admitting that people have a right "freely and prudently to propagate ... what things soever are true and honorable," he condemns the spread of falsehood and of things that would corrupt the moral life. The press has the right to discuss those things which God leaves free to human discussion. 13 pages.

[242] Lott, Theodore F. "Religion on the Air." *The Beam.* 16.8 (August 1965): 26-30.

Billed as "a significant statement of Southern Baptists' philosophy of broadcasting," this address by the director of radio production for the Radio and

Television Commission of the Southern Baptist Convention outlines three key points: the importance of freedom of speech, the need to solicit decisions for Christ, and the need to produce quality programming. "The summation of our philosophy of religion on the air would [be], then, that man wants a fundamental change, that the changed man wants an increased faith, and that tortured spirits want the serenity and objectiveness religion can bring." 5 pages.

[243] Mole, John W. "The Communications Decree of the Second Vatican Council: Charter of the Communications Apostolate." *Social Justice Review* 59 (December 1966): 274-350.

In a general commentary on the decree, *Inter Mirifica* [268], Mole notes that it is noteworthy for giving a juridical definition of freedom of information and for shifting away from the focus on questions of truth in earlier papal statements on communication to a focus on freedom and moral responsibility. Third, the decree shifts responsibility for the media to the reader, listener, or viewer and not only to the journalist or producer. Fourth, the Decree moves away from an elite view of communication (that is, communication to serve culture) to one which mandates that "all media education must be inspired by the social teachings of the Church" (pages 276-277). 77 pages.

[244] Mole, John W. *Citoyen et chrétien face à la révolution des communications.* Quebec: Éditions Paulines, 1969.

This extended commentary on *Inter Mirifica,* the Vatican II decree on social communications [268], considers the mass media under two headings: their civil usage and their apostolic usage. In the former section Mole underscores the Council's recognition of a right to communication and information as well as its insistence on moral aspects of communication. In the latter section, he looks at how communication can benefit the work of the Church. 198 pages.

[245] Mole, John W. "Die Pastoralinstruktion 'Communio et Progressio' und das Konzilsdekret 'Inter Mirifica.'" *Communicatio Socialis* 5 (1972): 108-117.

In this essay, Mole—an expert commentator on the communication decree of the Second Vatican Council—compares it to the more recently issued, *Communio et Progressio* [257], noting the development of themes and the additions of further materials. 10 pages.

[246] Morley, Hugh. *The Pope and the Press.* Notre Dame, IN: Notre Dame University Press, 1968.

This book documents and discusses Pope Paul VI's statements on the press from June 1963 until the end of the Second Vatican Council in Decem-

ber 1965. It divides the 36 papal documents on the press into five categories: journalists, journalism, the general press, Catholic journalism, and
the Catholic press. ("Journalism" refers to the nature of the work while
"press" refers to its functions.) For example, the pope notes that while
journalism cannot substitute for Christian preaching, it does have a lofty
calling—to educate, to inform, and to shape public opinion. This book
quotes extensively from various papal documents; unfortunately, it does
not provide the full texts for any of them. 143 pages.

[247] Pascual, Javier María. *Los medios de comunicación social en la doctrina de la iglesia.* Madrid: Servicio de Publicaciones del Ministerio de
Educación y Ciencia, 1976.

This history of and commentary on the Catholic Church's recent documents
on communication (Vatican II's *Inter Mirifica* [268] and the Papal Commission's *Communio et Progressio* [257]) traces the fascinating story of the
development of the decrees from the preparatory commission through the
Council to the follow up commission. Besides the chronology, this text also
traces the doctrinal development within the documents and the shifting
Church attitude toward using the mass media. 350 pages.

[248] Paton, David M., ed. *Breaking Barriers—Nairobi 1975: The Official
Report of the Fifth Assembly of the World Council of Churches, Nairobi, 23
November-10 December, 1975.* London: SPCK; Grand Rapids, MI: Wm.
B. Eerdmans, 1976.

While no specific document addresses the concerns of Christian communication, these emerge as a part of the methodology section of the main
document, "Confessing Christ Today." This section notes the availability
of a comprehensive set of means of communication ranging from literature
to the electronic media. Even with these, the document notes, it is the
living witness of the local community which brings people to the Lord. In
a different context, the general secretariat also mentions communication,
recommending that the WCC's own communications be geared more to the
parish level. 411 pages.

[249] Patterson, Ronald P., ed. "Standing General Commission on Communication." *The Book of Discipline of the United Methodist Church, 1980.*
Nashville, TN: The United Methodist Publishing House, 1980. 419-426.

This juridical description of the Communication Commission of the United
Methodist Church includes the Church's statement on communication.
While all have the duty to communicate their faith, some functions can
be performed better on behalf of the whole Church by a few: public relations, consulting, media production work, advocacy, etc. 8 pages.

[250] Paul VI. "A Call to Action. Apostolic letter to Cardinal Maurice
Roy, on the Occasion of the 80th anniversary of *Rerum Novarum*, May 14,

1971." *Official Catholic Teachings.* Ed. Vincent P. Mainelli. Wilmington, NC: McGrath Publishing Co., 1978.

Pope Paul addresses the issue of communication in the midst of a larger section detailing some of the issues facing modern society. In paragraph 20 he sketches the role of the mass media and then reminds people that these media are intimately connected with the quest for justice, that they have an obligation to the truth, and that they should serve the common good.

[251] Pius XI. *"Vigilanti Cura."* 1936. *The Papal Encyclicals.* Ed. Claudia Carlen. 5 vols. Wilmington, NC: McGrath Publishing Co., 1981. 3: 517-523.

In this letter Pope Pius XI urges caution and vigilance toward the movies, noting how they can easily influence audience members. He commends the American Bishops for the Legion of Decency approach and reminds all bishops and priests of their duties to teach the people how to take suitable measures to protect themselves against films. 7 pages.

[252] Pius XII. "Allocution to Representatives of the Italian Film Industry. [*Ci tourna sommamente*]" *The Pope Speaks* 2 (1955): 101-112.

Films possess great power for people and over people due to technical advances in film making and to the psychology of the film itself. Because of this power, state and church officials sometimes step in to rate or censor films; however, this would better be left to the film industry itself. As guidance in this, Pius XII suggests some attributes of "the ideal film." In relation to its audience, the ideal film should show a respect for the human being, an affectionate understanding of the human, a fulfillment of its own promises, and an exalted purpose. 12 pages.

[253] Pius XII. "Allocution to the International Union of Theater Owners and Film Distributors. [*Nel Dare.*]" *The Pope Speaks* 2 (1955): 351-363.

A continuation of Pius XII's treatment of the "ideal film," this address takes up the theme of the film in relation to its content and in relation to the community. In terms of content, the film must meet the demands of truth, goodness, and beauty; therefore, film should not attempt to portray "plots which defy objective presentation, which are unsuitable for visual presentation" or which offend natural delicacy or prudence. Films can and should show nature, human events, and religious themes, including questions of evil. In terms of the community, the film influences and can build up the family, the state, and the Church. 13 pages.

[254] Pius XII. "Address at the Dedication of the New Vatican Radio Station." [*Attendite Populi*]" *The Pope Speaks* 4 (1957): 313-317.

People must use radio as they do any other creature—for the glory of God. Guarding against evil, radio should "inculcate virtue, propagate sound doctrine, provide recreation for the listeners by means of wholesome entertainment," and relieve worry. Radio should also aid in the proclamation of the Gospel. 5 pages.

[255] Pius XII. *"Miranda Prorsus." The Pope Speaks* 4 (1957-1958): 319-346.

Issued on September 8, 1957, this encyclical deals with motion pictures, radio and television. In this letter, the Pope claims the Church's right to use all media since Church has a greater right than all to announce what is truly good news. Further, the purpose of this letter is to "set down norms and instruction" regarding the media. Clearly hierarchical in scope, the letter claims that the Church has first right to communicate, then the civil government (for the common good) and then individuals for enrichment of all. Communication is not to be used primarily for political or economic matters. The letter calls for education of viewers to fully appreciate and discriminate among programs, but also would ban any objectionable show. It also calls for rating motion pictures and gives instructions to all laity involved in film work. The third section of the letter deals with radio and the last with television. Both must bear great responsibility since both enter the home. Pope Pius calls for diocesan offices dealing with both and for the fostering of religious programming, particularly liturgical and doctrinal shows. Throughout there is a warning about possible harm caused by the communication media. Good in themselves, they can be put to evil ends by the people using them. 28 pages.

[256] Pontifical Commission "Justitia et Pax." "The Church and Human Rights." *Official Catholic Teachings.* Ed. Vincent P. Mainelli. Wilmington, NC: McGrath Publishing Co, 1978.

The commission notes that the communication media, through their portrayals, can make the public less sensitive to injustice. It also reaffirms the right of all to express their opinion and to be completely informed about public events.

[257] Pontifical Commission on the Instruments of Social Communication. "Pastoral Instruction on the Means of Social Communication *Communio et Progressio.*" *Vatican Council II: The Conciliar and Post Conciliar Documents.* Austin Flannery, ed. Collegeville, MN: Liturgical Press, 1975. 293-349.

This lengthy instruction on communication, commissioned by the Bishops of the Second Vatican Council, begins with a Christian view of communication media and offers Incarnational and inculturation models for communication—noting that Christ forms the perfect communicator. Major sections deal with the role of communication in human society, human rights to communicate, the contribution of Catholics to communication (both within and outside of the Church), and the possibilities of the various media for evangelization. 57 pages.

[258] Radio Vaticana. *Documenti Pontifici sulla Radio e sulla Televisione (1929-1962)*. Vatican City: Tipografia Poliglotta Vaticana, [1962].

This collection contains 75 pontifical statements about radio and 10 about television, each in its original language with an Italian translation and an Italian summary. Besides the usual chronological and subject indices, the book also presents a systematic index, which orders the statements according to theme and gives a nice overview of papal teaching regarding broadcasting. For example, the advantages of broadcasting accrue through its service of humanity, through its assistance to public worship, through its aid in moral teaching, through its promotion of international life, through its diffusion of information, and through its promotion of fraternal love (page xxiii). 425 pages.

[259] Rzepkowski, Horst. "Evangelisierung und Kommunikation nachdem Puebla-Dokument." *Communicatio Socialis* 12 (1979): 348-353.

This essay gives an introduction and an appraisal of the documents produced by the Latin American bishops meeting at Puebla, with the focus on those parts that concern evangelization and communication. 6 pages.

[260] Schmidthüs, Karlheinz. "Einleitung zum Dekret über die Sozialen Kommunikationsmittel." *Lexikon für Theologie und Kirche. Das Zweite Vatikanische Konzil*. Freiburg: Herder, 1966. 1: 112-115. English translation: Schmidthüs, Karlheinz. "Decree on the Instruments of Social Communication." Ed. Herbert Vorgrimler. *Commentary on the Documents of Vatican II*. 5 vols. New York: Herder and Herder, 1967. 1: 89-104.

The history of the decree forms the most valuable part of the commentary which Schmidthüs writes. After noting the membership of the secretariat charged with the decree's preparation, he outlines the original schema and then follows it through the first sessions of the Second Vatican Council. He also outlines the chief objections against the decree, formulated by a group of journalists and theologians. The decree passed the Council nonetheless, more for extrinsic reasons: "Thus the whole career of our Decree shows that it was treated as a stop-gap between deliberations which seemed a good deal more vital to the Fathers. It represents a compromise between irreconcilable attitudes: one which would have little time wasted over this matter, and another which would not neglect a subject of such importance from the pastoral point of view" (page 94). 4 pages.

[261] Spoletini, Benito D. *Comunicación social e iglesia: Documentos de iglesia latinoamericana, 1959-1976*. Bogotá, Colombia: n.p., 1977.

This collection of Catholic Church documents includes the statements on communication (film, the press, radio and television) of the bishops, of congresses and meetings, and of special interest seminars as well as a chronology for the period. An introductory essay places them within the context of the Church's thought and activity in Latin America since the 1830's. 272 pages.

[262] Spoletini, Benito D. *Los medios de comunicación social: La Iglesia ante el desafío de la prensa, del cine, de la radio y de la televisión, desde Pío XII al Concilio Vaticano II y Pablo VI.* Bogotá, Colombia: Ediciones Paulinas, 1978.

This is a collection of Catholic Church documents on communication (*Miranda Prorsus* [255], *Inter Mirifica* [268], *Communio et Progressio* [257], and 12 allocutions of Paul VI to journalists. The editor provides a brief overview of the situation of Church communication as an introduction. 187 pages.

[263] Synod of Bishops. "Justice in the World." *Official Catholic Teachings.* Ed. Vincent P. Mainelli. Wilmington, NC: McGrath Publishing Co, 1978.

In the context of a discussion of the ways in which justice is violated today, the synod notes that people today demand truth in the communications system and in the images it offers. In addition, all people have a right to suitable freedom of expression and thought.

[264] Thorn, William J., ed. *A Vision All Can Share: Report on the Conference at Marquette University.* [Washington, D. C.]: United States Catholic Conference, 1985.

This book contains the recommendations, conference papers and proceedings of a 1984 meeting of Catholic communication professionals. It marks the culmination of a five year process of "grass roots" reflection on common policies and shared goals for the various Church communication efforts. Papers include "The Church as Communicator to Society" (Kenneth Briggs), "Church Communications Among Catholics" (Joseph O'Hare), and "The Ministry of Communications: Theological Reflections" (James Bacik). 85 pages.

[265] Ugarte, Felix Placer. *Desacralización y catequesis: La sociología de la desacralización y la comunicación del mensaje de la fe según la constitución pastoral "Gaudium et Spes."* Madrid: Propaganda Popular Católica, 1973.

This study combines two themes: an analysis of contemporary culture with a focus on the religious crisis of secularization and language, and an analysis of the communication proposed by the Second Vatican Council's dogmatic constitution, *Gaudium et Spes.* In the first part, Ugarte examines the situation of language and models of religious communication, using

the usual sociological tools of codes, channels, programs, and the sender-
message-receiver model. Part two comments on the Catholic document and
examines the functions of communication in the Church. 221 pages.

[266] United States Bishops. "Pastoral Letter of the Second Plenary Council of Baltimore." 1866. *Pastoral Letters of the United States Catholic Bishops.* Ed. Hugh J. Nolan. 4 vols. Washington, D. C.: United States Catholic
Conference, 1983. 1:185-208.

As a part of a longer pastoral letter noting the situation of the Catholic
Church in the United States, the American bishops urge Catholics to support a Catholic press, particularly to inform themselves about issues which
become confused by a secular press. The bishops also oppose attacks on
the Catholic Church made by the non-Catholic press. 24 pages.

[267] United States Bishops. "Pastoral Letter of the Third Plenary Council
of Baltimore." 1884. *Pastoral Letters of the United States Catholic Bishops.* Ed. Hugh J. Nolan. 4 vols. Washington, D.C.: United States Catholic
Conference, 1983. 1: 209-240.

In their third pastoral letter the American bishops continue to call for
support for a Catholic press. They again sketch out the situation of the
Church and indicate the obligation that Catholics have to stay informed of
Church teachings. 32 pages.

[268] Vatican II. "Decree on the Means of Social Communication *Inter Mirifica.*" *Vatican Council II: The Conciliar and Post Conciliar Documents.*
Austin Flannery, ed. Collegeville, MN: Liturgical Press, 1975. 283-292.

This short conciliar decree begins by listing the moral demands of the
media, noting people's right to information and right to communicate. It
also reminds people of their duty to make careful use of the communications
media—including a duty to educate children for the proper understanding
of the mass media. A second chapter calls Catholics to use the media for
the spread of the Gospel. 10 pages.

[269] Visser 'T Hooft, W. A., ed. *The New Delhi Report: The Third Assembly of the World Council of Churches, 1961.* New York: Association
Press, 1962.

Communication appears twice as a concern in the Third Assembly, first on
a theoretical basis and then on a practical basis. The report of the section
on Christian witness notes the effectiveness of dialogic communication and
in this context raises the issue of the use of the mass media. These can bring
about an intimate address and so should be used in this way. In the Report of the Committee on the Department of Information, practical issues
come to the fore. This committee, established at the Evanston Assembly,
performs the general role of public relations and publications. Its report

sets forth the policies followed by the department in regards to the press, to publications, to broadcasting, and to film. 448 pages.

[270] World Association for Christian Communication. "Christian Principles of Communication." *Communication Resource* 8 (July 1986).

This official statement of the World Association for Christian Communication outlines basic principles: Christian communicators follow Christ poor by interpreting the Gospel from the perspective of the poor, give witness to the corporate Church, and show respect for God's mysteries. Christian communication creates community, is participatory, liberates, supports cultures, and is prophetic. 4 pages.

[271] World Council of Churches. *Evanston Speaks: Reports from the Second Assembly of the World Council of Churches, Evanston, Ill., U. S. A., August 15-31, 1954.* London: SCM Press, 1954.

In the context of the report on Evangelism (the mission of the Church to those outside her life), the Assembly addresses the aspect of communication. The Church itself forms the medium of the Gospel. Recognizing that "no strategy of communication is itself a guarantee of success," the Assembly does note some demands of communication upon the Church. "First, there must be encounter with the world. ... Second, there must follow the speaking of a word which is intimately related to the problems of the individual in his world. ... Third, too often our words have been impotent because they have not been embodied in works of service, compassion and identification. ... Fourthly, in order to possess the power to evangelize, the Church must nourish its life on the Bible." 115 pages.

[272] World Council of Churches. "The Church and the Media of Mass Communication." *The Uppsala Report 1968.* Geneva: World Council of Churches, 1968. 389-401.

This statement recognizes the role of the media and their impact on society and recommends that the churches become more involved in the world of the media, learning about them, training seminarians in their use, and cooperating with those who are working for a more just media society. A brief theological section (pages 394-397) suggests that two theological approaches to the media are possible: one that focuses on the individual and relationships between people (especially reconciliation) and one that looks to the social function of each medium. This latter needs the churches' attention, working for the restoration of communication to its proper place, as Jesus did. 13 pages.

[273] Yzermans, Vincent A., ed. *Valiant Heralds of Truth: Pius XII and the Arts of Communication.* Westminster, MD: The Newman Press, 1958.

This book is a collection of statements by Pius XII on the press, public opinion, film, radio, and television. Apart from the text of *Miranda Prorsus,* the book simply gathers materials out of their proper context, but sorted according to topic. The editor's comments seem uncritical and overly in awe of the person of the pope. The book ends with a bibliography of relevant journal articles. 201 pages.

Ethics

[274] Alley, Robert S. *Television: Ethics for Hire?* Nashville, TN: Abingdon, 1977.

This book deals with morality on television primarily through commentaries on television programming and through interviews with television producers. Alley sees the producers and production talent as seeking moral/ethical shows while at the same time facing network pressure to increase audience size. He rejects the general criticism of television as lowering moral standards as inaccurate. The difficulty here (which Alley admits) is that he never defines what he means by moral or ethical, preferring the general use of the terms. Specific chapters look at the family viewing hour, tv drama, tv humor, stars, sports, and the family. 192 pages.

[275] Boventer, Hermann. *Ethik des Journalismus: Zur Philosophie der Medienkultur.* Konstanz: Universitäts-Verlag, 1984.

This collection of papers deals with journalism and ethics in a broader context. 507 pages.

[276] Christian Conference of Asia. *The Communication Revolution and New World Information and Communication Order: The Challenge to the Churches.* Singapore: Christian Conference of Asia, [1985].

Three sets of documentation make up this book: (1) Bible studies by the Rev. Dr. Somen Das on communication in the service of a new heaven and a new earth which provide grounding principles for this reflection; (2) national reports from throughout Asia on the status on Christian media and international communication; and (3) resources papers for further study, giving summaries of the NWICO debate, the WACC positions, and Third World perspectives. 131 pages.

[277] Christians, Clifford G., Kim B. Rotzoll, and Mark Fackler. *Media Ethics: Cases and Moral Reasoning.* 2nd ed. New York: Longman, 1987.

A general text in media ethics, this volume presents cases drawn from many areas (censorship, children, confidentiality, conflict of interest, deception, economic pressures, sexuality, fairness, minorities, privacy, sensationalism, stereotyping, and violence) in a range of media (books, magazines, motion pictures, newspapers, photography, radio, and television). Aiming to improve ethical awareness, the book follows the "Potter Box" method of defining the issue, stating values, elucidating principles, and identifying loyalties. Five different ethical principles form the basis for judgment in the cases: Aristotle's Golden Mean, Kant's Categorical Imperative, Mill's Principle of Utility, Rawl's Veil of Ignorance, and the Judeo-Christian ethic of love (persons as ends). 344 pages.

[278] Deussen, Giselbert. *Ethik der Massenkommunikation bei Papst Paul VI.* München: Schöningh, 1973.

This study examines various aspects of mass communication ethics in the writings of Pope Paul VI. 354 pages.

[279] Guissard, Lucien. "Aspects éthiques des techniques d'information dans la press." *Revue Théolgique de Louvain* 6 (1975): 31-40.

The ethics applied to journalism must take shape from the ends of journalism: a paper providing entertainment differs greatly from one providing information. Furthermore, the situation of the contemporary press must be judged by contemporary standards, including the effects of technologies and the pressures which they bring to journalism. Finally, both economic and ideological factors play a role in determining the performance of the press. 10 pages.

[280] Häring, Bernard. *The Law of Christ: Moral Theology for Priests and Laity.* Trans. Edwin G. Kaiser. 3 vols. Westminster, MD: The Newman Press, 1966. 3: 626-682.

One section of this treatise on Catholic moral theology deals explicitly with "Communication Technique." Within the context of truth, fidelity, and honor, the means of communication have a duty to convey the truth and to build up the human community in God's image. Looking first at the meaning and function of the press, film, radio and television, Häring sees them as directed primarily to service of family, information, education, entertainment, and religion. He next surveys the same ground from the perspective of personal and social responsibility of the media and follows a traditional Catholic focus on the role of public opinion. The two final sections prove somewhat interesting—a note on the control of the media (self-regulation rather than censorship) and a note on the "new psychic consciousness created by mass media." A brief bibliography follows. This work, a solid summary of the Catholic position that informs most recent Church writing, is a bit dated now—not in its reasoning or grounds but in its view of the communication media and the context of contemporary society. 57 pages.

[281] Haselden, Kyle. *Morality and the Mass Media.* Nashville, TN: Broadman Press, 1968.

Writing from his perspective as a Baptist minister and an editor of *Christian Century,* Haselden situates his own moral position between legalism
and situationism. He then applies these norms to the uses of the mass media; to questions of censorship and obscenity; and to the media of radio,
advertising, film, and television. He concludes with some general reflections
on morality and the sense of God's presence. 192 pages.

[282] Hertz, Anselm. "Bildmedien in moraltheologischer Sicht und
Möglichkeiten zur Verwicklichung christlicher und allgemein sittlicher
Grundsätze in der pluralistischen Gesellschaft." *Fernsehen under Kon-
trolle?* Eds. Karl Becker and Karl August Siegel. Frankfurt/Main, 1960:
9-30.

This essays deals in a sound and open way with the morality of images and
sets forth some principles for their production. 22 pages.

[283] Jorgenson, Lawrence Joseph. *The Freedom of the Press and the
Right to Information.* Diss. Catholic University of Louvain, 1981. *Dissertation Abstracts International* 43.3C (1983): 432. Ann Arbor: UMI, 1981.
8170053.

This dissertation contrasts two approaches to an ethics of the press: the
freedom of the press (a negative formulation which tries to limit state en-
croachment on communication) and the right to information (a positive
assertion of a fundamental right of human beings). The issues are situated in terms of Church perspectives and documents. A personalist moral
theology is adduced as a solution to the dilemma. 364 pages.

[284] Kelly, David C. "Cross-Cultural Communication and Ethics." *Missiology* 6 (1978): 311-322.

Kelly sketches out a model of ethical reflection, noting the places in which it
parallels the process of intercultural communication—especially in the step
in becoming an "outsider" to the discourse. He then isolates two competing
concepts of a moral sense (duty and aspiration) and shows how each receives
different emphasis in different cultures. 12 pages.

[285] Kirtland, Robert. "Art, Movies, and Morals." *Catholic Educational
Review* 51 (1953): 617-624.

Morality must always stand judge over beauty or art, particularly in regards
to the cinema with its powerful persuasive force. Moviegoers should educate
themselves to become more critical viewers lest they succumb to the "art
for art's sake" mentality of film makers. 8 pages.

[286] Lee, Philip, ed. *Communication for All: The Church and the New World Information and Communication Order.* Indore, Madhya Pradesh, India: Satprakashan Sanchar Kendra; Maryknoll, NY: Orbis Books; Ibadan, Nigeria: Daystar Books, n.d.

The essays in this volume address the issues of the New World Information and Communication Order (NWICO) from the perspective of the Christian churches. For the most part, the churches see the necessity of supporting the NWICO as an aspect of their option for the poor and of their support for dialogic and popular communication.

In the essays themselves, Washington Uranga describes the NWICO and puts it in the context of the Catholic Church's communication in Latin America. He also gives a brief history of church communication in that context. Paul Ansah sketches African Responses to NWICO. Robert White gives a more specifically Christian approach to the topic, exploring options and questions as well as proposing a series of case studies to guide one's reflection. Gaston Roberge examines the Church's response to the NWICO in India. Other essays consider women and the NWICO and the overall impact of the NWICO on the nations of the world. 158 pages.

[287] Meiden, Anne van der. "The Basic Issues of Media Ethics." *WACC Journal* 26.4 (1979): 3-6.

This brief overview of media ethics provides both a theoretical grounding and a practical discussion. Key issues include freedom of speech, the right to communicate, the right to refuse communication, the right to be informed, the right to participate, the right to freely gather information, and the protection of local cultural value systems. Christian ethics should address these questions on three levels: developing moral criteria; applying Gospel values; and inserting the Church in the world. 4 pages.

[288] O'Sullivan, J. L. "Conflict over Freedom of Information." *America* 88 (February 28, 1953): 589-91.

This article briefly states the issues involved in freedom of information cases, both on the national and international levels. Newspapers demand too much by seeking total openness of all government records; yet some access is vital. The author calls for further study of the issue, particularly by religious groups who could add their own moral outlook to the debate. 3 pages.

[289] Phelan, John M. *Disenchantment: Meaning and Morality in the Media.* New York: Hastings House, 1980.

This collection of essays on the mass media focuses on morality writ large: rather than addressing the usual topics of media ethics, Phelan examines the contexts that shape those topics: method in the social sciences and humanities; censorship and consumerism; and technology. Along the way he deals engagingly with such things as the orality-literacy hypothesis, the workings of the Legion of Decency, and the shift from mechanical Christianity to mass culture. The essays stimulate thought and challenge easily accepted assumptions. 191 pages.

[290] Rubin, Bernard, ed. *Questioning Media Ethics.* New York: Praeger Publishers, 1978.

This collection of essays on media ethics simply raises issues pertinent to the United States (and, occasionally, Great Britain) without much theoretical grounding of an ethical system. Some historical material introduces the volume, followed by probings of the media by reporters and editors, a sketch of the players (owners, unions, government, etc.), a discussion of the fairness doctrine, and longer essays dealing with various publics. Among these latter are women, children, and the third world. Section on law and media images complete the volume. 308 pages.

[291] Sanchez Agesta, Luis, ed. *Los medios de comunicación de masas ante la moral.* Anales de Moral Social y Económica 23. Madrid: Centro de Estudios Sociales del Valle de los Caidos, 1970.

Each of the essays in this volume deals with a different aspect of communication ethics. The more general ones address the question from the perspective of liberty, truth or integrity of information. Other essays deal specifically with information and public opinion in the Catholic church, the Church's teachings on communication and individual rights, and moral problems which the Catholic church has noted in films and television. The essays include the following: Andrés Romero, "La libertad en los medios de comunicación de masas"; Ramón Cunill, "La veracidad en los medios de comunicación de masas"; César Vaca Cangas, "La integridad de la información"; Rodolfo Argamentería García, "Derechos y obligaciones de los cuidadanos y del Estado en relación con los medios de comunicación de masas"; José Luis Martin Descalzo, "Información y opinión pública en las Iglesia"; Manuel Olivencia Ruiz, "Las Empresas de Medios de comunicación de masas"; José María Sánchez de Muniáin y Gil, "Tensiones Éticas de l'arte en la cultura actual"; and Carlos Staehlin, "Problemas morales específicos de las cinematografía y las televisión." 276 pages.

[292] Souchon, Michel. "Ethique de Communication." *Recherches de Science Religieuse* 62 (1974): 541-562.

After noting the influence of the mass media on social behavior and on public opinion, Souchon sketches out some ethical tasks for communication. Apart from urging the examination of the structures of communication, he also suggests that one might examine the moral influence of opinion leaders or the varied weight of competing moralities in the media. 22 pages.

[293] UNDA. "On the Road to NWICO ...with Latin America." *the wide world of UNDA* Supplement 2.3 [1983]: 1-38.

The brief supplement to the newsletter of the International Catholic Association for Radio and Television contains the texts of three Latin American Catholic church documents dealing with the New World Information and Communication Order. First, the 8th Congress of the Latin American Catholic Press Union (UCLAP), meeting at Belo Horizonte, Brazil in 1981, called for the Church to focus on liberating communication and to support alternative communication. Second, a seminar on NWICO sponsored by UCLAP and UNESCO in 1982, called for an understanding of the link between the new order and human rights. Third, a conference convened by just about every Latin American association for Catholic and Christian communication, meeting in Sao Paulo in 1982, issued a more detailed statement of the situation in Latin America and possible responses for the Church in terms or the New Information Order. 38 pages.

[294] Veenstra, Charles Dewayne. *A Reformed Theological Ethics of Speech Communication*. Diss. University of Nebraska at Lincoln, 1981. *Dissertation Abstracts International* 42.9A (1982): 3810. Ann Arbor: UMI, 1982. 8203224.

Although described as an ethics for speech communication, this study actually examines the ethics of a series of broadcast sermons by Dr. Joel Nederhood. The Reformed tradition supplies the context and basic principles for the communication ethics proposed: "Communication links man with God and thus God must be honored in all communication." From this overarching principle five other principles flow: honesty, correct attitudes toward others, proper word choice, respect for human intellectual capacities, and attempt to satisfy others' needs. 311 pages.

Critiques of Media Use

[295] Bachman, John W. *Media—Wasteland or Wonderland: Opportunities and Dangers for Christians in the Electronic Age*. Minneapolis: Augsburg Publishing, 1984.

This well-written and challenging book examines television and the ways in which the Christian churches might respond to it and utilize it. The author refuses to condemn television or to accept the "party line" among religious communicators that broadcasting cannot evangelize. Unfortunately the popular nature of the book leads away from sustained argument and documentation. Chapters deal with negative and positive images of television, possibilities for churches, and views of the audience. 175 pages.

[296] Berton, Pierre. *The Comfortable Pew.* Philadelphia: J. B. Lippincott Company, 1965.

This "critical look at Christianity and the religious establishment in the new age" takes a 1960's view of the Canadian churches and their adaptation to modernity. The third section considers communication, judging it a failure; examinations of language and media use show how the churches have lost touch with the people. 137 pages.

[297] Bluck, John. *Beyond Neutrality: A Christian Critique of the Media.* Geneva: World Council of Churches, 1978.

Rather than choosing either an outright condemnation of the media or a full acceptance of them for mission, Bluck recounts the arguments for both and chooses a more nuanced position–what he terms a Gospel way of relating (a personalism), of seeing and of measuring. Where he punches holes in most "Christian approaches" to the media, he doesn't offer much beyond an appeal for a Gospel or community based approach. 68 pages.

[298] Bluck, John. *Beyond Technology: Contexts for Christian Communication.* Geneva: World Council of Churches, 1984.

A continuation of the author's *Beyond Neutrality,* this volume raises more questions about the quality of communication and about the news values of a Christian communication. It also includes the text of the Vancouver Assembly (1983) of the World Council of Churches on communication as well as a series of essays on religious communication by representatives from different parts of the world. Noteworthy is Michael Traber's essay in which he sets out as guidelines for Christian communication that which is based on human dignity, respect, justice, equality, and freedom (Traber, "Communication for Peace and Justice," pages 61-70). 101 pages.

[299] Boyd, Malcolm. *Crisis in Communication: A Christian Examination of the Mass Media.* Garden City, NY: Doubleday & Company, Inc., 1957.

This relatively early commentary on the culture of communication raises issues which still await an answer. How can the church both use the means of communication and stand in judgment over those means? How can the church avoid exploitation when it uses mass communication? What is the responsibility of a Christian who works in the mass media? Why can't the church be creative in its use of communication? Boyd also discusses the need for targeting audiences for religious communication, negative and positive witness through dramatic presentations, the danger of sentimentality, the possibility of commercial sponsorship of religious programming, etc. The book, despite its somewhat disjointed style, challenges the reader even thirty years after its first publication. 128 pages.

[**300**] Boyd, Malcolm. *Christ and Celebrity Gods: The Church in Mass Culture*. Greenwich, CN: The Seabury Press, 1958.

In an attempt to provide a bridge between theology and contemporary culture, Boyd demonstrates a model of Christian interpretation and witness in his review of films, plays, and television programming. Two brief chapters— the first and the last—set the argument that Christian faith must be lived in culture and that the Christian laity must witness to neighbor, taking advantage of the openings provided by mass communication's themes. The bulk of the book, however, consists of reviews, observations, and commentary on Hollywood and New York. 145 pages.

[**301**] Carnell, Edward John. *Television: Servant or Master?* Grand Rapids, MI: Wm. B. Eerdmans, 1950.

This study by a professor of systematic theology must surely form one of the earlier evaluations of television from a Christian and Biblical perspective. Carnell attempts, what he terms, "an anticipatory balance sheet," noting the virtues and vices of television and encouraging people to understand the new medium and its role in their lives. Writing in an clear and easy style, he marks both the good and bad sides of television in terms of its bringing entertainment, fostering knowledge, educating people, and influencing children. He concludes that television. like all creation, possesses a mixture of good and evil. 196 pages.

[**302**] Colwell, Gary. "Technology and False Hope." *Crux* 20.3 (September 1984): 17-26.

Within a larger discussion of technology, Colwell offers a Christian critique of television. Television shares the basic assumptions of techno-optimism that knowledge will save us, that humans are basically good, and that human beings are malleable. He rejects these assumptions and warns that television has ill effects based in its ability to hold our attention, render us passive, and shape us in a secular world view. 10 pages.

[**303**] Costigan, Michael E. "The Media in General." *Australasian Catholic Record* 61 (1984): 259-264.

In this essay a Catholic journalist reflects on the role of the media. 6 pages.

[**304**] Deskur, André Marie. "Kirchliche Kommunikation der Zukunft." *Communicatio Socialis* 10 (1977): 258-263.

Because technical developments will make communication even more important in daily life by the year 2000, Deskur argues that the Church has to defend the freedom of both communicator and receiver. In addition, the Church must give a clear view of the dignity and meaning of human life to guide both conscience and creativity. 6 pages.

[305] Dupree, James Vincent. *A Burkean Analysis of the Messages of Three Television Preachers: Jerry Falwell, Robert Schuller, and Jimmy Swaggert.* Diss. Pennsylvania State University, 1983. *Dissertation Abstracts International* 45.1A (1985): 16. Ann Arbor: UMI, 1984. 8409030.

Taking its lead from the rhetorical analysis of Kenneth Burke, this study examines the world views and motivations for action demonstrated in the sermons of Falwell, Schuller, and Swaggert. Noting that all three ministers "see a simple, largely causal world where people merely need to understand the 'truth' to solve their problems," Dupree argues that whatever their differences—and there are certainly differences—all three ministers call their hearers to "join the individual minister, not Christianity." 391 pages.

[306] Ellul, Jacques. *The Humiliation of the Word.* Trans. Joyce Main Hanks. Grand Rapids, MI: William B. Eerdmans, 1985.

Ellul offers a Christian critique of contemporary society and its communication through a commentary on the Word and its rejection in favor of the image. He develops a kind of phenomenology of the Word and reviews the presence of the Word in the Old and New Testaments. On this basis he draws a distinction between reality (which he says is visual) and truth (which he says is verbal). He then recounts how modern society has disvalued the Word and truth itself through a cult of images and a contempt for language. He offers a hint of salvation, though, in the contemplation of icons and in a meditation on the Gospel of John. 285 pages.

[307] Fischer, Edward. *Everybody Steals from God: Communication as Worship.* Notre Dame: University of Notre Dame Press, 1977.

This collection of essays deals with the different ways of finding God in the communicative dimensions of daily living. Specific topics include design, prose writing, the gospel in the mass media, films, ritual, and education. This is less a guide to communication than a Christian appreciation of communication as inherently religious. 170 pages.

[308] Fore, William F. *Image and Impact: How Man Comes Through in the Mass Media.* New York: Friendship Press, 1970.

This well done, but somewhat dated, commentary on the social effects of the mass media in the United States applies Biblical perspectives to media images of human beings, to news, to technology, and to advertising, as well as to other social situations created by the communication industry. 111 pages.

[309] Forster, Karl. *Glaube und Kirche im Dialog mit der Welt von heute.* Würzburg: Echter, 1982.

This collection of theological essays deals primarily with pastoral issues arising from modern problems in the relationship of the Church and the world. The essays are well informed and helpful. 702 pages.

[310] Gibbs, Mark. *Christians with Secular Power.* Philadelphia: Fortress Press (Laity Exchange Books), 1981.

This book which contains both ecumenical and evangelical materials, examines the leadership role of the Christian laity in various occupations. The chapter on the mass media offers both a critique and some suggestions, and encourages Christians to support those other Christians who work in the communication industry. 135 pages.

[311] Hoover, Stewart M. *The Electronic Giant: A Critique of the Telecommunications Revolution from a Christian Perspective.* Elgin, IL: The Brethren Press, 1982.

Hoover both introduces the various aspects of the communications revolution (television and cable, primarily) and offers the basis for a Christian reading of these media. His chief approach lies in ethics and he questions the authority of the media as well as sketching a picture of controllers and regulators. Beside debunking a series of myths about television (for example, television "is a mirror of society"), he reviews national and international communication policies of the U. S. government, noting how these too foster a series of myths. The final section introduces the media reform movement (including Action of Children's Television and the Communication Office of the United Church of Christ). His brief history of people and issues fills a gap in the popular knowledge of this movement. 171 pages.

[312] Horsfield, Peter G. "Larger than Life: Religious Functions of Television." *Media Information Australia* 47 (February 1988): 61-66.

Starting with a sociological definition of religion, Horsfield argues that television has become the functional equivalent of religion for many contemporaries. He notes that it provides a ritual which enables people to "transcend present profane time," a hermeneutic which enables people to relate meaningfully to their environment, and a common body of belief which enables people to form a community. 6 pages.

[313] Jenkins, Daniel. "The Word, the Media, and the Marketplace." *The Princeton Seminary Bulletin* 76 (1983): 88-94.

This essays calls attention to some of the dangers to Christian communication occasioned by the expansion of the mass media. These dangers include the volume of material communicated, the distraction of the ease of the media, and the trivializing tendency of the media. Christians should exercise caution in using the media with its salesmanship and celebrity status. 7 pages.

[314] Johnson, Merle Allison. *How to Be Happy in the Non-Electric Church.* Nashville, TN: Abingdon, 1979.

This delightfully written book takes a humorous, yet serious, look at the local church which must of necessity compete with the televised evangelists. Indirectly critical of the electronic church, the book provides real insight into communication on the local level. Told with anecdotes and wit ("Will you acknowledge that you can't quite fathom why the world's best-known faith healer is building the world's best medical facility?"), each chapter proposes rules to guide local ministers and congregations in their own process of communicating with each other. 112 pages.

[315] Kehl, D. G. "Peddling the Power and the Promise." *Christianity Today* 24 (March 21, 1980): 372-375.

A condemnation of "marketing" Christianity, this article calls for propagation of faith rather than propaganda for the faith. Unfortunately, many of the distinctions drawn in the article between the two methods are not clear. 4 pages.

[316] King, Michael. *It's the Mass Media That Matters.* Melbourne: Australian Catholic Truth Society, 1971.

This former archdiocesan priest director of a Catholic Communications office argues that the Church should take the media seriously.

[317] Lynch, William F. *The Image Industries.* New York: Sheed and Ward, 1959.

In this critique of American mass-media culture (particularly as shown in film and on television), Lynch alternates between the poles of criticism and theology as the anchors for his observations. Throughout the book he addresses artists, creative theologians, trained critics, and the universities in the hope of helping them to a deeper understanding of popular culture. Among his themes he includes fantasy and reality, sensibility, freedom and fixation, the imagination, and human values. His theological treatment of freedom and its application in the arts is excellent. 159 pages.

[318] Mills, John Orme. "The Church in a Media-Made World: What This Implies for Religious." *Multimedia International* 47 (1982): supplement.

The communications revolution has had its impact on the life style of Church members, forming a supermarket mentality (just shop around), raising expectations, and provoking a greater public examination of Church life. The Church needs to respond by noting how it is perceived and adjusting that; by promoting communication education; and by studying how better to use the media.

[319] Muggeridge, Malcolm. *Christ and the Media*. Grand Rapids, MI: William Eerdmans Publishing Company, 1977.

In these, the 1976 London Lectures in Contemporary Christianity, British broadcaster Muggeridge, alternating between anecdote and argument, questions whether television can adequately portray the seriousness of Christianity given its emphasis on entertainment. He further notes the contradiction between television's necessary focus on image and fantasy and the Christian attention to reality and word. 127 pages.

[320] Nelson, John Wiley. *Your God Is Alive and Well and Appearing in Popular Culture*. Philadelphia: The Westminster Press, 1976.

Arguing the thesis that "popular culture is to what most Americans believe as worship services are to what the members of institutional religions believe," this book examines the forms of popular culture and illustrates and critiques the religious forms of contemporary America. 217 pages.

[321] Reid, Gavin. *The Gagging of God: The Failure of the Church to Communicate in the Television Age*. London: Hodder and Stoughton, 1969.

Criticizing church communication, Gavin argues that "the greatest threat to the gospel today in our Western industrial societies ...is this breakdown of communication not only from the Church to those outside, but also a breakdown of communication in every field of daily life." Analyzing the problem as stemming from urbanization as well as from new forms of communication, he tends to follow McLuhan and argue the orality-literacy hypothesis. He asks for a new reformation that would make organized Christianity a cause, a community with the world in the deepest sense of community. And this, of course, finds its foundation in communication. 126 pages.

[322] Schneider, Louis and Sanford M. Dornbusch. *Popular Religion: Inspirational Books in America*. Chicago: The University of Chicago Press, 1958.

This study in the sociology of religion examines 46 religious best sellers in America from 1875 to 1955 through a rigorous content analysis. It finds that this literature is strongly oriented toward this world and its goods. Changes in its content reflect changes in the general American cultural outlook rather than in religious thought as such. Finally, the authors note that this literature "is preoccupied with power, success, life-mastery, and peace of mind and soul and not with salvation in older senses of the term." 174 pages.

[323] Schultze, Quentin J. *Television: Manna from Hollywood?* Grand Rapids, MI: Zondervan Publishing House, 1986.

This critique of television from an evangelical Christian perspective has a clearly educational purpose. Rather than assuming television promotes evil, the author provides a way of examining television as a cultural storyteller and encourages Christians to attend to its themes and effects. Because the book is directed to parents and church groups, it avoids close analysis and technical language, using anecdotes and commentary instead. 160 pages.

[324] Shayon, Robert Lewis. "TV as Religion." *Saturday Review* (October 22, 1966): 74.

Television programming, with its reassurance that all is well, has supplanted the tradition role of religion and theology, just at the moment theologians call for religion to challenge society and call it to conversion. 1 pages.

[325] Short, John and Ray Brown. *All Done by Mirrors: Reflections on the Mass Media.* Liverpool: Liverpool Institute of Socio-Religious Studies, 1978.

This study paper, prepared for the [Catholic] Conference of Major Religious Superiors of England and Wales, examines the role of television in British society and its impact on values, self-image, and behavior. Taking a cultural studies approach, the authors argue that the Church should be concerned and active in debates about television policy and content. 34 pages.

[326] Sills, Mark R. "The Docetic Church." *Christian Century* 98.2 (January 21, 1981): 37-38.

Sills argues that the "electronic church" implicitly promulgates the Docetic heresy because it denies the reality of the Body of Christ—the church—by substituting the appearance of a community for the biblically ordained community itself. Electronic media are tools for evangelization and not substitutes for the church. 2 pages.

[327] Taylor, James A. "No Miracles from the Media." *Christian Century* 96 (May 30, 1979): 613-615.

The mass media have inherent limitations which make them basically unsuitable for evangelization. Among these, the greatest is the lack of personal contact, the distance they engender between communicators. 3 pages.

[328] UNDA-OCIC. "Cultures, Media and Gospel Values." *OCIC- Info* and *The Wide World of UNDA* special issue (May- June 1986).

This study paper for the 1987 OCIC-UNDA convention in Quito, Ecuador provides background on the influence of the media on the development of local culture and the role of the Christian communicator. The paper presents various dichotomies: pessimism vs. optimism regarding culture and Christianity; Christianity in a non-Christian culture; cultural autonomy vs. cultural universalism; prophecy vs. accommodation; and the Church and culture. A final section provides a compendium of relevant Church texts. 15 pages.

[329] Wedel, Theodore Otto. *The Gospel in a Strange, New World.* Philadelphia: Westminster Press, 1963.

A volume of the Westminster Studies in Christian Communication, this book deals with evangelizing the secular society of the mid-twentieth century. After a brief cultural analysis, the author (an Episcopalian) poses the need for a greater lay ministry and for a ministry of reconciliation and calls for a witness by the Church, both gathered and scattered in the world. 141 pages.

Media Education

[330] Amgwerd, Michael. *Die Filmsprache: Ausdruck einer neuen Kulturform.* Sarnen: Kollegium Sarnen, 1965.

This introduction to film appreciation by an educator provides a valuable resource for a Christian guide to the media. 214 pages.

[331] Browning, Robert L. *Communicating with Junior Highs.* Nashville, TN: Graded Press, 1968.

Because of the "communications revolution," youths often find themselves in the awkward situation of trying to identify Christian values with what they see in the mass media. This book offers suggestions for better communication in youth ministry with pre-teens. 208 pages.

[332] Butler, John. *TV, Movies & Morality: A Guide for Catholics.* Huntington, IN: Our Sunday Visitor, Inc., 1984.

This introductory book forms a kind of "media education" guide for parents. Beginning with television, it sketches how television programs get on the air, the role of ratings and advertising, and the special interests of religious television and children's television. A guide to making intelligent and tactical choices about choosing programs concludes this first section. The second part of the book—devoted to the film industry—discusses movie ratings, moral issues, and how to choose films. This section seems weakened by an overemphasis on objections to nudity in films. The book ends with a viewer's guide to public interest activity regarding television, including sample letters to the FCC. 160 pages.

[333] Cameron, Regina and Charles Watt. *Growing with Media.* Sydney: St. Paul Publications, 1985.

This is a handbook for media studies in Catholic schools.

[334] Canavan, Kelvin. *Mass Media Education in Australia*. Sydney: Catholic Education Office, 1982.

This volume reports a study on the successes and failure of media education in Catholic schools in Australia.

[335] Chamberlin, Frederick. *You and the Movies*. Melbourne: Young Catholic Students Publications, 1952.

This guide to movie criticism for Catholic high schools reflects an earlier day's approach to media education.

[336] Consejo Episcopal Latinoamericano, Departmento de Comunicación Social (CELAM-DECOS). *Comunicación: Misión y desafío. Manual Pastoral de Comunicación Social*. Bogotá: Consejo Episcopal Latinoamerica, 1986.

This manual and study guide is designed to guide groups in critical thinking about communication, communication media, evangelization, the Church, and society in Latin America. It contains general reflections on communication, a history of the Catholic Church's thought on communication (both the universal Church and the Church in Latin America), theological reflections on communication, considerations of the ethical and moral dimensions of communication, and various liturgical, pastoral, and political strategies. 321 pages.

[337] Daughters of St. Paul. *Media Impact and You*. Boston: St. Paul Editions, 1981.

This book combines some basics of media education with catechetical materials based on various Catholic statements about the mass media. Each chapter gives a very simple overview, offers some reflections (including the activities of the Daughters of St. Paul in that area), and poses some study questions. The book ends with some prayers for those working in the media. ("The Daughters of St. Paul are an international congregation of religious women serving the Church with the communications media.") 124 pages.

[338] Fidelia, Sister Mary. "Values—Movies—Morality," *The Catholic Educator* 23 (June 1953): 502-505.

The teaching of critical viewing of film provides a good vehicle for developing values and inculcating a personal application of moral teachings. This article reports a project based on theories of moral education as applied to film study; among the project's findings is the fact that high school students quickly learned a greater appreciation of film and could readily apply a wide range of moral standards to films. 4 pages.

[339] Hawker, James F. "Are Catholic Educators Responding to the Powerful Presence of Television?" *Momentum* 17.1 (February 1986): 22-23.

Noting the impact of television and the duty of religious educators to "assist children and youth to examine and evaluate from a gospel perspective the values contained within the culture," this article introduces a method to aid teachers in their task. *The Media Mirror* is a joint U. S. Catholic Conference and National Catholic Educational Association project for media education; it contains student books and teacher guides addressing themes relevant to different age groups. 2 pages.

[340] Honeywell, William Paul. *Television Commercials and Biblical Motifs: A Theological Inquiry.* Diss. Drew University, 1983. *Dissertation Abstracts International* 44.11A (1984): 3412. Ann Arbor: UMI, 1984. 8402925.

This account of a media education adult Bible class which compared Biblical motifs (home, family, body, work, time, ageing) with the parallel images in television commercials remains fairly superficial, mainly due to a lack of methodology for such parallel evaluation. 231 pages.

[341] Horsfield, Peter G. *Taming the Television: A Parent's Guide to Children and Television.* Sydney: Albatross Books, 1986.

This guide for parents who want to control their children's television viewing habits is written by a Uniting Church minister who specializes in the study of religious television. 76 pages.

[342] Hudson, Mary, Petelo Falelavaki, et al. *Mass Media Education for Youth in the South Pacific: Training Manual.* Suva, Fiji: Lotu Pasifika Productions, 1983.

After a brief introduction spelling out the aims and assumptions of the program, this handbook outlines simple classroom strategies for teaching a media education course. The booklet does not treat any issue in depth but instead suggests approaches for teachers. 91 pages.

[343] Jones, G. William. *Sunday Night at the Movies.* Richmond, VA: John Knox Press, 1967.

This book argues that the churches and their members should be concerned with film. Films speak to contemporary people; films also teach and illustrate Christian truths. On the other hand, films can oppose Christian living. Jones, a professor of film and a Methodist minister, sketches a Christian film criticism in which he uses Christian principles to better appreciate film; he also shows how to use films to better understand Christianity. To take account of the harmful potential of film, Jones provides a guide to film (and television) study, urging media education for young people. 127 pages.

[344] Logan, Ben and Kate Moody, eds. *Television Awareness Training: The Viewer's Guide for Family and Community.* New York: Media Action Research Center, 1979.

This workbook for a Christian critique of television programming combines guided activities (complete with worksheets) and essays about the nature of television to be used in conjunction with the television awareness training program. The program seeks to develop a more attentive and critical viewer through various consciousness raising techniques. Despite its design for the program, the workbook can also stand alone as a resource about television in the United States for those seeking to become more critical viewers. 280 pages.

[345] McNulty, Edward N. *Television: A Guide for Christians.* Nashville: Abingdon, 1976.

This group study/discussion guide aims to help "the average intelligent Christian watch television more critically, and to have more fun while doing it." The book consists of six topics and exercises dealing with soap operas, adventure programs, advertising, children's shows, comedies, and news. Each unit contains introductory material, discussion guides, and activities. As in any television study guide, the material shows its age through dated examples but could provide ideas for group leaders. 96 pages.

[346] Perrotta, Kevin. *Taming the TV Habit.* Ann Arbor, MI: Servant Books, 1982.

Perrotta seeks to develop "a reasonable Christian use of television," claiming that television affects us by taking up time, displacing other (more worthwhile) activities, affecting our thinking and behavior, and providing a simplified "video view of life" which ignores God. While most of the book is devoted to this informed analysis, the last chapters present a thoughtful guide to a Christian world view and to positive action regarding television in the home. 162 pages.

[347] Pungente, John J. *Getting Started on Media Education.* London: Centre for the Study of Communication and Culture, 1985.

This introduction to media education provides an historical sketch of its development in the attempt to teach people how to respond to the media (film, radio, television, popular music, etc.). Defining media education as "education to create ... 'a critical awareness of mass media productions, an understanding of the language of image and sound, and some insight into the structure of the mass media,'" the book reports a survey of media education courses and methods from around the world and gives a 35 page annotated bibliography of relevant materials in English, French, German, and Spanish. 87 pages.

[348] Sacred Congregation for Catholic Education. "The Catholic School." *The Pope Speaks* 22.4 (1977).

In the context of a discussion of the Catholic school's mission to help its students synthesize faith and life, the Congregation calls for an education in the use of the media, both for information and for entertainment. Students should learn to choose consciously and freely, with personal critical evaluation, among the available mass communication materials.

[349] Secretariat for the Vatican Synod on the Family. "Preliminary Paper on the Role of the Christian Family in Modern Society." *Origins* 9.8 (June 19, 1979).

Listing communications media under modern problems for the family, this Catholic document counsels that families must work together for quality programming that does not offend the faith or morality of children.

Chapter 4

History

This chapter contains historical materials—either those which provide historical studies of various aspects of the religious communication of the Christian Churches or those which trace the biography of particular individuals associated with Christian communication. Other sources which contain some historical material appear under the section headings for the press, radio, and television. References to these appear at the end of the Historical Studies section on page 126.

Historical Studies

[350] Allen, Robert J. *Catholic Social Doctrine in National Network Catholic Television Programs in the United States, 1951-1968.* Diss. New York University, 1972. *Dissertation Abstracts International* 33.5A (1973): 2404. Ann Arbor: UMI, 1972. 7226581.

This survey of nationally broadcast Catholic television programs compares the program content with Catholic social teaching as found in papal documents and episcopal pronouncements. Only slightly involved in social issues until the late 1950's, the Catholic programs kept pace after that time with the church's thought in a generally orthodox way. The study is most thorough, with hundreds of pages of summary of Church teaching and lengthy summaries of network Catholic television. A parallel column presentation in chapter 5 brings the two bodies of material together, theme by theme. 810 pages.

[351] Allworthy, A. W. *The Petition Against God.* Dallas, TX: Christ the Light, 1975.

In 1974 Jeremy Lansman and Lorenzo Milam filed a petition for rulemaking with the Federal Communications Commission, asking it to restrict the ownership and activities of non-commercial educational radio and television stations and to freeze the granting of broadcast licenses to sectarian groups. This book contains the text of the original petition; the texts of the response petitions filed by the National Religious Broadcasters, the United States Catholic Conference, the United Church of Christ, and Dordt College; the text of the response petition of Lansman and Milam; texts of some of the 700,000 letters received by the FCC; and the final FCC decision (which rejected the petition). The tone of the author's introduction and his biography of Lansman and Milam is heavily fundamentalist and laced with biblical quotations; it fails to make clear (as the FCC decision does) that the original petition did not attack religious broadcasting per se and did not advocate the abandoning of Christian values. 149 pages.

[352] Anderson, Ruth D. *The Character and Communication of a Modern-Day Prophet: A Rhetorical Analysis of Dorothy Day and the Catholic Worker Movement.* Diss. University of Oregon, 1979. *Dissertations Abstracts International* 40.9A (1980): 4796. Ann Arbor: UMI, 1980. 8005750.

This study presents a history of Dorothy Day and the Catholic Worker movement and an evaluation of Day's rhetoric (mostly spoken, although examples do come from the newspaper). The rhetorical analysis consists mostly of a look at the extrinsic factors constituting her rhetorical situation and a look at the intrinsic factors forming the structure of her speaking style. 225 pages.

[353] Andrew, Agnellus. "Catholics and B. B. C. Policy." *The Clergy Review* 35 (1951): 217-224; 387-395.

In the first part of this article, Andrew reviews the work of the Beveridge Committee which evaluated the status of the B. B. C. He finds it unsatisfactory to Catholics in terms of the changes in religious broadcasting policy which it suggests. In the second part, Andrew reviews the kinds of Catholic programming that exist on the B. B. C. and provides a brief history of the development of religious radio in Britain. 17 pages.

[354] Arndt, Georg. *Pressearbeit und Verlag des Evangelischen Bundes: 1887-1928.* Berlin: n.p., 1928.

This volume provides a basic historical approach to publishing by evangelical church unions from 1887 to 1928.

[355] Augustine. *"De Doctrina Christiana* [On Christian Instruction]." Trans. John J. Gavigan. *Writings of Saint Augustine.* Vol. 4. New York: CIMA Publishing Co., Inc. 1947. 3-235.

In this lengthy treatise on Christian teaching, Augustine discusses signs and their relation to objects, language, and translation. In Book 4 he takes up the theme of rhetoric, asking whether it is proper for Christian teachers to use rhetorical arts and rhetorical images, in imitation of the pagan writers and speakers. He answers yes, noting that the Gospel need not stand rhetorically defenseless against pagan learning. 233 pages.

[356] Ayers, R. H. *Language, Logic, and Reason in the Church Fathers: A Study of Tertullian, Augustine, and Aquinas.* Hildesheim: Georg Olms Verlag, 1979.

This historical study of the understanding and use of language and semiotics in three church fathers examines the actual practice of religious predication in theology, long before the twentieth century noted the problematic nature of such predication. Applying contemporary linguistic, semiotic, and logical analyses to the work of Tertullian, Augustine and Aquinas, Ayers demonstrates that their sophisticated understanding of rhetoric helped them avoid problems of religious predication. He argues further that such rhetoric would supply "a necessary condition for the intelligible elucidation of any theology." 146 pages.

[357] Barrett, J. Pressley, ed. *The Centennial of Religious Journalism.* Dayton, OH: Christian Publishing Association, 1908.

This collection of essays and reprinted materials commemorates the 100th year of *The Herald of Gospel Liberty,* published by the Christian Church (an offshoot of the Methodist Church in the United States). The paper claims distinction as the oldest religious paper published in the U. S. Essays include materials dealing with the history of the paper and its editors, selected writings from the paper, the history of the denomination, and historical commentary on other church papers. 656 pages.

[358] Bauer, Gunther. *Kirchliche Rundfunkarbeit, 1924-1939.* Frankfurt: Knecht, 1966.

This standard historical work examines the engagement of the Catholic Church in broadcasting in Germany. More recent works, including those of Glässgen [375] and Vogt [1071], go beyond its scope and update it. 135 pages.

[359] Baumgartner, Appolinaris W. *Catholic Journalism: A Study of its Development in the United States, 1789-1930.* New York: Columbia University Press, 1931.

This book provides an historical introduction to the Catholic press, dividing its existence into three periods: formative years (1789-1840), Second Period (1840-1884), and Third Period (1884-1919). The discussion tends towards an annotated listing of newspaper and periodical titles and their years of publication. Baumgartner dates the first Catholic publication from 1789; although this newspaper had no specifically Catholic content, it had a Catholic editor and a "Catholic tone." Two additional chapters deal with

Catholic journalism education and the state of the Catholic press in the 1920's and 1930's (the period contemporaneous with the book's publication). 113 pages.

[360] Berger, Tom. *Baptist Journalism in Nineteenth-Century Texas.* Austin, TX: Department of Journalism Development Program, The University of Texas at Austin, 1966.

This short history places the development of the Baptist press in the context of the rise of the Baptist Church in Texas from the colonial period (1822-1836). The early Baptists received religious literature and tracts from Louisville until the publication of the *Texas Baptist* in 1855. Other Baptist papers—*Texas Baptist Herald, Texas Baptist Standard*—began in the following years; a circulation war led to the consolidation of two into *the Texas Baptist- Herald.* The book provides a look at the key individuals involved in each paper, their goals, and accomplishments as editors or publishers; it also gives a brief account of the content of the papers, with an eye to controversial issues like slavery, public conduct, and Catholicism. 73 pages.

[361] Boyle, Marjorie O'Rourke. *Erasmus on Language and Method in Theology.* Toronto: University of Toronto Press, 1977.

Erasmus bases a theological method on his humanist concern for language and learning, calling theologians to study Biblical and Patristic languages, because he recognizes that God's revelation (the Logos) forms the pattern for human language and true theological discourse. This fascinating study of Erasmus focuses on four key Latin terms, all possible translations of the Greek Logos: *Sermo, Oratio, Ratio,* and *Confabulatio.* Each of them provides a point of entry into the Erasmian method and each highlights a different role of the theologian. 265 pages.

[362] Breunig, Jerome. "Present Position of the Catholic Press." *America* 92 (February 19, 1955): 532-535.

This survey of the state of the Catholic press indicates 591 publications in 1955 and details 50 of the "new" journals (begun since 1925) noting their orientation (education, social comment, or professional); foundation; and editorial addresses. In addition, the survey notes several new diocesan papers and summarizes some current needs, including the better presentation of Catholic news, Catholic commentary on world events, and the safeguarding of morals. 3 pages.

[363] Bühler, Karl-Werner. *Presse und Protestantismus in der Weimarer Republik: Kräfte und Krisen evangelischer Publizistik.* Witten: Luther-Verlag, 1970.

This examination of the Protestant press in Germany between the wars looks at it in the context of evangelical theology and home missions. Topics include press ethics, critique of culture, faith and morality, and theology and the knowledge industries. 182 pages.

[364] Butcher, Harold. "Religion by Television." *Catholic Mission Digest* 7.9 (October 1949): 1-3.

A news report of a fifth grade religion class featured on the "Lamp Unto My Feet" series of CBS in 1949. 3 pages.

[365] Chrisman, Miriam Usher. *Lay Culture, Learned Culture: Books and Social Change in Strasbourg, 1480-1599*. New Haven: Yale University Press, 1982.

In attempting to answer what the "men and women of the sixteenth century" thought, believed, and knew, this intellectual history examines the books which provided the context for culture in Reformation Strasbourg. Apart from the Christian use of book publishing (which was not negligible), there also existed a strong lay culture, interested in vernacular works of entertainment, practical ideas, and highly polemic religion. This study surveys all the books printed in Strasbourg in the sixteenth century and arranges them according to audience, use, and language, providing a fascinating look at how book publishing entered into daily life and daily religion of the people. 401 pages.

[366] Cohen, Esther. "The Propaganda of Saints in the Middle Ages." *Journal of Communication* 31.4 (Autumn 1981): 16-26.

This examination of the medieval cult of the saints approaches it from the perspective of communication and examines how the Church used various means (or media) to promote its beliefs, including art, architecture, relics, legends, and so on. Cohen notes too the growing conflict between this form of popular religion and the dominance of Latin and writing as more official forms of religious discourse. 11 pages.

[367] Cohen, Esther and Sophia Menaché. "Holy Wars and Sainted Warriors: Christian War Propaganda in the Middle Ages." *Journal of Communication* 36.2 (Spring 1986): 52-62.

This essay provides an historical review of persuasive Christian communication in the medieval period, focusing particularly on recruiting for the Crusades. The authors note how symbolism and images combined in the visual images and folk memories associated with the cult of the saints. 11 pages.

[368] Consultation on Religious Telecasting. *Religious Telecasting in Australia: An Account of a Consultation held at Ormond College, University of Melbourne, August 1966*. Canberra: Advisory Committee on Religious Programmes, Australian Broadcasting Control Board, 1968.

These conference papers and discussion summaries give an interesting look at the status of religious television in Australia in the middle 1960's. The collection of background materials (statutes, agencies, commission reports) provides a nice bit of history; the conference presentations raise the fairly typical questions of use of resources, audience preferences versus ecclesiastical preferences, and critical evaluation of programming. While the questions are the same, the discussion provides some insight into another approach to televising religion. 102 pages.

[369] Craig, Hardin. *English Religious Drama of the Middle Ages.* Oxford: Clarendon Press, 1955.

A general history of religious drama in England from its origins in liturgical drama to the Reformation, this work examines the range and location of the plays, the various cycles, and the liturgical occasions for each. It contains an extensive bibliography. 421 pages.

[370] Dickey, Dale Franklin. *The Tent Evangelism Movement of the Mennonite Church: A Dramatistic Analysis.* Diss. Bowling Green State University, 1980. *Dissertation Abstracts International* 41.10A (1981): 4209. Ann Arbor: UMI, 1981. 8106885.

This historical study of the tent revival movement in American Mennonite churches traces a crisis in the church regarding the acceptability of mass evangelism. Burke's dramatism, as modified by Cathcart, provides a model to account for the failure of the challenge to change Mennonite practice. This study raises the question of the appropriateness of mass evangelism as a mode of communication for various kinds of Christian churches. 163 pages.

[371] Ferré, John Patrick. *A Social Gospel of Millions: The Religious Bestsellers of Charles Sheldon, Charles Gordon, and Harold Bell Wright.* Diss. University of Illinois, 1986. *Dissertation Abstracts International* 47.9A (1987): 3223. Ann Arbor: UMI, 1987. 8701482.

This study in cultural history examines the effects of a particular form of Christian communication—the religious novel. Prescinding from whether or not these novels, published between 1897 and 1917, persuaded their readers to adopt a given view, Ferré argues that the novels do indicate the salience of the terms of the debate about the Social Gospel Movement (the merits of individualism, community, and institutions). Among the common beliefs reflected in the novels are the following: (1) evil results from individual selfishness; (2) institutions cause evil; (3) individuals can cooperate only by strongly resolving to do so; and (4) enlightened individuals are the source of good. 215 pages.

[372] Foik, Paul Joseph. *Pioneer Catholic Journalism.* United States Catholic Historical Society Monograph Series 11. 1930. New York: Greenwood Press, 1969.

This monograph presents a brief narrative history of each of 43 Catholic newspapers or magazines which began publication in the United States between 1809 and 1840; the histories continue to the early twentieth century. In each instance, Foik gives a sense of the situation in which the paper began, a sketch of the editor's (or publisher's) life, and a sample of the periodical's content. The book provides a valuable resource despite its sometimes dated writing style. 221 pages.

[373] Fore, William F. "A Short History of Religious Broadcasting." A. William Bluem. *Religious Television Programs: A Study of Relevance.* New York: Hastings House, 1969. 203-211.

This outline history, while necessarily sketchy, covers the years 1920-1967 and includes the major topics of religious broadcasting from the perspective of the Broadcasting and Film Commission of the National Council of Churches. Evangelical, Catholic, or Jewish efforts are mentioned only in passing. 9 pages.

[374] Gallo. Max. "Luther et les médias." Rev. of *Eglise, culture et société, essais sur Réforme et Contre-Réforme.* by Pierre Chaunu. *L'Express* 1541 (24 janvier 1981): 22-23.

According to this review of Chaunu's history of the Reformation (from 1517-1620), Chaunu argues for a central role of the printing press in the reform. The new technique for the diffusion of information provided a journalism *avant la lettre* and gave an impetus to the spread of ideas throughout Europe. This amplification transformed a religious debate into an affair of state and drew in the reigning powers. 2 pages.

[375] Glässgen, Heinz. *Katholische Kirche und Rundfunk in der Bundesrepublik Deutschland 1945-1962.* Berlin: Verlag Volker Spiess, 1983.

This is a detailed history of Catholic Church involvement in radio and television broadcasting in the Federal Republic of Germany from the end of World War II until 1962. The study sets the political scene starting with the Weimar Republic and the religious scene starting with the Papacy of Pius XII; it then traces the debate within the Church as well as its efforts in setting up religious programming and religious broadcasting stations. 329 pages.

[376] Gosselin, Marcel and Jean Cabriés. *La télévision et les protestants; Les protestants et la télévision.* Paris: Les Éditions du Cerf, 1984.

The essays in this volume, by two Protestant producers, tell the 25 year story of the Protestant religious weekly programs on French television.

Other essays, dealing with audiovisual communication and the Protestant tradition, ecumenical relations, and theological questions regarding communication, are also included. 307 pages.

[377] Hadden, Jeffrey K. and Anson Shupe. *Televangelism: Power and Politics on God's Frontier.* New York: Henry Holt and Company, 1988.

Focusing on America's television evangelists as a sociological phenomenon, this book provides a good history of the movement, tracing its roots to various 19th century evangelical and fundamentalist churches. The authors situate the movement in terms of American history and in terms of the population segments in which it finds its greatest support. Within this overall setting, they discuss the growth of the movement, the debate over audience size, and the increased political clout of the group, paying particular attention to Pat Robertson and the Rev. Jerry Falwell. 325 pages.

[378] Hadden, Jeffrey K. and Charles E. Swann. *Prime Time Preachers: The Rising Power of Televangelism.* Reading, MA: Addison-Wesley Publishing Co, 1981.

A general overview of the electronic church in the U. S., this carefully researched book presents a history of televised religion; sketches the major evangelists, their business and political involvements; and discusses the religious and political controversies that follow them. Addition material gives a sense of program content and audience make up. 217 pages.

[379] Haims, Lynn Maria. *The American Puritan Aesthetic: Iconography in Seventeenth-Century Poetry and Tombstone Art.* Diss. New York University, 1981. *Dissertation Abstracts International* 42.2A (1982): 702. Ann Arbor: UMI, 1981. 8115550.

This study presents an intriguing aspect in the history of Christian communication: the ways in which a religious group which had rejected the use of images (artistic and sometimes even mental) communicated their religious beliefs. Where the Puritan divines banished art from churches, they admitted it in civic and funeral affairs as well as in some poetry. This dissertation provides interesting background on the role of image in Christian life and communication. 227 pages.

[380] Hardison, O. B., Jr. *Christian Rite and Christian Drama in the Middle Ages: Essays in the Origins and Early History of Modern Drama.* Baltimore: The Johns Hopkins Press, 1965.

These essays in the history of drama explore the medieval period when drama and religious acts coincided. "Religious ritual *was* the drama of the early Middle Ages and had been ever since the decline of the classical theater." Essays examine the origins of medieval drama, the Mass as drama, particular plays, and cycles of plays. An epilogue notes the continuity of ritual form in European drama. 328 pages.

[381] Hill, George H. *Airwaves to the Soul: The Influence and Growth of Religious Broadcasting in America.* Saratoga, CA: R. & E. Publishers, 1983.

This primarily anecdotal work provides an historical introduction to religious broadcasting in the United States. While no one person or operation merits more than a few pages of discussion, all of the key people and stations appear in the narration. The chapter on black evangelists fills an important gap in the usual histories of religious communication. 152 pages.

[382] Hoeren, Jürgen. *Die katholische Jugendpresse 1945-1970: Daten und Fakten zur Entwicklung.* Münster: Deutsches Institut für Wissenschaftliche Pädagogik, 1974.

This volume provides a basic historical study of the post-war Catholic youth press. 146 pages.

[383] Hood, John L. "The New Old-Time Religion: Aimee Semple McPherson and the Original Electric Church." Thesis: Wheaton College, 1981.

This study of Aimee Semple McPherson aims not at history but at a description and analysis of her impact on 20th century Christian communication. Hood focuses on her communication model and use of media rather than on her theology. 93 pages.

[384] Hostetler, John A. *God Uses Ink: The Heritage and Mission of the Mennonite Publishing House after Fifty Years.* Scottdale, PA: Herald Press, 1958.

Written on the occasion of the 50th anniversary of the Mennonite Publishing House, this volume gives a history of Mennonite efforts in publishing in the United States from colonial times to the present. The first part of the book address various independent Mennonite printers and publishers, beginning in 1727; chapters trace the careers of John F. Funk, the Mennonite Book and Tract Society, and the Gospel Witness Company. The second part of the book follows the Mennonite Publishing House from its foundation as an official, or church-owned, printing operation. It includes among its products books (under the imprint of the Herald Press); periodicals (the *Gospel Herald,* the *Christian Doctrine Supplement,* etc.); tracts; and educational materials. 264 pages.

[385] Jennings, Ralph. M. *Policies and Practices of Selected National Religious Bodies as Related to Broadcasting in the Public Interest, 1920-1950.* Diss. New York University, 1968. *Dissertation Abstracts International* 29.8A (1969): 2438. Ann Arbor: UMI, 1969. 693180.

This historical study provides a look at the development of Protestant religious radio in the United States, giving much valuable general information in addition to its stated focus on public interest questions. The study covers, first, major ecumenical groups, particularly the Federal Council of Churches, and second, the initiatives of individual church bodies. 529 pages.

[386] John of Damascus. *Writings.* Vol. 37 of *The Fathers of the Church: A New Translation.* Ed. Roy J. Deferrari. Trans. Frederic H. Chase, Jr. New York: Fathers of the Church, Inc., 1958.

In his work, "An Exact Exposition of the Orthodox Faith," John of Damascus defends the use of images and icons in the Church. In a summary section (book 4, chapter 16) he argues that because humans are made in the image of God, we can adore one another since that adoration leads to God ("The honor paid to the image redounds to the original," as Basis put it). Further, the Incarnation means that we must make an image since Jesus is the image of the invisible God. Third, images remind us to adore; they themselves cannot form the object of adoration. Finally, we are stirred to imitate that which we see. 426 pages.

[387] St. John of Damascus. *On the Divine Images: Three Apologies Against Those Who Attack the Divine Images.* Trans. David Anderson. Crestwood, NY: St. Vladimir's Seminary Press, 1980.

John of Damascus upholds the veneration of images against the iconoclasts by arguing that such veneration is an inevitable result of the Incarnation. As God has become flesh, it is praiseworthy to depict in matter what is matter (II.5). In the discourses (especially the first and third), John distinguishes various kinds of images and then argues that images form an essential part of our human understanding; as such we need their help in conceptualizing intangible things (I.11). "For just as words edify the ear, so also the image stimulates the eye. What the book is to the literate, the image is to the illiterate." Included with the translations of the three discourses is John's documentation and commentary on material from the Fathers of the Church. 107 pages.

[388] Jones, Clarence W. *Radio: The New Missionary.* Chicago: Moody Press, 1946.

This book narrates the founding and development of missionary radio station HCJB [Heralding Christ Jesus' Blessings], the voice of the Andes, in Quito, Ecuador. In addition to the history, Jones has added a few chapters on the rationale for the station; he argues that missionary radio meets the urgency of the need for world evangelism; that it covers a wide area simultaneously; that it allows repetition of the message; and that it achieves better penetration than a missionary on foot. 147 pages.

[389] Kapner, Gerhardt. "Heiligenfiguren und Theater im Wiener Barock." Ed. Franz Loidl. *Aspekte und Kontakte eines Kirchenhistorikers: Kirche und Welt in ihrer Begegnung.* Wein: Dom-Verlag, 1976. 149-163.

This historical study examines the role of the baroque theatre in Counter-Reformation Vienna. After looking at the symbolic and didactic functions of the theatre and after situating the Viennese theatre in the larger context of Austria, Kapner examines specific plays and characters to isolate common characteristics of this religious and controversialist use of the theatre. 15 pages.

[390] Kehoe, Richard Joseph. *The Marprelate Tracts: Religious Polemics and Humor in Elizabethan England.* 2 vols. Diss. Temple University, 1981. *Dissertation Abstracts International* 42.12A (1982): 4973. Ann Arbor: UMI, 1982. 8210511.

Included in this literary, historical, and rhetorical study of the Marprelate tracts is an historical account of the use of humor, satire, and irony in rhetoric, not only in the classical world, but also in Christian communication from Justin Martyr through Augustine and on to the medieval and renaissance preachers. 516 pages.

[391] Kennedy, Thomas Frank. *Jesuits and Music: The European Tradition, 1547-1622.* Diss. University of California, Santa Barbara, 1982. *Dissertation Abstracts International* 44.6A (1984): 1619. Ann Arbor: UMI, 1983. 8321525.

This historical study traces the position and use of music in Jesuit education in the second half of the 16th century. Despite some suspicion of music as sensual, it formed not only part of the educational effort of the Society of Jesus but also part of its evangelization efforts. The communication of the Gospel, the teaching of Christian doctrine, the performance of drama and ballet all featured music. This study details these uses and notes that music seemed to have had a larger place in the Roman schools than in others throughout Europe. 291 pages.

[392] Kersten, Kevin F. *The Structures, Activities, and Policies of UNDA, The International Catholic Association for Radio and Television.* Diss. University of Wisconsin, 1979. *Dissertation Abstracts International* 40.8A (1980): 4288. Ann Arbor: UMI, 1979. 7928649.

This official history of UNDA provides an in-depth examination of the organization's membership, structures, activities and policies at the international, continental, national and local levels. The materials—exhaustively assembled from UNDA's archives—provide a narrative look at the people and issues which shaped UNDA's policies as it emerged as a truly international organization. 2287 pages.

[393] Kochs, Anton. "Zur Geschichte der Pastoralinstruktion 'Communio et Progressio.'" *Communicatio Socialis* 5 (1972): 108-117. This essay contributes background information to the understanding of the historical de-

velopment of the Pontifical Communication Commission's *Communio et Progressio.* 10 pages.

[394] Kriebel, Claire. *A Study of the Portrayal of Saints Peter and Paul in French Gothic Art.* Thesis: Western Michigan University, 1980. *Masters Abstracts* 19.1 (1981): 47. Ann Arbor: UMI, 1980. 1315387.

This study of the changing images of Saints Peter and Paul in Christian art illustrates not only some principles of art but also—and more importantly—how the images worked as educational tools for the unlettered and as a means to keep Christianity alive through the medieval period. The text comments on some 60 illustrations from Roman times to modern. 84 pages.

[395] Lee, John A. *The Communication of the Roman Catholic Church to the World, 1968-1970.* Diss. University of Minnesota, 1970. *Dissertation Abstracts International* 32.9A (1972): 5259. Ann Arbor: UMI, 1971. 7118869.

This study gives a chatty look at Roman Catholic communication structures and institutions, both internal and external. It provides some interesting material and a fair introduction to the area but is not well written enough nor comprehensive enough to be a good resource. The bibliography seems thorough, though. 776 pages.

[396] Löwenthal, Rudolf. *The Religious Periodical Press in China.* 1940. Chinese Materials Center, Inc. reprint series 86. San Francisco: Chinese Materials Center, 1978.

This survey provides valuable historical documentation of the various religious presses operating in China in the first half of the twentieth century. "The book serves to indicate the methods by which people of different creeds approach the problem of stimulating their own religious life and of communicating their ideas and ideals to their co-religionists and others." A collection of a series of monographs, the work contains looks at nine different press groups: the Catholic press in China, the Catholic press in Manchuria, the Protestant press in China, the Buddhist press in China, the Taoist Press, the Confucian press in China, the Islamic press in China, the Jewish press in China, and the Russian Orthodox press in China. For each group, the survey gives the name, location, circulation, and sponsoring organization or mission as well as a brief indication of the contents of the publication. Geographical locations appear on maps throughout the volume. 294 pages.

[397] Lucey, William L. *An Introduction to American Catholic Magazines.* Philadelphia: American Catholic Historical Society of Philadelphia, 1952. [Reprinted from *Records of The American Catholic Historical Society* 43.1-4 (March-December 1952].

This overview of Catholic magazines published in the United States between 1865 and 1900 provides basic information for later use by journalism historians. Arranged year by year from 1865, each publication is listed along with all available information about its origin, publishing history, editors, and extent of existing copies in library holdings throughout the country. The monograph provides fascinating reading despite the fact that much of it consists of raw historical data. 96 pages.

[398] Luther, Martin. "Against the Heavenly Prophets in the Matter of Images and Sacraments." Trans. Bernhard Erling. *Luther's Works.* Ed. C. Bergendoff. 55 vols. St. Louis: Concordia Press; Philadelphia: Muhlenberg Press (Fortress Press), 1958-1986. 40: 79-223.

In this essay Luther argues against Karlstadt and other reformers who sought to remove images from church buildings and to prohibit sacramental celebration. In the course of his argument, Luther spells out his own theological approach to images and notes that Word and image should not be separated. 145 pages.

[399] Marsicano, Vincent Anthony. *Medieval Old Testament Drama as Biblical Exegesis.* Diss. Indiana University, 1980. *Dissertation Abstracts International* 41.1A (1981): 237. Ann Arbor: UMI, 1980. 8016454.

The purpose of this study "is to distinguish between historical and normative-mode actions in Old Testament plays of the middle ages." However, a detailed introductory chapter provides an historical insight into two competing strategies for religious communication that have contemporary significance: the literal and the spiritual. Medieval plays tend to be either historical or analogical and, as such, reflect two distinct trends in Christianity and in Christian patterns of communication. In the first, the particular thing or event matters; in the second, the particular represents something beyond itself and becomes a sign. This study traces these trends in the philosophical, theological, social, and dramatic environment of the middle ages. 402 pages.

[400] Max-Wilson, Peter. *Stars on Sunday.* Pinner, Middlesex: Pentagon, 1976.

This souvenir book of the Yorkshire Television religious series, *Stars on Sunday,* narrates the history of the program from its inception in 1969. The book also features photographs of the various stars who participated in the program, the texts of the talks given by Dr. Donald Coggan, and the texts of the most requested hymns. 163 pages.

[401] McClintock, Marilyn Joy Hull. *The Pictorial Nonverbal Communication System of the Medieval Church: Its Development and Use as a Method of Providing Religious Instruction in the Christian Faith During*

the Fourth Through the Fifteenth Centuries: with Implications for Visual Literacy. Diss. The Florida State University, 1980. *Dissertation Abstracts International* 41.7A (1981): 2829. Ann Arbor: UMI, 1981. 8101972.

This study looks at the historical events which affected the development of the pictorial communication system in Western Christianity and applies its findings to contemporary studies of visual literacy. Before and after the Iconoclastic debates, Christianity used images in churches for decoration and for learning—the pictures served as the "Bible of the unlettered." By the medieval period, the Church supplied not only a theology which could use images but also guides for artists in creating religious images for the Church. Examinations of Chaucer's *Troilus and Criseyde* and Robert Campin's *Merode Altarpiece* illustrate the visual communication system in the Middle Ages.

[402] McEldowney, James E., ed. *FRAM: A Report of the Oslo Assembly, June 1968.* London: The World Association for Christian Communication, 1968.

The 1968 Oslo Assembly resulted in the merger of the World Association for Christian Broadcasting and the Coordinating Committee for Christian Broadcasting to become the World Association for Christian Communication. This book contains the conference proceedings, a history of each organization, and the constitution and by-laws of the new organization. Many of the prepared papers deal with the nature of Christian communication, Christian broadcasting, or the Christian message. Unfortunately, some are little more than homilies. More fascinating and of greater enduring value are the historical pieces and the planning documents for the future. 144 pages.

[403] Mehnert, Gottfried. *Evangelische Presse: Geschichte und Erscheinungsbild von der Reformation bis zur Gegenwart.* Bielefeld: Luther-Verlag, 1983.

This volume gives the history of the evangelical press in Germany from its beginnings with special detail on the 19th century. Final chapters deal with questions of the relationship between the press, the church, and theology, noting theological starting points for reflection. 419 pages.

[404] Murphy, James J. "Saint Augustine and the Debate about a Christian Rhetoric." *Quarterly Journal of Speech* 46 (1960): 400-410.

Augustine's *De Doctrina Christiana* did more than advocate the use of rhetoric in the service of Christian instruction; it also opposed a contemporary revival of the notion that truth needed no art in its presentation. This essay describes the ecclesiastical situation in which Augustine wrote and notes the very real debate about pagan learning as the context for Augustine's thought. Even in this early day, the dictum of the neutrality of communication technology (in this case, rhetoric) found expression in the Church. 11 pages.

[405] Neeb, Martin J., Jr. *An Historical Study of American non- Commercial AM Broadcast Stations Owned and Operated by Religious Groups, 1920-1966.* Diss. Northwestern University, 1967. *Dissertation Abstracts International* 28.6A (1968): 2368. Ann Arbor: UMI, 1967. 6715303.

This valuable study tells the history of non-commercial religious radio stations in the United States, concentrating on their early history and foundations and on the personalities who made them a reality. Fifteen stations are featured, with material on their background, licensing, conflicts with the FRC and FCC, and broadcast schedules and programming. 679 pages.

[406] Nord, David Paul. "The Evangelical Origins of Mass Media in America, 1815-1835." *Journalism Monographs* 88 (1984).

This study traces the history of the American Bible Society, arguing that it played an important role in the popularization of print in the United States. The attempts of the Bible Society and the Tract Society—spurred on by missionary motives—to place the same printed materials in the hands of every citizen pioneered mass media. The Bible Society made full use of new printing technologies, of new paper making technologies, and of a distribution system that for the first time allowed a mass media. This study not only presents a fascinating history but also documents materials on production costs and distribution. 30 pages.

[407] Norton, Wesley. *Religious Newspapers in the Old Northwest to 1861: A History, Bibliography, and Record of Opinion.* Athens, Ohio: Ohio University Press, 1977.

This book chronicles the growth of religious journalism in the Old Northwest (the area of the United States now known as Ohio, Indiana, Illinois, Michigan, and Wisconsin). Readable and entertaining, the book recounts the adventures of different editors and the key issues of the day, including religious bigotry, public policy issues, and contemporary moral issues ranging from slavery to literature. A bibliography and library holdings of the various papers completes the volume. 196 pages.

[408] Reilly, Mary Lonan. *A History of the Catholic Press Association, 1911-1968.* Metuchen, NJ: The Scarecrow Press, Inc., 1971.

This standard historical treatment traces the Catholic Press Association from the pre-association meetings, held sporadically from 1890, to its foundation in 1911, through to 1968. The study follows the various disputes that characterized each decade of the organization's history (especially those dealing with finances and freedom from or longing for ecclesiastical supervision and the need for greater professionalism). The selective bibliography seems quite thorough. 350 pages.

[409] Riegler, Edward Ronald. *Printing, Protestantism and Politics: Thomas Cromwell and Religious Reform.* Diss. UCLA, 1978. *Dissertation Abstracts International* 39.1A (1979): 416. Ann Arbor: UMI, 1978. 7811375.

This historical study of Thomas Cromwell's role in the printing of English religious works (the Great Bible, primers, devotional and instructional works, propaganda, and education) concludes that Cromwell used the printing press and his control of the patent monopoly as a means of accomplishing Protestant reform in the 1530's. 428 pages.

[410] Roberts, Nancy L. *Dorothy Day and the* Catholic Worker. Albany: State University of New York Press, 1984.

Based on the author's doctoral dissertation at the University of Minnesota, this book traces the history of *The Catholic Worker,* from its foundation in 1933 as the organ of the Catholic Worker Movement by Dorothy Day and Peter Maurin, to 1982. A content analysis of the paper "indicates that the monthly has hewed to a remarkably consistent editorial line, espousing communitarian Christianity, pacifism, non-violent social justice, and personal activism." The well-written work includes biographical sketches of Maurin and Day. 226 pages.

[411] Sarno, Ronald A. *Modern Communication Theory and Catholic Religious Education, 1950-1980.* Diss. New York University, 1983. *Dissertation Abstracts International* 45.7A (1985): 2054. Ann Arbor: UMI, 1984. 8421468.

This study summarizes the communication work of Lewis Mumford, Norbert Wiener, Jacques Ellul, Harold Innis, Marshall McLuhan, Walter Ong, and Neil Postman. From the framework of their thought (a blend of technological determinism and humanism), Sarno analyzes the documents of the Second Vatican Council dealing with the mass media and with education and applies his findings to catechetical theory. He notes that the Council alternated between an incarnational and a trancendentalist view, with the former supporting dialogic communication and the latter, proclamation. Both these trends emerge in the educational debate about methods and about the use of the media. 464 pages.

[412] Saunders, Lowell Sperry. *The National Religious Broadcasters and the Availability of Commercial Radio Time.* Diss. University of Illinois, 1968. *Dissertation Abstracts International* 29.8A (1969): 2663. Ann Arbor: UMI, 1969. 6901436.

This study traces the history of the National Religious Broadcasters from its foundation in 1944 to 1968, noting its purposes and development and disputing its claim that the Federal (National) Council of Churches prevented conservative religious views from being aired. Rather, Saunders argues, limits to radio time stemmed from the poor reputation of conservative Christian broadcasters, from the poor quality of their programming, and from economic considerations. 261 pages.

[413] Schultze, Quentin J. "Evangelical Radio and the Rise of the Electronic Church, 1921-1948." *Journal of Broadcasting & Electronic Media* 32 (1988): 289-306.

The prehistory of the electronic church occurs in radio programming, particularly on the local level where evangelical churches either owned stations or used paid-time broadcasts for the preaching of the Gospel. This essay reviews both strategies and evaluates their success in the face of "restrictive network and regulatory policies." The historical material makes it abundantly clear that the electronic church did not simply emerge as a television phenomenon in the late 1970's. A lengthy bibliography concludes the essay. 18 pages.

[414] Siedell, Barry C. *Gospel Radio.* Lincoln, NE: Back to the Bible Broadcast, 1971.

Situating the challenge of Gospel radio broadcasting in terms of evangelism and nurture in a world dominated by communist or nationalist governments, this book sets out to tell some success stories of religious radio. Its brief history of religious radio pioneers introduces John Zoller, Paul Rader, New York's Calvary Baptist Church, R. R. Brown, Charles E. Fuller, the Moody Bible Institute, Donald Grey Barnhouse, T. Myron Webb, the Lutheran Hour, Clarence Jones and Reuben Larson of HCJB, Clarence Erickson, Paul Meyers ("First Mate Bob"), J. Harold Smith, M. R. DeHan and the Radio Bible Class, Theodore Epp, and Harry Schultze. In addition to contemporary programs in the United States, the book also looks at Trans World Radio and the Far East Broadcasting Company. 158 pages.

[415] Strand, Kenneth A. *Reformation Bibles in the Crossfire.* Ann Arbor, MI: Ann Arbor Publishers, 1961.

This biography of Jerome Esmer focuses on his work of Bible translation during the Reformation and on his critique of the Lutheran Bible. It provides some historical background to the competing uses of the printing press by Lutheran and Catholic parties in the 1520's. The text avoids polemics as well as theological issues and presents material from an historical survey of relevant sources. 116 pages.

[416] Vauchez, André et al. *Faire Croire: Modalités de la diffusion et de la réception des messages religieux du XIIᵉ au XVᵉ siècle.* Rome: École Française de Rome, 1981.

This collection of historical essays explores the questions of intention and methods in the Church's attempt to catechize "Christian" Europe in the

high middle ages. Contributers discuss means of presentation and persuasion (preaching, images, actions, clothing, etc.), views of the supernatural
(cult of the saints, hagiography, Masses for the dead), and popular responses and resistance. This collection provides a different view of Christian communication, rooting it in the common practices of the medieval
Church. 406 pages.

[417] Wolfe, Kenneth M. *The Churches and the British Broadcasting Corporation 1922-1956: The Politics of Broadcast Religion.* London: SCM Press,
Ltd., 1984.

This thorough and detailed history of religious broadcasting in Britain
traces the relations between the churches (particularly the Church of England and the Catholic Church) and the broadcasting institution up to the
advent of independent television. A second volume is planned to carry the
story from 1956 to the present. Of particular interest is the central concern of both church and broadcaster not to offend anyone, a concern that
notably weakened religious broadcasting. 652 pages.

[418] Yum, Pil Hyung. *Rhetoric of the Korean Protestant Church: The
Changing Patterns of the Christian Message in the Korean Methodist
Church from 1885 to 1961.* Diss. Ohio University, 1979. *Dissertation Ab-
stracts International* 40.5A (1980): 2356. Ann Arbor: UMI, 1979. 7924435.

This study is a history of the Methodist mission in Korea, with attention
given to the preaching styles as the situation of the nation changes. The
overall study serves to provide a context for different communication efforts
in more recent years. 260 pages.

Other works listed in this bibliography do contain some historical sections. Works on the history of the religious press include [74], [701], [732],
[747], [749], [751], [759], [764], [767], and [786]. For more on the history of
the religious film, see [833]. Materials dealing with religious broadcasting in
general include [703], [903], [906], [921] while [965], [970], [978], [989], and
[992] treat religious radio. Some historical material on religious television
appears in [1017], [1022], [1071], and [1077].

Many of the works on religious art take the historical approach; some
of these are [1152], [1160], [1170], [1172], and [1175]. Historical background
on religious dance appears in [1239], [1244], [1247], and [1252]. Finally,
[1266] and [1270] give some consideration to the history of religious music.

Biographies

[419] Aikman, Duncan. "Savonarola in Los Angeles," *American Mercury*
21.84 (December 1930): 423-430.

This journalistic, anecdotal account sketches the career of the early radio preacher, Rev. Robert (Bob) Shuler, in Los Angeles during the 1920's, including his campaign to clean up the city by publicly reciting the sins and failings of politicians, policemen, and show business leaders. 8 pages.

[420] Ashman, Chuck. *The Gospel According to Billy.* Secaucus, NJ: Lyle Stuart, Inc., 1977.

An unforgiving biography of Billy Graham written in an expose style of journalism, this book criticizes Graham for his friendship with Richard Nixon and attacks the business organization and style of his Gospel campaigns. 240 pages.

[421] Bakker, Jim with Robert Paul Lamb. *Move That Mountain!* Plainfield, NJ: Logos International, 1976.

This autobiography of evangelist Jim Bakker narrates the account of his early ministry and the founding of the PTL Club and the building of the theme park, Heritage Village. 183 pages.

[422] Barr, Browne. "Finding the Good at Garden Grove." *Christian Century* 94 (May 4, 1977): 424-427.

Barr reports on his attendance at Robert Schuller's Institute for Successful Church Leadership. Based on Schuller's own television ministry, the program provides concrete help for parish ministry. Schuller's own theology gears him to reach out to the unchurched by appealing to their sense of religion; hence many criticize him for not preaching a strong enough Gospel. However, Schuller holds that the nurture of souls and the growth in Christian living comes after people enter the church. 4 pages.

[423] Cogley, John. *A Canterbury Tale.* New York: Seabury Press, 1976.

This autobiographical account of a Roman Catholic editor's spiritual journey to the Episcopal communion provides intriguing, but cursory, accounts of the world of the Catholic press in the 1930's and 1950's, particularly the *Catholic Worker* and *Commonweal.* 126 pages.

[424] Comstock, Sarah. "Aimee Semple McPherson: Prima Donna of Revivalism." *Harpers Magazine* 156 (December 1927): 11-19.

This somewhat detailed portrait of Aimee Semple McPherson in action suggests that her church and radio ministry consists more of show business than of the Gospel, dependent upon McPherson's talents as an actress and director. Her written sermons fall into the simplistic and pietistic; in their delivered form they captivate the audience as part of the worship/show. 9 pages.

[425] Dabney, Dick. "God's Own Network: The TV Kingdom of Pat Robertson." *Harpers* 261.1563 (August 1980): 33-52.

This magazine report on Pat Robertson's ministry sketches the outline of the ministry and raises questions about its fund raising and integrity, particularly in the attitudes of the ministers toward the people. There's not a lot of new information here and Robertson comes across as a hard-bitten politician using the media ministry to build a base of support. 20 pages.

[426] Day, Dorothy. *The Long Loneliness: The Autobiography of Dorothy Day*. San Francisco: Harper & Row, 1952.

This wonderfully written autobiography chronicles Day's life and conversion through the death of Peter Maurin, the co-founder with her of the Catholic Worker movement and its newspaper, *The Catholic Worker*. Much of the work focuses on people; her account of those who worked with her on the newspaper makes this era of religious journalism take on new life. 288 pages.

[427] Duncan, Ray. "'Fighting Bob' Shuler: The Holy Terror." *Los Angeles* 8.3 (March 1964): 38-41, 65-67, 72.

This magazine essay narrates the story of the Rev. Bob Shuler, one of the most controversial radio preachers in Los Angeles. Active in the 1920's, Shuler would denounce sinners, including local politicians and socialites, from his radio pulpit. 7 pages.

[428] Epp, Theodore H. *Adventuring by Faith*. Lincoln, NE: Back to the Bible Publishers, 1952.

This pamphlet tells the autobiographical story of Dr. Epp and the beginnings of his Back to the Bible radio ministry. 72 pages.

[429] Epp, Theodore H. *Twenty-Five years of Adventuring by Faith*. Lincoln, NE: Back to the Bible, 1964.

A revision of Dr. Epp's 1952 autobiography, this edition adds some doctrinal material and updates the history of the Back to the Bible broadcasts. 78 pages.

[430] Falconer, Ronnie. *The Kilt beneath my Cassock*. Edinburgh: The Handsel Press, 1978.

Falconer, long-time director of religious broadcasting in Scotland for the BBC, describes in this autobiography many of the details of the setting up and carrying out of that religious service. His descriptions of the gradual working out of program types (especially those for television) and of his fruitful collaboration with William Barclay hold particular interest. 254 pages.

[431] Frady, Marshall. *Billy Graham: A Parable of American Righteousness*. Boston: Little, Brown and Company, 1979.

A detailed, journalistic biography of Graham, this book situates his career in terms of American culture and sees him as a symbol of a particular American vision. The work seems thorough and balanced. 558 pages.

[432] Freed, Paul E. *Towers to Eternity.* Waco, TX: Word Books, 1968.

This evangelical autobiographical account of the founding of Trans World Radio takes the reader from the beginnings of the author's missionary life through the negotiations for and building of the various transmitters to the growing world coverage of the stations. 154 pages.

[433] Freed, Paul E. *Let the Earth Hear.* Nashville, TN: Thomas Nelson Publishers, 1980.

This volume continues the story of Trans World Radio, first narrated by Dr. Freed in *Towers to Eternity.* Inspirational in tone and autobiographical in style, the book tells how TWR founded more broadcasting sites around the world and how it continues its radio ministry. 207 pages.

[434] Fuller, Daniel P. *Give the Winds a Mighty Voice.* Waco, TX: Word Books, 1972.

This biography of Charles E. Fuller, written by his son, gives a complete account of his life, from his birth in Los Angeles through his early ministry and founding of the "Old Fashioned Revival Hour" to his radio ministry. 247 pages.

[435] Fuller, J. Elwin. *The Old Fashioned Revival Hour and the Broadcasters.* Boston: The Fellowship Press, 1940.

This inspirational account combines a biography of Charles E. Fuller and a history of the Old Fashioned Revival Hour. Much of the book describes the program: its early difficulties and later successes (including pages of testimonies received at the station). 251 pages.

[436] Kernohan, R. D., ed. *William Barclay: The Plain Uncommon Man.* London: Hodder & Stoughton, 1980.

This collection of works by and about Barclay discusses his contributions to Christian education and communication. Of special interest are "Barclay as Broadcaster" by Ronald Falconer (with a postscript by Douglas Aitken) and "Communication Across the World" by T. B. Honeyman. The former traces Barclay's career in broadcasting while the latter focuses on his writing. 159 pages.

[437] Lord, Daniel A. *Played by Ear.* Chicago: Loyola University Press, 1956.

Lord, the Jesuit writer, critic, and publisher, casts his autobiography as a series of letters to relatives and friends describing his various activities. His chapters on his career as a writer and on his involvement with the United States film industry and with the origins of the Legion of Decency merit particular attention. He, together with Martin Quigley, authored the now-famous Hollywood production code. This book, which introduces Lord in his own words, reads easily and fills in many gaps in the previous histories of the Hollywood religious film. 383 pages.

[438] Lyons, Robert S., Jr. "Television's Unique Success: Religious Drama on 'Insight.'" *U.S. Catholic* 31.11 (March 1966): 49-53.

This article provides a history and overview of the activities of Fr. Ellwood Kieser in producing the "Insight" television programs. Written as a basic news magazine piece, it traces Kieser's involvement in television and his decision to use a dramatic series to reach a wider audience. 5 pages.

[439] Maier, Paul L. *A Man Spoke, A World Listened: The Story of Walter A. Maier and the Lutheran Hour.* New York: McGraw-Hill Book Company, 1963.

This biography of Walter Maier, written by his son, follows his life from childhood through his ministerial studies and teaching to his preaching on the "Lutheran Hour" radio program. Filled with details, the book also summarizes some of his sermons and the issues he addressed on the program. 411 pages.

[440] Marcus, Sheldon. *Father Coughlin: The Tumultuous Life of the Priest of the Little Flower.* Boston: Little, Brown, and Co., 1973.

The first biography of Father Coughlin written with access to the priest's files, this volume outlines Father Coughlin's life with special emphasis given to his political activities and to the contradictions between his recollections and those of his opponents. His radio ministry figures in the early history but is overshadowed by his other activities; the radio career, though, clearly prefigures that of more contemporary religious broadcasters—in terms of both political involvement and fund raising techniques. 317 pages.

[441] McLoughlin, William G. "Aimee Semple McPherson: 'Your Sister in the King's Glad Service.'" *Journal of Popular Culture* 1 (1967): 192-217.

This brief biography of the Pentecostal evangelist notes the chief details of her life and also the innovations of her ministry, especially her use of radio and her use of telephone counselors. 26 pages.

[442] Morgan, Dewi, ed. *Faith in Fleet Street.* London: A. R. Mowbray & Co, Ltd, 1967.

This inspirational book publishes the testimonies of 15 British journalists reflecting on their faith, their conversion to faith, and their work. Each takes a different tack, some staying at the level of biography and others reflecting on the relationship of the Christian faith to journalism. The book reads well as spiritual reading and encouragement. 153 pages.

[443] Nason, Michael and Donna Nason. *Robert Schuller: The Inside Story.* Waco, TX: Word Books, 1983.

This edifying biography of television evangelist Robert Schuller traces his career through his theological preparation in the Dutch Reformed Church to his founding of the Garden Grove Community Church and his television ministry. Largely anecdotal, the book does have one chapter which details Schuller's "Theology of Self-Esteem." 264 pages.

[444] Neely, Lois. *Come up to this Mountain: The Miracle of Clarence W. Jones & HCJB.* Wheaton, IL: Tyndale House Publishers, 1980.

An anecdotal and inspiring account of the life of Clarence W. Jones and his part in building radio station HCJB in Ecuador, this book provides an overview to Jones' work but tends to stress more his family and crises rather than the work of the missionary radio station. 194 pages.

[445] Noonan, D. P. *The Passion of Fulton Sheen.* New York: Dodd, Mead & Company, 1972.

This uncritical biography of Fulton Sheen uses his life to narrate the events of the Catholic Church in the United States in the middle twentieth century. The material dealing with Sheen's broadcasting career is helpful but the style is distracting. 182 pages.

[446] Orr, J. Edwin. *The Inside Story of the Hollywood Christian Group.* Grand Rapids, MI: Zondervan Publishing House, 1955.

This account of the formation and growth of a Bible study and prayer group at the First Presbyterian Church in Hollywood, with membership drawn from among the stars, gives an example of ministry to the Hollywood community. 134 pages.

[447] Pepple, R. Ted. *His Master's Voice: The Story of Father Eugene Murphy and the Worldwide Sacred Heart Program.* [St. Louis: Christian Board of Publication], 1975).

Within the context of an admiring biography of Fr. Murphy and as a tribute to him, this book tells the story of the Catholic Sacred Heart program from its beginnings on radio in 1939 through its television debut to the present day. 196 pages.

[448] Robertson, Pat with Jamie Buckingham. *Shout it from the Housetops.* Plainfield, NJ: Logos International, 1972.

This inspirational autobiography traces Robertson's life from his decision to enter into the ministry to the founding and growth of the Christian Broadcasting Network. 253 pages.

[449] Routh, Eugene C. *Adventures in Christian Journalism*. Nashville, TN: Broadman Press, 1951.

The autobiography of the editor of *The Commission* tells not only of his life but also narrates the story of Southern Baptist journalism in Texas and parts of the South from 1855 to 1950. 92 pages.

[450] Sheen, Fulton J. *Treasure in Clay: The Autobiography of Fulton J. Sheen*. Garden City, NJ: Doubleday, 1980.

This autobiography more or less follows the course of Sheen's life and career but each chapter detours through a variety of topics, allowing Sheen to comment on the Church, mission work, radio and television, prominent personalities, and so on. Written in a conversational style, the book devotes only a chapter to his radio and television preaching. 366 pages.

[451] Sholes, Jerry. *Give Me that Prime-Time Religion: An Insider's Report on the Oral Roberts Evangelistic Association*. New York: Hawthorn Books, 1979.

This expose of the Oral Roberts organization by a former employee details deception, misconduct, and hypocrisy largely through anecdotes. 224 pages.

[452] Strober, Jerry and Ruth Tomczak. *Jerry Falwell: Aflame for God*. Nashville, TN: Thomas Nelson Publishers, 1979.

This biography gives the full course of Falwell's life, with an emphasis on the development of the Liberty Baptist College and on his television ministry. 188 pages.

[453] Sveino, Per. *Orestes A. Brownson's Road to Catholicism*. Oslo: Universitetsforlaget; New York: Humanities Press, 1970.

This biography of Brownson traces his early life through his various journalistic writings and essays in the religious press of his day. His different religious stages—Presbyterianism, Universalism, Unitarianism, and Catholicism—all appear clearly in his writings. 339 pages.

[454] Tansey, Anne. "Canada's TV Priest: Father Matt Meehan, C. SS. R." *Ligourian* 68.5 (May 1980): 2-6.

This article is a feature on Fr. Meehan, his life, his activity in broadcasting, and his ministry. 5 pages.

[455] Voskuil, Dennis. *Mountains into Goldmines: Robert Schuller and the Gospel of Success*. Grand Rapids, MI: William B. Eerdmans, 1983.

This fairly credible biography of Dr. Schuller traces the growth of his Garden Grove "Crystal Cathedral" ministry and the development of his "theology of self-esteem." Different from most biographies of religious figures, this volume also situates Schuller within the frame of American popular religion and offers a fairly balanced, but on the whole somewhat critical assessment of Schuller's theology. 176 pages.

[456] Wayne, Joseph L. "Pioneer Priest in Radio." *Sign* 31.9 (April 1952): 58-59, 75.

This is a brief biography of Father Lambert H. Perquin, O. P., the founder of KRO—the Catholic broadcasting Company of Holland. Journalistic in tone, the article reports Perquin's beginnings in the 1920's through to the growth of the station which broadcasts in Dutch as well as in various European and world languages via short wave. 3 pages.

[457] Wolseley, Roland E. *Still in Print: Journey of a Writer, Teacher, Journalist.* Elgin, IL: David C. Cook Foundation, 1985.

In this autobiography Wolseley outlines his career as a journalism teacher and as a writer, paying particular attention to his own involvement in "religion journalism." In his years of teaching at the Newhouse School of Public Communications at Syracuse University, he started and sustained this program to train writers to write about religion and to work for religious publications. The book also include Wolseley's observations about religion, about journalism, and about a career as a writer. 171 pages.

[458] Wyler, Alain. *Recherche sur la communication de l'Evangile.* Publications Universitaires Europeenenes, ser. 23. Vol. 124. Berne: Peter Lang, 1980.

This qualitative study investigates the ways in which Christian belief is communicated through an analysis of 88 religious biographies: those of 56 major historical figures and those obtained by interviews with 32 contemporaries. Important elements leading to Christian faith include parental belief, church environment, Christian education, and personal witness. 487 pages.

Chapter 5

Rhetoric

This chapter includes materials on speaking and writing. Some homiletic material appears here; however, for a full reference to the literature on homiletics, see [51], [69], and [75]. A few other titles which combine homiletics with other communication forms appear listed under group communication; for example, see [575] and [578]. The remainder of the materials here deals with religious language, narrative theology, literature and religion, oral forms of religious expression, and religious writing. For more specific material on religious writing, see the material on the religious press, beginning on page 199.

Proclamation and Homiletics

[459] Lerg, Winfried B. and Rolf Zerfass. "Modelle der Kommunikation." *Konfrontation: Massenmedien und kirchliche Verkündigung*. Ed. Willi Massa. Stuttgart: Katholisches Bibelwerk, 1972. 17-47.

This reprint from the *Jahrbuch der Arbeitsgemeinschaft Katholischer Homiletiker* presents a dialogue between a social scientist and a pastoral theologian who try to apply the criteria of communication studies to Christian proclamation. 31 pages.

Language

[460] Alonso-Schökel, Luis. *The Inspired Word: Scripture in the Light of Language and Literature*. New York: Herder and Herder, 1965. German translation: *Sprache Gottes und der Menschen: Literarische und sprachpsychologische Beobachtungen zur Heiligen Schrift*. Düsseldorf: Patmos, 1968.

This work investigates the Bible and biblical inspiration, asking how God communicates with human beings. The book summarizes a great deal of scholarship and seems particularly helpful in looking at the psychology, sociology and language of inspiration. 284 pages.

[461] Altizer, Thomas J.J. *The Self-Embodiment of God.* New York: Harper & Row, 1977.

This search for a language of theology looks primarily into speech as "the most immediate and intimate arena of our life and identity." Trying to find a way to speak of God, Altizer begins with the possibility of speaking: speech differs from silence; speech is self-division; speech brings division but also intimacy; speech embodies a presence different from itself. From these beginnings, Altizer proceeds with a kind of meditation on language and God, arranged under the biblical headings of Genesis, Exodus, judgment, incarnation, and Apocalypse. 96 pages.

[462] Bochenski, Joseph M. *The Logic of Religion.* New York: New York University Press, 1965.

An application of the domain of symbolic and modern logic to religious discourse, this book is interesting and relates to the topic of Christian communication as a foundational discipline. 179 pages.

[463] Bourgeois, Henri. *Le salut comme discours: Analyse semiotique du discours et analyse theologique.* Lyons: Éditions du Chalet, 1974.

Less a study of Christian communication than an application of linguistic and communication tools to a theological problem, this work investigates the meaning and function of "salvation" in Indian and Biblical discourse. Insofar as it proposes and exemplifies a methodology for studying communication (in this case language), the book offers some guidelines for foundational thought in the area of theology and communication. 174 pages.

[464] Bucher, Ephrem-Josef. *Religiöse Erzählunger und religiöse Erkenntnis: Erste Schritte zur Bestimmung des kognitiven Gehalts religiöser Texte.* Bonn: Linguistica Biblica, 1978.

Beginning with a review of the debates about the meaningfulness of religious language in Ayer and Heimbeck, this study explores the possibilities of religious meaning in various texts. Asking whether there might be a "religious semantics," the study looks at the different kinds of predication embodied in religious discourse. (As a published thesis, it also contains over 20 pages of bibliographic information.) 326 pages.

[465] Burke, Kenneth. *The Rhetoric of Religion: Studies in Logology.* 1961. Berkeley: University of California Press, 1970.

Consisting of an introductory chapter, three extended essays commenting on religious texts, and a concluding dramatic epilogue, this is Burke's attempt to apply his theories of language and rhetoric to religious discourse. On one level he takes a lead from Christian theology and reads its tenets back into language, finding six analogies between words and the Word. On another level, he shows how the Christian thematic is woven out of the text of language itself and that language best predicts the ways of theology. The commentaries on Augustine's *Confessions* and on the early chapters of Genesis provide stimulating reading and a good look at Burke's method in action. 327 pages.

[466] Campbell, James I. *The Language of Religion.* New York: The Bruce Publishing Company; London: Collier-Macmillan, 1971.

This introduction to the philosophy of religious language begins with an historical overview of analytic philosophy's development and then moves to the consideration of specific questions. The material treated includes the meaning of religious statements, the functions of religious statements, analogy, symbol, and proofs for the existence of God. The volume ends with a lengthy bibliography. 183 pages.

[467] Casper, Bernhard. *Sprache und Theologie: Eine philosophische Hinführung.* Freiburg: Herder, 1975.

This book examines religious language and the religious use of language from the perspective of speech-act theory and functionalism. Following J. L. Austin and Ludwig Wittgenstein in this analysis, the book goes on to examine the theological possibilities of speaking of faith. 208 pages.

[468] Charlesworth, Maxwell John, ed. *The Problem of Religious Language.* Englewood Cliffs, NJ: Prentice-Hall, 1974.

The editor has divided this collection of essays into two parts: those which claim religious language is descriptive and those which claim for it a non-descriptive status ("meaningless," evocative, emotive, practical, poetic, or separated in language game). For the most part the collection reprints well-known pieces. The editor's introduction is lucid and well worth reading for the statement of the problem and its historical perspective. 253 pages.

[469] Christian, William A. *Meaning and Truth in Religion.* Princeton, NJ: Princeton University Press, 1964.

From within the general discussion of the philosophy of language, Christian explores the possibility of religious truth claims and the ways in which these claims may be judged. As background he considers theories of religion, inquiry, and judgement; from this he develops a category of "proposals" for religious truth claims. 273 pages.

[470] Coulson, John. *Religion and Imagination: In Aid of a Grammar of Assent.* Oxford: Clarendon Press, 1981.

This book examines how language works and how a literary language aids the understanding of religious language. Coulson examines various forms of the imagination, illustrating his concepts with examples from the works of Cardinal Newman, various 19th century British poets and novelists, and T. S. Eliot. He then applies this investigation to religious language and the explication of faith. 192 pages.

[471] Crystal, David. *Linguistics, Language and Religion.* Twentieth Century Encyclopedia of Catholicism Series 126. New York: Hawthorn Books, 1965.

The first half of this volume gives a readable and fairly good general introduction to linguistics, taking into account both classical and twentieth century approaches. The second part of the book raises the question of language and religion, and then addresses three issues: theological language; language and liturgy; and language and logical positivism. 191 pages.

[472] Crystal, David. "Language and Religion." *Twentieth Century Catholicism.* Vol. 3. Ed. Lancelot Sheppard. New York: Hawthorn Books, 1966. 11-28.

This look at language examines both language in itself and language in its social context. Every speaker must take into account the subject matter, the audience, and the needs of that audience. Religious discourse produced by the church must seek for maximum intelligibility, whether one preaches, engages in ritual, or seeks publicity through the media. 18 pages.

[473] Dalferth, Ingolf U., ed. *Sprachlogik des Glaubens: Texte analytischer Religionsphilosophie und Theologie zur religiösen Sprache.* München: Chr. Kaiser Verlag, 1974.

This volume publishes a collection of papers from a symposium dealing with philosophical problems in religious language such as verification, falsification, and the "grammar of faith." Presenters include Flew, Hare, Mitchell, Crombie, Hick, Braithwaite, Palmer, and Phillips. 313 pages.

[474] Delzant, Antoine. *La communication de Dieu: Par-delà utile et inutile.* Paris: Éditions du Cerf, 1978.

This volume applies the findings of contemporary French scholarship in communication to theological discourse and concepts, particularly to the concept of the covenant. Methods include symbolism, structuralism, and linguistics. Scholars whose work inform this study include de Saussure, Levi-Strauss, Greimas, Serres, Lacan, and Baudrillard. 358 pages.

[475] Dilley, Frank B. *Metaphysics and Religious Language*. New York: Columbia University Press, 1964.

This treatment of the grounding of religious language and communication looks at specific problems, particularly those of symbol, transcendence, and proof. "The thesis that the nature of metaphysical thinking is best described in terms of a 'root-metaphor' or 'confessionalist' or 'tentative hypothesis' theory of metaphysics is presented at length and defended." 173 pages.

[476] Donovan, Peter. *Religious Language*. New York: Hawthorn Books, 1976.

As a review of the various debates about meaning in religious discourse, this book provides a basic introduction to the key questions and opinions. However, despite the author's tendency to situate the questions rather than answer them, he does raise the challenging issues of empty talk, the validity of stories, religious claims in the present and in a future life, the validity of witness, religious language as action language or as language game, and truth in religious language. 114 pages.

[477] Durrant, Michael. *The Logical Status of "God" and the Function of Theological Sentences*. London: Macmillan, 1973.

This essay in the philosophy of language concludes pessimistically that "there are fatal difficulties for any scheme in which 'God' is introduced as having a single status such that we can offer a coherent and consistent account of the form of proposition expressed by sentences of the form 'God is F.'" To get to this point, Durrant reviews the work of many linguistic philosophers and attempts to clarify many of the issues. He does hold out the hope that philosophy can indeed address this issue and in such a way that it will benefit Christian theology. 117 pages.

[478] Edwards, Bruce L., Jr. "Thy Speech Betrayeth Thee: Theological Implications of Language Study." *Center Journal* 3.3 (Summer 1984): 69-80.

In a first person narrative, Edwards indicates how he discovered in language study the traces of "a God who is the Word. A universe made out of words. A man created to participate in creation by naming the other creatures." Because language goes beyond any particular communication, it takes us beyond ourselves. 12 pages.

[479] Fenn, Richard K. *Liturgies and Trials: The Secularization of Religious Language*. New York: The Pilgrim Press, 1982.

Using the Karen Ann Quinlan case as a focus and the Eden myth as a hermeneutic tool, Fenn examines human language and its necessary demand for interpretation. Where religious contexts or rituals provide the authority for language, no doubt can enter as to intention or responsibility; when these are removed by (or to) the courts, ambiguity and doubt enter. "The myth of the Fall claims that uncertainty about the content and the force of expressed or implied intentions is at the root of all evil, and the Western religious tradition accords this type of uncertainty a very high place indeed in its catalogue of human dilemmas." The book goes on to examine types of speech and speech contexts, drawing on both the religious tradition and on that of contemporary linguistic philosophy and sociolinguistics. 215 pages.

[480] Funk, Robert W. *Language, Hermeneutic, and Word of God: The Problem of Language in the New Testament and Contemporary Theology.* New York: Harper & Row, Publishers, 1966.

This important book first introduced much of the debate about language and interpretation in the Scriptures and in Christian communication to a wide audience. Grounded in the theological work of Bultmann, Heigegger, Fuchs, Ebeling, Van Buren, Ogden, and Ott, the argument calls attention to language and language forms. Specific topics include the role of parable in the New Testament (including an interpretive reading of Mt. 22:2-10), and the phenomenology of the New Testament letter form. While providing only a remote background to communication study in the church, this book gives an excellent introduction to the thought of key theorists on religious language in use. 317 pages.

[481] German, Terence J. *Hamann on Language and Religion.* Oxford: Oxford University Press, 1981.

This historical study examines the 18th century philosopher/theologian's writings on language, noting in particular his possible contributions to the contemporary discussions on the status of religious language. 187 pages.

[482] Gill, Jerry. "Religious Experience and the Language of Popular Culture." *Concilium* n.s. 5.9 (1973): 107-113.

This essay notes the points of contact between the rhetoric of contemporary English and religious expression. Three areas of this rhetoric show promise for a religious understanding of culture: slang, rock music, and radical political discourse. 7 pages.

[483] Goldstein, Robert Morris. *On Christian Rhetoric: The Significance of Søren Kierkegaard's "Dialectic of Ethical and Ethical-Religious Communication" for Philosophical and Theological Pedagogy.* Diss. Princeton Theological Seminary, 1982. *Dissertation Abstracts International* 43.3A (1983): 824. Ann Arbor: UMI, 1982. 8218352.

This dissertation investigates the possibilities of using Kierkegaard's dialectic of communication as the grounding of a Christian rhetoric. The rhetoric in question takes into account the individual characteristics of the receiver and differentiates between the knowledge of an object and self-knowledge. In the latter category fall aesthetic knowledge, ethical knowledge, and religious knowledge. 306 pages.

[484] Grisez, Germain. *Beyond the New Theism: A Philosophy of Religion.* Notre Dame, IN: University of Notre Dame Press, 1975.

One part of this philosophy of religion textbook deals explicitly with religious language—examining the meaningfulness of talking about God. Inspired by Thomistic philosophy, the book moves beyond Thomas and examines religious questions inspired by more contemporary philosophies including realism, idealism, reductionism, and humanism. 418 pages.

[485] Hall, James. *Knowledge, Belief, and Transcendence: Philosophical Problems in Religion.* Boston: Houghton Mifflin Company, 1975.

This textbook in the philosophy of religion devotes its second half to problems in the language of theism. After a consideration of various alternative interpretations of theistic language (mythic, psychological, social, metaphysical, emotive, moral, and perspectival), it develops a category-based approach. It argues that there exist "some basic linguistic acts that do for religious description the same sorts of things that the theoretical construction of 'space,' 'matter,' 'time,' and 'causation' do for physical description." 237 pages.

[486] Hallett, Garth L. *Darkness and Light: The Analysis of Doctrinal Statements.* New York: Paulist Press, 1975.

This extended foray into linguistic philosophy ("of a late-Wittgensteinian variety") attempts to introduce this tool to theologians through an application to doctrinal statements of the Catholic Church. After a basic review of the problem (the nature of meaning and meaningfulness), Hallett carefully examines moral meaning in the contraception debate. In passing, he notes that communication takes place when the speaker's meaning coincides with the words' meaning and all hearers discern without difficulty what the speaker means to say. This ideal situation does not always occur in the context of church documents. 174 pages.

[487] Hamilton, Kenneth. *Words and the WORD.* Grand Rapids, MI: William B. Eerdmans Publishing Co., 1971.

This expansion of the 1970 Payton Lectures at Fuller Theological Seminary examines religious language and philosophy from the side of theology. While most studies ask what analytic philosophy can contribute to theology, this one asks what theology, with its heightened sensitivity to language, can contribute to philosophy. For Hamilton, language is the human context for divine revelation. 120 pages.

[488] Heinbeck, Raeburne S. *Theology and Meaning: A Critique of Metatheological Scepticism.* Stanford, CA: Stanford University Press, 1969.

This work of linguistic philosophy examines carefully and in detail the "philosophical charge that 'God'-talk is nonsense." Working in the domain of philosophical logic, it reviews the history of metatheology and the main positions which reject the meaningfulness of theological discourse (specifically that discourse which predicates anything of 'God'). As befits its nature, the book makes careful distinctions among sentence and statement, actual statement and putative statement, conventional meaning and contextual meaning, and so on. A lengthy bibliography appears at the end of the book. 276 pages.

[489] Hick, John. *Theology's Central Problem.* Birmingham, England: University of Birmingham, 1967.

In this his inaugural lecture as H. G. Wood Professor of theology, Hick sketches out the contemporary situation in theology with regards to religious language and the meaningfulness of religious discourse. This problem gives rise to several others in theology: the problem of evil, the problem of conflicting interpretations, and the problem of conflicting truth-claims by different religions. 15 pages.

[490] High, Dallas M. *Language, Persons, and Belief: Studies in Wittgenstein's* Philosophical Investigations *and Religious Uses of Language.* New York: Oxford University Press, 1967.

After essays introducing Wittgenstein's general notions of meaning, use, language game, and form of life, High applies these concepts to religious language. He examines the category of "belief utterances" and argues that they constitute a separate language game; he also criticizes Barth, Tillich, and Bultmann for capitulating too easily to the logical positivists' approach to language and religion. 216 pages.

[491] Hordern, William. *Speaking of God: The Nature and Purpose of Theological Language.* New York: Macmillan, 1964.

The problem of Christian communication cuts across Christianity: preaching, counseling, education, evangelization, etc. This study looks at the the conditions for the possibility of that communication through a consideration of language. After reviewing the concerns and history of linguistic philosophy, Hordern posits theology as a language game suiting a community of faith and discusses the concerns of theology as it enters into a dialogue with linguistic philosophy. 209 pages.

[492] Horne, Janet. "The Sacramental Rhetoric of Thomas Merton." *Journal of Communication and Religion* 11 (1988): 1-9.

Horne reports some unpublished lectures by Merton in which he develops a three-fold characterization of rhetoric: proclamatory, hermeneutic, and sacramental. Within Christian discourse, the sacramental rhetoric refers to speaking in which words "are used as signs of...meanings that can't be communicated in any other way...symbols and mysteries and so forth." 9 pages.

[493] Lantz, William Carson. "Rhetoric and Theology: Incompatible?" *Western Journal of Speech Communication* 19.2 (March 1955): 77-82.

Lantz raises a question asked by many with the traditional Christian view of God—"Why should we study rhetoric when we are only God's instruments by which God speaks to men?" Wondering whether we deny God by studying rhetoric, Lantz reviews both the "mystical personal experience" theory and the rhetorical theory of communication and argues that this should not be an either/or question. Studying and using rhetoric, he believes, is not a denial of God but a recognition that God can use and work through rhetoric. 6 pages.

[494] Lau, Ephrem Else. "Symbole in der Vermittlung: Symbolische Kommunikation in säkularisierter Gesellschaft." *Ordenskorrespondenz* (1985): 6-16.

This is the text of a lecture to the major superiors of women religious in the Federal Republic of Germany on the function of symbols in communication. 11 pages.

[495] Lucier, Pierre. *Empirisme logique et langage religieux: Trois approches anglo-saxonnes contemporaines.* Tournai: Desclée & Cie; Montréal: Bellarmin, 1976.

This introduction to contemporary logical empiricism and religious language reviews the work of R. B. Braithwaite, R. M. Hare and I. T. Ramsey in depth. Key issues for each thinker are placed in the context of his work and in the context of the history of philosophy. A 40 page bibliography concludes the book. 461 pages.

[496] MacCormac, Earl R. *Metaphor and Myth in Science and Religion.* Durham, NC: Duke University Press, 1976.

This study examines the nature of religious language using scientific discourse as a counterpoint. After sketching out the state of the question in linguistic philosophy, MacCormac focuses on the analogic role of metaphor in each meaning domain. "The conclusion of this study is that one cannot reject religious language primarily because of the forms of expression which it uses." 167 pages.

[497] Macquarrie, John. *God-Talk: An Examination of the Language and Logic of Theology.* New York: Harper & Row, 1967.

This book gives a good general introduction to the debate about language and meaning in theology. In short, it asks, "Can such language [theological discourse] communicate to the people of our time?" Exploring the ways in which theological language might communicate, Macquarrie takes the reader through the ways different theologians and philosophers have stated the problem, and through a discussion of various kinds of theological discourse, including myth, symbol, and analogy. He often borrows from Heidegger in forming his argument and presentation. 255 pages.

[498] Mascall, E. L. *Words and Images: A Study in Theological Discourse.* New York: The Ronald Press Company, 1957.

In this small volume, Mascall surveys the state of the philosophical question about religious language in the mid-1950's. He considers verification, falsification, the nature of sense experience, the nature of theological knowledge, and the communication of religious experience in theological discourse. In the last section, his examination of the writings of John of the Cross and of those dealing with the Atonement provide a good introduction to an analysis of analogy and imagery in theological discourse. 132 pages.

[499] Mathieson, Eric. *Religion of Cliche.* Leighton Buzzard, Beds: The Faith Press, 1974.

This brief book assails the use of cliches in religious discourse (whether in the liturgy, in preaching, in the media, or in interpersonal pastoral conversation). Filled with examples of how cliches lead to a lack of communication, the book calls for clarity and simple expression. 80 pages.

[500] McClendon, James Wm., Jr. and James M. Smith. *Understanding Religious Convictions.* Notre Dame, IN: University of Notre Dame Press, 1975.

Beginning with the question of religious language, this book sets out to develop a philosophical theory of religious conviction. Theology itself becomes a science of convictions, expressing not individual beliefs but those of a community. The study moves from the objections of philosophers to speech-act theory to a process of justification for conviction, part of which involves a linguistic process. 230 pages.

[501] McFague, Sallie. *Metaphorical Theology: Models of God in Religious Language.* Philadelphia: Fortress Press, 1982.

This exploration of the basis for theological language sets the ground for any investigation of Christian communication. Though specific to theology, it notes some key differences between the Protestant and the Catholic traditions (arguing, for example, that "metaphorical" describes Protestantism while "symbolical" or "analogical," Catholicism). Beginning with the parables of Jesus, the book examines religious discourse and suggests that metaphor in language leads to models in systematics. It concludes with a case study of God as Father and feminist theology. 225 pages.

[502] Nida, Eugene A. *Signs, Sense, Translation.* Cape Town: Bible Society of South Africa, 1984.

In these three lectures, Nida discusses recent advances in the theory of translation, focusing "on semantics and its importance for translating Greek texts." In keeping with his own interests and background, Nida uses Biblical texts to illustrate his lectures and places the overall discussion in terms of communicating the Gospel. 143 pages.

[503] Paus, Ansgar. *Die Analogie als Prinzip religiöser Rede.* Salzburg: Univ.-Verlag Anton Pustet, 1974.

This brief essay explores the status of analogy as a theological mode of discourse. After reviewing the now classic summary of Aquinas, Paus applies the concept of analogy to religious texts. 28 pages.

[504] Penn, C. Ray. "Competing Hermeneutical Foundations and Religious Communication: Why Protestants Can't Understand Each Other." *Journal of Communication and Religion* 11 (1988): 10-21.

Arguing that religion is a linguistic enterprise, Penn seeks to account for Christian differences by noting basic differences in language use between those who seek for exactly defined, unambiguous langauge and those who accept metaphor, ambiguity, and the "edge of language." The former group has roots that go back to the Antiochian school of biblical interpretation and reach forward to branches among the fundamentalists; the latter trace their heritage to the Alexandrians and include the liberal Protestants. 12 pages.

[505] Peterson, Thomas D. *Wittgenstein for Preaching: A Model for Communication.* Lanham, MD: University Press of America, 1980.

This book gives a fairly straightforward introduction to the linguistic philosophy of Wittgenstein and then applies it to developing a model for communication. While Peterson's interest lies chiefly in preaching, the concepts he develops could well apply to any other form of religious communication. He notes in particular the need to develop a "grammar circle" in order to support the transmission of religious messages. 192 pages.

[506] Ping, Charles J. *Meaningful Nonsense.* Philadelphia: Westminster Press, 1966.

An investigation into the nature of religious language, this book quickly accepts the positivist thesis that such language is meaningless and then argues somewhat too simply that the nature of religious language is rather to be the language of commitment and communion. Such language is verified not in direct observation but in the life process. 143 pages.

[507] Preller, Victor. *Divine Science and the Science of God: A Reformulation of Thomas Aquinas.* Princeton, NJ: Princeton University Press, 1967.

This book presents an attempt to rethink the question of meaningfulness of religious language "in the context of an explicit rejection of the epistemological presuppositions of traditional empiricism." Using the writings of Thomas Aquinas as a model of religious language because of his importance in the theological tradition, this volume explores the foundational level of communication about religious themes. The title reflects Thomas' distinction between two kinds of theology: knowledge about God that comes from human reasoning and the knowledge of God that comes from faith. 281 pages.

[508] Ramsey, Ian T., ed. *Words about God: The Philosophy of Religion.* New York: Harper & Row, Publishers, 1971.

This book presents in a single collection a number of short philosophical works on religious language. In the "classical discussion" section, we see the readings from Plotinus, Maimonides, Aquinas, Berkeley, Mansel, Lotze and Bradley, and Otto. Under "recent empiricism" there is listed Russell, Moore, Wittgenstein, and Ayer. Other figures whose work also appears include Waismann, Ryle, Strawson, Hare, Austin, Odgen and Richards, Black, Hepburn, Ramsey, and Evans. 244 pages.

[509] Reith, Karl Friedrich. *Mikrologie: Reflexionen zu einer kritischen Theologie.* Vol. 93, series 20, Europäische Hochschulschriften. Frankfurt am Main: Peter Lang, 1982.

This essay examines the grounding of theological discourse and fundamental theology. It focuses particularly on several communication themes: Pannenberg's notion of criticism as hermeneutic and Peukert's re-reading of the communication theory of Habermas in the light of fundamental theology. Ten pages of bibliographic references conclude the volume. 126 pages.

[510] Root, Howard E. "The Christian Vocabulary: The Problem of Communication." *Modern Churchman* 42.3 (September 1952): 279-297.

Essentially a philosophical exploration into the meaning of "Christian communication," this essay begins by noting the common or ordinary language uses of "communication." Holding that in order to be meaningful, the expression must refer to a distinctive content, Root explores just what that content might be. Prescinding from doctrinal statements, he opts to look at things like lives of holy individuals or at the evocations of the holy through poetry. Little by way of conclusion comes out but one does get the sense that the best way to communicate Christianity involves inviting one into the experience of Christianity. 19 pages.

[511] Santoni, Ronald E., ed. *Religious Language and the Problem of Religious Knowledge*. Bloomington, IN: Indiana University Press, 1968.

This book collects 22 essays on religious language into an introductory volume. The editor's initial comments situate the problems and group the issues addressed by the essays into four divisions: (1) the logical status of religious language; (2) the question of the literalness of religious language; (3) cognitivity and the possibility of religious knowledge; and (4) justification, verification, and falsifiability. Each section contains essays from philosophers and from theologians; each balances critics with defenders. Current to its 1968 publication, the book now needs some supplementary material. 382 pages.

[512] Sherry, Patrick. *Religion, Truth and Language Games*. New York: Barnes & Noble, 1977.

Noting that religion is "a response to experience, like art, science, and many other spheres of life," Sherry asks how the later Wittgenstein might illuminate issues of religion and religious language. Convinced that previous treatments of Wittgenstein have side-stepped questions of religious truth, he chooses to explore the consequences of Wittgenstein's philosophical ideas for religion. For example, such a reading would focus the debate about the meaning of religious doctrine on the "possibilities of spiritual transformation" which the doctrines evoke in believers. 234 pages.

[513] Smith, Wilfred Cantwell. *Belief and History*. Charlottesville, VA: University Press of Virginia, 1977.

This book examines religious language and argues that the meaning of various terms has shifted linguistically such that moderns put too much emphasis on "belief" when, in fact, the Scriptural focus falls on "faith." 138 pages.

[514] Stahmer, Harold. *"Speak That I May See Thee": The Religious Significance of Language*. New York: Macmillan, 1968.

This volume provides an introduction to the writings of J. G. Hamann, Eugen Rosenstock-Huessy, Franz Rosenzweig, Martin Buber, and Ferdinand Ebner on the religious significance of language and of the spoken word. Most of this group belonged to the Patmos Circle just after World War I and followed the lead of Hamann in exploring the unitative functions of language. The book provides biographical material on each author as well as a summary of writings; however, the summaries are often confusing. 304 pages.

[515] Stowell, Joseph M. *Tongue in Check*. Wheaton, IL: Victor Books [SP Publications], 1983.

This book treats verbal communication and the many ways in which we abuse it: lying, gossip and slander, boasting, swearing, contentious words, and so forth. A second section suggests positive ways to change bad verbal habits. Each chapter provides anecdotes and homiletic encouragements, making the book suitable for group study as well. 132 pages.

[516] Sweitzer, Eric K. *The Symbolic Use of Religious Language among Evangelical Protestant Christians from the Perspective of James Fowler's Faith Development Theory.* Diss. Boston University, 1984. *Dissertation Abstracts International* 45.4A (1985): 1145. Ann Arbor: UMI, 1984. 8416865.

Seeking to determine whether differences in the use of religious imagery by Evangelical Protestants correlate with different levels of faith development (as defined by James Fowler), this research study collected common "word-symbols" from Evangelical pastors and measured how a select group of 36 subjects defined them. Subsequent analysis showed that the individual subjects did indeed fall along a continuum of faith development; the language use matched this continuum. Perhaps more valuable than the experimental part of the study is the contextual investigation into the nature of symbolism, religious language, and faith. 288 pages.

[517] Swinburne, Richard. *The Coherence of Theism.* Oxford: Clarendon Press, 1977.

This set of essays on religious language argues that such language is indeed coherent and that one can well argue coherently that there exists "an omnipresent spirit, perfectly free, the creator of the universe, omnipotent, omniscient, perfectly good and a source of moral obligation." The text works within the highly technical discourse of linguistic philosophy. 302 pages.

[518] Tilley, Terrence W. *Talking of God: An Introduction to Philosophical Analysis of Religious Language.* New York: Paulist Press, 1978.

As an introductory text this book serves well, providing an accessible view of key problems—including meaning, verification, falsification, and reference. The author gives his readers a coherent look at philosophers of language arranged in schools from narrow empiricists (Hume, Ayer, Flew) to cognitivists (Aquinas, Arnold, Zuurdeeg, and Evans) and non- cognitivists (Spinoza, Braithwaite, Hare, et. al) to personal empiricists (High and Ramsey). Each section poses the key questions which a philosophy of religious language must answer. 131 pages.

[519] Track, Joachim. *Sprachkritische Untersuchungen zum christlichen Reden von Gott.* Göttingen: Vandenhoeck & Ruprecht, 1977.

This book represents a "dialogue" between analytic philosophy and religious language. Track provides an overview of analytic philosophy, attending to communication theory and to the work of Wittgenstein, Carnap, Morris, Austin, and the constructivists. He brings this material to bear upon Christian religious language examining the nonsense theory, the pseudo-meaning theory, the syntactic category theory, and the place-holding theory. 337 pages.

[520] Tracy, David and John B. Cobb, Jr. *Talking about God: Doing Theology in the Context of Modern Pluralism.* New York: Seabury Press, 1983.

In their separate discussions of the "problem of God today" (the topic for the 1977 Tuohy Chair lectures at John Carroll University) Tracy and Cobb explore the possibility of communicating about God in the contemporary world. Where Cobb examines specific problems of belief, Tracy discusses more fundamental issues dealing with the possibility of communication. Particularly helpful is his treatment of analogical predication in theology, its history, and its current uses; this discussion applies equally well to forms of Christian communication other than language. 91 pages.

[521] Vergote, Antoine. *Interprétation du langage religieux.* Paris: Éditions du Seuil, 1974.

This volume approaches religious language from the perspective of psychoanalysis and proposes a hermeneutic for religious discourse similar to that used in exploring inner symbolism and dramatizations. Its topics include the quest for the originary, the semiology of religious symbolism, faith and myth, naming, dogmatism, and ritual. 221 pages.

[522] Webster, Jonathan James. *Some Sociolinguistic Aspects of Religious Communication.* Diss. State University of New York at Buffalo, 1981. *Dissertation Abstracts International* 42.1A (1982): 199. Ann Arbor: UMI, 1981. 8114728.

This dissertation provides an empirically-based method to describe religious language and its usage rules among members of socio-culturally defined groups. Linguistic solidarity extends beyond the denomination and beyond purely denominational differences. 372 pages.

[523] Wilder, Amos N. *The Language of the Gospel: Early Christian Rhetoric.* New York: Harper & Row, 1964.

Accepting that we cannot separate "what the early Christians said" from "how they said it," Wilder examines the forms and modes of Christian rhetoric in the Scriptures and in the first century: dialogue, story, parable, and poem. A final chapter explicitly considers the metaphorical and symbolic character of each of these forms. In his careful analysis of these forms, he simultaneously sheds light on the conditions of Christian communication throughout the centuries. 143 pages.

Narrative

[524] Bausch, William J. *Storytelling: Imagination and Faith*. Mystic, CT: Twenty-Third Publications, 1984.

This volume provides a readily accessible but simple introduction to narrative theology and to storytelling as a form of Christian communication. Illustrating the text with an abundance of stories, the author suggests 13 characteristics (for example, stories provoke curiosity, stories help us to remember) and six paradoxes (for example, prayer is offered through study) exemplified by stories. Later chapters explore the links among story, theology, spirituality, and the Church. 232 pages.

[525] Cameli, Louis John. *Stories of Paradise: The Study of Classical and Modern Autobiographies of Faith*. New York: Paulist Press, 1978.

A study in narrative theology, this book proposes a nine-step method for the study of spiritual autobiographies. Focusing on four principal stories—those of Augustine, Teresa of Avila, Therese of Lisieux, and Thomas Merton—the book calls attention to the ways in which faith flows from the stories and from the Catholic tradition of theology. 86 pages.

[526] Crossan, John Dominic. *The Dark Interval: Towards a Theology of Story*. Niles, IL: Argus Communications, 1975.

Borrowing heavily from structural analysis, this exploration of the story form proposes that the story creates "world so that we live as human beings in, and only in, layers upon layers of interwoven story." As a form of Christian communication, story functions as myth and parable; Crossan focuses on parables, closely reading several of the parables of Jesus as models for the genre. The book introduces many key concepts for a narrative theology; it also supplies a helpful bibliography. 134 pages.

[527] Dyer, George J., ed. "Storytelling and Christian Faith." *Chicago Studies* 21 (1982).

This theme issue of *Chicago Studies* addresses the general topic of narrative and theology. The authors generally regard storytelling as *the* Christian medium of communication. Articles include "A Pastoral Theological Reflection on Storytelling" (Eugene W. King); "Storytelling and Religious Identity" (John Shea); "The Demands of a Truthful Story: Ethics and the Pastoral Task" (Stanley Hauerwas); and "The Narrative Quality of Christian Liturgy" (Mark Searle). 103 pages.

[528] Goldberg, Michael. *Theology and Narrative: A Critical Introduction*. Nashville, TN: Abingdon, 1982.

Narrative theology raises many issues of genre and interpretation which writers often ignore in developing their own kinds of narrative. Intending a work of the philosophy of religion, Goldberg attempts to map out a strategy for "critically exploring the different ways that different types of narrative have recently been used in theology." He includes discussions of the different kinds of narrative (fable, myth, history, etc.), the truth claims of narrative, the usefulness of narrative, and the paradigmatic function of narrative. The work itself provides an interesting critique of the ground for a Christian communication. 288 pages.

[529] Kelsey, Morton T. *Myth, History and Faith: The Remythologizing of Christianity.* New York: Paulist Press, 1974.

In the genre of narrative theology, this work examines the nature of myth (in the larger sense) as essential to Christian faith. 185 pages.

[530] Kort, Wesley A. *Narrative Elements and Religious Meanings.* Philadelphia: Fortress Press, 1975.

In this study of literature, Kort argues "that modern narratives can so often be found to carry or imply religious or religiously suggestive meanings because the elements of narrative ... have a natural relation to corresponding moments in religious life and thought." The book examines various elements of narrative (atmosphere, character, plot, tone) and demonstrates how each finds a complement in religious meaning. Kort resists the temptations of separating form and content and of finding religious meaning only in overtly religious works. 118 pages.

[531] Lischer, Richard. "Luther and Contemporary Preaching: Narrative and Anthropology." *Scottish Journal of Theology* 36 (1983): 487-504.

This study examines Luther's preaching from the aspect of narrative, noting how Luther moves from rhetoric to anthropology. Major sections look at the functions of narrative for Luther in expounding Christian doctrine and at narratives as the points of contact with the lives of his hearers. 18 pages.

[532] Luera-Whitmore, Mark Willard. *The Role of Story/Storytelling in Christian Spiritual Formation.* Diss. School of Theology at Claremont, 1980. *Dissertation Abstracts International* 41.3A (1981): 1092. Ann Arbor: UMI, 1980. 8019022.

After reviewing process theism and epistemology, this essay argues that story and storytelling are "excellent mediums for accomplishing an integration of belief and action which can be useful and meaningful for people in the local parish." The theological argument hinges on the assertion that narrative best suits theology because human life naturally takes on a narrative form. The study concludes with a set of exercises designed for small group settings in a local parish. 179 pages.

[533] McClendon, James W., Jr. *Biography as Theology: How Life Stories Can Remake Today's Theology.* Nashville: Abingdon Press, 1974.

After situating the issues of contemporary theology in terms of their developing an "ethics of character," McClendon sketches out an ethics concretely based in biographical narrative. The communicative form allows both a pastoral and an illustrative approach and speaks more powerfully to the contemporary generation than do abstract theological systems. 224 pages.

[534] Navone, John J. *The Jesus Story: Our Life as Story in Christ.* Collegeville, MN: The Liturgical Press, 1979.

In this collection of his essays, Navone examines various aspects of narrative theology, including a theology of story, the Christ story as normative for all human stories, Biblical travel stories, and medieval allegories. Particularly helpful are the first and last essays: a treatment of the Gospels on the narrative level as analogic guides for human living and a review essay, summarizing the work of 22 contributors to the theology of story. 244 pages.

[535] Roth, Robert Paul. *The Theater of God: Story in Christian Doctrines.* Philadelphia: Fortress Press, 1985.

Written from the perspective of Lutheran theology, this work explores the possibilities of communicating Christian teaching through story. "I want to explore what it will do to Christian theology if we substitute story as a category in place of all the philosophical metaphors and scientific models." Chapters of the book explore specific doctrines and fill in the gaps through stories of historical context and stories of illustration. 191 pages.

[536] Scott, Bernard Brandon. *Jesus, Symbol-Maker for the Kingdom.* Philadelphia: Fortress Press, 1981.

This study of the parables of Jesus works from the language itself, using a kind of semiotic analysis, to achieve a deeper understanding of the Kingdom of God symbol and of the life of Jesus. The focus on symbol also brings with it a emphasis on the communication event of the parables and an insight into the sender, the receiver, and the referent of the parable-sign. 182 pages.

[537] Shea, John. *Stories of God: An Unauthorized Biography.* Chicago: The Thomas More Press, 1978.

Examining the possible roles of storytelling and narrative in theology, Shea looks at the patterns of human stories dealing with mystery: stories of hope and justice; stories of trust and freedom; and stories of invitation and decision. He illustrates each theme with stories and then examines how God figures in each one, as its plot.

[538] Shea, John. *Stories of Faith*. Chicago: The Thomas More Press, 1980.

Examining the use of language and the use of images in dealing with God, Shea continues his exploration of narrative theology. Through story we move to an awareness of the communicative moments in human life and we become more sensitive to the context of our living: the relationship with mystery. Shea expands this material into the more usual theological categories: Christ, the Church, tradition, and so forth.

[539] Stroup, George W., III, et al. "Story and Narrative in Theology." *Theology Today* 22.2 (July 1975).

This issue includes a symposium on story and narrative in theology. The participants and their articles are George W. Stroup, III, "A Bibliographical Critique"; James H. Cone, "The Story Context of Black Theology"; James B. Wiggins, "Re-imagine Psycho-History"; Sallie McFague TeSelle, "The Experience of Coming to Belief"; and Robert McAfee Brown, "My Story and 'The Story.'"

[540] Tilley, Terrence W. *Story Theology*. Wilmington, DL: Michael Glazier, 1985.

This attempt to develop a fundamental narrative theology makes stories primary and doctrines derivative. Tilley argues that stories gave definite meaning to key Christian doctrines (in other words, that the communication patterns of Christian thought influenced the content of Christian thought). To develop this he sketches a history of narrative theology, attending particularly to the functions and forms of narrative, and provides an exploration of the parables, actions, and myths of Jesus. Further development of the thesis comes with the analysis of Christian stories (hagiography) and with a look at eschatology in its narrative and non-narrative forms. Each chapter ends with review of relevant literature; the book also contains a lengthy bibliography. 242 pages.

[541] Wijngaards, J. N. M. *Communicating the Word of God: Practical Methods of Presenting the Biblical Message*. Bangalore, India: Theological Publications in India, 1979.

"This book offers a 'do-it-yourself' course on scriptural communication," prepared by the author, a member of the faculty at the Catholic seminary in Hyderabad, India, to aid in the exposition of scripture. Techniques include narration, sketching biblical personalities, finding motifs, use of perspective, imagination or mystery, oral reading, and witnessing. 304 pages.

Literature

[542] Carnell, Corbin Scott. *Bright Shadow of Reality: C. S. Lewis and the Feeling Intellect.* Grand Rapids, MI: William B. Eerdmans, 1974.

This work examines Lewis specifically as a Christian writer, as a writer of Christian literature. Focusing on *Sehnsucht,* what Lewis termed the "dialectic of desire," the study looks at Lewis's life and writing, noting the images and concerns which make both Christian. 180 pages.

[543] Detweiler, Robert. "Christ in American Religious Fiction." *The Journal of Bible and Religion* 32 (1964): 8-14.

After reviewing the use of Christ in American novels, Detweiler argues that Americans "apparently want Christ, but they do not want him straight." In other words, the novels bend the Christ figure to serve the nationalist, secularist or moralist ends which will appeal to an American audience. 7 pages.

[544] Detweiler, Robert. "Mass Communication Technology, Postmodern Fiction, and Theological Considerations." *Union Seminary Quarterly Review* 35 (1980): 201-209.

Noting that mass communication technology correlates with several traits of postmodern fiction, Detweiler uses the theological-literary theories of Walter Ong to comment on some implications of this relationship. For example, the postmodern emphasis on multiple perspectives ties in both to a narrative point of view and to Ong's observations that print led to a closed system (like that of Descartes) while the voice leads to an open system, to a system capable of mystery and moral choice. Detweiler illustrates each of four observations about postmodern fiction with appropriate examples. 9 pages.

[545] Dunne, John S. *A Search for God in Time and Memory.* New York: Macmillan, 1967.

This important book explores the communicative possibilities of religious autobiography. As much a theoretical work as a demonstration, it begins with a look at "what is involved in bringing the lifetime to mind, how this is done from an autobiographical standpoint." With that background the study then turns to the lives of Jesus in the Gospels, the life of Augustine in the *Confessions,* and the life of Kierkegaard. Other examples of the narrative of religious experience come from Luther, Rousseau, and Sartre. In each case the method remains the attempt to pass over by sympathetic understanding to another and then to come back with a new understanding of oneself. 237 pages.

[546] Edwards, Michael. *Towards a Christian Poetics.* Grand Rapids, MI: William B. Eerdmans, 1984.

This volume attempts to frame a grounding "theory of life" for literature and human expression by looking to the Christian tradition and the Bible. For example, a typical movement in literature from greatness to wretchedness to hope finds its archetype in the Biblical account of the Fall and Redemption. Beginning with this Christian dialectic, the book examines various modes of artistic expression: tragedy, comedy, story, music, and painting. A final chapter considers language itself and the critique of language posed by Christianity and by contemporary deconstructionism. 246 pages.

[547] Jarrett-Kerr, Martin. *Studies in Literature and Belief.* New York: Harper & Brothers, 1954.

This set of essays explores the relationship of theology to literary criticism, of belief to poetic expression. Noting two exaggerations (which the critic must avoid)—to say that the beliefs of the poet do not affect the poetry or to say that "good belief" makes good poetry—Jarrett-Kerr examines how theology and literature have influenced one another historically. He includes among his considerations the ballads of England, Norway, and Iceland; and the writings of Calderón, Manzoni, Dostoevsky, Ramuz, Kafka, Greene, Mauriac, and others. The essays pose a theoretical question that informs a reflection on the nature of Christianity and communication media. 203 pages.

[548] Lynch, William F. *Christ and Apollo: The Dimensions of the Literary Imagination.* New York: Sheed and Ward, 1960.

Lynch argues that literature must have its own autonomy, but that it also has dimensions or limits to its images (of psychology, metaphysics, theology, and so forth.) This book explores these dimensions against the backdrop of two contrary poles: Apollo, who represents a kind of infinite dream, and Christ, who stands for the completely definite. Chapters illustrate different dimensions through a discussion of various literary works; topics include the definite, time, tragedy, comedy, equivocality, the analogical, the theological imagination, and the Christian imagination. In this work as in his others Lynch seeks out the place of the theological or the Christian in the artistic expression of a secular age. 254 pages.

[549] Lynch, William F. *Christ and Prometheus: A New Image of the Secular.* Notre Dame, IN: University of Notre Dame Press, 1970.

This book explores the possibility of a "Christian" anything (literature, communication, art, and so forth) by raising the prior question of the religious imagination in a secular age. To do this properly, one must take the secular seriously and not abandon its own principles (autonomy, unconditionality, self-identity); at the same time one must also "never betray the long-term vocation of the religious imagination, which is to bring total unity to the universe under God and total internal unity to its own imaginings." The book uses the model of the plays of Aeschylus to explore this ground and challenges those who would truly seek a religious world to truly grasp the freedom of the world that they seek. 153 pages.

[550] Lynch, William F. *Images of Faith: An Exploration of the Ironic Imagination.* Notre Dame, IN: University of Notre Dame Press, 1973.

This volume continues Lynch's exploration of the foundations of any Christian communication. Remaining within his particular area of literature, he asks what images of faith appear in the world and, simultaneously, how faith would image the world. "When I say that faith is a form of imagining *and experiencing* the world, I am also hypothesizing, and I think correctly, that there is an equation between the imagination and experience." He then argues that the Judeo-Christian faith functions as the "prime imaginer" of the world—that it forms a creative, moving, ironic paradigm modelled on the irony of Christ. Through meditations and commentaries on literary masterpieces, Lynch defines and illustrates each of the terms, bringing the reader to a new understanding of faith and of the world. 184 pages.

[551] Mursillo, Herbert. *Symbolism and the Christian Imagination.* Baltimore: Helicon Press, 1962.

Written from a Catholic perspective, this historical study of Christian communication argues that a specifically Christian form of communication does exist and that it emerges precisely in the symbolic imagination. "From the psychological point of view it would seem that there is, or at least should be, a specifically Christian imagination, one, that is, that has been elevated by Baptism into the Mystical Body, and has been impregnated by the truths, symbols, and liturgy of Revelation." This study examines that Christian imagination as it appears in the imagery of the New Testament and follows it through the Apostolic Fathers, the martyrs, St. Augustine, early Christian poetry, the monastic age, to the end of the middle ages. 188 pages.

[552] Scott, Nathan A., Jr. "Prolegomenon to a Christian Poetic." *Journal of Religion* 35.4 (October 1955): 191-206.

Noting that the Protestant tradition has said little about understanding the literary imagination, Scott offers such a reflection and suggests that a Christian understanding of the office of a poet is that this vocation "is to *stare,* to *look* at the created world,and to lure the rest of us into a similar act of contemplation." However, the whole of modern life has moved to a kind of angelism, following Descartes' move to interiority. Such a move leaves poetry separated from the world and absorbed in technique. The Christian critic (or the Christian poetic) must take up the theological task of bringing the poet back to the world and of teaching the poet courage in the fact of boundary situations. This latter move follows Augustine rather than Aquinas (who, leading the Roman tradition, counsels wisdom). Here Scott follows Tillich in holding that a Protestant understanding of culture leads more deeply into the culture. 16 pages.

[553] Smith, James Ward and A. Leland Jamison, eds. *Religious Perspectives in American Culture.* Religion in American Life 2. Princeton: Princeton University Press, 1961.

This general overview of religion in American life includes chapters on the religious novel (Willard Thorp), the Bible in American fiction (Carlos Baker), religious poetry (Richard P. Blackmur), religious music (Leonard Ellinwood), and religious architecture (Donald Drew Egbert). Though dated as a general commentary, the volume's historical material provides a solid foundation on each subject. 427 pages.

[554] Smith, John E. "Poetry, Religion and Theology." *The Review of Metaphysics* 9 (1955): 253-273.

This review essay discusses The Poetry of Meditation by Louis L. Martz, *Spiritual Problems in Contemporary Literature* edited by Stanley R. Hopper, and *Poetry and Dogma* by Malcolm Mackenzie Ross. While each of these works deals with the relationship between poetry and theology (and often in terms of the Metaphysical Poets), Smith uses the review to raise the question of the theological underpinnings for any kind of aesthetic. His discussions of the tradition of meditation and mediation stemming from Augustine, and of the debate about sacramental representation are particularly helpful. 21 pages.

[555] Stewart, Randall. *American Literature and Christian Doctrine.* Baton Rouge, LA: Louisiana State University Press, 1958.

Assuming a strong Christian influence on American culture and literature, this book examines the writings of key individuals (Edwards, Paine, Jefferson, Emerson, Whitman, Hawthorne, Melville, Crane, Norris, Dreiser, Eliot, Hemingway, Faulkner, and Warren) with an eye to their acceptance or rejection of key doctrines of Christianity, particularly that of original sin. Eschewing academic neutrality, the author seeks a religiously committed literary criticism rather than a theological or theoretical statement. 168 pages.

[556] Tennyson, G. B. and Edward E. Ericson, Jr., eds. *Religion and Modern Literature: Essays in Theory and Criticism.* Grand Rapids, MI: Eerdmans, 1975.

This collection, designed as a college level anthology, deals with three main topics: (1) the relationship between religion and literature; (2) the religious backgrounds of modern literature; and (3) the religious dimensions of modern literature. Because it does deal so specifically with literature, it provides only an indirect resource to the study of other kinds of communication. The material of the first section does offer some perceptive comments for a wider study; the others do not. 424 pages.

[557] TeSelle, Sallie McFague. *Literature and the Christian Life.* New Haven, CN: Yale University Press, 1966.

While specifically addressing the question of the relationship between literature and Christianity, this book indirectly sheds light on the theology and communication debate. TeSelle describes and criticizes three approaches that Christians have taken to the arts: Christian amiability (an openhanded acceptance), Christian discrimination (an opposition to any art or culture that is not Christian), and Christian aesthetics (the construction of an aesthetics based on Christian principles). In addition she claims that each attempts theological criticism of literature, with varying measures of success. Her most telling criticism of such criticism is that it does not treat literature as literature. Each part of the discussion examines the works of representative theologians and writers. The rest of the book examines the function of literature, the definition of the Christian life, and the relationship between the two. 238 pages.

[558] Wilder, Amos N. *Modern Poetry and the Christian Tradition: A Study in the Relation of Christianity to Culture.* New York: Charles Scribner's Sons, 1952.

This cultural commentary from the perspective of a Christian examines poetry as the site of contemporary theological reflection. Wilder sees the arts as a means of communication, perhaps not of Christian truth but of a modern spirituality. This volume examines the communication of the Christian culture as a background and then looks at the works of various poets, both Protestant and Catholic, as expressive of Christian belief. 287 pages.

[559] Ziolkowski, Theodore. *Fictional Transfigurations of Jesus.* Princeton: Princeton University Press, 1972.

This informative work of literary criticism explores the use of postfigurative technique in the literature of the late 19th century to the present, as it uses the figure of Jesus as model. The author examines parallels to the life of Jesus as they appear in Christian Socialist novels, in the novels which explore the psychology of messiahship, in novels focused on the mythic dimension, in the novels of the Marxist Christ, and in "fifth gospels" or Evangelium Judae. In each chapter a working definition is followed by the discussion of exemplary novels. The work includes reference to 22 specimen novels. 315 pages.

Orality

[560] Allen, Ronald J. *Our Eyes Can Be Opened: Preaching the Miracle Stories of the Synoptic Gospels Today.* Washington, D.C.: University Press of America, 1982.

Hearing the miracle stories as stories allows us to appreciate them in their "presentational form." After explaining his hermeneutic method, Allen examines six miracle stories, beginning with a recovery of the oral tradition and ending with the use of the story in preaching. While the book deals somewhat with homiletics, it raises important questions regarding oral forms and narrative styles. 129 pages.

[561] Bailly, Chantal (Isha). "Rhythmo-Catechesis: An Oral and Rhythmic Memorizing of the Gospel." *Lumen Vitae* English edition 36 (1981): 479-496.

Arguing that God's word is living and active and that the Scriptures were mainly oral in composition, this article proposes that children learn the Gospels following the methods of an oral culture: in recitatives that stress rhythm, movement, and formulism. The method has the advantage of making learning participative, unitative, and celebratory. 18 pages.

[562] Bertone, Tarcisio. "Communicazione e predicazione." *Seminarium* ns 19 (1979): 176-199.

In the context of a special issue on preaching, this article looks at the problems for preaching posed by the mass media, by new discoveries in communication science, and by the arts of oral communication. 24 pages.

[563] Kelber, Werner H. *The Oral and the Written Gospel: The Hermeneutics of Speaking and Writing in the Synoptic Tradition, Mark, Paul, and Q.* Philadelphia: Fortress Press, 1983.

This work of biblical scholarship focuses on the communicative form of the Gospel traditions. Reacting against what he terms the "disproportionately print-oriented hermeneutic" of biblical studies, Kelber examines the various New Testament narratives from the aspect of their oral telling. Oral pressures (the need to memorize, the entertainment value of stories, etc.) shaped the mode of dramatization of the Gospel accounts. This volume applies some findings of orality-literacy studies to the scriptures in an imaginative and revealing way. 254 pages.

[564] Klem, Herbert V. *Oral Communication of the Scripture: Insights from African Oral Art.* Pasadena, CA: William Carey Library, 1982.

Beginning with a case study of evangelism in West Africa (through the Evangelical Churches of West Africa), Klem examines the nature of the oral cultures in Africa and compares it to that of first century Palestine.

He then reports an experiment in teaching biblical materials through the use of oral forms. The study provides a fascinating look at an oral culture and at the attempt to adapt missionary methods to it. 256 pages.

[565] Ong, Walter J. *Orality and Literacy: The Technologizing of the Word.* New York: Methuen, 1982.

This book summarizes much of Ong's previous work in the study of oral and literate cultures. Here, he sets for the characteristics of each culture and notes how each has been studied. He gives little explicit attention to Christian or religious communication; however, the book provides a theoretical model for understanding the verbal basis for Christian practice and indeed for the Scriptures. 201 pages.

Writing

[566] Anderson, Margaret J. *The Christian Writer's Handbook.* New York: Harper & Row, 1974.

This handbook, filled with illustrations, reviews many different kinds of writing—bits, devotions, poetry, quizzes and puzzles, columns, nonfiction, journalistic pieces, and fiction. In addition, it offers many practical suggestions for the beginning writer on topics ranging from setting up a work space to keeping records. Each chapter concludes with a series of exercises which one can use to polish the skills taught in the chapter. 270 pages.

[567] Browne, Benjamin P., ed. *Techniques of Christian Writing.* Philadelphia: The Judson Press, 1960.

The volume continues the publication of lectures delivered at various Christian Writers' Conferences, but concentrates on materials not sufficiently covered in previous publications. After a short introductory chapter on the role of the Christian writer, Browne has arranged the material into the following sections: fiction writing, article writing and features, play writing, book writing, poetry writing, writing for children, special writing fields, techniques of writing, and challenges to Christian writing. For the most part, the essays focus on practical details and aspects of writing, including topic ideas and marketing tips. 382 pages.

[568] Gentz, William H. and Elaine Wright Colvin. *The Religious Writer's Marketplace.* Philadelphia: Running Press, 1980.

This is a valuable reference book listing publishers for religious writing. It contains titles, addresses, and editorial information for religious periodicals and newspapers and general information regarding editorial offices for religious book, drama, music, and greeting card publishers. 237 pages.

[569] Nichols, Sue. *Words on Target: For Better Christian Communication.* Richmond, VA: John Knox Press, 1963.

This brief book, addressed to Christian preachers, teachers, and writers, focuses on language, composition, and rhetoric. It encourages people to communicate (speak/write) with economy, energy, and subtlety. A kind of style book, it comes complete with checklists to help improve writing and speaking. 90 pages.

[570] Schell, Mildred. *Wanted: Writers for the Christian Market.* Valley Forge, PA: Judson Press, 1975.

Primarily a how-to book, this volume introduces the basics of free-lance writing and outlines the Christian church market. After reviewing the basics (equipment, style, practice, markets, etc.), Schell examines the needs of the church market for short fiction, nonfiction, curriculum resources, books, and short items. The book includes a brief bibliography, a writer's prayer, and a code of ethics. 160 pages.

[571] Unger, Henry F. *Writers in Roman Collars: Free-Lancing for Catholics.* Fresno, CA: Academy Guild Press, 1959.

This somewhat dated writer's guide proposes to introduce the Catholic priest or seminarian to a career in non-fiction writing for the popular magazine press. Avoiding theory, it "explains the writing business as it applies particularly to the priest- seminarian on a rock-bottom level." The book includes sections on physical preparation, the article formula, article ideas, interviews, short items, copyright, letters to editors, and the market place of Catholic periodicals. 193 pages.

[572] Wirt, Sherwood Eliot with Ruth McKinney. *Getting into Print: Solid Help for Christian Writers.* Nashville, TN: Thomas Nelson Inc., 1977.

Largely anecdotal, this book urges Christian writers to start with the right attitudes (prepared, responsible, free, Spirit-filled) and to know deeply their own culture. As an ideal the authors suggest a renaissance knowledge of culture combined with a Reformation passion for evangelization. A brief theological reflection offers a meditation on God as a writer, uttering the Word. The book provides more inspiration than practical help. 132 pages.

[573] Wolseley, Roland E., ed. *Writing for the Religious Market.* New York: Association Press, 1956.

The authors of this book (religious writers, all) aim to give instruction to those who wish to write on religious topics, not in a how-to manner, but in an intelligent discussion of the problems and methods of religious writing. Their specialties run the gamut of written communication: fiction (novel, short story, drama, poetry); non-fiction (news, public relations, features, editorials, reviews, juvenile materials, biographies, inspirational works);

and scripts for radio, television, and film. Appendices contain information
on marketing religious writing and bibliographic suggestions. The book
suffers its age a bit but does have some useful material. 304 pages.

[574] Yost, F. Donald. *Writing for Adventist Magazines.* Nashville, TN:
Southern Publishing Association, 1968.

This writer's handbook addresses a particular audience: members of the
Adventist church and those who write for the publications of that church.
Its treatment of the basics (process of writing, forms of writing, illustrations, submitting manuscripts) seems solid and consistently geared to the
Adventist church. Two lengthy chapters list general interest magazines and
Adventist magazines, briefly describing each as well as supplying editorial
addresses, types of work accepted, and editor's comments for potential contributors. An initial chapter examines "the ministry of writing" and sees
writing as important as preaching or teaching in conveying the Christian
message. "The clearest examples of Christian writing are those articles and
stories that have both Christian content and Christian purpose." 144 pages.

Chapter 6

Interpersonal Communication

This chapter contains materials dealing with communication between individuals or in groups. While some of this communication occurs in an unassisted manner, in other instances it occurs aided by various audiovisual equipment. Thus those works which deal explicitly with AV techniques appear under the small group heading. Material dealing with organizational communication—the communication within the Church, for example—appears here as well. Finally, some studies of communication in the liturgy and of communication through the telephone conclude this chapter.

General Interpersonal Communication

[575] Abbey, Merrill R. *Communication in Pulpit and Parish*. Philadelphia: The Westminster Press, 1973.

A homiletic textbook, this volume presents the material in the light of communication theory and attempts to integrate preaching and the larger communication environment. The book itself is an admirable example of an awareness of the impact of new communication practices. While the second part deals exclusively with homiletics, the first part touches on theoretical material applicable to interpersonal communication as well as to preaching. 237 pages.

[576] Arn, Win. "Mass Evangelism—The Bottom Line." *Church Growth: America* 4.1 (January-February, 1978): 4-7, 16-19.

Mass evangelistic appeals could become more effective by following these counsels: (1) change the goal from registering decisions to making disciples;

(2) train local pastors and laity; (3) elevate the importance of the local church; (4) train the laity to evangelize; (5) use natural networks of friends and relatives; and (6) structure a year-round strategy in local churches. 8 pages.

[577] Arnett, Ronald C. "A World in Need of Dialogue." *Brethren Life and Thought* 26.4 (Autumn 1981): 230-236.

Humanist theories of interpersonal communication propose that people should use non-judgmental transactional patterns in relationships with others. Arnett counters this with a theory of Christian dialogue, grounded in caring judgment. In this approach, communicators have a concern for what is right and loving rather than for their image. 7 pages.

[578] Baldwin, Earl David. *Dialogical Communication in Preaching: A Venture in Encouraging and Enabling Reciprocal Participation Between Pulpit and Pew in the Preaching Event.* Diss. Drew University, 1982. *Dissertation Abstracts International* 43.4A (1983): 1186. Ann Arbor: UMI, 1982. 8219944.

This D. Min. project developed a method for congregation members to meet with their pastor to discuss the biblical texts for the coming Sunday's sermon. Out of this dialogue grew a sense of enrichment and a satisfaction with communication on the parish level. 170 pages.

[579] Barclay, William. *Fishers of Men.* Philadelphia: The Westminster Press, 1966.

A series of essays on Christian teaching primarily, this book focuses on the aim of teaching, the people (a kind of audience analysis), the faith, and the methods of teaching. It is geared to the YMCA movement and self-consciously examines it. 113 pages.

[580] Bossart, Donald E. *Creative Conflict in Religious Education and Church Administration.* Birmingham, AL: Religious Education Press, 1980.

This book applies the insights gained from conflict studies to church situations. After setting forth some basic principles from sociology, psychology, and theology, Bossart suggests making use of conflict to enhance human functioning, self-acceptance, reconciliation, and affective instruction. He urges readers to regard conflict as potentially positive and as a daily reality in the lives of local congregations. 284 pages.

[581] Cotterell, Peter. *Look Who's Talking! The Christian's Guide to Better Communication.* Eastbourne: Kingsway Publications, 1984.

This general guide to interpersonal communication provides basic material on listening, steps of communication, the effects of culture, group communication and family communication. While nothing specifically addresses

Christian communication, the examples and exhortations presume a Christian audience. 158 pages.

[582] DeWire, Harry A. *The Christian as Communicator*. Philadelphia: The Westminster Press, 1961.

This book, one of the Westminster Studies in Christian Communication series, examines the role of the laity in communicating the Gospel, particularly through interpersonal communication. Largely Lutheran in approach, it explores topics as diverse as listening and speaking skills, manifesting love, authority, dealing with other Christians, and dealing with those outside the Church. Unfortunately, the author does not follow the standard divisions of interpersonal communication study but tends to borrow eclectically from psychology. 198 pages.

[583] DeWire, Harry A. *Communication as Commitment*. Philadelphia: Fortress Press, 1972.

This book, based on a lecture series at Concordia Seminary, examines interpersonal communication from the perspective of Christianity. Intrapersonal dialogue forms the beginning of commitment; for the Christian, the goal of this commitment is "to maintain and develop a community of thought and action based upon the will and work of God's spirit." Communication manifests and accomplishes this goal. The six sections of the book (each of them well-grounded in communication theory, psychology, linguistics, and so on) cover the intrapersonal dialogue, witness, listening, language, conflict, and commitment to the world. 115 pages.

[584] Ellis, E. Earle. "Communicating the Gospel to a Secular World." *Christianity Today* 5 (August 28, 1961): 987-988.

This essays argues that Christians should be aware of the need to communicate through involvement in the world as well as through preaching at the world. This involvement can lead to personal contact—for example through home missionaries. 2 pages.

[585] Erickson, Kenneth A. *The Power of Communication for Richer Interpersonal Relationships*. St. Louis: Concordia Publishing House, 1986.

This general introduction to interpersonal communication combines basics of communication study with anecdotes and scriptural citations to give a readable overview of the area. Many of the examples and case studies come from church situations; the book itself seems to address a church audience. Topics include dialogue, listening, writing, nonverbal communication, and blocks to communication. Among the latter are façades, one-way communication, poor listening, and fuzzy symbols. Many chapters contain lists of pointers which, while accurate, need more supplementary explanation. 96 pages.

[586] Faulkner, Brooks R. *How to Communicate: A Communication Workbook for Church Leaders.* Nashville, TN: The Sunday School Board of the Southern Baptist Convention, n.d.

This workbook sketches the characteristics of several styles of interpersonal communication that can help or hinder ministry and church relations: the constructive communicator (one who listens, understands, encourages, inspires, stimulates, informs); the dominative communicator (one who threatens, disapproves, forces); the evasive communicator (one who compromises, avoids involvement); and the explosive communicator (one who vents anger, resentment, and suspicion). The book provides exercises to identify each type, suggests reasons to account for that behavior, and offers a series of steps to help one improve or change one's style. 74 pages.

[587] Ferder, Fran. *Words Made Flesh: Scripture, Psychology & Human Communication.* Notre Dame, IN: Ave Maria Press, 1986.

Attempting to "reflect on the relationship between the psychological and spiritual dimensions of human communication," this book argues that faith and psychological integration go together. The author, a clinical psychologist and Catholic minister, begins each chapter with a reflection on a biblical text dealing with some aspect of communication; she then explores the same aspect from the side of interpersonal communication. Topics include listening, expressing emotions, dealing with anger, caring for others, words in relationships, dealing with conflict, and self-disclosure. 183 pages.

[588] Griffin, Dale E., ed. *What Has God Done Lately?* St. Louis: Concordia Publishing House, 1970.

This collection of essays, originally published in *Interaction,* addresses primarily an audience of church school teachers and suggests ways in which they can better communicate God's word. Written from a Lutheran perspective the essays discuss the Church as God's communicator, methods of communicating God's word, issues in communicating a sense of God's grace, and communicating specific church doctrines (the Incarnation, the Atonement, etc.). 106 pages.

[589] Griffin, Emory A. *The Mind Changers: The Art of Christian Persuasion.* Wheaton, IL: Tyndale House, 1976.

Through the use of anecdotes and first person experience, this delightful book reviews persuasion research and applies it to Christian communication, both interpersonal and mass-mediated. Chapters deal with target audiences, resistance, guilt and fear as motivators, incentives, credibility, conformity, and sustaining belief. A particularly good chapter presents "an ethic for the Christian persuader," noting that the end does not justify the means, particularly means which Griffin describes as non-loving, flirting, seducing, raping, smothering, and legalism. 228 pages.

[590] Hendricks, Howard. *Say It With Love.* Wheaton, IL: Victor Books, 1972.

This book deals with communicating and sharing God's love with others more effectively. Hendricks breaks communication down into three components: (1) concept—the better you know your subject, the better you will communicate it; (2) feeling—the way you feel about a message affects how you communicate it; and (3) action—you must live the message as well as speak it. Hendricks also gives tips on improving communication and training communicators. 143 pages.

[591] Hilde, Reuben. *In the Manner of Jesus.* Mountain View, CA: Pacific Press Publishing Association, 1977.

This book presents a collection of meditations and educational illustrations in order to improve communication. The overall direction of the book takes "a careful look at the manner in which Jesus labored" in order "to discover His methods of communication." Each chapter begins with a basic principle, illustrated by Scriptural quotations, and then develops the idea through stories, through materials from communication studies, and through common sense reasoning. Some of the chapters deal with individual communication, authorship, values, climate, goals, preparation for communication, educating the whole person, and continuing efforts at communication. 143 pages.

[592] Howard, J. Grant, Jr. "Interpersonal Communication: Biblical Insights on the Problem and the Solution." *Journal of Psychology and Theology* 3 (1975): 243-257.

This biblically based analysis of the problems of interpersonal communication places their origins in the Fall and attributes the failure of communication to pride which hides the self and hurls its guilt toward others. The solution to the problem lies in opening the self to another; a relationship with God provides the opening through the work of the Holy Spirit. Such communication is active, complete, positive, expressive, and enabling (confession and forgiveness). The overall perspective of the article comes from the Baptist tradition. 15 pages.

[593] Hunter, George G., III. *The Contagious Congregation: Frontiers in Evangelism and Church Growth.* Nashville: Abingdon, 1979.

Less about the congregation than about the works of a congregation, this book details a method of personal evangelism, building on the findings of interpersonal communication and rhetorical studies. It stresses an inductive approach to Christian witness based on human needs and an Aristotelian rhetoric as well as on an analysis of the results of secularization. 160 pages.

[594] Jahsmann, Allan Hart. *Power Beyond Words: Communication Systems of the Spirit and Ways of Teaching Religion.* St. Louis: Concordia Publishing House, 1969.

This book examines Christian communication—particularly that of the educator—in the light of scripture and communication theory. The first half of the book deals with revelation and the knowledge of God. "Any Christian communicator (parent, preacher, teacher, writer, artist) is a person who speaks for God. He is a minister (servant) of the Word in the functioning sense of the term." To serve the Word means to experience the Word and the Spirit of the Word. Only with this understanding can one proceed to the study of communication in its human aspects: learning theory, nonverbal communication, media for communication. Under the last heading, the book treats the arts as well as worship and sacrament. 180 pages.

[595] Kelsey, Fred S. *The Development of Pastoral Listening Skills in order to Ascertain the Common Elements Leading to Institutional Commitment or Lack of It in the Religious Life Stories of Members of a Local United Methodist Church.* Diss. Drew University, 1986. *Dissertation Abstracts International* 47.10A (1987): 3781. Ann Arbor: UMI, 1987. 8703142.

This study examines the role of listening in pastoral work and in church planning. As a D. Min. project, though, much of it deals with the personal experience of the author in designing and carrying it out. The overall plan does hold interest for a look at the possibilities of this interpersonal skill in the day-to- day life of a congregation. 133 pages.

[596] Lawyer, John W. and Neil H. Katz. *Communication Skills for Ministry.* Dubuque, IA: Kendall/Hunt Publishing, 1983.

This communication skills training manual focuses on five areas: communication in general, reflective listening, problem solving, assertiveness, and conflict resolution. The first three sections seem rushed with the greater part of the material devoted to the final two sections. Only the nature of the role playing exercises (illustrating situations drawn from ministry or parish life) merits the label, "religious communication"; the rest comes straight from basic interpersonal communication texts. 118 pages.

[597] Leas, Speed and Paul Kittlaus. *Church Fights: Managing Conflict in the Local Church.* Philadelphia: The Westminster Press, 1973.

This guide applies standard conflict-management techniques to local church groups, presenting material in a "how-to" fashion. Flow charts and illustrations of materials make the presentation clear and effective; theoretical reflections in each chapter allow the interested reader to make wider applications of the topics. The authors also urge people to regard conflict as a natural and healthy activity in any group. 186 pages.

[598] Lewis, G. Douglass. *Resolving Church Conflicts: A Case Study Approach for Local Congregations.* San Francisco: Harper & Row, Publishers, 1981.

Lewis begins with a theoretical perspective on conflict and conflict management, examining the nature of conflict, principles of conflict management, and styles of conflict management. He also cites various religious perspectives to provide a grounding for the process. Throughout, he illustrates with examples drawn from different religious traditions and situations. The last part of the book consists of cases for individual and group learning. 182 pages.

[599] Lynch, Barbara Ann. *Sacred Space: Spatial Communication Patterns in an Irish-American and Slovak-American Roman Catholic Parish.* Diss. University of Pennsylvania, 1984. *Dissertation Abstracts International* 45.9A (1985): 2694. Ann Arbor: UMI, 1984. 8422926.

This ethnographic study of religious patterns draws heavily on the notion of space and time as key to communicative interaction. This study's value lies not so much in the actual observations of two ethnic Catholic parishes as in the summaries of prior research and the methodological directions for applying this body of data to the understanding of an often overlooked kind of religious communication. 398 pages.

[600] Markham, Meeler. *This Confident Faith.* Nashville, TN: Broadman Press, 1968.

A book of inspirational stories and folksy reasoning, this volume argues that the Christian faith must be expressed. The communication of the Christian faith takes many forms, but Christian witness ranks first. 128 pages.

[601] Nelson, Carl Ellis. *Where Faith Begins.* Atlanta, GA: John Knox Press, 1971.

Nelson, whose background is in religious education in the Presbyterian Church, argues that faith is communicated by a community of believers and that the communication model most appropriate to Christianity is one based in the socialization process by which one is integrated into a given society. Setting aside concepts of communication through the mind (teaching concepts), through experience (teaching individuality), through selfhood (teaching self-realization), and through the Church (teaching an institutional affiliation), he presents faith as a category of communication, a faith which comes through a culture. The cultural model offers a self-identification out of personal relations with a social group (a Church), a perceptive system in relation to a world view (as in the Bible), and a formation of conscience according to a value system. 231 pages.

[602] Noyce, Gaylord. *The Art of Pastoral Conversation*. Atlanta, GA: John Knox Press, 1981.

This guide to conversation for church ministers, visitors, and laity introduces the general art of conversation through situations, suggestions, and examples. Cultivating positive skills (self-disclosure, listening, testimony) and avoiding negative habits (indirection, images) form a foundation for the more demanding pastoral roles of dealing with the bereaved, the shut-in, and the hospitalized. Additional chapters describe group learning exercises for a pastoral team. 140 pages.

[603] Patterson, Ward L. *Holy Humor: The Religious Rhetoric of Grady Nutt*. Diss. Indiana University, 1983. *Dissertation Abstracts International* 44.10A (1984): 2925. Ann Arbor: UMI, 1984. 8401529.

This study of Southern Baptist humorist Grady Nutt examines his speaking style and manner of storytelling, humor, and preaching. While much of the dissertation contains transcriptions of his routines, an introductory chapter gives a nice overview of the church's attitudes towards humor—which it has historically opposed. However, Patterson ties humor to a theology of story and parable in an attempt to integrate humor and religion. 609 pages.

[604] Piper, Hans-Christoph. *Kommunizieren lernen in Seelsorge und Predigt*. Göttingen: Vandenhoeck & Ruprecht, 1981.

This textbook places an emphasis on "communication" in pastoral work as well as in preaching. 130 pages.

[605] Pippert, Rebecca Manley. *Out of the Salt-Shaker & into the World*. Downers Grove, IL: InterVarsity Press, 1979.

Told largely in an anecdotal, autobiographical style, this guide to person-to-person evangelism presents a model for religious conversation. Based on the evangelical theory of the InterVarsity Christian Fellowship, the book examines the process of the communication of the Gospel and illustrates each aspect through a first person account. Three different conversational models (investigation, concentric circles, relationship) are proposed. 188 pages.

[606] Poster, Sandra Sollod. *Confession as Communication: A Communications Analysis of the Apparent Efficacy of the Confessional Experience*. Diss. New York University, 1984. *Dissertation Abstracts International* 45.2A (1985): 343. Ann Arbor: UMI, 1984. 8412355.

This study examines the forms of confession in Judaism, Catholicism, Protestantism, and psychotherapy, noting their history, usual practice, rules, symbolic actions, environment, purposes, and relationships between confessant and confessor. Nonverbal and verbal constituents are also described. After listing the features common to all rituals, the study proposes an interpretation based on the role of language and interpersonal communication. 331 pages.

[607] Sanford, John A. *Between People: Communicating One-to-One.* New York: Paulist Press, 1982.

Written solidly from within the Jungian perspective, this book introduces the issues of interpersonal communication, noting places of conflict and failure. Specific topics include identifying the agenda, creative listening, dealing with emotions, the animus/anima problem, the Proteus problem, guilt, and nonverbal communication. While not strictly Christian in orientation, many of the examples come from Christian ministry or marriage. The book tends to stay at the anecdotal level and away from analysis or instruction. 92 pages.

[608] Stoppe, Richard L. *Leadership Communication: A Scriptural Perspective.* n.p.: Church of God Department of General Education, 1982.

Thoroughly grounded in interpersonal communication studies and principles, this book applies them to ministerial communication, finding confirmation in the Scriptures. While not presenting "Christ as a communicational psychologist," the study does find in Jesus a model of communication: "You persuade a person only to the extent that you come into his world of experience, speak his language, and identify your message with his needs, motives, and desires." Chapters include reviews of four basic elements: persuasion, trust, love, and provisionalism. These are then applied to empathic understanding, possibility thinking, problem solving, and leadership. 254 pages.

[609] Underwood, Ralph L. *Empathy and Confrontation in Pastoral Care.* Philadelphia: Fortress Press, 1985.

Within an overall view of ministry as communication, Underwood defines pastoral care as "the communication of the gospel verbally, dynamically, and symbolically in interpersonal relationships that refer, however implicitly, to the community of faith." Seeing pastoral care as a kind of conversation, he lists the following attributes for it: interpersonal, disclosing, process, culturally conditioned, dialogic, and respectful. He counsels a balance between empathy (listening) and confrontation. The approach seems basically sound but does tend to borrow more from psychological models than from either theological or communication models. 127 pages.

[610] Wright, H. Norman. *Energize Your Life Through Total Communication.* Old Tappan, NJ: Fleming H. Revell Company, 1986.

This solidly-based book on communication applies the findings of interpersonal communication and conversational communication study to daily life. Geared to a Christian audience, it draws supporting evidence from biblical materials and includes chapters on communicating with God. Highly anecdotal in presentation, the book covers active listening, non-verbal communication, building rapport, expressing feelings, and dealing with interior thoughts. Each chapter ends with some suggested activities to aid one's understanding of the material. 159 pages.

Small Groups and Group Media

[611] Babin, Pierre, ed. *The Audio-Visual Man.* Trans. Arca. Dayton, OH: Pflaum, 1970.

This book, a translation of *L'Audio-Visuel et la Foi,* presents an examination of contemporary culture as characterized by an audio-visual orientation and examines the consequences of this for religious education. Essays range from the effect of the mass media on catechetics to instructional aids to selecting AV equipment. In an essay on "audio-visuals and revelation" H. Kunzler argues that the Biblical prohibition against idols stresses that "no one medium alone can adequately express God" (p. 61) and that revelation must appeal to all human senses. 218 pages.

[612] Bamberger, Stefan. "Reflections on the Ecclesiological Aspects of Group Media." *1978 Multimedia International Yearbook.* Rome: Multimedia International, 1978. 5-18.

This essay which introduces a volume devoted to case studies of group media in church settings discusses the role and use of such media by Christians as they rediscover the central place of community. Group media lead to greater exchange among members of a group, bring group members closer to reality, and carry the message more effectively to other groups. 14 pages.

[613] Barlow, T. Ed. *Small Group Ministry in the Contemporary Church.* Independence, MO: Herald Publishing House, 1972.

Written from the experience of the Restoration Church, this book details how a church can grow spiritually and demographically through small group meetings. The book contains materials on small groups, the dynamics of group processes, as well as lots of anecdotes about the use of small groups in church meetings and Bible study. 190 pages.

[614] Betz-Howard, Carla Gail. *Development of an In-Service Guide for Utilizing Media in a Church Education Program.* Thesis. University of Northern Colorado, 1980. *Masters Abstracts* 19.3 (1981): 217. Ann Arbor: UMI, 1980. 1316196.

This thesis presents eight training workshops for Christian education teachers who would utilize the Alleluia Series from Augsburg Publishing House, a series of Bible study lessons following the common three-year lectionary cycle. Aiming to prepare teachers to use a variety of small group media (puppets, bulletin boards, videotapes, films, photographs, slides, cassettes, etc.), the training includes basic materials on learning theory, group communication, and classroom media. The workshops come complete with lesson plans, evaluation sheets, and detailed instructions. 147 pages.

[615] Church, Peter. "Go-Tell Communications." *International Christian Broadcasters Bulletin.* First Quarter, 1973: 6, 14.

A basic news report on the activities of the Go-Tell organization which works in South Africa for Christian communication. 2 pages.

[616] Cousineau, Jacques, ed. *Audiovisuales y evangelización: Primer Congreso Mundial. Acta Congressus AV-EV.* [Lima, Peru]: OCIC, 1977.

The acts of this congress on audiovisuals and evangelization contain reports on Catholic Church activities in communication from each part of the world and presentations by Bartolino Bartolini, Pierre Babin, and Jesús Montero Tirado on theological, pedagogical, and pastoral approaches to communication in evangelization. The English language edition [618] provides somewhat more information. 304 pages.

[617] Cousineau, Jacques. *Audiovisual Media and Evangelization, World Congress, November 1977–Munich: Global Report on the Questionnaire.* Vatican City: SM-OCIC [Organisation Catholique Internationale pour le Cinema, 16 Piazza San Calisto, 00120 Vatican City], 1977.

This report presents the responses to a world-wide survey of Catholic Offices or organizations concerned with small group communication for evangelization. Almost 600 centers provided information on their general structure, production, distribution, training, and utilization. While the material is not always presently clearly, it is of great value in giving a picture of world issues in small group religious communication. 84 pages.

[618] Cousineau, Jacques, ed. *Audiovisual and Evangelization, World Congress, Munich, 6-10 November 1977: Acta Congressus AV- EV.* Vatican City: SM-OCIC, 1977.

The 1977 Audiovisual and Evangelization Congress brought together delegates from over 60 countries; its acta, valuable as a sourcebook, include reports from each region represented as well as presentations on the theological (Bartolino Bartolini), pedagogical (Pierre Babin), pastoral (Jesús Montero Tirado), and technical (Walter Cappel) aspects of small group communication. Both Bartolini and Babin take the approach that a-v media call for a new language, an emotive language rather than the linear language of print. For Bartolini ("Audio- visual and Theology," pages 96-109) a-v is like the Biblical word in that both are community-based, speak a popular language, and are fundamentally connotative. He then examines specific topics: using the language of the image (both present and historical), conversion, evangelization of culture, and witness. Babin ("Policy and Methodology for Group Media," pages 110-120) examines three characteristic methods of group media: experience, direct communication, and the group. 262 pages.

[619] Engstrom, W. A. *Multi-Media in the Church: A Beginner's Guide for Putting It All Together*. Richmond, VA: John Knox Press, 1973.

This simplified technical guide covers basic information regarding cameras, slides, sound, filmstrips, and 8 mm films and suggests uses for them in church worship. 128 pages.

[620] Ferreras-Oleffe, Gregorio and Jeanne-Marie Ferreras-Oleffe. "New Language, New Formation: The Requirements of Audiovisuals." *Lumen Vitae* 33 (1978): 233-244.

The authors argue that since the means of communication have significantly altered human beings, any religious discourse or instruction must take this into account. While they recognize this as a cultural shift and while they seek a different training for religious educators, they opt for group media as their preferred solution. 12 pages.

[621] Ford, LeRoy. *Using Audiovisuals in Religious Education*. Nashville: Convention Press, 1974.

This self-instruction book on audiovisuals teaches teachers how to incorporate a variety of audiovisual materials into their classes. The book seems rather simple in its approach. 128 pages.

[622] Gilbert, Milton Heath. *The Utilization of the Medium of Marionettes as a Legitimate Resource for the Proclamation of the Gospel of Jesus Christ as Demonstrated Through the Production of Three Original Marionette Dramas*. Diss. Drew University, 1982. *Dissertation Abstracts International* 43.9A (1983): 3018. Ann Arbor: UMI, 1983. 8302397.

This D. Min. project explores the use of puppets for Christian communication. An initial chapter attempts to lay a theological groundwork by referring to the role of art in creation; it largely fails through a too instrumental view of art. However, a second chapter does a nice job of tracing the use of puppets in Christian preaching and teaching from the third century. The rest of the study outlines the project and scripts the dramas produced by the author. 298 pages.

[623] Greer, Clark F. *Multi-Media Methods for Christian Ministries*. Schaumburg, IL: Regular Baptist Press, 1982.

After a brief introduction detailing the necessity for Christian ministries to take advantage of different means of communication, this volume gives practical suggestions for working with multi-media presentations, particularly slide-sound presentations. Chapters deal with preparing a script, photographic techniques, sound recording, projection equipment, displays, overhead displays, and various other technical details. The book concludes with an extended example of a presentation by the author. 79 pages.

[624] Jensen, Mary and Andrew Jensen. *Audiovisual Idea Book for Churches.* Minneapolis, MN: Augsburg Publishing House, 1974.

This book "is designed to be a starter for creative thinking about audiovisuals in the church." Each chapter, which discusses a different audiovisual medium, both suggests possible uses of the medium and provides a brief guide to its use. Media considered include tape recorders, phonographs, camera, filmstrips, slides, overhead projectors, puppets, television, visual boards, posters, drama, banners, and maps. Some ideas are quite helpful; others, simplistic. 160 pages.

[625] John Paul II. "Catechesis in Our Time *Catechesi Tradendae.* Vatican Council II: More Post Conciliar Documents. Ed. Austin Flannery. Collegeville, MN: The Liturgical Press, 1982. 762-814.

A general letter on Christian teaching, in response to the synod of bishops in 1977, this document includes a section (VI) on the means of catechetics. Among other things, the pope writes, "I think immediately of the great possibilities offered by the means of social communication and the means of group communication: television, radio, the press, records, tape recordings—the whole series of audio-visual means. The achievements in these spheres are such as to encourage the greatest hope. Experience shows, for example, the effect had by instruction given on radio or television, when it combines a high aesthetic level and rigorous fidelity to the magisterium" (#46). The pope goes on to discuss literature, catechisms, and conversation as ways of spreading the Gospel. 53 pages.

[626] McLaughlin, Raymond W. *Communication for the Church.* Grand Rapids, MI: Zondervan Publishing House, 1968.

Drawing on general semantics and interpersonal communication theory, the author discusses communication within churches, paying particular attention to common errors and barriers. Theoretical issues predominate in the first half of the book but give way to practical problems in second, including a nice overview of group communication. The book contains many examples throughout, many of which come from the author's experiences in the Baptist church. 228 pages.

[627] McSwain, Larry L. and William C. Treadwell, Jr. *Conflict Ministry in the Church.* Nashville: Broadman Press, 1981.

Weaving Biblical and interpersonal communication sources, the authors propose ways to deal with conflict in the local church. In their view conflict arises from stress and should not be regarded as wholly bad. Their treatment includes many case studies which invite the participation of the reader; a final chapter lists resources—both printed materials as well as films and simulation games. 202 pages.

[628] Nagy, Szabolcs S. G. *Developing a Videotape Statement of Congregational Mission Through a Group Process.* Diss. Drew University, 1983. *Dissertation Abstracts International* 44.11A (1984): 3413. Ann Arbor: UMI, 1984. 8402929.

This D. Min. project combines group communication with video in the production of a mission statement by a local congregation. Apart from the project narrative, this study contributes a summary of some of the theological literature on church groups and on the theology of communication. 219 pages.

[629] National Catholic Education Commission. *Report on a Survey to Gather Information and Views about the Use of Media by the Church in Education.* Canberra: National Catholic Education Commission, 1984.

This study reports a survey of teachers and others in the Catholic education system on views about the best use of the media in the Catholic education enterprise.

[630] O'Donnell, John. "Group Media for Evangelization." *Australasian Catholic Record* 61 (1984): 252-258.

This article, by priest-director of Catholic AudioVisual Centre production house, Sydney, outlines how group media can be used effectively for catechetical and evangelizing purposes. 7 pages.

[631] OCIC [Organisation Catholique Internationale pour le Cinéma]. *OCIC World Congress General Assembly: Mass Media and Group Media— New Challenges for OCIC. Study Session, The Cultural and Social Influence of Foreign Films.* Manila: OCIC, 1980.

This study guide contains the texts of several addresses on the influence of foreign films and other media in the Third World as well as reports on the activities of OCIC around the world. 298 pages.

[632] OCIC. "Audiovisuals and Evangelization." *Lumen Vitae* 33 (1978) 139-246.

This theme issue deals with audiovisuals and evangelization, printing the papers and discussion of an international congress on the subject, organized by the International Catholic Film Organization. Many of the papers deal with small group media and examine current practice as well as theological, educational, pastoral, and technical theories which ground church use of the media. The articles include the following: Lucien M. Metzinger, "Audiovisuals and Evangelization"; Jean-Pierre Dubois Dumée, "An Approach to the Problems of Communication"; Bartolino Bartolini, "Evangelization and Audiovisual Communication"; Pierre Babin, "Policy and Methodology for Group Media"; Jesús Montero Tirado, "Audiovisual Communication and Pastoral Work"; Walter Cappel, "Audiovisual Technique"; Anthony Scannell, "Group Media in a New Age of Evangelization"; Guy Martinot, "Pastoral Value of the Social Communication Media"; and Gregorio and Jeanne-Marie Ferreras-Oleffe, "New Language, New Formation." 108 pages.

[633] Riddle, Norman George. *Church Growth and the Communication of the Gospel in Kinshasa.* Thesis: Fuller Theological Seminary, 1971. *Masters Abstracts* 20.1 (1982): 106. Ann Arbor: UMI, 1971. 1317063.

Primarily an analysis of missionary work in the city of Kinshasa, this thesis does include a consideration of various communication strategies used by the chief Baptist congregations in the city. Apart from overarching categories like preaching, teaching, worship and music, these include small group discussion, filmstrips, flannel boards, and drama. The study has value as a social study of Kinshasa but breaks no new ground in missionary communication. 196 pages.

[634] Sarno, Ronald A. *Using Media in Religious Education.* Birmingham, Alabama: Religious Education Press, 1987.

This general introduction to contemporary theories of mass media and of religious education argues for an "immanentist" approach to religious education—allowing students to grow as Christians rather than indoctrinating them with theological formulae. The approach has as a foundation primarily the McLuhan theories, but also cites work by Babin, Ong, and Postman. After quickly reviewing this material, Sarno discusses various approaches to religious education by reviewing the work of representative theorists. Finally, he suggests concrete teaching strategies using various media. 300 pages.

[635] Saunders, Denys J. "Visual Aids and the Communication of the Gospel." *International Review of Missions* 45 (1956): 314-322.

Although pictures aid learning, they cannot replace the human contact needed for the proclamation of the Gospel. With this in mind, visual aids can work in the missions as long as the media match the message, the media are appreciated by the audience, and the media can be used by all Christian workers. The mass media should also be used, but carefully. 9 pages.

[636] Scholz, Marlene. *Communication in Pastoral Work.* Eldoret, Kenya: Baba Publications, 1980.

An "experimental source book for religious education," this small volume provides a basic introduction–in an African context–to various aspects of communication and evangelization (theological, catechetical, pastoral, cultural, etc.), to audiovisual language, and to techniques for production of audiovisuals. A final section gives concrete suggestions and hints for everything from posters to film to dramatic productions. 104 pages.

[637] Wedel, Theodore O. "The Group Dynamics Movement and the Church." *Theology Today* 10 (1954): 511-524.

The findings of the Group Dynamics Movement have a place in the church for the knowledge of group experience can lead to the better formation of community and the better sense of participation by all group members. The churches need to learn these lessons because of the growing sense of individualism and isolation in the church. 14 pages.

[638] Wilson, Ron. *Multimedia Handbook for the Church: How to Use Sight and Sound and Motion to Make your Church's Programs Come Alive.* Elgin, IL: David C. Cook Publishing, 1975.

This non-technical guide to photography, film, filmstrips, audiotapes and video contains many ideas and suggestions for the pastoral minister, presented in a folksy style. 142 pages.

Other materials that offer some information about small group communication appear in [37], [107], [136], and [314].

Organizational Communication

[639] Baum, Gregory and Andrew M. Greeley, eds. *Communication in the Church.* New York: The Seabury Press, 1978.

This collection of essays focuses on the internal communication of the Catholic Church, the relations among its various elements: country to country, hierarchy to priests and laity. A final section proposes a more theoretical look and features essays on "communication without domination" and on theology and communication. Contributors include Reyes Mate, Osmund Schreuder, Brian Smith, Kenneth Westhues, André Rousseau, Greeley, Janice Newson, Giovanni Cereti, Ed Grace, Rudolf Siebert, and Wolfgang Bartholomäus. 112 pages.

[640] Hormell, Sidney James. *The Presbyterian Communication System: An Examination of the Formal Mass Communication System of the United*

Presbyterian Church, U. S. A. Diss. University of Illinois, 1966. *Dissertation Abstracts International* 27.2A (1967): 450. Ann Arbor: UMI, 1966. 6607755.

This study approaches the communication activities of the Presbyterian church from an organizational perspective, examining the technological and ideological factors in its growth. The historical material is of interest to church communicators, but the theoretical material addresses questions of voluntary associations more than ecclesiological questions. 302 pages.

[641] Rammenzweig, Willi Guy. *Kirchliche Kommunikations und Entscheidungsprozesse: Analysen, Modelle, Alternativen, Thesen zur Innovation.* Mainz: Inaugural-Dissertation zur Erlangung des Doktordiploms des Evangelisch-Theologischen Fachbereichs der Universität Mainz, 1975.

This dissertation examines communication in the church from the perspective of organizational communication studies. Within this overarching theme a variety of approaches appear: group theory, systems theory, functional theory, leadership theories, and the communication of innovations theory. The variety of perspectives clarifies the material and offers some stimulating suggestions for examining the life of the church and its process of decision making. 238 pages.

[642] Schmidthüs, Karlheinz. "Die öffentliche Meinung und die Katholiken." *Die neue Ordnung* (1966): 405-415.

In this essay, the author calls for the recognition of public opinion and more freedom of communication within the Catholic Church. 11 pages.

Liturgy

[643] Baragli, Enrico. "L'uso dei 'mass media' nelle azione liturgiche." *La Civiltà Cattolica* 126.1 (1975): 144-157.

This essay examines Catholic Church policy regarding the use of the mass media in liturgical and para-liturgical settings, with particular attention to the concepts of participation and presence. After considering general themes and historical background, Baragli turns to specific questions: the cases of marriage, of sacramental confession, and of the Eucharist. In all cases one must be personally present. 14 pages.

[644] Benson, Dennis C. *Electric Liturgy.* Richmond, VA: John Knox Press, 1972.

This rambling reflection on planning a "relevant" liturgy of the early 70's is clearly dated. While some of the thoughts on liturgy and communication within liturgy remain valid (knowing the congregation, touching their experience), the book itself is an historical curiosity. The book comes with two phono discs. 96 pages.

[645] David, Lucien. "Liturgie et radiophonie." *Vie Spirituelle* 125 (février 1930): 197-203.

Glossing a 1928 Vatican prohibition of broadcasting the Mass by radio, David suggests that the reason for the prohibition lies in the separation of the actions of the worshippers from their presence at the eucharist. He then raises the question of whether a televised broadcast would evoke the same difficulty and compares the situation to another prohibition—of the use of phonograph recordings in worship as a substitute for choirs. The latter decision he accepts on the basis of living action as opposed to mechanical action. 7 pages.

[646] Donovan, Kevin. "Liturgy and Communication." *The Way* 12.2 (1972): 91-98.

"Communication" applies to liturgy in two ways: God communicates with humans through word and ritual, and humans communicate with one another in such a way as to witness to God's revelation. Since liturgy forms a communication system, it can benefit from improvements in style and form; liturgists should not hesitate to look to the study of communication for insights. 8 pages.

[647] Greeley, Andrew M. "Empirical Liturgy: The Search for Grace." *America* 157 (November 21, 1987): 379-383, 90.

In a reflection based on his sociological work, Greeley argues that Catholic liturgy should seek out the experiences of God's presence found in the secular world and correlate these with sacramental experience. He notes particularly moments of reconciliation, love, life, and community. This search for grace should include people's stories and narratives, especially those found in popular culture. The liturgist should become a storyteller. 6 pages.

[648] Guardini, Romano and Heinrich Kahlefeld, eds. *Apparatur und Glaube: Überlegungen zur Fernsehübertragung der heiligen Messe.* Würzburg: Werkland Verlag, 1955.

The collection contributes to the German discussion of the reasons for and against television the Catholic Mass. The essay by Guardini, "Fotographie und Glaubenszweifel," takes a critical approach to the possibilities of using technological means to spread the faith (pages 7-22). A more negative view comes from Clemens Münster in his essay, "Mysterium und Apparat" (pages 23-32).

[649] Houtart, François. "Aspects sociologiques du role de la liturgie dans la vie ecclésiale: communication, socialisation, appartenance." *La Maison-Dieu* 91 (1967): 105-128.

The liturgy has three functions in terms of the Catholic Church as a social body: communication, education (socialization), and belongingness. The changes introduced by the Second Vatican Council make it more important than ever to understand these sociological functions because they will ultimately influence the theological understanding of the Church. Communication structures all community and within the Church's liturgy it has the role of teaching, creating an atmosphere, and evoking mystery. It does this verbally and nonverbally and by bringing all the groups or "publics" of the Church together. Communication questions which still remain open in terms of the liturgy have to do with inculturation, biblical language, the image of the Church, and the use of the mass media for liturgy. The other functions (of socialization and belongingness) in some ways derive from the communication question and reveal different aspects of the liturgy. 24 pages.

[650] Lardner, Gerald Vincent. *Liturgy as Communication: A Pragmatics Perspective.* Diss. Temple University, 1980. *Dissertation Abstracts International* 41.5A (1981): 2170. Ann Arbor: UMI, 1980. 8025139.

Following the work of Bateson, Wiener, Wazlawick, and others, this study applies the tools of cybernetics and transactional communication to the understanding of Catholic liturgy. Although the investigation remains on an abstract level, developing a language of analysis (semiotics and systems), it does propose a different view of Christian worship that might well serve to better prepare pastoral workers. 159 pages.

[651] McLuhan, Marshall. "Liturgy and the Microphone." *The Critic* 33.1 (October-November-December 1974).

This article argues that the popular response the liturgical changes result more from the introduction of amplified sound than from anything else. The shift of acoustic space changes all other relationships within worship— a phenomenon similar to the shift to a visual culture with the spread of print.

[652] Pieper, Josef. "Zur Fernsehübertragung der heiligen Messe." *Weistum, Dichtung und Sakrament.* Ed. Josef Pieper. München, 1954. 271-276.

In this contribution to an ongoing discussion in the early 1950's, Pieper sounds a cautious warning about the televising of the Eucharist. 6 pages.

[653] Rahner, Karl. "The Mass and Television." *Mission and Grace: Essays in Pastoral Theology.* Vol 1. Trans. Cecily Hastings. London: Sheed and Ward, 1963. 255-275. German original: "Die Messe und das Fernsehen." *Apparatur und Glaube.* Ed. R. Guardini and H. Kahlefeld. Wurzburg, 1955.

An early essay of Rahner, this piece argues that the Roman Catholic Mass should not be televised because the Mass should not be shown to non-

Catholics (on the principle of excluding catechumens) and because television does not allow active participation. 21 pages.

[654] Rodgers, John Bryden. *Liturgy and Communication: 'An Uncertain Sound?'* Slough, England: St. Paul Publications, 1975.

This is an attempt to apply some elementary aspects of communication theory to the Catholic liturgy and to the training of priests. The book goes step by step through the Mass in a folksy style, pointing out how the communication might be improved. 133 pages.

[655] Semmelroth, Otto. "Die Messe im Fernsehen." *Stimmen der Zeit* (1952/53): 442-449.

This article, by a liturgist, provides a balanced contribution to the controversy on the television transmission of the Eucharist. 8 pages.

[656] Tuttle, James E. *The Communicative Impact of Focused Worship.* Diss. Drew University, 1982. *Dissertation Abstracts International* 43.9A (1983): 3036. Ann Arbor: UMI, 1983. 8302423.

Worship takes place in a media-rich, culturally multi-dimensional environment. Therefore worship should take advantage of all available communicative elements to create a single thematic focus. This D. Min. project reports a study of planned worship done in the Protestant free church tradition. The project found that worshippers did notice thematic worship; those who attended some classes in worship had an even greater sensitivity to the themes. 160 pages.

Telephone

[657] Arn, Win. "A Church Growth Look at ...Here's Life America." *Church Growth: America* 3.1 (January/February 1977): 4-9, 14-15, 27, 30.

This article evaluates the multi-media "I found it!" campaign of the Campus Crusade for Christ and notes that despite its publicity and methods, it succeeded in recruiting relatively few new church members. The telephone method of contact did not prove especially effective. 10 pages.

[658] Dowdy, Jr., Augustus W. *Phone Power.* Valley Forge, PA: Judson Press, 1975.

The telephone gives the minister an effective pastoral tool, allowing contact with parishioners who cannot come to the church or who do not welcome home visits. Other telephone pastoral ministries include crisis lines, information lines, and a variety of help lines. This book sketches some of these ministries and gives a brief "theology of telephone pastoral care." 96 pages.

[659] Mitchell, Hubert. *Putting your Faith on the Line.* San Bernardino, CA: Here's Life Publishers, 1981.

This manual for telephone visitation follows the method of the Campus Crusade for Christ and guides outreach workers through the steps of a typical visitation. It suggests methods of interviewing and offers scripts and stories of successful interviews. Among the benefits of telephone visitation, it notes these: time, convenience, comfort, economy, courtesy, legality, and safety. 99 pages.

[660] Rogers, Mickie and Marjie Thompson. *God ... Where Are You?* Glendale, CA: G/L Regal Books, 1971.

This book of testimonies introduces the work of "People Who Care," a Christian telephone counseling group. The group uses Christian radio station KBIQ in Seattle to introduce individuals to Christian concepts and to advertise their work. Each chapter of this book, written in an inspirational style, narrates a different "salvation story" of a person helped by the group. 109 pages.

[661] Walker, Alan. *The Life Line Story.* London: Fontana Books, 1967.

This story of the founding and early years of the Life Line telephone ministry not only traces the history of the organization but also describes the training program for the laity who staff it. Each of the many divisions and services of Life Line appears through anecdotes and personal reminiscence. The whole book shows how the telephone can become a powerful means of ministry in contemporary society. 126 pages.

Chapter 7

Mass Communication

This chapter includes materials that address the Christian use of the various means of mass or social communication—primarily the press, film, radio, and television. The first section lists those materials which refer to mass communication in general or which refer to several media together. The second section deals with the press, in terms of both publishing and newspapers. The third section deals with a specific use of the mass media: public relations. Section four treats the Christian use of film. The second half of the chapter deals with broadcasting and includes sections on radio, television, audience studies, and cable distribution of television programming.

Mass Media

[662] Baacke, Dieter. "Massenmedien." *Practisch theologisches Handbuch.* Hamburg: Otto G., 1975. 428-444.

This chapter in a general theological handbook gives a brief description of the mass media and their relevance to Christian practice. 17 pages.

[663] Bachman, John W. "Media Evangelism." *LWF Documentation* 17 (March 1984): 3-10.

Broadcast evangelism evokes both positive and negative reactions; media specialists often conclude that at best televised religion can have only an indirect effect on its viewers. Bachman isolates three different approaches to media evangelism: nominally Christian (highly verbal and message oriented); sub- Christian adaptation (preoccupation with the medium); and post- Christian posture (interaction model). He then proposes a multidimensional model which would use the best features of message, medium, and process. 8 pages.

[664] Bailey, Raymond, et al. "The Church and the Media. *Review and Expositor* 81.1 (Winter 1984).

This theme issue of the Baptist theological journal examines the Church and the media from several angles. Raymond Bailey looks at the Church and the media in general while Lucien Coleman reviews the history of the Southern Baptist Convention and the Media. Bill J. Leonard provides an interpretive essay on the electronic church while Ben Armstrong weighs in in its defense. Gary Barkley supplies a bibliography of books and articles on the electronic church. Two others essays, by William Hendricks [193] and by Robert Hughes [910] are reviewed separately in this volume.

[665] Baragli, Enrico. *Elementi di sociologia pastorale sugli strumenti della comunicazione sociale.* 2nd ed. Roma: Studio Romano della comunicazione sociale, 1970.

A seminary textbook on mass communication, this volume presents a comprehensive look at communication and the Catholic Church. Beginning with a history and commentary on Vatican II's *Inter Mirifica,* the text continues with examinations of the themes of the conciliar decree: the cultural context of communication, information and public opinion, propaganda, morality and art, and relations of media to the state. A second part examines specific media: the press, the cinema, radio and television, and other new technologies; each section concludes with pastoral and moral reflections. The book is very thorough but generally remains on an elementary level. [666] is a more recent edition of this book. 291 pages.

[666] Baragli, Enrico. *Comunicazione e pastorale: sociologia pastorale degli strumenti della comunicazione sociale.* 3rd ed. Rome: Studio Romano della comunicazione sociale, 1974.

Basically a textbook on pastoral communication, this volume presents a thorough treatment of church communication from the Catholic perspective. After a general look at communication and pastoral work, the author reviews theological perspectives on communication (particularly based on Church pronouncements), the pastoral possibilities of each medium (press, cinema, radio, and television), and then considers some general questions on publicity, public opinion, and information within the Church. 566 pages.

[667] Baragli, Enrique. *Comunicación social y comunión: Historia, teología, pastoral, liturgia de los medios de comunicación social.* Trans. Jos. E. Fuquen C. Bogotá: Ediciones paulinas, 1980.

A translation and abridgment of Baragli's *Mass media e chiesa* (on the Catholic Church and the instruments of communication), this book reviews the history and theological thinking in Rome about communication and then discusses in more depth the pastoral and liturgical applications of the media. 159 pages.

[668] Bastian, Hans Dieter. *Kommunikation: Wie christlicher Glaube funktioniert.* Stuttgart: Kreuz Verlag, 1972.

This book, approaching communication from a Protestant perspective, deals with various aspects of communication and applies the results of social science mass communication research to pastoral theology. The book needs updating. 176 pages.

[669] Boyd, Malcolm. "Communicating as Christians." *Religion in Life* 26 (Winter 1956-57): 62-74.

This article reports a variety of experiments in communicating the Gospel which the author witnessed during a year's study in Europe. They include the work of a minister in editing both religious and non-religious comic books for children, discussion groups on contemporary films in France, conferences of Christians and scientists to discuss values, and the discussions on art and Christianity at St. Anne's House in London. 13 pages.

[670] Bühler, Karl-Werner. *Die Kirchen und die Massenmedien.* Hamburg: Furche-Verlag, 1968.

This books deals with the approach of the churches to the mass media in a rather negative and unspecific manner. Its criticism appears dated. 134 pages.

[671] Coleman, John. "The Church and the Media—The New Zealand Scene." *The Australasian Catholic Record* 61 (1984): 125-129.

Coleman, the editor of the leading Catholic paper in Australia, reviews the situation in New Zealand. 5 pages.

[672] Dinechin, Olivier de. "Parole d'Eglise au crible des médias." *Cahiers de l'actualité religieuse et sociale* 240 (1 février 1982): 123-128.

The Catholic Church today addresses people primarily through television and radio and thus must submit to the filters imposed by these media. These include reporting only the outlines of events, stressing the novel, examining effects produced by the messages, and personalizing the news. This situation creates difficulties for the Church: presenting a universal message in a pluralist society, engaging people's religious attention, speaking with authority, treating moral questions, and demonstrating economic and social consequences of the Gospel. 6 pages.

[673] Duffy, Paul J. *To Bring the Good News: Evangelization and Communications: Report of the National Enquiry into the Communications Apostolate.* Canberra: Australian Catholic Bishops' Conference, 1987.

This report commissioned by the Australian Catholic Bishops' Conference contains the results of 16-month study of the Catholic Church's work in the electronic and print media in Australia. 168 pages.

[674] Dunnam, Spurgeon M., Jr. "Guidelines for the Church for Ministry Through the Mass Media." *The Perkins School of Theology Journal* 28.4 (Summer 1975): 25-35.

After noting that Church use of mass media suffers from the high cost of broadcast time and from the lack of training of pastoral workers in media, Dunnam examines the mass media under the heading of the nature of media, the nature of the audience, the nature of the message, and the role of the church communicator. The article contains good summary but little new material. 11 pages.

[675] Düsterfeld, Peter. "Kommunikative Diakonie: Überlegungen zum Verhältnis der Kirche zu den Massenmedien." *FUNK-Korrespondenz* 13-14 (1988): 1-6.

This lecture to the German Catholic bishops deals with various aspects of the mass media and the possibilities of service by the mass media. 6 pages.

[676] Esposito, Rosario F. "Mass-media e annuncio evangelico." *Vita pastorale* 62.2 (febbraio 1974): 50-54; 62.3 (marzo 1974): 44-51.

From an analysis of communication models, Esposito argues that the mass media have a role in evangelization. Since criticism of the media apply just as much to other church communication (the liturgy, for example), one needs a better understanding of the overall communication process before planning any use of media. 13 pages.

[677] Evans, W. Glyn. "Preaching the Gospel Via the Mass Media." *Bibliotheca Sacra* 126 (1969): 132-145.

After reviewing some material on audiences for religious programming, Evans suggests five possibilities for church television programming: (1) documentaries, (2) interviews, (3) discussion programs, (4) musical programs, and (5) dramatic programs. 14 pages.

[678] Falconer, Ronald. *Message, Media, Mission: The Baird Lectures, 1975.* Edinburgh: The Saint Andrew Press, 1977.

Falconer, a past director of the BBC's Scotland religious broadcasting service, combines anecdote and theory to sketch out an overview of the potential of religious radio and television. Taking the general stance that broadcasting can serve as "an instrument of Christian education and evangelism," he describes its key message as the person of Jesus. "All the television, film and mass communication facilities in the world will in no way forward the Christian Cause if the Message of Christ is not at the heart of communication." Describing some of the programs he produced, he notes some of the ways one can use the broadcast media to serve the Gospel. 138 pages.

[679] Flake, Carol. *Redemptorama: Culture, Politics and New Evangelicalism*. New York: Anchor Press, 1984.

Three chapters of the book examine various kinds of evangelical communication: the electronic church, Christian book publishing, and Christian music. Anecdotal in nature, the treatment tends toward a critique of the alliance between evangelical religion and marketing or fund raising. 300 pages.

[680] Folliet, Joseph, et al. "The Mass Media in Priestly Formation." *Seminarium* 11 (1971) 1-199.

This special issue on the mass media in priestly formation collects essays which provide a background for Catholic seminaries which wish to fulfill the various conciliar and post-conciliar calls for integrating communication study in the seminary curriculum. The essays include Folliet, "La révolution audio-visuelle" (general considerations on the role of the mass media in contemporary society); Giacomo Martegani, "Gli strumenti audiovisivi: nuovi mezzi de comunicazione sociale" (contemporary debates: NWICO, satellites, technical details, new outlooks, types of training); Jules Gritti, "Les mass-media: de la communication technique à l'expression artistique" (aesthetics of media, based on Jakobsen's types of speaking); Enrico Baragli, "L'aspetto personale e morale" (seminarians and priests must make choices about their own use of the media: how much time to spend with media, what programs to watch, media education for themselves and for their parishioners, etc.); Rosario F. Esposito, "L'apostolato dei mass-media nella formazione sacerdotale" (mass media shape society, form public opinion, and convey information; they are a place the church should be); Renzo Giacomelli, "I mass-media strumenti di apostolato" (possibilities for using the mass media for evangelization); Réal Fréchette, "Utilisation des moyens de communication sociale: paradoxes de la mission sacerdotale" (qualities for a priest who would use the mass media and some guidelines in its use); and Andrea M. Deskur, "La Pontificia Commissione per le Comunicazioni Sociali e l'applicazione del Decreto Conciliare 'Inter mirifica'" (historical review of some church documents on mass media and a guide on future application of these to contemporary situations).

[681] Frost, Francis P., ed. *A Vision All Can Share: Toward a National Plan for Church Communication*. New York: United States Catholic Conference Department of Communication, 1982.

This collection of papers argues for a more unified effort in communication by the Catholic Church in the United States. After an initial overview of the current situation by the editor, scholars and practitioners discuss six main topics: the press, intra-church communication, media research, communication and religious education, Church activities in public media policy, and television. The book gives an historical background for contemporary Catholic activities in communication. 121 pages.

[682] Fuchs, Ottmar. "Überlegungen zu einer kirchlichen Medienpolitik." *Stimmen der Zeit* (1985): 111-124.

Commenting on the media policy of the Church, Fuchs takes a critical stance against both a naive and a radical use of the mass media. In each instance he warns against an adjustment to the power of economy. 14 pages.

[683] Hart, Norman, ed. *The Lively Word: Christian Publishing and Broadcasting in East Africa.* Limbe, Malaŵi: Popular Publications, 1975.

This booklet publishes the talks and papers from an ecumenical meeting—a Christian communicators' workshop—at Blantyre, Malaŵi, devoted to developing professional communication skills. Bishop Patrick Kalilombe gives a general "theology of communication," noting that communication serves the social nature of human life and reveals God to human beings. The texts from the workshops on publishing and radio broadcasting complete the book. These stress that the Christian nature of such communication places it at the service of the people. 68 pages.

[684] Hazlewood, John. "The Use the Church Does or Might Make of the Mass Media." *St. Mark's Review* 74 (July 1973): 18-21.

Religious use of the mass media in Australia, as elsewhere, often gains only poor ratings. Churches should work to improve their television and radio programs as well as their newspaper columns. Other possibilities include church publicity, commenting on current events (despite the disagreements this might cause), ministry to the men and women who work in the media, and the ongoing personal preaching of the Gospel. 4 pages.

[685] Horsfield, Peter G. "Evangelism by Mail: Letters from the Broadcasters." *Journal of Communication* 35.1 (Winter 1985): 89-97.

This survey of the mailings sent out by religious broadcasters in the United States indicates that direct mail forms an essential part of the electronic church. Broadcasters' initial mailings often acknowledge the addressee's religious quest; subsequent mailings show "that the broadcasters view convert-respondents to their programs less as candidates for referral to local churches and more as candidates for membership and support of their own organizations." 9 pages.

[686] Kanzlemar, Joseph. *The Relationship of Mass Media Courses in Ministerial Curriculum on the Subsequent Behavior of Ministers.* Diss. University of Cincinnati, 1980. *Dissertation Abstracts International* 41.10A (1981): 4268. Ann Arbor: UMI, 1981. 8107492.

This comparative study of mass media use for pastoral purposes by pastors who had taken mass media courses and those who had not finds that academic study of the media influences later practice. The author recommends that at least an introductory course in radio, newspaper, direct mail, and television be included in seminary curricula. 101 pages.

[687] Kaufmann, Willy. *Katholische Medienarbeit in der Schweiz: Bestandsaufnahme—Strukturanalyse—Entscheidungsgrundlagen.* Freiburg: Universitätsverlag, 1974.

After reviewing Catholic activity in the Swiss media (publishing, journalism, film, radio, television), this study recommends changes in organizational structure, geared to greater cooperation, within existing financial and ecclesiastical constraints. Particularly interesting is the review of Catholic organizations involved in the media, their history, aims, and current activities. 154 pages.

[688] Klaus, Bernhard. *Massenmedien im dienst der Kirche: Theologie und Praxis.* Berlin: Verlag Walter de Gruyter & Co., 1969.

This study examines mediated communication as a theological problem, reviewing first the history of journalism and its theory as it applies to the church. The communication process itself has theological significance, both from the point of view of the community and from the role of information in the church. The larger part of this study reviews various media—the press, radio, and television—noting their forms, their uses by the church, and their potential for the church. 215 pages.

[689] L'Hour, Jean. "Les nouveaux médiateurs de la bible." *Lumière et vie* 30.155 (octobre-novembre-décembre 1981): 70-87.

The advent of the mass media has changed people's access to and understanding of the Bible. In the past people depended on the local parish priest for instruction (or even for reading) in the Bible. However, today, they have access to the latest in exegesis in various public journals or on television. This essay examines how people use these methods and how the Church responds to these other channels. 18 pages.

[690] Lee, Robert E. A. "New Approach to Media: Constructive Engagement." *Lutheran Forum* 20.1 (Lent 1986): 9-13.

After making the case for greater Lutheran involvement in television, Lee suggests a five point strategy for the church. (1) Lutherans should engage in constructive criticism and media education. (2) Lutherans should engage in ministry with media professionals. (3) Lutherans should promote visibility for their newsmakers. (4) Lutherans should engage in selective production efforts. (5) Lutherans should engage in media marketing development. He also proposes that the Lutheran church establish a "Christian Institute for Communication Development," a center that would promote program ideas, research, and so forth. 5 pages.

[691] Lorey, Elmar Maria. *Mechanismen religiöser Information*. München: Kaiser, 1970.

This book offers a critical study of the way religious information is spread. Unfortunately, the author is too dependent upon stereotypes of the late 1960's. 139 pages.

[692] Lott, Theodore. *Mass Media Communications: A Comprehensive Handbook*. Fort Worth, TX: Radio and Television Commission of the Southern Baptist Convention, 1971.

By and large a practical guidebook to radio, television, and print media, this book provides tips and suggestions for those who wish to utilize "the various media of communications to take the Good News of Jesus Christ to the lost people of this world." Topics it covers include radio and religion, writing for radio, using a microphone, various kinds of radio shows, appearance on television, writing for television, producing for television, news writing, advertising, and church publicity. 174 pages.

[693] Lowe, Kathy. *Opening Eyes and Ears: New Connections for Christian Communication*. Geneva: World Council of Churches; London: World Association for Christian Communication, 1983.

This is a collection of stories about communication efforts which illustrate credible communication as it is described in the WCC Vancouver Statement: committed to justice, culturally authentic, participatory, open to dialogue, and so forth. Some of the groups described are the Philippine Educational theatre Association, a Lutheran church paper in the German Democratic Republic, the Inter Press Service, Radio Enriquillo in the Dominican Republic, and a women's journal in India. There is also an excellent afterword by Martin Marty. 118 pages.

[694] Martinot, Guy. "Pastoral Value of the Social Communication Media." *Lumen Vitae* 33 (1978): 223-232.

This article offers some guidelines for discernment on the use of the mass media by the Church. For example, Martinot suggests that the Church should consider (1) whether it can control the effectiveness of a medium; (2) whether it knows anything about the structure of the media; and (3) whether it knows anything about the level of trust that exists between people and media. He then analyzes the use of the media in terms of various needs of the Church, noting especially the uses and gratifications and the diffusion of innovations research traditions. 10 pages.

[695] Marty, Martin E. *The Improper Opinion: Mass Media and the Christian Faith*. Philadelphia: The Westminster Press, 1961.

This thought-provoking study of Christianity and the mass media argues that the best Christian use of the media is to form the "improper opinion"— the rejection of the proper popular opinion of religion that "in some vague future I shall receive some vague reward" (p. 84) and the acceptance that God is faithful and that Christ's love touches us. Marty sees the media in general as forming proper opinions—of ideas, of commerce, of power—into which religion all too easily fits. In the face of this the Christian response is not to preach (for that either reaches only believers, simplifies and distorts the Christian message, or fails to reach those in most need of the message); instead Christian communication should focus on *didache* or imaginative teaching and on witness, service, and Christian activity. The one-way nature of mass communication best serves to show these aspects of Christianity, which can function as "masks" of God's activity in the world. 144 pages.

[696] Marty, Martin E. "Needed: A Christian Interpretation of the Media World." *Lutheran World* 19.2 (1972), 105-114.

The opportunities for Christian communication have shrunk: costs have increased; a localism distrusts central church offices and impersonal communication; secularization and dechristianization have increased; Christians have lost power in controlling the secular media. In response to this Christians should find new ways of interpreting the existing the media: to seek the good in them, to use them to confirm the celebratory aspects of Christianity and to intervene in them in a "therapeutic" manner. 10 pages.

[697] McElwain, Alan. "The Media, Warts and All." *Australasian Catholic Record* 61 (1984): 115-124.

A former international journalist and Sydney Catholic Archdiocese press officer reflects on the Church's relations, good and bad, with the media. 10 pages.

[698] Murray, James. "An Outsider Looks at the Catholic Church." *Australasian Catholic Record* 61 (1984): 137-145.

An Anglican priest, who writes a weekly column on religion in a national daily newspaper, reflects on the Catholic Church's use of the media. 9 pages.

[699] Olson, George L. et al. *Japan Multimedia Evangelism Project: A Case Study of the Lutheran Churches' Quest for Total Communication.* Tokyo: Lutheran Office of Communication, 1979.

This is a report of a five year project sponsored by the Lutheran churches in Japan to create a unified media project in order to present the Gospel through radio, television, slides, posters, newspapers, and so on. The report includes a description of the project, its chronology of activities, and a detailed critique. 80 pages.

[700] Pawlowsky, Peter. "Kirche und Massenmedien nach den öster-reichischen Synoden." *Communicatio Socialis* 9 (1976): 233-254.

This article gives a clearly-written concise report of the discussions about the Catholic Church's relationship to the media at the Austrian synod of bishops in 1976. 22 pages.

[701] Phy, Allene Stuart, ed. *The Bible and Popular Culture in America.* Philadelphia: Fortress Press, 1985.

This collection offers an historical view of the Bible in America, focusing mostly on the American South and its culture. For the most part the es-says are fascinating, dealing with topics ranging from American humor to country music to popular fiction to the electronic church (a particularly good essay by Perry C. Cotham). 248 pages.

[702] Rahner, Karl. "Probleme der kirchlichen Verkündigung." *Universitas* 25 (1970): 387-390; *Universitas,* English edition 13 (1970): 53-56.

Following his usual style, Rahner gives some theses regarding the mass media and the proclamation of the Gospel. Noting that the distinction between information and appeal separates two aspects that usually go to-gether, Rahner accepts that the Church can use the mass media but not in a purely informational way. "It is appropriate that the propagation of the Christian faith, like Christianity in general, should be conducted in public" since it deals with a public religious question. Hence the media can help but the nature of the media and their independence must also be respected. 4 pages.

[703] Roberge, Gaston. "The Roman Catholic Church in Asia and the Me-dia of Mass Communication—Press, Film, Radio and Television." *East Asian Pastoral Review* 20 (1983): 151-166.

Based on a study paper and discussion guide for a 1982 bishops' meeting, this essay outlines the changing Roman Catholic Church practice regard-ing communication (from suspicion and censorship to indiscriminate use to critical understanding and compassionate service) through an overview of Church documents. It does a nice job presenting Church policy and then outlines various problem areas including the NWICO debate, forms of Church communication ministry, and the relation between group and mass media. 16 pages.

[704] Roegele, Otto B. and G. Bauer. "Kirche und Massenmedien." *Hand-buch der Pastoraltheologie.* Freiburg/Brsg.: Herder, 1966.

This brief essay makes two points: it defends the use of the mass media by the church and it criticizes the abuses of the media by journalists. 1 page.

[705] Ruszkowski, André. "Communications sociales et penseé chrétienne." *Cahiers d'études et de recherches* 9 (1968): 1-52.

In these three lectures addressed originally to clergy, Ruszkowski outlines the mass media prevalent in contemporary society, the effects they might have on the faith of Christians, and the possibilities of their use in evangelical work. Among the positive aspects of mass communication, he lists their ability to open people to the transcendent and their distillation of human longing into concrete forms in mass culture. He also addresses the problems of the freedom of information, the morality of the form itself of the various media, and the roles of Christians working in the communication industry. 52 pages.

[706] Secretariado Nacional de la Comisión Episcopal de M. C. S. [España]. *La Iglesia ante los medios de comunicación social: Ponencias de la XXIX Asamblea Episcopal Española.* Madrid: Ediciones Paulinas, 1978.

This collection of presentations to the Spanish bishops includes papers on the mass media in general, the "language" of the media, the impact of specific media on Spanish society (newspapers, records, etc.), pastoral and theological reflections on the media, and ethical issues dealing with the media. The papers are quite detailed and complete and include bibliographic references. 287 pages.

[707] Shumaker, C. Richard, ed. *Africa Wide Christian Communications Congress Report.* Kijabe, Kenya: Africa Inland Church Press, 1971.

This volume contains the papers presented at the congress, meeting at Nairobi from March 14-21, 1971. Mostly evangelical in outlook, the papers deal with communication in general, Christian literature and publishing, radio and television, and film. Additionally, the volume contains the status reports from the various language areas in Africa as well as reports from the business meetings. 276 pages.

[708] Smith, Jerry Ray. *The Professional Preparation of Theological Students in the Seminaries of the Lutheran Church in America in the Use of Educational Communication and Mass Media.* Diss. Temple University, 1973. *Dissertation Abstracts International* 34.4A (1974): 1724. Ann Arbor: UMI, 1973. 7323363.

Based on a survey of the nine seminaries of the Lutheran Church in America, this study concludes that courses in media and proclamation, communication and Christian eduction, communication theory, interpersonal communication, and public relations should be included in the seminary curriculum. 122 pages.

[709] Sodepax. *Church—Communication—Development.* Geneva: Committee on Society, Development and Peace, 1970.

This report from the SODEPAX consultation on the mass media, held in Driebergen, Holland in March 1970, presents the papers and documentation of the discussions which addressed "how the extensive facilities of Catholic and Protestant churches can be coordinated and better used for the purposes of promoting development and peace." Each of the participants provides a brief overview of church communication in his or her area and highlights problems. The findings included the recognition that the churches collectively own and operate more communication installations around the world than any other group; the difficulty that those charged with communication in the churches have little input on policy making; and the call for greater strategic planning and the move away from parochialism. The group published its working bibliography in a separate volume. 111 pages.

[710] Strategic World Conference for Evangelical Communicators. *The 80's and Beyond.* Hilversum, The Netherlands: Evangelische Omroep, 1981.

This volume collects the plenary speeches and seminar papers delivered at the Strategic World Conference for Evangelical Communicators held in Amsterdam in October 1980. Topics addressed covered a wide range: Christian media in the Eighties; the role of the mass media in the end times; the domination of the Western mass media by unscientific and destructive Marxist doctrine; religion in the on-line age; communication training; a profile of a Christian communicator; and the potential of satellites. For more information or report copies: Evangelische Omroep; P.O. Box 565; 1200 An Hilversum; The Netherlands. 398 pages.

[711] Sullivan, Edmund V., ed. "The Formation of the Public: Mass Media." *Religious Education* 78.1 (Winter 1983).

This special issue of *Religious Education* examines the impact of the mass media on North American society. Among the articles are Sullivan's "Mass Media and Religious Values"; Peg Slinger, "Television Commercials: Mirror and Symbol of Societal Values"; Jeanne Cover, "Theological Reflections: Social Effects of Television"; and John Kavanaugh, "Capitalist Culture as a Religious and Educational Formation System." The articles deal with a variety of media topics, most from a critical point of view. Some urge educational action to counteract the effects of the media; however, they show no in-depth analysis of media functions or content.

[712] Suter, Keith D. "Media, the Churches and Peace: From Gloom and Doom to Vision and Hope." *Media Information Australia* 42 (November 1986).

An outline of the ways the churches can use the media for pursuing the cause of peace.

[713] Thorn, William. *Catholic Communication: Electronic Media Access in the 1980's.* Washington, D. C.: United States Catholic Conference, 1983.

This research report contains four studies of Catholic communication: a survey of diocesan radio use, a survey of program syndicators, a survey of diocesan communication directors, and a survey of selected commercial radio and television station managers. The results show a fragmented, low-budget effort in the Catholic Church communication plan in which the mass media have lacked any significant priority among Church resources. The study calls for a more balanced approach to national and local interests and resources. 49 pages.

[714] Todd, Wayne E., ed. *Media on the Move: Reaching Out with Resources.* Nashville, TN: Convention Pres, 1974.

Designed as a textbook for the Southern Baptist Church Training program, this book discusses the ways to use media in home visitations. Although books and paperbacks form the majority of media resources, this text also encourages the use of filmstrips, records, and other media; it also suggests ways of setting up branch or mobile church libraries. Several chapters discuss the training of home visitors and their preparation in using media resources. The text concludes with a list of 213 suitable books, magazines, filmstrips, and so on. 123 pages.

[715] Wolseley, Roland E. "The Role of the Church in Communications." *Concern* 4.8 (April 15, 1962): 17-18.

As much as it would like to, the Church does not use the mass media to further its own work, to cooperate with the secular world, or to evaluate the media. The churches in the United States are not in enough agreement to achieve these ends; a first step would be to provide more national church newspapers like the *Christian Science Monitor.* Similarly, united action could give more weight to advocacy for better media and improved media content. 2 pages.

[716] Zöchbauer, Franz. *Verkündigung im Zeitalter der Massenmedien.* München: Kösel, 1969.

A positive study of Christian proclamation in the mass media. 198 pages.

Press

[717] Baker, Richard T. *The Christian as a Journalist.* New York: Association Press, 1961.

Directed primarily to students, this book examines journalism as a Christian vocation. While much of the book addresses common journalistic themes (freedom of the press, accuracy in reporting, the commercial press, limitations of journalists), it does so within a religious context. The journalist's attention to words (as born from the Word), to the formation of community, and to history (sanctified in the Incarnation) gives added value to this vocation. 121 pages.

[718] Beaufort, L. J. "Freedom of Information." *Catholic Mind* 46 (September 1948): 545-551.

In this address to the United Nations Conference on Freedom of Information, Father Beaufort, representing the Netherlands, seeks clarification of key terminology and notes the difference in interpretation of freedom of information between the East and the West. He also seeks to link freedom and responsibility and limit both the absolute freedom of the state and the absolute freedom of the individual. In this, he represents an early statement of the Catholic position, elaborated in later papal and conciliar documents. 7 pages.

[719] Bieger, Eckhardt. *Die Redakteure der Bistumspresse: Ergebnisse einer Umfrage.* München: Verlag Ferdinand Schöningh, 1978.

This study reports the findings of a survey of editors of the "official" Catholic press in Germany, that is, diocesan Catholic papers. Editors were polled on a variety of questions regarding Church policy and beliefs. 140 pages.

[720] Bowen, Francis A. *How to Produce a Church Newspaper ... and Other Ways Churches Communicate.* Janesville, WI: F. A. Bowen Reports, 1974.

This guide provides information on newspaper publishing for churches. The material covered is extensive—planning, mechanics, type style, layout, writing, photography, style sheets, and so forth—but perhaps too quickly presented. Besides the practical information, the guide also surveys some outstanding church papers and outlines a possible communications clinic for a local church. The guide contains a bibliography and glossary. 76 pages.

[721] Browne, Benjamin P., ed. *Christian Journalism for Today.* Philadelphia: The Judson Press, 1952.

This resource book contains the lectures from the Christian Writers and Editors' Conferences from 1948 to 1951. Sponsored by the Baptist Church, the conferences set out to train Christians for work in journalism and freelance writing. After introductory material dealing with the Christian vocation of writing, the book's sections address practical issues, including the audience, the mechanics of writing, the editor's role, and marketing one's writings. Much of the material still has some value today. 252 pages.

[722] Buchs, Walter, ed. *Die Verantwortung der katholischen Journalisten für Kirche und Europa—La responsabilité du journaliste catholique envers*

l'Eglise et envers l'Europe. Fribourg: Universitätsverlag/Éditions Universitaires, 1987.

This volume, the first of a proposed series by UCIP—the International Catholic Press Union—publishes the acts of a symposium on the Catholic journalist and Europe held in Yugoslavia in 1985. For the most part each participant provides an overview of the situation of the Catholic Church in his/her country; some note, additionally, the role of the religious press. Apart from the welcome addresses and the general introductions to the state of the Church in Europe, papers presented include those discussing Yugoslavia, Italy, Scandinavia, Ireland, Germany, Poland, and Hungary. Papers appear in the language of presentation (German, French, Italian, or English). 130 pages.

[723] Buddenbaum, Judith M. *Survey of Religion News Editors and Writers: Summary of Findings.* Geneva: Lutheran World Federation Information Bureau, 1982.

This pamphlet reports the results of a 1981 telephone survey of 62 religious news editors conducted on behalf of Lutheran World Information in order to collect data on the effectiveness of LWI and to evaluate its news service. The survey also includes some material on how these editors define and report religious news. 38 pages.

[724] Carty, James W., Jr. "Religious Journalism on the African Continent." Paper presented at the 18 th Annual meeting of the African Studies Association, San Francisco, CA. October 30, 1975.

This paper describes the major African organizations devoted to Christian communication: The African Literacy Centre, Daystar Communications, Unbowo, Multimedia Zambia, Radio Voice of the Gospel, Tele-Star, Lutheran Radio Center in Tanzania, and the World Association for Christian Communication. 15 pages.

[725] Catholic Media Council. *Organisational Principles of Newspapers in Developing Countries.* Aachen, Germany: Catholic Media Council, 1974.

After noting the role of Christian missionaries in introducing printing and publishing in African and Asian countries, this report addresses the issue of newspaper management for the religious press. It sets forth some principles of editorial work, gives several sample organizational charts, and suggests an accounting system for a mixed press enterprise. Additionally, it reprints the job descriptions of the editorial staff of the Catholic paper, *Munno.* 38 pages.

[726] Chenu, M. D. "Journalism and Theology." *Faith and Theology.* Trans. Denis Hickey. New York: Macmillan, 1968. 158-167.

Attempting to explain the link between journalism and theology "which can be found in their very nature," Chenu examines each in terms of their response to the world: the journalist's which is immediate and the theologian's which is reflective. Both must assess the human implications of real events, but each in a different light. To the journalist falls the duty of speaking out, applying Christian ideals and truth of day-to-day events while the theologian must provide the tools to assist the journalist. The essay seems a bit dated and reflects more the role of journalist as commentator on affairs rather than reporter. 10 pages.

[727] Coleman, John. "The Role of the Catholic Newspaper." *Australasian Catholic Record* 61 (1984): 282.

The editor of the leading Catholic weekly newspaper in Australia continues his review of Catholic publishing. 1 page.

[728] Deedy, John G., Jr. "What's Missing in the Catholic Press?" *America* 104 (February 4, 1961): 590-592.

Deedy argues that the Catholic press is not what it could be because the lay editors, well versed in the newspaper business, lack theological education. By appealing to past examples (Orestes Brownson, James J. Roche) and present work by priest-journalists, he suggests that Catholic periodicals can do more in presenting the opinions and interests of the Church. 3 pages.

[729] Dimnet, Jean. *La Religion dans Paris-Match.* Paris: Éditions du Centurion, 1967.

This study reports a content analysis of *Paris-Match* from September 1963 to September 1964. Religious issues, particularly the Catholic Church, get good coverage in the commercial press as represented by this leading French news-photo magazine. Religious personalities (popes, prelates, priests and religious) appear as well as do simple faithful. In addition, the readers see religious practices from around the world. 249 pages.

[730] Duke, Judith S. *Religious Publishing and Communications.* White Plains, NY: Knowledge Industry Publications, Inc., 1981.

An examination of the religious book publishing business, this volume presents a detailed marketing survey of Bible publishing, religious book clubs, books, magazines, recordings and broadcasting as well as an analysis of distribution, market size and structure, and demographic and economic trends. While this latter material will be somewhat dated, the overall survey, including the profiles of organizations in religious communication, is excellent. 275 pages.

[731] Dörger, Hans Joachim. *Theologie und Kirche in "Spiegel," "Zeit" und "Stern": Zur Darstellung und Beurteilung der Funktion von Theologie*

und Kirche in der Gesellschaft. Diss. Johannes Gutenberg-Universität zu Mainz, 1971.

This inaugural dissertation for the faculty of evangelical theology at Mainz examines the way that theological questions and church issues were treated in the German popular press and magazines from 1946 to 1970. By and large a content analysis which identifies themes like religious renewal, theology and politics, the status of the Church in Germany, and church reform, the study also presents some interesting prefatory material on the possibilities for the Church in taking advantage of popular media. 457 pages.

[732] Eilers, Franz-Josef. *Christliche Publizistik in Afrika: eine erste Erkundung.* Veröffentlichungen des Missionspriesterseminars St. Augustin, Seigburg 13. N.p.: Steyler Verlag, 1964.

This study gives a history of the Christian press in Africa and then analyzes its present status under the headings of the communicator, the medium, and the recipient. A brief look to the future concludes the book. 103 pages.

[733] Federazione Italiana Settimanali Cattolici. *Cultura e informazione sul territorio: Il ruolo del settimanale cattolico locale.* Rome: FISC, [1982].

This collection of papers, presented at the 1981 Italian Federation of Catholic Weekly Newspapers meeting (a meeting on the occasion of the centenary of *Il Resegone*) includes a history of the Catholic Press in Italy, discussion of the role of the Catholic press in the culture, and a presentation by Carlo Martini on the relationships among communion, community, and communication. 165 pages.

[734] Feldblum, Esther Yolles. *The American Catholic Press and the Jewish State, 1917-1959.* New York: Ktav Pub. House, 1977.

This combination content analysis and interpretation focuses upon the Catholic Press in the United States and its attitudes towards the founding of a Jewish state in Palestine. Beyond the development of this major topic, the book also sheds light upon the workings of the Catholic Press, its role in opinion formation among the Catholic community, and its relationship with the hierarchy. 199 pages.

[735] Gabel, Emile. *L'enjeu des media.* Paris: Mame, 1971.

This posthumous collection of the writings of Emile Gabel, the general secretary of the International Catholic Press Union, contains 28 essays, talks, and conferences on the Catholic press and journalism, public opinion in the Church, and the Church and mass communication in the light of Vatican II. The writings on public opinion are excellent as is his sketch on theological approaches to mass communication. 472 pages.

[736] The Gallup Organization. *U. S. Catholics and the Catholic Press.* Princeton, NJ: The Gallup Organization, 1973.

The document reports the findings of a national survey sample regarding the Catholic Press in the United States. The findings include the following: (1) The Catholic press should focus to a greater extent on the key concerns of Catholic families. (2) Catholics disagree with the Church's position on key issues but remain in the Church. (3) The Church's position on key issues has an important impact on Catholic public opinion. (4) The survey results point to the teaching function of the press. (5) Attitudes toward the Catholic press are largely favorable. 103 pages.

[737] Goonan, Michael. "Catholic Book Publishing in Australia." *Australasian Catholic Record* 61 (1984): 146-150.

This essay by the publisher of St. Paul Publications, surveys the successes and problems of Catholic book publishing in Australia. 5 pages.

[738] Gritti, Jules and André Rousseau. *Trois enquêtes sur les catholiques: Un essai de lecture critique.* Lyons: Chalet, 1977.

This volume reports several surveys about Catholic attitudes and opinions in France and among the readership of three Catholic periodicals in France: *Panorama aujourd'hui, La Vie Catholique* and *Témoignage Chrétien.* While not specifically devoted to a study of Christian communication, the content analysis of the Catholic periodicals does give a flavor of Catholic journalism. Following the methods of structuralism, the authors examine the form of the messages in each publication, the cultural values, and the image of the readership they project. 127 pages.

[739] Gritti, Jules. *Jean XXIII dan l'opinion publique: Son image à travers la presse et les sondages d'opinion publique.* Paris: Éditions du Centurion, 1967.

This case study of the image of the Catholic Church in the press focuses on Pope John XXIII's pontificate. Beyond the specific data, the author raises several significant sociological issues: the church's public existence when it no longer controls its own public image; the role of journalists as filters for theological reflection; and the church's (or the papacy's) use of the mass media as a platform to address the people. 198 pages.

[740] Gritti, Jules. *La "pilule" dans la presse: Sociologie de la diffusion d'une encyclique.* Tours: Mame, 1969.

This diffusion of information study applies the standard sociological tools to a particular instance of church communication: the reporting in French-language papers and magazines (in France and Canada) of Paul VI's encyclical *Humanae Vitae.* The study holds interest for the larger question of Christian communication for it demonstrates how the Church has lost the ability to set the rhetorical or even informational tone for its own pronouncements. Gritti shows how journalists focussed on "the pill" no matter how much church voices tried to situate the issues in terms of a theology of marriage or family life. This indicates, for him, a shift in the status of church utterances away from performatives towards other categories. 158 pages.

[741] Hart, Charles A. "Freedom of the Press and Forbidden Books." *Catholic Action* 26.2 (February 1944): 6-7.

This articles explains the Index of Forbidden Books of the Catholic Church, noting its principles and parts. 2 pages.

[742] Hemels, Joan and Michael Schmolke, eds. *Katholische Publizistik in den Niederlanden*. München: Verlag Ferdinand Schöningh, 1977.

This is a collection of articles, most published in *Communicatio Socialis*, on the history and present situation of Catholic communication activities (particularly the press) in the Netherlands. Schmolke's introduction surveys the structure of Dutch mass communications according to ideological and religious criteria. Other articles deal with the Catholic Press Bureau and with Catholic broadcasting efforts. 124 pages.

[743] Herr, Dan and Clem Lane, eds. *Realities: Significant Writing from the Catholic Press*. Milwaukee: Bruce Publishing Company, 1958.

This collection of essays, published in the Catholic press from 1951 to 1957, gives an indication of the themes and opinions in the Catholic community. While nothing specifically deals with Christian communication, this work provides a look at a change in the Catholic press as it grew more independent and professional. Topics include everything from politics and the arts to race relations to the family. 296 pages.

[744] Herrera Oria, Angel. "The Patrimony of Every Normal Society." *The Tablet* 197.5792. (May 26, 1951): 424-425.

In this speech, Bishop Herrera Oria comments on an address by Pius XII defending the rights of the press. Public opinion, a necessity for every society, must have an outlet—a function which a press free from governmental censorship can well serve. 2 pages.

[745] Hess, Geraldine. *Planning the Church Bulletin for Effective Worship*. New York: Exposition Press, 1962.

This very complete, very practical guide gives suggestions for the preparation of Sunday worship folders. Though dated in terms of printing technologies and directed solely to Protestant churches, the book contains some valuable suggestions for planning and organizing church bulletins. 141 pages.

[746] Jackson, Gordon Stuart. *The Secular and the Sacred: A Comparative Study of the Daily and Religious Press in South Africa.* Diss. Indiana University, 1983. *Dissertation Abstracts International* 44.10A (1984): 2915. Ann Arbor: UMI, 1984. 8401571.

This groundbreaking study of the religious press in South Africa surveys publications of every church and language and situates them in terms of the other media and in terms of society as a whole. Based on interviews and questionnaires completed by representatives of 67 religious publications, this study notes the theological and ideological diversity in the religious press as well as its range of publications and frequency of publication. While the religious press in South Africa tends to reflect the racial tensions in that country, few papers take political stances. Some literally cannot afford to while others feel that such positions go against their nature as religious publications. 348 pages.

[747] Kessemeier, Siegfried. *Katholische Publizistik im NS- Staat.* Münster: Regensberg in Komm., 1973.

This historical study presents a rather critical view of the Catholic Press during the Nazi era in Germany and Austria. 472 pages.

[748] Makunike, E. C., ed. *Christian Press in Africa: Voice of Human Concern.* Lusaka, Zambia: Multimedia Publications, 1973.

Historically situating the Christian press in Africa, this book sets out guidelines for Christian communications development as agreed to at a regional meeting of [Catholic] Episcopal Conferences of East Africa in September 1973. In addition the book contains essays by Patrick Kalilombe on a theology of communications and by Burgess Carr on the place of the Christian periodical in Africa. 61 pages.

[749] Malgreri, Francesco. *La stampa cattolica a Roma dal 1870 al 1915.* Brescia: Morcelliana, 1965.

This historical review of the Catholic press in Rome during the years of struggle between the Italian government and the papacy over the papal states gives a brief account of each paper, its years of publication, its editor, its editorial policies and general outlook. The papers are arranged chronologically with indices of names and newspaper titles to provide an alternative method of searching for information. 367 pages.

[750] Maritain, Jacques. *Integral Humanism: Temporal and Spiritual Problems of a New Christendom.* 1936. Trans. Joseph W. Evans. Notre Dame, IN: University of Notre Dame Press, 1973.

In an appendix first published in 1935, Maritain—following Gilson—posits three realms of action: the spiritual, the temporal, and a third which falls in between. Catholic Action takes place in the first and third areas; Catholics should show unity when acting as part of the Church but may take diverse positions when acting in the temporal realm. The Catholic press has a role in both the second and third realms: to make temporal judgments and to assist in religious formation. Given the difference between the two realms, the Catholic press should take greater care to differentiate its functions. 308 pages.

[751] Marty, Martin E., John G. Deedy, et al. *The Religious Press in America*. New York: Holt, Rinehart and Winston, 1963.

A collection of essays (on the Protestant, Catholic, and Jewish presses), this volume provides an historically interesting overview and evaluation of the religious press as it was in 1963. Each essay also sketches the history of its respective press in the United States. 184 pages.

[752] McDonald, Erwin L. *Across the Editor's Desk*. Nashville, TN: Broadman Press, 1966.

This "story of the state Baptist papers" examines not only the papers themselves but also looks at the work of an editor and the ministerial aspect of Christian journalism. The book contains brief histories of 14 long-established Baptist publications in Alabama, Arkansas, Florida, Georgia, Kentucky, Louisiana, Mississippi, Missouri, North Carolina, Oklahoma, South Carolina, Tennessee, Texas, and Virginia. 128 pages.

[753] Micewski, Andrzej. *Das Deutschlandbild in der katholischen Publizistik Polens, 1969-1974*. München: Kaiser, 1976.

This book provides a critique of stereotypes regarding Germany in the Polish Catholic press. 89 pages.

[754] Mitchell, R. Gordon. "Bookselling as a Ministry." *Christianity Today* 2.10 (February 17, 1958): 22.

This is a brief article in praise of Christian bookselling, based on the value of God's word. 1 page.

[755] Nevins, Albert J. "A Profile of the Catholic Press in the United States." *Twentieth Century Catholicism*. Vol. 3. Ed. Lancelot Sheppard. New York: Hawthorn Books, 1966. 29-50.

This overview provides a brief look at the Catholic press, its history, and the qualities of a "Catholic" editor. Nevins devotes the greatest amount of space to the latter topic, suggesting that a good Catholic editor must inform the readers, interpret the news for the readers, professionally prepare the material in the paper, and have a clear and integrated sense of the Catholic faith. 20 pages.

[756] Noling, Kathleen Strutt. *Profile of an Industry: The Marketing of Religious Books to General Bookstores*. Thesis: California State University,

Fullerton, 1980. *Masters Abstracts* 18.4 (1980): 301. Ann Arbor: UMI, 1980. 1314911.

This case study of the marketing of five evangelical books to general bookstores presents some useful observations about Christian bookselling and supplies interesting background information about various Christian publishing houses. 178 pages.

[757] Norton, William B. *Church and Newspaper.* New York: The Macmillan Company, 1930.

Drawing on his experience as a pastor and as religion editor of the *Chicago Tribune,* Norton tries to introduce ministers and church workers to newspapers and publicity. Almost a textbook, the volume covers all the basics of writing and editing. It also makes some suggestions—still helpful today—for using the news in preaching and reaching people's lives. 271 pages.

[758] Oertel, Ferdinand. *Dialogforum Kirchenpresse.* Limburg: Lahn-Verlag, 1972.

In this book, Oertel sketches out a model for the religious press, arguing that it should enable dialogue with the world and with other churches. 111 pages.

[759] Ortmann, Ernst-Albert. *Motive einer kirchlichen Publizistik: Dargestellt an den Gründungsaktionen des Evangelischen Bundes, der "Christlicher Welt" und des evangelischsozialen Preßverbandes für die Provinz Sachsen (1886-1891).* Diss. Theologischer Fakultät der Universität Hamburg, 1966. Berlin: Ernst-Reuter- Gesselschaft, 1966.

This study gives the historical situation of the publication, *Christlicher Welt,* as well as an historical overview of the evangelical press and its various justifications in the late 19th century: polemic, apologetic, social, and missionary. The study suggests that two abiding principles for the religious press are to provide information and to promote discussion. It includes a lengthy bibliography. 286 pages.

[760] Ortmann, Ernst-Albert. *Motive evangelischer Publizistik: Programme der Gründerzeit als Frage an die Theologie.* Witten: Luther-Verlag, 1969.

Beginning with a review of the Evangelical Church press in the 19th century, this study goes on to see the press as a function of the church. The press serves a teaching role; it has a polemical or dialogic role in terms of other churches; it has a apologetical and missionary role with non-believers; and it has a social role in influencing society. 172 pages.

[761] Osmer, Harold H. *U. S. Religious Journalism and the Korean War.* Washington, D.C.: University Press of America, 1980.

This study examines the responses to the Korean War and to the U. S. foreign policy of containment by the religious press in America. Based on a review of leading Catholic, Protestant and Jewish periodicals, it summarizes reactions; unfortunately, it never states why these reactions or opinions are important. 143 pages.

[762] Piehl, Mel W. *The Catholic Worker and the Origin of Catholic Radicalism in America.* Diss. Stanford University, 1980. *Dissertation Abstracts International* 40.11A (1980): 5980. Ann Arbor: UMI, 1980 8011694.

Within the larger topics of the Catholic Worker movement and Catholic radicalism in the United States, this study provides a look at the Catholic Worker newspaper as an example of a particular kind of religious communication. 340 pages.

[763] Pius XII. "Allocution to North American Editors and Publishers." *The Unwearied Advocate: Public Addresses of Pope Pius XII.* 3 vols. Ed. Vincent A. Yzermans. St. Cloud, MN: private, 1954. 2: July 11, 1946.

Freedom of the press, like any freedom, allows people a choice for the good. "It should guarantee a man against being shackled by material or selfish interests, when he pursues the laudable purpose of exposing truth and vindicating right and justice." The press should exercise an influence to change the world and put an end to injustice. 1 page.

[764] Prélot, Robert. *La press catholique dan le tiers monde.* Paris: Librairie Saint-Paul, 1968.

This valuable work provides an introduction to and history of the Catholic Press in the mission territories of the Church. Beginning with a discussion of the press in the 15th and 16th centuries and its role in the diffusion of the Bible to the missions, this discussion then traces the parallel growth of printing and evangelization. The heart of the book, however, treats the contemporary scene. Noting the different kinds of Catholic publications (as well as those of the Protestant churches), it illustrates the difficulties these face: problems of freedom, problems with language and literacy, problems with materials, and problems with political interference. Finally, for each region of the third world, the book lists papers and their circulations, and other printed works and their audiences. The second part of the book traces the history of those religious congregations devoted to the work of missionary printing. Other Catholic agencies (the Catholic Press Union, the Missionary Institute of the Press in Paris, and so on) are also indicated. 320 pages.

[765] Quezada, Maribel and Giovanna Riveri. *Los micromedios de iglesias cristianas en Chile: funcionamiento y discurso.* Santiago, Chile: CENECA [Centro de Indagación y Expresión Cultural y Artistica], 1984.

This report of a combined quantitative/qualitative research project describes the rise of small circulation print media in post-Allende Chile and compares the publications of the Catholic Church with those of the Evangelical Church. Besides the general data, the report includes a content analysis of the materials published, including themes, worldview, values, and Church perspectives. 163 pages.

[766] Quezada, Maribel, Giovanna Riveri, and Eduardo Goldstein. *Destinatarios y recepción de micromedios de la iglesia.* Santiago, Chile: CENECA, 1985.

A follow up study of the 1984 survey of small print media in the churches, this qualitative research examines the audiences for six papers, describing their characteristics, views of the Church, sacraments, and Christian life, and their uses of the small media. 144 pages.

[767] Real, Michael R. "Trends in Structure and Policy in the American Catholic Press." *Journalism Quarterly* 52 (Summer 1975): 265-271.

After recounting the history of the Catholic press in the United States, Real updates that history through interviews with editors and surveys of papers. Where the standard histories end with a note of expansion in 1960, Real divides the American experience into six phases, each with its own policy: (1) independent, 1822-1889—immigrant defensive; (2) cooperative, 1890-1918—increasingly Church oriented; (3) consolidated, 1919-1945—sectarian; (4) expanded, 1946-1961—professionalized; (5) liberalized, 1962-1968—controversial; and (6) re-institutionalized, 1968-present—stabilized. He argues that the Catholic bishops made a concerted effort to rein in the church press after the brief liberal period during the Second Vatican Council, substantiating his claims with stories of restricted editors, cut subsidies, and forced resignations. 7 pages.

[768] Richter, Klemens. *Katholische Presse in Europa.* Osnabrück: Fromm, 1969.

This book, somewhat dated now, provides a survey of the Catholic press in Europe. 173 pages.

[769] Rimmer, William, ed. *The Church Presented in "The Age" and "Sun News-Pictorial."* Melbourne: Victorian Council of Churches and Catholic Communications Centre, 1982.

A study of the way the two leading Melbourne daily newspapers treated news items on religion.

[770] Ringlet, Gabriel, ed. *Dieu et les journalistes.* Paris: Desclée, 1982.

The Catholic University of Louvain invited 16 French journalists to review with them the state of religious reporting twenty years after the Second Vatican Council. This volume includes reflections of the journalists (divided into thoughts on the daily press, the periodical press, television reporting, the specialized press, and public relations) and an analysis by several faculty members of the actual practice of religious journalism. 248 pages.

[771] Robinson, Ron. "The Role of the Catholic Newspaper." *Australasian Catholic Record* 61 (1984): 130-136.

The editor of a leading Catholic weekly archdiocesan newspaper describes the function of the Catholic newspaper in today's church. 7 pages.

[772] Ross, Robert W. *So It Was True: The American Protestant Press and the Nazi Persecution of the Jews.* Minneapolis, MN: University of Minnesota Press, 1980.

After recounting in a single narrative the events of Nazi Germany, the persecution of the Jews, and their coverage in a widely representative sample of the Protestant press in the United States (52 periodicals), Ross concludes that "the Protestant Christians who read the periodicals published by their denominations and independent sources did know what was happening to the Jews in Germany under the Nazis from 1933 on." Much of the narrative consists of material which appeared in various issues of the Protestant press. Concluding chapters of this powerful work raise the question whether complicity or complacency accounted for the lack of response of American Christians to this news. 374 pages.

[773] Rowles, George. *The Technique of the Church Magazine for the Clergy and the Skilled Laity.* London: Samuel Bagster & Sons, 1955.

After an introductory chapter discussing the need for church news and church publications, this book gives an overview of the technical processes of magazine and newspaper production. One part covers editing and editorial questions; another, technical details of copy preparation; a third, notes on illustrations and layout. Appendices introduce more restricted topics such as style sheets, type sizes, paper sizes, and so on. The book has limited contemporary value since its technical sections review only linotype typesetting and letterpress printing methods. 124 pages.

[774] Schmid, Gilbert. *Lebensberatung durch Publikumszeitschriften: Konkurrenz oder Chance für kirchliche Pastoral?* Frankfurt/Main: Haag & Herchen Verlag, 1979.

This book analyzes popular advice columns in newspapers and magazines, arranging them in typologies after a process of content analysis. It argues that these columns provide a clear pastoral opportunity for the church and gives examples of how this format might be used. 378 pages.

[775] Sheppard, Lancelot. "A Profile of the Catholic Press: The English Catholic Press." *Twentieth Century Catholicism.* Vol. 3. Ed. Lancelot Sheppard. New York: Hawthorn Books, 1966. 51-57.

This review gives a succinct history of the Catholic Press in Britain and offers a capsule characterization of each of the leading weeklies and monthlies. As opposed to the United States, the Catholic press in England—apart from the journals run by religious orders—operates under lay control. 7 pages.

[776] Shumaker, C. Richard. *An Evangelical Literature Survey of Africa.* Nairobi, Kenya: Africa Evangelical Office, 1969.

This survey report provides a country-by-country review of the Evangelical Press in Africa, noting publications, trends in printing, involvement of nationals, evangelical cooperation, and planning needs. The countries surveyed include Ethiopia, Kenya, Tanzania, Zambia, Malawi, Zimbabwe, South Africa, Kinshasa, Nigeria, Ghana, the Ivory Coast, and Liberia. 60 pages.

[777] Simonsson, Bengt K. D. *The Way of the Word: A Guide for Christian Literature Workers.* London: United Society for Christian Literature; New York: The Committee on World Literacy and Christian Literature, 1965.

Acknowledging that a Christian literature program cannot be separated from Christian life (it gains from the witness of believers and it nourishes those believers in their faith), this book sets out to provide information about book publishing and literacy for the church. According to the author, Christian literature serves three functions: (1) to help the Church in the task of evangelism; (2) to strengthen and build up the faith of the individual church member; and (3) to bring to bear Christian insights upon social, national and international issues. Apart from specific material on the organization of a Christian Council Literature Committee, the book also explains how to find manuscripts for publication, how to prepare materials for printing, how to estimate costs, how to distribute materials, and how to plan the financial side of a Christian book ministry. 206 pages.

[778] Sorge, Bartolomeo, "I compiti dei giornalisti cattolici dopo il convegno 'Evangelizzazione e promozione umana.'" *La Civiltà Cattolica* 128.4 (1977): 161-170.

In the light of a conference and a bishops' statement on evangelization, Sorge examines the role of Italian Catholic journalists in working either in the Church or in building up human society, particularly looking toward the 1980's. Among other things he recommends a program of spiritual and professional formation for journalists, more cooperation and coordination among media professionals in cultural programming, and a greater dialogue in determining what is truly cultural. 10 pages.

[779] Stritch, Samuel Cardinal. "Freedom of Speech, Censorship and the Responsibility of a Free Press." *Books on Trial* 12 (1954): 323-324, 358-360.

Originally presented as an address to the Catholic Press Association, this piece argues that the press has the freedom to present the truth but not to deceive or to damage the community. The Catholic press has the added responsibilities of reporting the news that is important to the life of the Church, of filling in the religious backgrounds of stories, of making known Papal pronouncements, and of commenting on current affairs. 5 pages.

[780] Thaman, Mary Patrice. *Manners and Morals of the 1920's: A Survey of the Religious Press.* 1954. Westport, CN: Greenwood Press, 1977.

This book paints a social history of the 1920's in the United States by providing quotations from the religious press of the day (primarily Catholic, Baptist, Episcopal, Lutheran, and Presbyterian newspapers and magazines). Topics range from finance to dancing, from drinking to films, from sex to sports. The book reports less about the press and more about the roaring twenties. 215 pages.

[781] Thomas, T. K., ed. *Ecumenical Communication in Asia.* Singapore: Christian Conference of Asia, 1981.

This booklet contains the set of papers delivered at a conference of Christian journalists in Asia: two dealing with ecumenism and two with communication. In one of the latter, John Bluck argues that Christian journalism has failed where it adopts the news values of the journalism profession. He and Michael Traber both hold that ecumenical news should use the Gospel as a standard. Bluck holds that ecumenical news is confident in God's word but incomplete since it moves to an ideal of face-to-face encounter. Traber sees the ecumenical news as a sign of contradiction for the churches. 75 pages.

[782] Thorn, William J. and Bruce Garrison. "Institutional Stress: Journalistic Norms in the Catholic Press." *Review of Religious Research* 25.1 (September 1983): 49-62.

This article reports a study of the attitudes of bishops and editors to the role of the Catholic press in local dioceses. Both agree on three major roles (news reporting, diocesan communication, religious education), but rank them in opposite ways, illustrating the tension between two definitions of the Catholic press: an adversarial model and a public relations model. 14 pages.

[783] Wagner, Hans. *Das Ende der katholischen Presse.* 3 vols. Aschaffenburg: Pattloch, 1974.

Using the case of the Catholic weekly, "Publik," the author argues that the time for a "Catholic Press" is gone.

[784] Wolseley, Roland E. "The Influence of the Religious Press." *Religion in Life* 26.1 (Winter 1956-57): 75-86.

This article presents the results of an informal survey of 14 editors of Catholic and Protestant magazines, asking them about the purposes, readership, and influence of their publications. Many could not state the purpose except in the most general terms. Most relied on mail and an occasional readership survey to inform them of the influence of their publications. Most feel that they do exert a positive influence on their readers. 12 pages.

[785] Wolseley, Roland E. *Careers in Religious Communications.* 3rd ed. Scottdale, PA: Herald Press, 1977.

This new edition of *Careers in Religious Journalism* is intended for guidance counselors or job seekers. The book provides an overview of the various kinds of religious communication and gives suggestions for career planning, with the idea that communication can indeed be a religious vocation. The press is emphasized and three general types of positions discussed: working for a religious newspaper or as a church publicist; working as a religious writer for a secular paper; and providing a Christian witness in a secular paper. The book also contains sketches of many men and women working in religious communication. 243 pages.

[786] Wood, Donald J. *Needed: A Media Doctor: The Catholic Press— 1972.* Oakland, CA: Am Cal Company, 1973.

This published dissertation tells the history of the Catholic press in the United States from the first Catholic paper in 1808 to the range of papers issued in 1972. Dividing the history into three periods (The Pilgrim Church—to 1900; the Age of Control—to 1961; and the Open Window—to 1972), Wood briefly notes the issues facing the Church and its journalists as well as the individual editors and papers founded in those years. A second part of this study reports a survey of the Catholic press in the United States. Editors provided information on their editorial philosophies, circulation, salaries, employees, advertising, and production methods. Suggestions for improvement appear at the end. Appropriate to its scholarly origin, a 13 page bibliography concludes the book. 199 pages.

[787] Zachariah, Mathai, ed. *Christian Communication in India: Problems and Prospects.* New Delhi: ISPCK [The Indian Society for Promoting Christian Knowledge], 1981.

A report of the 1981 National Seminar for Communication Workers, this booklet contains the conference papers and the findings of the working groups. While in this instance Christian communication deals largely with the press, T. K. Thomas defines it as "the communication of the good news of Jesus Christ" and Richard Taylor discusses "Communication through art forms." The latter essay reviews visuals, performance, and slogans and posters as means for Christian communication. Another essay, by

Fr. D. S. Amalorpavadass, seeks to attune Christian communication to the cultural and spiritual values of India and reviews carefully the Indian lifestyle as it affects public communication. 104 pages.

Bibliographic material on the religious press appears in chapter 2; these include [54], [57], [68], [73], and [74]. Directories of religious newspapers and publishers appear in [81] and [83]. Chapter 3 lists materials dealing with ethical issues and the press: [275], [279], [283], and [288]. Several histories of the religious press, noted in chapter 4, include [359], [360], [363], [371], [372], [382], [384], [396], [397], [406], and [407].

Public Relations

[788] Allen, Mary E. *127 Ideas for Promoting Church Training.* Nashville, TN: Convention Press, 1973.

This brainstorming collection of ideas to promote church training and education applies as well to any church activity. Geared to various age groups, the ideas are grouped according to media: handouts, mailouts, posters, telephone, mass media, etc. And, there are actually 134 ideas in the collection! 82 pages.

[789] American Lutheran Church, Commission on Public Communication. *Communication.* Minneapolis: American Lutheran Church, 1961.

This brief guide provides information for church public relations, including how to prepare news releases, advertising, parish newsletters, and bulletins. The material is very general and not terribly helpful except for a beginner. 44 pages.

[790] Austin, Charles M. *Let the People Know: A Media Handbook for Churches.* Minneapolis: Augsburg Publishing House, 1975.

This brief guide on how to use the media for church public relations focuses primarily on the local newspaper, the church newspaper, and flyers. Many examples and anecdotes fill the book but it seems too simple to satisfy the needs of most congregations. 91 pages.

[791] Barrows, William J., Jr. *How to Publicize Church Activities.* Westwood, NJ: Fleming H. Revell Company, 1962.

Defining the purpose of church publicity as placing "the work and witness of the church before the eyes of its membership and the countless thousands who have little or no contact with the church," this booklet reviews how to use church publications, personal contacts, the newspapers, radio and television, and a variety of other ways to increase the visibility of the church. Though somewhat dated in its approach, many of the suggestions are still workable, given a bit of adaptation. 62 pages.

[792] Binet, Jacques. "L'Eglise a-t-elle sa place dans la publicité sociétale?" *Cahiers d'études et de recherches* 31 (1984): 1-36.

Asking how the Church might find its place in contemporary society, Binet proposes a public relations campaign modelled on those of Jacques Bouchard which sell "social images" rather than corporate products. In this monograph he describes such "social publicity" and explores ways of applying it to the Church. As an illustration he details a campaign dealing with the family and Christian values. 36 pages.

[793] Brodie, W. Austin. *Keeping Your Church in the News.* New York: Fleming H. Revell Company, 1942.

This guide to church public relations addresses itself to print media alone. Defining what makes news, the newspaper field, and editors' views on religious news, it goes on to present a careful review of the mechanics of press relations—copy preparation, placing stories, planning publicity and campaigns, and using photography. Although dated, the book's basic introduction to journalistic conventions seems sound. 125 pages.

[794] Brodie, William Austin. *Keeping Your Church Informed.* Old Tappan, NJ: Fleming H. Revell Company, 1944.

This book discusses how to prepare church literature and use direct mail as a means of encouraging individuals' religious interest and activity. 121 pages.

[795] Brown, Richmond O. *Practical Church Publicity.* Nashville, TN: Broadman Press, 1953.

Brown discusses the practical application of church publicity and methods for promoting the local church. 171 pages.

[796] Carty, James W. "Get Your Message Across." *Christianity Today* 3.17 (May 25, 1959): 14-17.

A systematic study of communication will benefit clergy by showing them the interrelationship of all communication and improving their use of each medium available to them. Public relations can help churches since the mass media better call attention to the vitality of religion in society than preach the Gospel. 4 pages.

[797] Carty, James W., Jr. *Advertising the Local Church.* Minneapolis, MN: Augsburg Publishing House, 1965.

This booklet explores the various aspects of church advertising as a "special and valuable form of religious communication." Written from an interdenominational perspective, it presents some basic advertising principles and then explains ad preparation, budgeting, choice of media, intended audience, and ad campaigns. The many illustrations, though dated, help to make the text clearer. 63 pages.

[798] Carty, James W., Jr. and Ricardo Pastor Poppe. *Comunicación y relaciones públicas: Un guía para las iglesias.* Mexico City: Casa Unida de Publicaciones, 1978.

This primer gives an introduction to the history of public relations and illustrates its various branches and their potential for service to the churches. It includes sections on communication in general, printed materials, photography, periodicals, public opinion, correspondence, and newsletters. An appendix by Rolando Zapata Reséndiz covers group media, mostly through how-to-do-it illustrations. 92 pages.

[799] Chabot, Louis. "Les relations publiques et l'Eglise." *Cahiers d'études et de recherches.* 10 (1970): 1-62.

This fine treatment of church public relations begins with a long theoretical section, establishing the Church as the People of God and its need for determining its own public opinion, its relationship with the larger society, and its self-critique. From there, Chabot sketches out public relations historically as the identification of audiences or publics and their relationship with an organization. Only with this introduction does he begin to identify the publics of the church and the techniques of public relations, firmly insisting on the basic need for research into the audience. 60 pages.

[800] Colle, Raymond. *La comunicación del mensaje cristiano: Orientaciones prácticas.* Santiago, Chile: CENCOSEP [Centro Nacional del Comunicaciones Sociales del Episcopado de Chile], 1979.

A correspondence course in Church communication, this set of 11 lessons introduces the structure of Catholic communication offices in Chile, the functions of communication, and communication planning. Practical lessons include writing notices, preparing parish bulletins, producing radio spots, and arranging public exhibitions. 76 pages.

[801] Craig, Floyd A. *Christian Communicator's Handbook: A Practical Guide for Church Public Relations.* Nashville, TN: Broadman Press, 1969.

Public relations forms an essential part of the tool kit of the contemporary Christian communicator because it involves making oneself known and making oneself understood. This guide, prepared for Baptist churches, sketches the history of public relations and defines major terms (publicity, news, advertising, promotion, audience, media). It explains how to state objectives, identify audiences, and look for motivation. It introduces the tools of public relations which include media directed to the church (bulletins, newsletters, etc.) and media used indirectly by the church (newspaper, radio, television). The book concludes with a case study of a church and includes samples of media products. 96 pages.

[802] Crockett, W. David. *Promotion and Publicity for Churches.* New York: Morehouse-Barlow Company, 1974.

Written from the author's experiences as an Episcopalian pastor, this guide to public relations covers the basics of newsletter production, newspaper relations, and radio and television work. More practically, it also suggests guidelines for setting up a promotion-publicity committee on the parish level and gives a raft of suggestions regarding the often-neglected aspects of communication in the parish: the look of the buildings and grounds, signs, bells, displays, telephone directories, scrapbooks, and so on. 43 pages.

[803] DeVries, Charles, ed. *Religious Public Relations Handbook.* New York: The Religious Public Relations Council, 1982.

This attractively designed booklet covers all the bases for public relations by churches. Initial essays introduce the concept of public relations and urge churches to plan their information so that their communities learn about them. The later sections deal with newsletters, local newspapers, cable television, photography, advertising, special events, signs, and community relations. The booklet includes a bibliography. The booklet, updated periodically, is available from the Religious Public Relations Council; Room 1031; 475 Riverside Drive; New York, New York   10027. 56 pages.

[804] Donaldson, Margaret R. Phinn. *The Complete Parish Communications Handbook.* Columbus, OH: Donaldson Publishers, 1987.

Born from the author's experience in church public relations, this "how-to" manual takes the reader through the basics of press releases, newspaper relations, tabloid publishing, religious television, and much more. Filled with creative ideas for the novice, the book remains somewhat sketchy and distracted by personal anecdotes. 136 pages.

[805] Dubost, Michel. *Guide des relations extérieures d'une communauté chrétienne.* [Paris]: Le Centurion, 1979.

This general guide and reference book offers a well written rationale for church communication and then provides brief "how-to" sections on public speaking (preaching, radio, television), the press, mail and telephone campaigns, and other kinds of communication. 104 pages.

[806] Dunkin, Steve. *Church Advertising: A Practical Guide.* Nashville: Abingdon, 1982.

Based on the author's personal experience, this book is an elementary primer on advertising as applied to building church membership. 126 pages.

[807] Fields, Wilmer C., ed. *Religious Public Relations Handbook.* New York: The Religious Public Relations Council, 1976.

This general guide to public relations is concise, well-ordered, and marvelously helpful. It includes sections on press relations, broadcasting, advertising, congregational publications, audio-visual aids, photography, displays, community relations, direct mail, etc. Each section includes a bibliography. 61 pages.

[808] Greif, Edward L. *The Silent Pulpit: A Guide to Church Public Relations.* New York: Holt, Rinehart and Winston, 1964.

This general introduction to public relations for churches provides a brief survey of advertising, promotion, and publicity, sketching how each serves the church and the news media. The book also indicates basic techniques for news releases, spot announcements, church ads, setting up a public relations committee, communicating with the congregation, and telling the church's story to non-members. 213 pages.

[809] Johnson, Philip A., Norman Temme, and Charles C. Hushaw, eds. *Telling the Good News: A Public Relations Handbook for Churches.* St. Louis, MO: Concordia Publishing House, 1962.

This collection of essays, gathered around the theme of public relations for the church, offers brief reflections from various practitioners associated with the three main Lutheran church bodies in the United States. Topics include dealing with people, the church building, neighbors, parish papers, direct mailing, advertising, press relations, conventions, and public relations as a vocation. 208 pages.

[810] Knight, George W. *How to Publish a Church Newsletter: An Illustrated Guide to First-Class Editing, Design, and Production.* Nashville: Broadman Press, 1983.

This guide covers all the basics in newsletter design and production. Key features include an insistence on and tips for good editorial content and advance planning. The analysis of three model newsletters and a resource guide add to the booklet's value. 96 pages.

[811] Leidt, William. *Publicity Goes to Church.* Greenwich, CT: The Seabury Press, 1959.

Leidt describes the "principles of effective publicity" that can be applied to any Christian group so that they can communicate the Christian message more effectively to those around them. 119 pages.

[812] Lesch, Gomer R. *Public Relations at Work.* Nashville, TN: Convention Press, 1962.

A textbook for the Southern Baptist Convention Church Study course, this book introduces public relations and suggests ways of using it to reach people both inside and outside the church. An interesting chapter asks whether public relations is scriptural and answers by looking at figures from the Old and New Testaments and seeing in their actions the equivalent of modern public relations. To confirm this point other, more contemporary, examples from within the Baptist Church are adduced. 142 pages.

[813] Lessl, William M. *Church Publicity.* Camden, NJ: Thomas Nelson, Inc., 1970.

Almost a textbook, this guide contains basic principles and practices for churches in the area of publicity. After an overview of promotion programs, it contains a careful and complete chapter on layout and design and another on copy preparation and other basic techniques. A second part examines printing processes and addressing systems. 221 pages.

[814] Mecca, Raymond G. *Your Church Is News.* Valley Forge, PA: Judson Press, 1975.

The commercial media can help in communicating Christianity because their job entails telling their readers about the world. Mecca describes how the church itself, events, projects, and people in the church can become newsworthy. He also gives tips on gathering the news, telling it, and using it. Turning to internal church communication, he notes the beneficial uses of newsletters and suggests ways to set up a newsletter or improve on an existing one. 94 pages.

[815] Moore, Paul with William Proctor. *The Art of Christian Promotion.* Old Tappan, NJ: Fleming H. Revell Company, 1975.

Based on five autobiographical episodes, Moore suggests strategic actions to promote Christian evangelism through advertising techniques and public-relations ploys. Throughout each account, he lists a series of principles to guarantee that God leads the action. Among activities he mentions are a rock concert, flood relief work, and evangelization at singles bars. In all these things he sees a good since God has created them all. 127 pages.

[816] Morgan, Dewi and Michael Perry. *The Printed Word.* London: Epworth Press; SPCK: 1969.

This volume combines reflections on print communication for the church with an abundance of practical advice. Published jointly by the Church of England and the Methodist Church, the book presents material on parish magazines, relations with the secular press, advertising, religious publishing, church bookstalls and parish libraries. The press relations chapter narrates interesting and humorous stories about specialized publications running church stories—as long as the editors can see the link, as one could in a story on garbage hauling and dredging to prepare a cathedral site. 113 pages.

[817] National Catholic Welfare Conference. *The Church and Communications Arts.* 2nd ed. Washington, D. C.: National Catholic Welfare Conference, 1962.

This volume consists of the edited proceedings of a conference sponsored by the Bureau of Information of the National Catholic Welfare Conference.

Geared to train individuals in public relations positions for the Catholic Church, it touches on the basics of PR work: planning, publicity, special church challenges. A second section examines special needs of the Catholic Church: diocesan bureaus of information; public relations for religious communities, parishes, mission societies, and schools. Examples from successful operations punctuate the discussion. Finally, the last section of the book addresses practical topics, including religious news; how to meet the press; how to work with newspapers, magazines, radio, and television. The material draws from a "faculty" of over 40 communications professionals. 183 pages.

[818] Niese, Richard Beall. *The Newspaper and Religious Publicity.* Nashville, TN: The Sunday School Board of the Southern Baptist Convention, 1925.

Written especially for Christian workers, this book describes how to write religious news and publicity. 116 pages.

[819] Proulx, Jean-Pierre. "La publicité de l'Eglise." *Cahiers d'études et de recherches* 27 ([1980]): 1-28.

This monograph, based on the conclusions of the author's dissertation for the University of Montreal, argues that the ideology of Catholic diocesan press offices follows Vatican II's emphasis on the participation of the laity but that their practice tends to focus on the activities of the hierarchy. Interpreting data from four press offices in French-speaking Canada, Proulx bases his conclusions on an examination of the organization, specific practices, ecclesiology, information products, and publications of each office. The monograph devotes considerable space to an historical and biblical interpretation of the publicity (or public witness) of religious organizations. 28 pages.

[820] Proulx, Jean-Pierre. "Les bureaux de presse diocésains: Un modèle d'analyse." *Cahiers d'études et de recherches* 28 (1981): 1-98.

This monograph continues the publication of the author's dissertation for the University of Montreal on Catholic press offices in French-speaking Canada. This number spells out the model of analysis (ideology, organization, information, product, and publication) and examines the working of the press offices. In addition, it publishes an extensive bibliography on communication research and on the church and communication. 98 pages.

[821] Reagen, Michael V. and Doris S. Chertow, eds. *The Challenge of Modern Church-Public Relations.* Syracuse: Syracuse University, 1972.

This volume publishes the papers of the 1971 Institute on Modern Religious Communication Dilemmas, held at Syracuse University. After introductory presentations on the future of religion (Warren L. Ziegler), the crisis in belief (T. William Hall), and a social theory of human communication (William P. Ehling), the conference considered case studies of religious journalism and public relations. Among the cases are that of *Event* magazine, a United Methodist Church information area survey, and several others proposed by the conference participants. In addition to these, Jack B. Haskins adds a very pragmatic paper on religion as a marketing problem and the uses of research to resolve that problem. 67 pages.

[822] Riley, Miles O'Brien. *Training Church Communicators for Television News Interviews.* Diss. Graduate Theological Union, 1981. *Dissertation Abstracts International* 42.6A (1982): 2348. Ann Arbor: UMI, 1981. 8121872.

An alternative approach to religious communication involves the church's use of the news media, particularly television news, to carry its message. This study examines how the news media work, sketches their strengths and limits, and develops a workshop to train church leaders "to communicate their faith through the mass media." The workshop aims to educate but also to demonstrate the power of the mass media available to churches without the churches having to produce their own programming or buy their own air time. Workshop materials include interview techniques, pointers for communication planning, checklists for audience analysis, and sample materials (news releases, press conferences, etc.) 517 pages.

[823] Schütte, Manfred. *Kirchliche Werbung: Aufgaben, Ziele, Möglichkeiten.* Düsseldorf: Econ-Verlag, 1966.

This study analyzes various aspects of church publicity, placed in the context of contemporary society. It looks not only at the functions of communication inside and outside of the church, but also at questions of the limits and the ethics of such activity. 188 pages.

[824] Stewart, John T. *How to Get Your Church News in Print.* St. Louis: The Bethany Press, 1960.

Stewart, formerly church editor for the *St. Louis Post-Dispatch,* provides an editor's perspective on church news in the commercial press. He describes the kinds of stories editors look for (large meetings, ordinations, calls and resignations, anniversaries, etc.) and those editors avoid (social events, advertising for fund raisers, etc.). He then describes how to prepare the church news, and how to decide what makes news and what makes for church advertising. A last section gives suggestions for contacting newspapers. 64 pages.

[825] Stuber, Stanley I. *Public Relations Manual for Churches.* Garden City, NY: Doubleday & Co, 1951.

Addressed to pastors and religious leaders, this guide to public relations suggests techniques and skills to keep the local church in the news. The book's arrangement follows a series of key "how to" questions, including church appearance, programs, bulletins, mailings, newspaper stories, etc. Though dated, the book does present sound basic principles, particularly that "the local church must remain the Church." 284 pages.

[826] Suggs, James C., ed. *Handbook on Church Public Relations for Local Congregations of all Denominations*. New York: The Religious Public Relations Council, 1969.

This general introduction and commentary on public relations, updated periodically by the publishers, covers the definition and background of public relations and applies these to parish publications and church operations. Specific topics include broadcasting, advertising, audio-visuals, photography, signs and displays, and organizing. The booklet, written by expert contributors, also contains a bibliography. 61 pages.

[827] Sumrall, Velma and Lucille Germany. *Telling the Story of the Local Church: The Who, What, When, Where, and Why of Communication*. New York: The Seabury Press (Crossroad), 1979.

This guide covers all the basics of church public relations but does so less in a how-to manner than in a thoughtful, planned-out fashion. Beginning with the people and the communication plan, it has chapters on the church bulletin, the parish newsletter, mailings, surveys, cassette ministries, slides, film, advertising, in-house television, radio, and broadcast television. 117 pages.

[828] Swann, Charles E. *The Communicating Church: How to Tell Your Church Story to Congregation and Community*. Atlanta, GA: Office of Media Communications of the Presbyterian Church in the U. S. 1981.

This is a general handbook and how-to guide for all kinds of church communication, from news releases to posters to broadcasting. It is directed primarily to the U. S. situation. 122 pages.

[829] Toussaint, Carol Towers, ed. *Public Relations for Your Church*. Lake Mills, WI: Rural Life Publishing Co. (The Wisconsin Council of Churches), n.d.

A collection of essays designed to introduce the concept of public relations to the churches, this booklet defines public relations and suggests how churches can use it to aid in fund raising and membership drives, and suggests techniques for dealing with the press, radio, and television. 57 pages.

[830] Webley, Simon and John Capon. *Loud and Clear: A Practical Handbook on Local Church Publicity*. London: Falcon Books, 1970.

"This book has been compiled to assist local churches, and particularly their hard-pressed incumbents and ministers, with the task of publicity and public relations." The authors suggest that publicity includes communicating with both members and non-members and should include announcements, printed or duplicated materials, church magazines, displays, and press announcements. Geared to a British audience, the book lists suppliers and services available in the London area. 112 pages.

[831] Westmoreland, Reg. *A Guide to Church Publicity*. Austin, TX: Sweet Publishing Company, 1971.

"This book is for ministers, educational directors, youth workers, and others on the congregational level. It is intended to show these people how to cooperate with the mass media in the local community." Providing a general introduction to the media, it discusses news writing and other story types, radio and television basics, and internal communication. 101 pages.

[832] Wolseley, Roland E. *Interpreting the Church Through Press and Radio*. Philadelphia: Muhlenberg Press, 1951.

This early book on religious journalism and publicity introduces the media, syndicated religious news, and a variety of printed church materials. In addition, it provides practical suggestions for the "churchman as reporter," the "churchman as news writer," "the churchman as feature and article writer," as well as for editors and advertisers. Changing technology and practice make the book superfluous for anything but historical interest. 368 pages.

Film

[833] Ayfre, Amédée. *Dieu au cinéma: Problèmes esthéthques du film religieux*. Toulouse: Editions Privat, 1953.

This examination of religious film restricts itself to a consideration of the aesthetics of such film and brackets for the moment the theological or philosophical approaches to film. Religious film originated early in the history of the cinema—by 1897, parts of the Passion Play of Omerammergau had been filmed. After reviewing the history of religious films, the book moves on to a more specifically aesthetic consideration. The material is divided into films about historical personnages, films about social types (pastor, women religious, etc.), films with a psychological perspective, and films with a more phenomenological view. For each, the books gives historical background, a discussion of the relevant aesthetics, a discussion of the values in the films under discussion, and a discussion of specific issues raised by the films. The book concludes with a bibliography and filmography divided according to the materials in each chapter. 210 pages.

[834] Ayfre, Amédée. *Cinéma et mystère*. Paris: Éditions du Cerf, 1969.

This volume consists of a series of essays, several by Ayfre—dealing with cinema as a sacred art, with religious films, and with a theology of the image—and one by Alain Bandelier dealing with the image and its relation to mystery. Most of the essays begin with commentary on specific films and then move to the more general question. Ayfre's essay on a theology of the image remains at a more theoretical level, tracing the Church's attitudes towards images from pre-Christian times through the early church councils to the synthesis of medieval philosophy. The proper place to begin a discussion of image lies in the Incarnation, in Jesus as the image of the invisible God. Throughout, the book provides a fairly good application of film criticism to larger (religious) questions. 130 pages.

[835] Bamberger, Stefan. *Christentum und Film*. Aschaffenburg: Pattloch, 1968.

This study attempts to give an orientation for Christians on film. 148 pages.

[836] Bedouelle, Guy. "Film and the Mystery of the Person." *Communio* 13 (Spring 1986): 84-94.

Borrowing a distinction from Marie-Alain Couturier, Bedouelle remarks that sacred art insists on separation, on transcendence, since it takes place in the context of sacred functions; religious art, on the other hand, insists on immanence for this art is present in daily living. Film, then, is an icon of the human, shown in its great subjects—life, death, God, love and its refusal, time, and history. To illustrate his thesis, Bedouelle comments on the film, *L'Argent* by Robert Bresson. 11 pages.

[837] Bedouelle, Guy. *Du Spirituel dans le cinéma*. Paris: Les Éditions du Cerf, 1985.

Following a "literary" rather than a technical approach, the author seeks to discover the theological or spiritual in the contemporary cinema. The first part of the book examines in detail the works of Bresson and Rohmer; the second provides a commentary on the works of 16 other directors, from Wim Wenders to Woody Allen. 211 pages.

[838] Bieger, Eckhardt. "Gibt es eine Theologie des Filmes?" *Filmdienst* 25 (1976): 1-4.

Bieger argues that there is a theology of film. In general he takes a rather open approach to the question. 4 pages.

[839] Blake, Richard Aloysius. *The Lutheran Milieu of the Films of Ingmar Bergman*. New York: Arno Press, 1978.

This theological exploration of the films of Bergman aims not so much to list "references to God" as to "understand a basic viewpoint on life."

Blake argues that the Lutheran culture in which Bergman grew up has formed his thinking and use of images in all of his films. This study (a reprint of his 1972 dissertation at Northwestern University) examines a series of themes—sin and guilt, silence and wrath, faith and reconciliation, love and sexuality, and society and institutions. For each Blake sketches the background in Lutheran theology and then notes how this world view emerges in the films. 333 pages.

[840] Boyd, Malcolm. "All Films Are Theological," *The Christian Century* 71 (December 1, 1954): 1456-1457.

Theological meaning inheres in all films because they deal—at one level or another—with creation, God, Incarnation, sin, salvation, and so forth. The subject matter does not make the film religious; the Christian interpretation of the film does. 2 pages.

[841] Boyd, Malcolm. "Theology and the Movies," *Theology Today* 14 (October 1957): 359-375.

Starting with Tillich's method of correlation, Boyd asks how we can find a religious point of contact with the contemporary world and then argues that "all media of communication are implicitly theological" insofar as they realistically mirror the human condition. He then considers various films, noting the human or religious issues in each and concludes with sections on explicitly religious films and Christian cinema. 17 pages.

[842] Burns, Francis T. J. "The Impact of the Motion Picture." *Homiletic and Pastoral Review* 47 (1946): 165-171.

The author criticizes the film industry on five points: (1) mass production of films leads to low standards; (2) films appeal to the emotions rather than the intellect and indirectly lead to the cheapening of literature; (3) films contribute little of value; (4) films enshrine entertainment and sexuality; and (5) films lack any sense of the supernatural. 7 pages.

[843] Butcher, Maryvonne. "The Church and the Cinema." *Twentieth Century Catholicism.* Vol. 3. Ed. Lancelot Sheppard. New York: Hawthorn Books, 1966. 117-157.

This essay provides a Europe-centered look at the work of the Catholic Church in cinema. Focusing largely on the role of OCIC (Office Catholique Internationale du Cinèma), it reviews 30 years of cinema history and frankly points out the benefits and drawbacks of film rating systems, film awards, and religious films. The article also includes brief comment on two major papal encyclicals dealing with film, *Vigilanti Cura* and *Miranda Prorsus.* 41 pages.

[844] Butler, Ivan. *Religion in the Cinema.* New York: The International Film Guide Series, 1969.

The book surveys religion in films, briefly summarizing the plots of films which deal with religious themes such as the Bible, the life of Christ, priests and ministers, evangelists and missionaries, monks and nuns, saints, allegories and parables, the devil, and so forth. 208 pages.

[845] Cameron, Ian, ed. *The Films of Robert Bresson.* London: Studio Vista, Ltd., 1969.

A book of film criticism, this volume consists of a general introduction to the films of Bresson by Amédée Ayfre and commentaries on each of Bresson's films to 1968. Most of the critics take the position that Bresson's work forms a corpus of religious films—sometimes in virtue of their subject matter and sometimes in virtue of their style. Some, like his "Le proces de Jeanne D'Arc" or his "The Diary of a Country Priest" achieve a religious theme on both counts. 128 pages.

[846] Civardi, Luigi. "Motion Pictures as an Occasion of Sin." *Homiletic and Pastoral Review* 51 (October 1950): 16-21.

Using the language of an older moral theology, Civardi explains the obligation of Catholics to observe the guidance of film boards like the Legion of Decency. Immoral films pose a danger and might lead to sin; therefore, the prudent individual should avoid them. 6 pages.

[847] Civardi, Luigi. "The Church, the State, and the Films." *Homiletic and Pastoral Review* 51 (August 1951): 987-992.

Because of its authority in questions of morality, the Church has a competence to speak of films and must encourage good films while rejecting immoral films. The state, too, has a duty in protecting its citizens from evil and should therefore exercise vigilance regarding films, especially those directed to minors. 6 pages.

[848] Cooper, John C. and Carl Skrade, eds. *Celluloid and Symbols.* Philadelphia: Fortress Press, 1970.

This collection of essays explores the ways in which contemporary films enter into a dialogue with contemporary theology. Many of the essays interpret particular films or directors, noting how these wrestle with the classic problems in theology (good and evil, God, the human person, etc.). Skrade contributes a lengthy essay on theology and film which sketches out five values of film for theology (from the examination of the sacred in daily life to a potential for proclaiming the Gospel). The other contributors include Cooper ("The Image of Man in Recent Cinema"); Robert Jenson ("Film, Preaching, and Meaning"); James Wall (on Biblical spectaculars); William Hamilton (on Bergman and Polanski); Anthony Schillaci (on Bergman); Harvey Cox (on Fellini); William Lynch ("Counterrevolution in the Movies"—on the relationship of word and image); and Robert Wagner ("Film, Reality, and Religion"). 143 pages.

[849] Coppenger, Mark. "A Christian Perspective on Film." Ed. Leland Ryken. *The Christian Imagination: Essays on Literature and the Arts.* Grand Rapids: Baker Book House, 1981. 285-302.

A Christian should attend movies to find him/herself, the world, and others; to find the way; and to lose the self for a time. This essay reviews the basics of film and film appreciation and urges wisdom regarding film and Christianity. The essay is written from a fundamentalist Christian perspective. 18 pages.

[850] Desser, David. "Transcendental Style in 'Tender Mercies.'" *Religious Communication Today* 8 (September 1985): 21-27.

Desser applies Schrader's [881] concept of "transcendental style" (a style resulting from the desire to express the transcendent and from the nature of film, a style which expresses the holy) to the film, "Tender Mercies." Both the film content with its explicit Christian setting and the film style reflect the transcendental. 7 pages.

[851] Drew, Donald J. *Images of Man: A Critique of the Contemporary Cinema.* Downers Grove, IL: InterVarsity Press, 1974.

This book gives a general review of films and film study from the perspective of a careful Christian critic. Early chapters examine the status of film as an art and the impact of film on culture. The middle chapters explore particular themes in the human search for meaning as portrayed in films: sex, violence, work, play, religion. The book concludes with some general guidelines for film viewing and with some directions to develop a Christian perspective on film. Throughout, the book remains positive and honestly religious. 121 pages.

[852] Fearson, John. "Movies and Morals." *America* 91 (June 5, 1954): 277-79.

The author argues that morality has a place in film and that the production code is realistic because it recognizes the moral impact of films on people due to the nature of film from a psychological point of view—modelling, suggestion, laws of association, and so forth. 3 pages.

[853] Ferlita, Ernest and John R. May. *Film Odyssey: The Art of Film as Search for Meaning.* New York: Paulist Press, 1976.

Based on a film course taught by the authors at Loyola University New Orleans, this volume collects commentaries on 21 films, grouped about three kinds of search for meaning: the personal, the social, and the religious. Additional essays highlight the specifically religious nature of this search through theological reflection upon the nature of hope and the journey to God. The authors suggest that the films from this course form a kind of "great books" curriculum for film. 163 pages.

[854] Ferlita, Ernest and John R. May John *The Parables of Lina Wertmüller.* New York: Paulist Press, 1977.

A commentary on the films of Wertmüller from a Christian perspective, this work examines those films as contemporary parables. After initial biographical data and film history, much of the book consists of simple plot explication of the films. An interview with Wertmüller concludes the book. 104 pages.

[855] Fitzmorris, Thomas J. "The Legion of Decency Saved Movies from Themselves." *America* 61 (August 5, 1939): 394-95.

This examination of the Legion of Decency provides a brief history of the rating service and its constituent groups and explains its functions in rating films, arguing that the Legion has brought about a renewed vigor in the film industry through raised standards of entertainment. Despite problems of rating "propaganda films," (for example, those dealing with communism), the Legion desires to promote "an artistic medium which will entertain a healthy-minded public in terms of intelligence and identity." 2 pages.

[856] Galatik, Michael. *Film, Fernsehen und Evangelisation: Zur Erschliessung der Ausdrucksweise der 'Cinema' für den Glauben.* Wien: Herder, 1982.

This investigation of the possibilities of the characteristic image-sound-montage of film and television for proclamation of the Gospel reviews theological and aesthetic background materials and explores the specialized "language" of each. The last chapter brings the material together, contrasting the differences between religious discourse and cinematic discourse but arguing that the two are complementary. 87 pages.

[857] Gerber, Hermann and Dietmar Schmidt, eds. *Christus im Film: Beiträge zu einer umstrittenen Frage.* München: Evangelischer Presseverband, 1967.

This collection of essays, first presented as papers to a conference on religious films sponsored by the German Evangelical Church in 1965, explores the various aspects of presenting Christ in films. Essays include Hermann Gerber (Worum es geht), Walter Först (Jesus Christus—Wort oder Bild?), Gerd Albrecht (Kanzel im Kino?), Werner Hess (Kann der Film verkünkigen?), Johannes Berger (In der Sicht der Gemeinde), Franz Everschoir (Wie ein Katholik essieht), Ulrich Gregor (In den Aigen der Filmkritik), Ernst Fr. Goldschmidt (Apologie der Filmwirtschaft), Eberhard Laubvogel (Aus der Geschichte des Bibelfilms), and Friedrich Thürigen (Versucheiner Bilanz). 146 pages.

[858] Getlein, Frank and Harold C. Gardiner. *Movies, Morals, and Art.* New York: Sheed and Ward, 1961.

The two essays which make up this volume examine film from the perspective of Christian art and Christian morality. Written in response to Pope Pius XII's call for the study of film by Catholics, the book presents a balanced view of art. Getlein's chapter on the relationship among art, sex, and religion is excellent as is Gardiner's guide to a moral evaluation of films. Basing their thought in the history of art and film, both reject an unthinking criticism of film content, preferring instead an evaluation of the ways in which films treat various themes. 179 pages.

[859] Graef, H. C. "Catholics and the Film: Thoughts on some Spiritual Possibilities." *The Tablet* 191.5631 (April 24, 1948): 258.

The author calls for films that deal with real religious issues rather than sentimentality in religion. Topics for such films would include ministry seen from a human dimension, contemplative life and its place in the modern world, the holiness of day-to-day living. However, the accomplishment of such films requires writers and actors who themselves seek holiness. 1 page.

[860] Hartung, Philip T. "How are the Movies?" *Commonweal* 30 (August 4, 1939): 358-359.

Comments on a Catholic approach to film rating drawn from American, French, Belgian and British sources show the range of responses to Pius XI's *Vigilanti Cura*. Where the Americans tend to be highly moralistic, the French tend to be aesthetic and the Belgians educational. 2 pages.

[861] Hayes, Paul. "Are the Motion Pictures Facing a Moral Crisis." *Pastoral Life* 2.3 (May-June 1954): 9-14.

After warning that the moral state of movies is slipping (due to efforts to modernize the industry), the author calls for greater vigilance in supporting the Legion of Decency on the parish level. The article also includes a brief overview of how the Legion operates. 6 pages.

[862] Henderson-Hart, Anne. "What Makes a Film Christian?" *Eternity* June 1982. 18-21.

Beginning with an examination of the commercial and artistic success of the film, "Chariots of Fire," Henderson-Hart looks at the idea of a Christian film. Not so much a theoretical piece, this article gives an overview of the work of the Christian Film Distributors Association and various other Christian film producers, noting the kinds of films acceptable to evangelical groups. Among films chosen for film production or distribution are those with themes of conversion or crisis. Others among the evangelicals hold open the possibility of film as promoting dialogue with the world. 4 pages.

[863] Herx, Henry, ed. *The Family Guide to Movies on Video*. New York: Crossroad, 1988.

This collection reprints some 5,000 film reviews from the U. S. Catholic Conference's office of motion pictures. Almost all "motion pictures in national release to American theatres during the years 1966-1987" are included. The guide reprints the USCC classification, the Motion Picture Association of American classification, and a brief evaluation of each film.

[864] Holloway, Ronald. *Beyond the Image: Approaches to the Religious Dimension in the Cinema.* Geneva: Film Oikoumene, World Council of Churches, 1977.

This work examines western cinema in an historical context, arguing that the same themes which dominated theology in the 20th century have also influenced the cinema. Films have moved from explicitly religious themes to melodrama to moral issues. Among these latter issues are progress, the role of the machine, and the focus on the human.

[865] Horstmann, Johannes, ed. *Kirchliches Leben im Film: Mission und konfessionelle Jugendund Sozialarbeit im Spiegel kirchlicher Filmproduktionen in Deutschland von den Anfängen des Films bis 1945.* Schwerte: Katholische Akademie Schwerte, 1981.

This collection of articles investigates the churches' role in youth work and social work in Germany, particularly as these were seen in early German films. The final article lists the relevant films, giving technical and archival information about each. 160 pages.

[866] Hurley, Neil P. *Theology Through Film.* New York: Harper & Row, Publishers, 1970. Also published under the title, *Toward a Film Humanism.*

Aiming "to impress upon theologians, educators, and representatives of the major world religions that for tens of millions of people the motion picture experience enjoys a psychological and pedagogical legitimacy that has as yet not been matched by a corresponding effectiveness in the modes of religious communication," Hurley sketches out an overview of film study that notes theological themes in this mass medium. Among his themes he includes religious and secular society; the individual as center; freedom; conscience; sex; evil; death; grace; and sacrificial love. For each Hurley develops the theme through comment and discussion of various films. The final chapter suggests a method of teaching theology through film. 212 pages.

[867] Hurley, Neil P. *The Reel Revolution: A Film Primer on Liberation.* Maryknoll, NY: Orbis Books, 1978.

Modelled on the idea of a Christian liberation theology, this book examines the theme of liberation in contemporary cinema. Commenting on films from both North and South America, Hurley notes the stages by which one comes to a consciousness of exploitation and the ways in which one seeks liberation. While not specifically Christian in orientation, the book does indicate how a "Christian" theme interpenetrates the secular media. 175 pages.

[868] Hurley, Neil P. "The Divine Comedies of Frank Capra." *America* 152.15 (April 20, 1985): 322-324.

Calling Capra's films "divine comedies," Hurley argues that Capra presumes a three-level universe similar to Dante's. Plots too reflect the *Divine Comedy*: "The politically naïve man-child hero ...finds himself entangled in a web of compromise, suffers the pangs of hell in terms of bad conscience and thoughts of disgrace, even suicide, then—with the help of a woman— purges himself through a public confession of complicity and atonement, thus leading to a happy ending." Hurley also notes the uses of biblical imagery and themes in Capra's work. 3 pages.

[869] Keyser, Les and Barbara Keyser. *Hollywood and the Catholic Church: The Image of Roman Catholicism in American Movies.* Chicago: Loyola University Press, 1984.

Through an analysis of films and of American culture, the Keysers argue that the Hollywood film industry has established and continues to foster a set of stereotypes about Catholics (including that Catholics are immigrants living in ghettos but desperately trying to be assimilated; that the older generation clings to traditional values; that women are guilt ridden and filled with repressed sexuality; and that their religion demands ritual, statues, penance, and unnatural postures). At its best this book provides penetrating cultural analysis through a close reading of films (regarding the epic, the crime movie, and the clerical melodrama); at its worst, through an uncritical film commentary, the volume reinforces the very stereotypes it seeks to explore (regarding the horror film and the romance). 295 pages.

[870] Konzelman, Robert G. *Marquee Ministry: The Movie Theater as Church and Community Forum.* New York: Harper & Row, 1972.

This book discusses ways of using popular films in church adult education programs. Taking the line that mass communication shapes people's perceptions and values, it presents a methods for dialogical film study and suggests ways to make use of local facilities (theater, church, homes) to foster that study. The book also contains a brief history of church-cinema dealings and a bibliography. 123 pages.

[871] Lefeber, T. W. "C. F. S. Movement in Holland." *Blackfriars* 20 (1939): 41-46; 97-103.

This article narrates the history of the Dutch equivalent to the Catholic Film Society from its beginnings as a ratings agency to an attempted incorporation of a film production company to an alliance with the Catholic Action movement. The resultant organization promoted film studies, local film circles, and consumer groups to demand better quality (moral and artistic) films. 13 pages.

[872] Lindsay, Gordon. *Should Christians Attend the Movies?* Dallas, TX: The Voice of Healing Publishing Co., 1964.

This determined critique of the film industry argues that Christians should not attend the movies. Beginning with a lengthy description of the dissolute lives of film stars and with critiques from the secular press, the book ends with a list of 14 reasons to avoid the movies. These include degrading themes, glorification of evil, the opposition of church leaders, offense against modesty, and the illustration of a false way of life. 36 pages.

[873] Linhart, Paula. "Bibelfilme auf dem akademischen Prüfstand." *Film-dienst* 14 (1978): 1-3.

This essays deals in a positive way with the production and distribution of Biblical films. 3 pages.

[874] Malone, Peter. *The Writing on the Wall.* Perth: Westbooks, 1974.

A priest student of film writes on creative criticism of films.

[875] Malone, Peter. *Two Hundred Movies.* Melbourne: Chevalier Press, 1975.

A critical analysis of 200 movies, as guide for students and parents, by a priest film critic.

[876] Malone, Peter. *Video At Home.* Melbourne: Australian Catholic Truth Society, 1985.

A critical guide to the use of video films by a priest film critic.

[877] Malone, Peter. *Movie Christs and Anti-Christs.* Sydney: Parish Ministry Publications, 1988.

An analysis of the heroes and anti-heroes of contemporary films by a priest expert in film criticism.

[878] Martin, Thomas M. *Images and the Imageless: A Study in Religious Consciousness and Film.* East Brunswick, NJ: Associated University Presses, 1981.

This theoretical investigation of the art form of cinema looks for its relations to religious consciousness at the common level of the image. Martin sees the image and the "imaginative construct" as proper both to film and to religious discourse; with this starting point, he explores in detail the nature of image, the nature of the imagination, the nature of story, and the use of each in both religion and film. The book sets an ambitious goal for itself: "to relate the film medium to religious studies by means of the spatial interpretation and orientation (the image, the sense of direction) that is common to both forms of reflection." 178 pages.

[879] May, John R. and Michael Bird, eds. *Religion in Film.* Knoxville, TN: University of Tennessee Press, 1982.

This collection of essays presents three different approaches to the religious interpretation of film, reviews various genres open to religious interpretation, and discusses the work of 13 directors (from Altman to Wertmüller). The theoretical approaches, particularly the excellent essays of May and Ernest Ferlita (visual story and analogy of action), argue that the religious quality of film results from structural aspects of film rather than content. The section on genres and cultural trends is strongest when most specific (genres of transformation of Jesus (Neil Hurley) or the demonic (May)). The section on directors, while interesting, remains the weakest due to the brief summary treatment of each director's works. 257 pages.

[880] Rule, Philip C. "Reflections on the Religious Dimensions of the Film." *Christian Scholar's Review* 7 (1977): 36-50.

Rather than explore theology of film (a task which he claims degenerates into dogma hunting), Rule looks to religion—the "set of symbolic forms and acts which relate man to the ultimate conditions of his existence" (page 37). Film also constitutes a symbolic form which if it cannot image God can image human beings and their quest for the ultimate. While few American films explore such ultimate questions (because of cultural or commercial reasons, he suggests), some European ones do, notably the films of Bergman and Fellini. Rule demonstrates his method of analysis with these films as well as with a few other European and American films. 15 pages.

[881] Schrader, Paul. *Transcendental Style in Film: Ozu, Bresson, Dreyer.* Berkeley: University of California Press, 1972.

Various artists have used a transcendental style to express the holy. This work by a film critic aims not so much to interpret that style but to demonstrate of what it consists. Through an examination of the films of Yasujiro Ozu, Robert Bresson, and Carl Dreyer, Schrader points out how the transcendental style maximizes the mystery of existence and draws one to the holy. Schrader further argues that the style results not from a common personality, culture, or morality, but from the desire to express the Transcendent in art and from the nature of the film medium. 194 pages.

[882] Skinner, Richard Dana. "The Morals of the Screen." *Catholic Educational Review* 33 (October 1935): 449-456.

This article presents a very clear discussion of some rules for determining whether a film is immoral or indecent, based on the author's experience as a film reviewer. After defining some basic terms (theme, plot, treatment),

Skinner distinguishes immorality, unmorality, and indecency. Noting that each group may well have different standards informing their definition of immorality and indecency, he urges all such film reviewing groups to specify their definitions and to indicate whether a given film is, for example, immoral in theme and decent or indecent in treatment. The article's importance lies in its later use by the Catholic Legion of Decency. 7 pages.

[883] Smith, Roy L. *Moving Pictures in the Church*. New York: Abingdon Press, 1921.

Consisting of reprints of the author's articles from *The Moving Picture Age*, this book explores ways in which churches can use films. Narrating his own experience, Smith suggests that theatrical motion pictures can serve church community outreach programs as well as church education programs. He discusses program design, proposes some suitable film titles, and addresses potential problems with commercial theaters or technical details. Thoroughly outdated today, the book does hold some historical interest and may also suggest some adaptations for similar contemporary programs. 74 pages.

[884] Sumner, Robert L. *Hollywood Cesspool: A Startling Survey of Movieland Lives and Morals, Pictures and Results*. Grand Rapids, MI: Zondervan Publishing House, 1955.

This book attacks the film industry, basing its condemnation on the moral failings of actors and directors, on the immorality portrayed in films, and on the effects of films on young people who easily imitate them. A final chapter examines a Biblical response to the problem: to be holy and to avoid the movies. 284 pages.

[885] Wall, James M. *Church and Cinema: A Way of Viewing Film*. Grand Rapids, MI: William B. Eerdmans Publishing Co. 1971.

This book provides both an argument for the church's role in film education and a method for that film education. Drawn loosely from Langer's distinction between discursive and presentational style, the method is elaborated and then applied to racism and sexuality in contemporary cinema. The book is well-written and sensible; it reprints some of Wall's reviews from *The Christian Advocate* as examples of his method. Often, however, there is less a theological basis for his critiques than there is a solidly cinematic one. 135 pages.

[886] Woollen, C. J. "Films and the Family." *The Clergy Review* 28.2 (August 1947): 105-112.

Woollen urges his readers to take action in the face of the appeal of films to young people, particularly films which are objectionable. He opposes not only immodesty in films but also the glorification of luxury and wealth and the attempts of cinema chains to get youngsters in the habit of attending films regularly. He encourages a greater critical attitude and the active participation of families in the teaching of their children about film. 8 pages.

Some other material that addresses the question of the religious film appears in the periodicals, [26] and [38]. More general guides to religious communication which include sections on film are [82], [124], [285], and [300]. Media education guides that devote some attention to film are [332] and [343].

Broadcasting

[887] Armstrong, Ben, ed. *Religious Broadcasting Sourcebook*. Revised ed. Morristown, NJ: National Religious Broadcasters, 1978.

A compilation of articles (mainly from the Evangelical-sponsored *Religious Broadcasting* magazine) intended for use in religious communication institutes, this book contains sections on Christian communication, Christian radio, radio programming, music, and overseas outreach as well as on research, careers, and the history of the NRB. Most of the material consists of short magazine pieces which make for interesting and inspirational reading. 218 pages.

[888] Armstrong, Ben. *The Electric Church*. Nashville, TN: Thomas Nelson Publishers, 1979.

A general history of the electronic church from its beginnings in the 1920's to its rapid growth in the 1970's, this book introduces key people, events, concepts, and issues (including selling air time, international broadcasting, fund raising, and the imperative to broadcast the Gospel). Written from a strongly favorable point of view by the director of the National Religious Broadcasters, the book is at times factual, at times uncritical, and at times defensive. The book includes the NRB code of ethics, principles and guidelines for fund raising, and honors and awards given to members of the NRB. 191 pages.

[889] Assmann, Hugo. *La Iglesia electrónica y su impacto en América Latina*. San José, Costa Rica: Departamento Ecuménico de Investigaciones, 1988.

This volume, commissioned by the Latin American section of the World Association for Christian Communication, reviews the electronic church in North America and examines its influence in Latin America. A second part examines other communication activities of the churches in Latin America—Protestant and Catholic radio and television—and argues for a more participatory communication model. 170 pages.

[890] Bachman, John W. *The Church in the World of Radio-Television.* New York: Association Press, 1960.

Bachman, writing from his experience in religious broadcasting and with the National Council of Churches of Christ, provides an introduction to and commentary on American broadcasting, treating the system itself, its programming, its effects, and its prospects for improvement. The churches' task requires it to keep in mind its double character of "in the world but not of it"; Bachman approvingly quotes Hendrik Kraemer, "The best communication does not necessarily guarantee success. The search for successful communication has no Biblical justification. Only the search for faithful, really interpretative communication has" (page 114). The scope of church communication must create both an institutional and ideological climate for people to come to conversion. He concludes with some specific recommendations for Christian communication work: cooperation, program influence, and so on. As usual, Bachman's writing is clear and to the point. 191 pages.

[891] Becker, Karl and Karl August Siegel, eds. *Rundfunk und Fernsehen im Blick der Kirche.* Frankfurt: Knecht, 1957.

This book of essays contains pre-conciliar discussions of radio, television, and the Catholic Church by representatives of the German bishops. 371 pages.

[892] Benson, Dennis C. *Electric Evangelism.* Nashville: Abingdon Press, 1973.

Based on the author's experiences in producing local religious programs for radio and television, this book introduces basic concepts of electronic communication and suggests ways of their utilization at the local level. The section on radio—by far the longest—provides good program and planning ideas, particularly for youth ministry. The anecdotal nature of the writing makes it highly approachable but somewhat limited in scope. 144 pages.

[893] Bethell, Tom. "The Common Man and the Electronic Church." *Harper's* 256.1535 (April 1978): 86-90.

Reporting on the annual convention of the National Religious Broadcasters, Bethell notes that speaking openly about religious issues, as do the evangelical broadcasters, marks out a class division in the United States, much more so than does money or social status. The broadcasters simply represent an additional manifestation of this largely unacknowledged issue in the United States. 5 pages.

[894] Bisset, J. Thomas. "Religious Broadcasting: Assessing the State of the Art." *Christianity Today* 24 (December 12, 1980): 1486-1489.

After reviewing the results of a *Christianity Today-* Gallup poll that indicates that Christian broadcasting (radio and TV) reaches only 4% of the population—those already belonging to evangelical churches—, Bisset proposes the strategy that churches close competing stations, pool their resources and buy VHF stations in the top markets, run them commercially except for editing of objectionable contents and running Christian public service announcements. 4 pages.

[895] Bisset, Tom. "Religious Broadcasting Comes of Age." *Christianity Today* 25 (September 4, 1981): 1106-1108.

After reviewing the first 25 years of religious television (and crediting Percy Crawford as the first to own and operate Christian FM and UHF stations), Bisset notes several current trends in programming: the debate among evangelicals about Gospel music, the use of religious broadcasting to carry ideas within the Christian community, and the need for cooperation. In looking to the future he sees the growth of a Christian satellite consortium and the challenge to reach those who do not watch religious television. 3 pages.

[896] Blake, Richard A. "Catholic, Protestant, Electric." *America* 142 (March 15, 1980): 211-214.

A report on the "Consultation on the Electronic Church" sponsored by the National Council of Churches, the United States Catholic Conference, UNDA-USA, and the World Association for Christian Communication, this article focuses on questions of economics, ethics, and theology in the electronic church. Both questions of economics and ethics have to do with fund raising and taking members away from the local church. Theological questions deal with the nature of the church, religious responses to complex social issues, and the distinction between a Catholic theological outlook and an evangelical Protestant outlook. 4 pages.

[897] Butler, Phill. "Research and Christian Broadcasting." *International Christian Broadcasters Bulletin* October 1969: 3, 5, 6.

Christian broadcasters need to do audience research both to clarify their own goals and to attract advertising. 3 pages.

[898] Butler, Phill. "Evangelism and the Media." *International Christian Broadcasters Bulletin* February 1972: 10, 12, 15.

Christian broadcasters need to know their goals (honestly), to understand the Scriptural process of evangelism, and to know their audiences. Further, the Christian broadcaster must seek to integrate the use of media into the local church. 3 pages.

[899] Butler, Phill. "The Christian Use of Radio and TV." *Interlit* 14.4 (December 1977): 2-3, 15.

Because of the great number of immigrants to the United States, evangelical broadcasters should look on the U. S. as a mission field. Programs should seek out the unreached as well as continue to succor the converted. To do this planning should include knowledge of broadcast markets, financing, analysis of the limits and benefits of owning broadcast properties, and the integration of broadcasting with print and personal witness. 3 pages.

[900] Clancy, Thomas H. "Nine and a Half Theses on Religious Broadcasting." *America* 140 (April 7, 1979): 271-275.

In a piece intended to provoke thought on the part of the Catholic community, Clancy argues these (and other) theses: religious broadcasting is booming, exposure on news is the best kind of religious broadcasting, liturgical actions have a build-in electronic advantage, Catholic broadcasting has neglected religious music, short spot broadcasting is better than long programs, and cable is the medium of the future. 5 pages.

[901] Cohn, Marcus. "Religion and the FCC." *The Reporter* January 14, 1965: 32-34.

Although no evidence exists to indicate that the Federal Communications Commission has ever awarded a license solely on the basis of religious programming, religious programming does figure into the licensing process and this seems to violate the Constitutional ban on governmental involvement in religion. The writer argues that the FCC should change this policy and that such a change would actually benefit religious broadcasting since more religious groups would have access to broadcasting. 3 pages.

[902] Cornehl, Peter and Hans-Eckehard Bahr, eds. *Gottesdienst und Öffentlichkeit: Zur Theorie und Didaktik neuer Kommunikation.* Hamburg: Furche-Verlag, 1970.

This collection of essays discusses the question of the public communication of religious worship from various angles. After a brief exposition of the problem by Bahr, others examine specific issues: preaching, the holy, worship, Christian teaching, and the uses of television by Christian groups. 264 pages.

[903] Coulson, John. "Broadcasting and Christian Responsibility: Radio and Television in Great Britain." *Twentieth Century Catholicism.* Vol. 3. Ed. Lancelot Sheppard. New York: Hawthorn Books, 1966. 74-100.

This article provides a history of radio and television work by the Catholic Church in England, situating it in terms of the governmental policy decisions establishing first the BBC and then the ITA. Further, Coulson argues that "religious programmes can never be separated from the context in which they appear." He ends with three principles for religious broadcasters: (1) the churches should acquire a more sophisticated appreciation of the way the media determine the handling of the subject matter. (2) The churches should not confuse the media with their subject matter. (3) The churches should be sensitive to the context in which their programs appear. 27 pages.

[904] Cox, Kenneth. "The FCC, the Constitution, and Religious Broadcast Programming." *George Washington Law Review* 34.2 (December 1965): 196-218.

Responding to Loevinger's article in the previous volume of the journal [917], Cox argues that the FCC does not promote religious practice by requiring the reporting of religious programming. After reviewing the authority of the Commission to consider broadcast programming, he notes that the inclusion of a religious category arose from the practice of the stations and not from any federal mandate. Turning specifically to the Supreme Court cases cited by Loevinger, Cox notes that the points of law do not apply to broadcasting. However, he agrees that the complexity of the issue merits further study and perhaps judicial review. 23 pages.

[905] De Vries, C. Michael. "Christian Broadcasting in Oecumenical Perspective." *EBU Review* 97B (May 1966): 70-72.

This article offers a short account of the broadcasting policies of the World Council of Churches and gives a bit of the history of its cooperation with the World Association for Christian Broadcasting. It also notes the ecumenical thrust of this work, the flexibility the WCC hopes to maintain, and its consciousness of the need to evaluate the effectiveness of Christian broadcasting. 3 pages.

[906] Ellens, J. Harold. *Models of Religious Broadcasting.* Grand Rapids, MI: William B. Eerdmans Publishing Company, 1974.

This well-written, well-thought-out book uses the idea of a model "to describe what has been and what is happening in the church's use of electronic mass media." Historically sound, the book sets the theme by recounting the early events of radio broadcasting in the United States and the interactions between the churches and the broadcasting industry. Over the years different practices and rationales for religious broadcasting have emerged. Ellens sorts these into four main categories: (1) the extended pulpit in which the broadcaster preaches to the people; (2) the spectacle in which the broadcaster entertains the people; (3) the classroom in which the broadcaster teaches; and (4) the leaven in which the broadcaster tries to provoke serious thought. In the first category, Ellens narrates the history of Bishop Fulton J. Sheen, the Lutheran Hour, the Back to God Hour, Father Charles Coughlin, and Bob Shuler. In the second, he places Aimee Semple McPherson, Rex Humbard, Oral Roberts, and Billy Graham. The third contains the efforts of the Presbyterian Church, the United Churches of Christ, the

Southern Baptist Convention, the Seventh-Day Adventist Church, and the Lutheran Church—Missouri Synod. The Presbyterian Church, the United Presbyterian Church, and the Franciscans make up the fourth category. Ellens concludes with a brief chapter on the advocacy and ethics work of Everett Parker, and Morality in Media. The work provides not only a good overview and history, but a good source of ideas for understanding religious broadcasting in the United States. 168 pages.

[907] Fore, William F. "Religion on the Airwaves: In the Public Interest?" *The Christian Century* 92 (September 17, 1975): 782-783.

This article briefly reviews the history of the Lansman-Milam Petition which asked the FCC "to prohibit the assignment of any additional educational television or radio licenses to applicants controlled either by sectarian religious groups or by state or local governments." Fore also reviews the law and the church-state issue while noting that the petition itself did not discriminate against any religious programming. 2 pages.

[908] Griswold, Clayton T. and Charles H. Schmitz, Charles. *Broadcasting Religion: Manual for Local Use.* New York: National Council of the Churches of Christ, Broadcasting and Film Commission, 1954.

A somewhat dated, practical guide to the use of radio and television for religious purposes, this book covers writing for radio and television, production ideas, possible types of shows, production aids, and deciding policy issues at the congregational level. 103 pages.

[909] Griswold, Clayton T. and Charles H. Schmitz. *How You Can Broadcast Religion.* New York: National Council of the Churches of Christ in the United States of America, 1957.

Following a listing format, this manual presents a quick look at radio and television production. It gives a brief description of programming types, hints for writing, common production guidelines, basics on legal issues and industry structures, and information about Christian broadcasting in the U. S. and overseas. Somewhat outdated, the book does provide a simple introduction to communication work. 128 pages.

[910] Hughes, Robert Don. "Models of Christian Missionary Broadcasting." *Review and Expositor* 81.1 (Winter 1984): 31-42.

The task of missionary broadcasting involves determining the audience, the gatekeeper of the message, and the cost-effectiveness of the overall project. In the past, five models have appeared in Christian missions: (1) the ecumenical committee model; (2) the international transmitter model; (3) the western evangelist model; (4) the geosynchronous satellite model; and (5) the independent producer model. The article describes each model and outlines its strengths and weaknesses. 12 pages.

[911] Interchurch Communications. *Submission to the Canadian Radio-Television and Telecommunications Committee Regarding Religious Broadcasting in Canada.* Ottawa: Interchurch Communication, 1982.

After tracing the context of Canadian religious broadcasting, the submission proposes ten recommendations, including the establishing of a religious broadcasting department in the CBC–English division; the setting of a minimum requirement for religious broadcasting by each CBC section or local affiliate; the establishing of a religious advisory committee; and a set of norms for religious broadcasting or religious stations. Signatories include Rev. W. E. Lowe, Anglican Church of Canada; Rev. Philip Karpetz, Baptist Convention of Ontario and Quebec; Mr. Walter Schultz, Lutheran Council in Canada; Mr. Donald I. Stephens, Presbyterian Church in Canada; Dr. John E. O'Brien, S.J., Canadian Conference of Catholic Bishops; and Rev. Dr. R. G. Brisbin, the United Church of Canada. 20 pages.

[912] International Christian Broadcasters. *Report: Tokyo International Communications Congress, April 13-18, 1970.* Colorado Springs, CO: International Christian Broadcasters, n.d.

The collection of conference papers from this evangelistic broadcasting gathering includes the keynote address by Max Atienza ("Mandate to Communicate"); position papers on topics ranging from cross-cultural communication to the use of the mass media and satellites, to communication barriers; and seminar presentations on a variety of technical developments and new equipment. Individual papers, such as "The Use of Mass Media to non-Christian Cultures" by Gollapalli John and "Communication Barriers" by Carl W. Lawrence provide good stimuli for reflection. 152 pages.

[913] Johnson, Daniel L. "Electronic Fundamentalism: Supply and Demand." *Christian Century* 97 (May 28, 1980): 606-607.

Explaining the rise of the fundamentalist television preachers by a vacuum in American culture, Johnson calls for the mainline churches to address that demand as well. He suggests that they purchase time for their own messages, that they use the local pulpit to point out to congregations the differences they have with the fundamentalists, and that they look to creatively address the American public. 2 pages.

[914] Lacey, Linda Jo. "The Electric Church: An FCC-'Established' Institution?" *Federal Communications Law Journal* 31 (Spring 1979): 235-275.

The article raises questions regarding the policies of the FCC in dealing with religious issues and broadcast properties: allocation of non-commercial licenses, commercial programming requirements, program content, on-air fund raising, ownership concentration, etc. Lacey asks whether the FCC policies could pass the Supreme Court's non-establishment criteria and concludes that they violate at least one of them. The FCC has favored religious broadcasting; whether it should is an issue that must be addressed. 41 pages.

[915] Lamb, Kenneth. "Freedom and Responsibility in Religious Broadcasting." *EBU Review* 97B (May 1966): 45-48.

Lamb, then head of religious broadcasting for the BBC, describes the BBC policy for programming religion, placing it in its historical context. He characterizes it as attempting to evoke a Christian response and to present a balanced view of each "responsible Christian viewpoint" in England. 4 pages.

[916] Loevinger, Lee. "Broadcasting and Religious Liberty." *Journal of Broadcasting* 9.1 (Winter 1964-1965): 3-24.

Reviewing and using the First Amendment of the U. S. Constitution and several judicial decisions as a background on which to base his conclusions, Loevinger questions the Federal Communication Commission's policies on religious broadcasting. He suggests that the FCC "has gone far beyond the limits that have been marked by the Supreme Court as permissible government action in the field of religion." 22 pages.

[917] Loevinger, Lee. "Religious Liberty and Broadcasting." *George Washington Law Review* 33 (March 1965): 631-659.

After reviewing relevant Supreme Court rulings regarding the First Amendment and religious rights, Loevinger turns to the policies of the FCC which govern religious broadcasting. From its beginnings in the Federal Radio Commission, the FCC has supported religious programming as part of a station's duties of serving the public interest. However, while acknowledging the complexity of the issue and of the historical background, Loevinger argues that the FCC should review its reasoning since much of that reasoning runs afoul of the Supreme Court decisions regarding state involvement in religious issues. 29 pages.

[918] Luce, Clare Boothe. "The FCC vs. God." *Catholic Digest* 14.4 (February 1950): 85-89.

This piece presents a somewhat partisan attack on the FCC's handling of the Scott case, a case in which the petitioner sought broadcast access to promote atheism. Although the FCC denied the petition, the language of the decision seems to suggest that the issue of religious broadcasting is open to question. 5 pages.

[919] Marty, Martin E. "The Electronic Church." *Missouri in Perspective* (March 27, 1978): 5.

Marty opposes the whole idea of the "electronic church" on the basis that it promotes a private Christianity at the expense of the local congregation.

He supports church use of broadcasting according to this rule of thumb: "if the use of media is *costing* someone, not earning for them, be ready to trust them at least a bit." 1 pages.

[920] McKay, Roy. *Take Care of the Sense: Reflections on Religious Broadcasting.* London: SCM Press, 1964.

McKay, the head of religious broadcasting for the BBC from 1955 to 1963, presents a series of reflections on religious broadcasting. Some of the material is historical and sheds light on particular decisions and programs which appeared on BBC radio or television during his tenure. Other material, grouped thematically, illustrates policy issues, the BBC's sense of its audience, or program types. 127 pages.

[921] Neuendorf, Kimberly A., Pamela Kalis, and Robert I. Abelman. "The History and Social Impact of Religious Broadcasting." Paper presented to the annual meeting of the Association for Education in Journalism and Mass Communication, San Antonio, Texas, August 1987.

This paper presents three views of religious broadcasting: an historical survey (drawing primarily on Armstrong [888], and Hadden and Swann [378]), a structural view of programming, and a review of research dealing with audiences. It provides a handy summary but breaks no new ground. 32 pages.

[922] Norris, William C. Jr. *An Evaluation of Federal Court Decisions on Religion in Broadcasting in the Light of the First Amendment.* Diss. University of Southern California, 1971. *Dissertation Abstracts International* 32.12A (1972): 7023. Ann Arbor: UMI, 1972. 7217496.

Abstracting 26 key court cases, this study provides a valuable resource for legal considerations of religious broadcasting. The author concludes that religious liberty has not been fostered by the system of broadcasting in the United States; in fact, courts have tended to avoid the issue by limiting cases dealing with churches outside the mainline denominations. 251 pages.

[923] Oberdorfer, Donald N. *Electronic Christianity: Myth or Ministry.* Taylors Falls, MN: John L. Brekke and Sons, 1982.

This clearly written book provides an excellent short introduction to the world of religious broadcasting in the United States. It combines a history with an analysis of program types, church types, and media theory. It also features an outstanding chapter on "theological implications for communications." Oberdorfer argues that a theology of communication must articulate some measure of understanding the Divine will, reflect the reality of the human condition, and encourage dialogue. Out of this comes his statement that Christian communication should aim less at proclaiming the Word and more at media ministry— that media should have a place in the ministry of the church and not be a separate "amplifier." Other chapters deal with concrete suggestions and issues which Oberdorfer has faced as director of television and films for the Media Services Center of the American Lutheran Church. 159 pages.

[924] Palmer, Donald C. *Religious Television and Radio*. Bathurst, 1983.

An Anglican priest's study of how the church can more effectively use the electronic media for preaching the Word; he is a lecturer in media studies at a tertiary institution in Australia.

[925] Robinson, Haddon W. "The Impact of Religious Radio and Television Programs on American Life." *Bibliotheca Sacra* 123 (1966): 124-135.

Reviewing then current literature on audiences for religious television, Haddon suggests that television does not serve evangelization well. First, television functions as an agent to reinforce existing beliefs (thus believers and not the unchurched watch religious programming); second, audiences judge television to be an entertainment medium, not suited to "serious" topics such as religion (thus audiences prefer religious programming on the radio). 12 pages.

[926] Ruf, Ambrosius Karl. *Fernsehen, Rundfunk, Christentum*. Aschaffenburg: Pattloch, 1960.

After giving a general introduction to radio and television from a Christian perspective, Ruf provides a remarkably open discussion of the problems a Christian use of these media faces. 128 pages.

[927] Schultze, Quentin J. "The Mythos of the Electronic Church," *Critical Studies in Mass Communication* 4 (September 1987): 245-261.

This article argues that broadcast evangelism appeals to large numbers of American Protestants because it ties into a "mythos" of "the Christian idea of progress, contemporary evangelical theology, and American technological utopianism." A rhetorical analysis of various evangelical broadcasters supports the argument. 17 pages.

[928] Smith, Desmond. "The Churches and the Airwaves." *The Christian Century* 82 (March 24, 1965): 364-367.

After briefly reviewing some of the interaction between American Protestantism and the broadcast industry, Smith argues that "by reason of their concern, competence, comprehension the churches have a responsibility to speak forthrightly on the subject of secular as well as religious TV programming." He urges a greater role on the churches for taking an interest in programming and petitioning the FCC to enforce the law calling for broadcasting in the public interest, convenience, and necessity. 4 pages.

[929] Smith, Robert R. "Broadcasting and Religious Freedom." *Journal of Broadcasting* 13.1 (Winter 1968-1969): 1-12.

Written in response to Lee Loevinger's "Broadcasting and Religious Liberty" [917] this article discusses the argument among theologians, communication lawyers, and broadcasters over FCC requirements in religious programming. Smith proposes as a compromise that broadcasters should take editorial responsibility for programs that help audience members understand religious problems outside of their geographic communities. This way the broadcasters would help to preserve religious freedom by aiding the audience's learning without promoting any particular church. 12 pages.

[930] Tatlock, Richard. *Proving, Preaching and Teaching.* London: The Faith Press, 1963.

This book is "an inquiry into the nature and technique of apologetics and communication in the context of the Christian religion." The first of the two essays deals with apologetics, describing its nature, techniques, and problems. The second essay deals with communication and draws on the author's experiences with the BBC in religious broadcasting for the Anglican communion. Much of this latter essay is highly pragmatic, discussing language, vocabulary, stories, timing, boredom, and audience motivation. 131 pages.

[931] Timmins, Leslie. *'Vision On!' Christian Communication through the Mass Media.* London: The Epworth Pres, 1965.

Rev. Timmins, a host for various religious broadcasts in Britain, reviews the use of television for religious purposes. After an historical and present day (1965) sketch, he addresses several questions that deal the suitability of the mass media for religion. While encouraging the churches to make use of the media, he nevertheless argues that the autonomy of the media of radio and television must be respected—the church must work through them, not dominate them. 132 pages.

[932] UNDA. *UNDA General Assembly: Dublin 1974.* Blackrock, Dublin: The Communications Centre, 1974.

A detailed report of the UNDA General Assembly in 1974, whose themes were "Broadcasting in the Service of Mankind" and "Mass Media as a Means of Evangelization," this book contains the transcripts of the three main presentations, the reactions, and the discussions. Two documents are noteworthy: "Theological Reflections on the Media of Social Communications" by Most Rev. Andre Marie Deskur of the Pontifical Commission for Social Communication, and comments by Manuel Olivera, S. J., on two different approaches to mass media, stemming from different approaches to Christian living–a private one and a public one. 396 pages.

[933] UNDA. *UNDA General Assembly, Namur 1977.* Brussels: UNDA [International Catholic Association for Radio and Television], 1977.

This document is basically a report of the business meetings at the 1977 UNDA general assembly. 126 pages.

[934] UNDA. *UNDA General Assembly: Manila 1980.* [Brussels: UNDA], 1980.

The acts of the 1980 UNDA General assembly, this volume features reports on Catholic communication activities around the world and presentations on religious programs for radio and television, media education, and popular music. 362 pages.

[935] UNDA. *General Assembly of Unda: Nairobi 1983.* [Brussels: UNDA], 1983.

Primarily a business report, this document does contain interesting looks at Catholic Church communication activities around the world for the 1980-1983 period. Each region has provided a detailed report, including statistical summaries and illustrations.

[936] Westerhoff, John H., ed. "The Electronic Media." *Religious Education* 82 (1987): 161-336.

This theme issue of *Religious Education* publishes the report of the National Council of Churches Study Commission on the Electronic Media. In addition, the volume includes papers by various commission members, among them: William Fore ("A Theology of Communication"); Thomas Boomershine ("Religious Education and Media Change: A Historical Sketch"); Robert Jenson ("The Church and Mass Electronic Media"); and James Capo ("Annotated Bibliography on Electronic Media"). 174 pages.

Radio

[937] Aske, Sigmund [sic]. "Radio Evangelism and Africa." *The Christian Broadcaster* 9.1 (January-April 1961): 9-12.

Working in the planning stages for Radio Voice of the Gospel, Dr. Aske outlines the project and the necessity of using radio despite some theological doubts about its suitability for evangelism. 4 pages.

[938] Aske, Sigurd. "Radio Voice of the Gospel." *International Review of Missions* 56 (1967): 355-364.

This brief introduction to the work of station RVOG in Addis Ababa sketches the history, the programming, and the missionary philosophy of the station. RVOG is a Protestant interdenominational radio, broadcasting in 16 languages; all programs are produced by the churches in the reception area and programming is balanced between secular and evangelical material. 10 pages.

[939] Bloom, Naomi L., ed. *Giving the Winds a Mighty Voice, 1949-1979.* N.p.: Northwestern College Radio Network, 1979.

The Northwestern College Radio Network provides a Christian counterpart to secular radio—"twenty-four hour daily inspirational, informational, exhortational radio whose format, musical preaching, teaching and speaking content bespeaks the excellence and beauty of the Christ we love and serve." This history of the network traces it from its first station, KTIS, in St. Paul, Minnesota, sponsored by Northwestern College and Billy Graham, through the addition of four other stations: KNWS (Waterloo, Iowa), KFNW (Fargo, North Dakota), KNWC (Sioux Falls, South Dakota), and WNWC (Madison, Wisconsin). 96 pages.

[940] B[ooth], P[hilip A.] *Ears that Hear: Some Thoughts on Missionary Radio.* London: Radio Worldwide, 1966.

Most of this short volume consists of directories: a directory of missionary radio recording studios, a directory of missionary radio stations, a directory of cooperative works in missionary radio, etc. In addition several introductory chapters address the effectiveness of Christian radio, financing Christian radio, and a philosophy of programming. Radio Worldwide attempts Christian radio in a manner different from North American efforts; this program-provider approach is described and explained as well. 85 pages.

[941] Booth, Philip A. *Slim Fingers.* Fort Washington, PA: Christian Literature Crusade, 1976.

Booth, the director of Radio Worldwide, narrates the history of this missionary radio service from its beginnings as a small part of the Christian Literature Crusade. This service differs from other missionary radio in that it produces programs for broadcast by others; further, its programs often indirectly preach the Gospel. Booth includes two more theoretical chapters in the course of his narrative: these specifically address the nature of programming for Christian radio and examine the potential audiences for that radio. 120 pages.

[942] B[romiley], G. "Evangelical Broadcasting Outlook." *Christianity Today* 2.7 (January 6, 1958): 28.

A news report on the continuing conflict between the evangelicals who favor paid time broadcasting (in this instance on radio) and the National Council of Churches which favors sustaining time broadcasting. The evangelicals feel discriminated against and assert that they are being forced off the air. 1 page.

[943] Cousins, Peter and Pam Cousins. *The Power of the Air: The Achievement and Future of Missionary Radio.* London: Hodder and Stoughton, 1978.

Written in a familiar style, this small volume tells the story of the Far Eastern Broadcasting Association's establishment in the Seychelles against the background of missionary radio in general. It includes chapters on the general history of the station, financing, programming, and audience analysis. 157 pages.

[944] Crowe, Charles M. "Religion on the Air." *The Christian Century* 61 (August 23, 1944): 973-975.

Crowe argues that the Christian churches cannot afford to let religious radio lie in the doldrums and offer only sermons or services. They must adapt the religious message to the medium and the audience if they would have any influence and if they would escape the network regulations designed to curb unbridled fund raising on the air. Entertainment programming can have a religious flavor; Crowe suggests four possible program formats to achieve this end. 3 pages.

[945] Di Giacomo, Maurizio. "Radios paroissiales en Italie." *Lumière et Vie* 30.155 (octobre-décembre 1981): 11-17.

After a 1975 Italian Supreme Court ruling allowed local private radio and television stations, the Catholic Church established almost 200 radio stations on the parish level throughout Italy. Many of the stations address local needs and allow their people a hearing on political issues (local traffic, etc.) and thus give the Church a measure of prestige; other stations offer popular courses in Bible study and religious practices. This church use of radio provides a new community focus for the Italian church. 7 pages.

[946] Dick, Donald David. *A Survey of Local Religious Radio Broadcasting in Los Angeles, California, with a Bibliography on Religious Broadcasting 1920-1964.* Diss. Michigan State University, 1965. *Dissertation Abstracts International* 26.8 (1966): 4884. Ann Arbor: UMI, 1965. 6514205.

This study reports a survey which measured 112 local religious radio programs and questioned station managers about this kind of programming. The majority of programming in Los Angeles at the time of the survey was produced by the evangelical and pentecostal churches. Most programs seek a general audience but few producers made much of an effort to study their audiences or to work with station management to position their programming. The study also contains over 100 pages of bibliography on religious broadcasting. 609 pages.

[947] Dinwiddie, Melville. *Religion by Radio: Its Place in British Broadcasting.* London: George Allen and Unwin Ltd, 1968.

This history of religious radio in Britain, written by the BBC's Scottish Regional Director for religious broadcasting, not only narrates the historical events but also includes reflections and observations on the nature of religious radio and television. The book follows a topical rather than a chronological organization, discussing worship programs, prayer, praise, preaching, teaching, and evangelism and their possibility on radio. 136 pages.

[948] Dolle, Charles F. "Religious and Educational Broadcasting and Some of its Problems." *Radio Law Bulletin of the School of Law of the Catholic University of America* (1931): 100-113.

This lecture by the executive director of the National Council of Catholic Men outlines in general terms the situation of church- owned broadcasting properties in the early days of the Federal Radio Commission. More specifically, it describes the seven stations owned by the Catholic Church and their interests and operations, particularly as these pertain to educational broadcasting. Finally, it discusses the plan, format, and implementation of the weekly *Catholic Hour* on the NBC radio network. 14 pages.

[949] Doyle, Michael W. *Cable Radio: A New Delivery System for Catholic Communications.* Milwaukee: Archdiocese of Milwaukee, 1984.

This pamphlet provides a very simple introduction to cable radio and suggests ways for Church groups to establish stations in cooperation with local cable companies. It will be of interest only to beginners. 32 pages.

[950] Durfey, Thomas C. and James A. Ferrier. *Religious Broadcast Management Handbook.* Grand Rapids, MI: Zondervan Publishing House, 1986.

Beginning with a brief history of broadcasting, this handbook sketches out the basics of setting up a broadcast station. Although it addresses the issues of broadcasting in general, its specific materials deal solely with AM and FM radio. More technical chapters describe the engineering reports necessary for an FCC application. Other chapters provide a more readable overview of programming—its history, its types, and its structures. Two other sections deal with financial aspects (sales, promotions, commercial and noncommercial operations) and with station management (including a chapter on Biblical perspectives on management). Most of the material could address a general audience; examples, however, come from Christian broadcast stations. 294 pages.

[951] Edmonstone, John "2CH—A Christian Station?" *Australasian Catholic Record* 61 (1984): 247-252.

This essay evaluates the operation of a metropolitan Sydney commercial radio station, operated by the Australian Council of Churches. 6 pages.

[952] Eldersveld, Peter. "Communication—For What?" *United Evangelical Action* 22.9 (November 1963): 12-13.

Introducing a general report on evangelical radio, Eldersveld notes that the purpose of communication outweighs the importance of audience numbers or equipment. The report itself, compiled by several authors, runs from pages 13-23 and covers evangelical radio in the United States and abroad. 2 pages.

[953] Frames, Robin, ed. "Radio Voice of the Gospel, Addis Ababa." *Multimedia International* 16 (1974): 1-12.

This collection provides a brief history and overview of operations of Radio Voice of the Gospel (station ETLF), run by the Lutheran World Federation and affiliated with the World Association for Christian Communication. 12 pages.

[954] Freed, Paul Ernest. *A Study of the Extent to which the Indicated Objectives of American-Produced Religious Radio Programs Prepared for Broadcasting to Europe Would Be Achieved According to French, German, and Spanish Religious Leaders.* Diss. New York University, 1960. *Dissertation Abstracts International* 21.10 (1961): 2998. Ann Arbor: UMI, 1961. 6100323.

This qualitative study attempts to predict the success of American produced Protestant programming in Europe through interviews with representative religious leaders. It reports mixed results and reactions to the programs, which included the Lutheran Hour, Temple Time (Reformed Church), and Light and Life Hour (Methodist Church). 450 pages.

[955] Freeman, Wendell K. *Why Not Broadcast the Gospel? Radio Broadcasting: Methods, Sermons, Questions.* Huntington, WV: n.p., [1952].

This early guide to religious broadcasting includes an exhortation to use the radio for evangelism (put in the form of a commentary on Mt. 13:3-9, the parable of the sower) and some guidelines for program preparation. The rest of the book consists of transcriptions of actual broadcasts, collections of sermons, and question and answer materials on biblical matters, suitable for broadcasting. The author has an affiliation with the Church of Christ. 180 pages.

[956] Gillies, John. *A Primer for Christian Broadcasters.* Chicago: Moody Press, 1955.

Directed to a "Christian who is interested in radio broadcasting," this booklet introduces basic concepts about radio but shows the greatest attention to matters of programming. Gillies reviews the most common types of religious radio programs and offers tips on everything from speaking voice to scripting and music. 79 pages.

[957] Graham, James Wilson. *And Now a Word from our God—A Local Church Uses Local Radio.* Diss. Princeton Theological Seminary, 1982. *Dissertation Abstracts International* 43.9A (1983): 2821. Ann Arbor, MI: UMI, 1983. 8302729.

This D. Min. project asks whether a local church can "use its own local electronic medium (radio) appropriately and with integrity to communicate its message to its immediate community." Motivated by the theological themes of proclamation and stewardship, the author designed a program to test whether a local church could clearly state what it wanted to communicate and produce a program to accomplish that. He found a tension between the message and the medium that constrained the communication in some ways and he also noted a tendency to focus on means rather than ends in the planning groups. 97 pages.

[958] Hughes, Don H. "The Use of Radio in Teaching Catechism." *Journal of Religious Instruction [The Catholic Educator]* 11 (February 1941): 552-555.

Told in the first person, this account suggests ways of writing radio scripts that combine instruction and entertainment. Hughes notes that such programming should feature children, use stories, and have a professional presentation. A sampling of scripts appears in the April 1941 issue, pages 737ff. 4 pages.

[959] Jordan, Max. "Radio Adds to the Story of Religion." *Catholic Mind* 41.969 (September 1943): 38-44.

This article, reprinted from RCA's *Radio Age,* sketches the activities of NBC in religious broadcasting, noting special programming as well as the regularly featured "Catholic Hour," "The National Radio Pulpit," and "Message of Israel" programs. Jordan also reiterates the NBC policy of not selling radio time for religious broadcasting because selling time "might result in according a disproportionate representation to those individuals or groups who happened to command the biggest purse." 7 pages.

[960] Josuttis, Manfred. *Beiträge zu einer Rundfunkhomiletik.* München: Kaiser, 1967.

This volume discusses the possibilities of preaching on radio and attempts to set up an overall didactic plan for it. 218 pages.

[961] Kimsey, James E. *How to Conduct Religious Radio Programs.* St. Louis: Bethany Press, 1958.

After a brief introductory chapter on the potential of radio for preaching the Gospel, this work describes the legal basis that makes a radio ministry possible in the United States. The larger part of the book outlines types of religious radio programs (news, documentaries, interviews, devotionals, round tables, etc.) and gives suggestions for developing workable radio scripts. The material is very basic and somewhat sketchy. 64 pages.

[962] Knutson, Franklin A. *A Survey of Religious Radio Broadcasting in St. John's, Newfoundland.* Diss. Michigan State University, 1969. *Dissertation Abstracts International* 30.11A (1970): 5096. Ann Arbor: UMI, 1970. 7009576.

This study contains lots of history of Newfoundland but only a cursory kind of account of the development of religious broadcasting there; briefly noted are the church sponsored stations and the gradual takeover by commercial operators. The survey is more one of religious attitudes than anything else.

[963] Kuehle, Donald Lawrence. *Developing a Strategy for a Radio Ministry in a Rural Setting.* Diss. Drew University, 1980. *Dissertation Abstracts International* 41.8A (1981): 3310. Ann Arbor: UMI, 1981. 8103465.

This report of a professional project for the D. Min. degree examines how a rural church began a radio ministry. After a first chapter which explores the theological bases of communication (the nature of God and the nature of redemption), the study rehearses the general history of radio and the specific history of radio in rural Missouri. With this background, the D. Min. project develops a strategy to enable a radio task force to engage in a radio ministry through audience analysis, program format design, and program production. 137 pages.

[964] Kushner, James Michael. *International Religious Radio Broadcasting in Africa: Program Policies and Problem Areas.* Diss. University of Minnesota, 1976. *Dissertation Abstracts International* 37.11A (1977): 6820. Ann Arbor: UMI, 1977. 7709964.

This dissertation presents general information about four evangelical radio stations in Africa: RVOG, FEBC, CORDAC, and ELWA, examining in particular the history, programming, economics, politics, and personnel of the stations. 290 pages.

[965] Ledyard, Gleason H. *Sky Waves: The Incredible Far Eastern Broadcasting Company Story.* Chicago: Moody Press, 1963.

This book narrates the history of the Far Eastern Broadcasting Company and its 17 stations. The story is told through the lives of its founders in a "thanks be to God" fashion. 229 pages.

[966] Leger, Robert Michael. *Counterprogramming among Religious Radio Stations in the Los Angeles Area.* Thesis: California State University, Fullerton, 1980. *Masters Abstracts* 18.3 (1980): 218. Ann Arbor: UMI, 1981. 1314304.

This study reports a survey of religiously oriented radio stations in Los Angeles, noting that little direct counterprogramming takes place. (Counterprogramming involves scheduling shows in an attempt to take listeners away from other stations.) Instead, stations tend to compete for listeners using larger measures such as format and musical styles. 87 pages.

[967] Lohr, Lennox R. *The Partnership of Religion and Radio.* New York: The Federal Council of Churches of Christ in America, 1938.

This pamphlet reprints an address by Lohr, speaking on behalf of NBC, in which he recounts the history of network religious broadcasting. In addition he describes the thinking behind NBC's religious broadcast policies that representative church groups receive free time on the air. The document holds some historic interest. 16 pages.

[968] Loveless, Wendell P. *Manual of Gospel Broadcasting.* Chicago: Moody Press, 1946.

This textbook of Gospel radio covers most of the technical aspects of radio (in the 1940's). After reviewing the purposes of Gospel radio as well as program principles, Loveless devotes over 100 pages to radio script writing and to sample scripts. The book holds historical interest rather than practical teaching today. 352 pages.

[969] Lowe, S. F., ed. *The Living Christ in the Life of Today.* Nashville, TN: Broadman Press, 1941.

This volume collects the first 13 addresses broadcast by the Southern Baptist Convention over radio. The broadcasts took place primarily in the South. Although no individual dates are given for the programs, speakers' names do appear. 128 pages.

[970] Lungren, Manfred. *Proclaiming Christ to His World: The Experience of Radio Voice of the Gospel, 1957-1977.* Geneva: Lutheran World Federation, 1983.

A detailed, official history of RVOG from its planning stages to its nationalization by the Ethiopian government, this study describes the operating partnership, the broadcast institution (technical, financial, ecumenical, and governmental aspects), the radio ministry, and the revolution that led to nationalization. Particularly noteworthy is the account of the ways RVOG used dispersed, local studios to produce programming for 17 language groups it reached throughout Africa, the Near East, and Asia. 329 pages.

[971] Maclin, H. T. "Religious Broadcasting in Africa." *EBU Review* 97B (May 1966): 53-58.

Maclin gives an overview of the African situation for religious broadcasters at the time of independence from colonial rule. Focusing principally on radio, he describes patterns of religious broadcasting in different geographic regions and by different Christian denominations. He also includes information on listener profiles and on training programs for domestic services. 6 pages.

[972] Maher, Frances, ed. "Communication and Development: Summary Report of the Consultation of African Churches, Limuru, Kenya, 1986." *LWF Documentation* 21 (December 1986): 3-48.

The report summarizes the findings of the conference on the Lutheran Church-sponsored Communication for Development Project, on the restructuring of the Madagascar radio studio to a communication center, and on the options for the Africa Radio Ministry Capital Fund. The report contains the recommendations as well as summaries of each major presentation. 46 pages.

[973] Mahoney, E. J. "Wireless and Liturgical Services." *Clergy Review* 16 (May 1939): 440-441.

In answer to a questioner, Mahoney, a canonist, gives an opinion that the 1927 restriction on broadcasting Catholic services no longer binds or that permission can be readily obtained. The 1927 ruling apparently applied just to the German bishops who inquired of the Vatican; it was never applied to the universal Church. 2 pages.

[974] Maier, Walter A. *The Lutheran Hour: Winged Words to Modern America, Broadcast in the Coast-to-Coast Radio Crusade for Christ.* St. Louis: Concordia Publishing House, 1931.

A collection of radio talks and sermons arranged in sequence of content; all originally broadcast on CBS as part of the Lutheran Hour. 324 pages.

[975] Maier, Walter A. *America, Turn to Christ! Radio Messages of the Lutheran Hour from Easter through Christmastide, 1943.* St. Louis: Concordia Publishing House, 1944.

This is exactly what it says it is: a collection of radio talks and sermons by the Rev. Maier. 341 pages.

[976] McLaren, Jim. *Crosstalk.* Melbourne: Collins Dove, 1986.

Australia's leading priest radio talk-back host assesses his fourteen years of broadcasting to youth on the most popular Sydney night-time talk-back/counselling radio program.

[977] McLaren, Jim. *Stories in the Night.* Melbourne: Collins Dove, 1987.

Father McLaren narrates some of the most significant life-stories from his popular radio talk-back program in Sydney.

[978] Miller, Spencer, Jr. "Radio and Religion." *Annals of the American Academy of Political and Social Science* 177 (1935): 135-140.

This essay briefly narrates the history of religious broadcasts on United States radio networks and describes the official policies of the NBC and CBS radio networks to religious radio. It proves helpful as an historical resource, particularly with its interview of Rev. Edwin Van Etten, rector of Calvary Episcopal Church in Pittsburgh—the site of the first religious broadcast. 6 pages.

[979] Mocellín, Luis. *La radio, instrumento de evangelización.* Quito: Asociación Católica Latinoamericana de Radio, Televisión y Medios Afines [UNDA- AL], [1983].

This brief account of Radio Católica in Brazil describes the station and its uses for evangelization; it also makes some general suggestions regarding techniques for using radio, giving some programming ideas. 16 pages.

[980] Münster, Clemens. "Christliche Rundfunkarbeit." *Frankfurter Hefte* (1949): 678-686.

In this early essay, Münster offers a definition of the standpoint for a Christian engagement in broadcasting. 9 pages.

[981] Murray, John. "Catholics and the BBC." *The Month* 177.924 (November-December 1941): 531-541.

This article gives an overview of the problems Catholics face in religious broadcasting–particularly dead air, the use of Latin, and the availability of non-Eucharistic devotions. Opportunities for ecumenical cooperation and common themes offset some of these problems and the advent of regular television service ("after the war") will offset others. 11 pages.

[982] Neves, Moreira das. "A Discussion on Religious Radio Programmes." *EBU Review* 97B (May 1966): 32-33.

This brief article restates the Catholic position on the use of radio broadcasting, drawing from the documents of the Second Vatican Council and the encyclicals of Pope Pius XII. 2 pages.

[983] Parker, Everett C. "Religion on the Air in Chicago." *The Chicago Theological Seminary Register* 31 (January 1942).

After personally interviewing station managers to compile a list of all religious programs airing in Chicago in November 1941 (77 programs, with a total time of 46 hours), Parker suggests that the programs feature too much talk (sermons or addresses), that production values lack dignity, and that too many of the programs originate outside of Chicago. He recommends that the churches explore alternative kinds of programming—including music, education, history, and discussion.

[984] Parker, Everett C. "Big Business in Religious Radio." *The Chicago Theological Seminary Register* 34.2 (March 1944): 20-23.

Noting that commercial religious radio programs generated over $200 million in income in 1943, Parker argues against these ventures because the sponsoring churches are not accountable to any denomination nor do they provide financial reports. Instead, Parkers urges greater use of sustaining time. He also notes that listener interest in religious programming could increase should the churches (a) use more program formats, (b) target specific audiences, (c) train people in broadcasting, (d) promote sustaining time programs, and (e) meet the needs of the average listener. 4 pages.

[985] Perry, Armstrong. "Religion's Raid on Radio." *Popular Radio* 7.1 (January 1925): 3-10.

While unopposed to religious programs in general, Perry attacks the religious broadcasters who try to monopolize the air waves or to jam out other programming. He briefly describes the situation and then documents his claims with listings of stations owned or operated by religious groups. This latter listing holds some historical interest, describing the situation in the mid-1920's before the United States Congress established the Federal Radio Commission. Of historical interest, too, is the argument of the essay since it foreshadows later controversies. 8 pages.

[986] Puga, Josefina. *La iglesia católica chilena y los medios de comunicación social.* Santiago: Centro Bellarmino, Departmeno de Investigaciones Sociológicas, 1983.

This research reports the involvement of the Chilean Catholic Church with the mass media, particularly the radio. After surveying the relevant Church documents, Church structures, and Church-sponsored or produced radio programs, it evaluates how well the actual communication efforts fit into the bishops' pastoral plan. 38 pages.

[987] Read, David H. C. *Overheard.* Nashville, TN: Abingdon Press, 1969.

This book publishes 13 talks first presented by Read on the "National Radio Pulpit," produced by NBC and by the Broadcasting and Film Commission of the National Council of Churches. Most of the talks address the relevance of Christianity in the modern world. 141 pages.

[988] Reed, Jane and Jim Grant. *Voice Under Every Palm: The Story of Radio Station ELWA.* Grand Rapids, MI: Zondervan Publishing House, 1968.

A straightforward narration by one of the founders of ELWA radio in Liberia, this book provides an evangelical witness to the possibilities of missionary radio and a testimony to the faith of those who built the station. ELWA broadcasts in multiple languages to bring the Gospel to Africa and to help solve the mission problems of "manpower, multiplication, mobility, and maintenance." 151 pages.

[989] Rodgers, W. W. "Broadcasting Church Services." *Radio Broadcast* 1 (August 1922): 321-329.

Rodgers, a member of the radio production team from KDKA that pioneered religious broadcasting at Calvary Episcopal Church in Pittsburgh, narrates the early history of this style of broadcasting. He describes some technical details of the link between church and station and then goes on to discuss listener response and the involvement of other churches in the efforts. Well illustrated with photographs, the article proves a good historical resource. 9 pages.

[990] Schmitz, Charles H. "Religious Radio in the United States." *Crozier Quarterly* 24 (October 1947): 289-315.

This article reviews radio broadcasting by various religious groups in the late 1940's, discussing each group (Catholic, minority Protestant, mainline Protestant, Jewish) and its programming in turn. 26 pages.

[991] Schultz, Hans Jürgen. "'Commentary on Life'—Church and Theology in Broadcasting." *EBU Review* 97B (May 1966): 20-23.

Considering radio primarily as a means of information, this article challenges the religious use of radio. Accusing churches of addressing only believers and of repeating meaningless phrases, Schultz calls for a real preaching of the "Good News"—one which would respect the intimacy of the medium and one which would articulate the faith in an idiom intelligible to modern society. Such a preaching flows from a converted life in which people truly share their lives in Christian love. 4 pages.

[992] Schultze, Quentin J. "The Wireless Gospel." *Christianity Today* 32.1 (January 15, 1988): 18-23.

Within the context of a history of evangelical radio broadcasting, Schultze attempts to lay to rest seven myths. (1) Evangelical broadcasting is a recent phenomenon. (2) Evangelical broadcasting became popular only in the last decade. (3) The total audience for evangelical broadcasts has increased enormously in recent years. (4) The power of televangelism threatens to destroy the local church. (5) Evangelical broadcasting is creating a powerful conservative political movement in America. (6) Most evangelical broadcasters preach a "health and wealth" gospel. (7) The latest communications technologies give media preachers unparalleled power. 6 pages.

[993] Smith, William C. "The Priest in Radio." *American Ecclesiastical Review* 119 (1948): 285-292; 367-374; 424-435; 120 (1949): 113-122.

Because the radio has such great power in persuasion, the Catholic Church should use it; therefore priests need to use radio and to encourage the laity in spreading the Church's teaching through radio. With this introduction, the essay continues to explain the nature of radio, the nature of the audience, adaptation of style to the radio style, preparation of the radio talk, delivery styles, and producing and directing radio programs. 30 pages.

[994] UNDA-AL. *La Misa radiofonica.* Quito, Ecuador: UNDA-AL [Asociación Católica Latinoamericana para la Radio, Television, Audiovisuales y Medios Afines], 1986).

This booklet gives simple instructions, illustrated with graphics, for producing the Mass on radio. 38 pages.

[995] Valente, Robert with Duane Nigh. *Backtalk.* Iowa City, IA: Future Productions, 1977.

This volume consists of transcriptions of the radio program, "Backtalk," on which Nigh interviews Valente about his Christian music and religious views. Valente, based in Florida, presents a fundamentalist reading of the scriptures and of life experience. 120 pages.

[996] various authors. "Missionary Broadcasting: 10 Years of Progress." *Christian Life* 20.7 (November 1958): 29-45.

This set of articles provides a journalistic overview of evangelical radio stations around the world. The special report also includes maps of stations and listings of support agencies. 17 pages.

[997] Walker, E. Jerry. *Religious Broadcasting.* Washington, D. C.: National Association of Broadcasters, 1945.

The National Association of Broadcasters prepared this pamphlet as a guide for people who would prepare or broadcast religious programs. Written from the broadcaster's point of view, it suggests community cooperation, governing committees, and program planning. In addition it reviews some basics of broadcasting and notes the rights and obligations of broadcasters. 19 pages.

[998] Windsor, Carl Douglas. *Religious Radio in the 1970's: A Uses and Gratifications Analysis.* Diss. The Ohio State University, 1981. *Dissertation Abstracts International* 42.5A (1982): 1841. Ann Arbor: UMI, 1981. 8121872.

This study is not so much a uses and gratifications analysis as it is a survey of religious radio stations, their numbers, formats, locations, and growth. While the assembled data is helpful, little interpretation or even definition of the categories is offered. 158 pages.

Some periodicals which report on Christian radio include [9], [22], [27], [31], [42], and[50]. Further bibliographic suggestions appear in [62] and [65] while [80], [87], and [89] offer directories of religious radio stations and their personnel. Historical materials on the use of radio by religious groups may be found in [353], [373], [375], [388], [405], [412], [413], [414], [417], [432], and [433].

Television

[999] Abelman, Robert and Kimberly Neuendorf. "How Religious Is Religious Television Programming?" *Journal of Communication* 35.1 (Winter 1985): 98-110.

A content analysis of a two-week sample of the "top-30" religious television programs indicates a wide variety of themes treated, with about 75% of programming content overtly religious. Social issues also appear; political issues, less often but usually in a conservative light. "Solicitations average $190 per hour." 13 pages.

[1000] Abelman, Robert and Kimberly Neuendorf. "The Cost of Membership in the Electronic Church." *Religious Communication Today* 8 (September 1985): 63-67.

Despite reports in the popular press, the television evangelists do not all ask for money all the time. This study of a sample of programs indicates that fund raising remains concentrated among a few of the most well known evangelists; the study also notes their justifications for asking funds and the promised rewards to the contributors. 5 pages.

[1001] Abelman, Robert. "Ten Commandments of the Electronic Church." *Channels of Communications* 4.5 (January-February 1985): 64-67.

This popularized account of Abelman's research notes that religious television now resembles the format of secular programming, that it features predominantly middle-aged white males, that it tends not to criticize television, and that it competes for the same audience as network programming. 4 pages.

[1002] Albrecht, Horst. *Kirch im Fernsehen: Massenkommunikationsforschung am Beispiel der Sendereihe "Das Wort zum Sonntag."* Hamburg: Furche-Verlag H. Rennebach KG, 1974.

This volume reports an extensive sociological study of the church sponsored program, "Das Wort zum Sonntag" on West German television. The study consists of several content analyses, an audience analysis, an investigation of the impact of the counter-cultural message of the program and a functional analysis of the program. 240 pages.

[1003] Alexander, Danny Lee. *A Rhetorical Analysis of Selected Television Sermons.* Diss. Texas Woman's University, 1983. *Dissertation Abstracts International* 45.1A (1985): 175. Ann Arbor: UMI, 1984. 8409203.

This study examines the speaking style and sermon invention of television evangelists. Taking a sample of the sermons of Jimmy Swaggart, James Robison, W. A. Criswell, Jerry Falwell, Robert Schuller, and Howard C. Estep, Alexander analyzes each of them according to the Aristotelian categories of ethos, pathos, and logos. 361 pages.

[1004] Allen, Robert L. *The Use of Television in Wesley United Methodist Church, Oklahoma City, Oklahoma, as an Alternative to Current Religious Programming.* Diss. Drew University, 1983. *Dissertation Abstracts International* 44.4A (1984): 1107. Ann Arbor: UMI, 1983. 8318257.

This D. Min. professional project narrates how one church decided to make use of television as a part of its ministry and illustrates that decision with accounts of several televised services. Reacting strongly against the electronic church, Allen argues on theological grounds that pastoral presence in the community defines the church. He lists three assumptions for a valid broadcast ministry: an essential relationship to Christ, a supportive fellowship of the church, and a personal involvement in ministry. 140 pages.

[1005] Barton, Michael. "What a Friend They Have in Jesus." *Christian Century* 96 (September 19, 1979): 886-888.

Viewing Pat Robertson's "700 Club," Barton observed the personalized religious language—people are not born again, they "know the Lord." He attributes this to a cultural change in the United States, one correlated with the rise of electronic media. This personalism covers for the impersonal quality of the media; basically a good thing, it runs the risk of letting people turn to something else when religion becomes demanding. 3 pages.

[1006] Bechara, Assad. *Religious TV Spots: Guidelines for Developing a Mass Media and Follow-up Strategy.* Diss. Andrews University, Seventh-Day Adventist Theological Seminary, 1980. *Dissertation Abstracts International* 42.10A (1982): 4191. Ann Arbor: UMI, 1982. 8205789.

This thesis reports a study of religious television spots as part of a evangelical campaign in Brazil. After a review of the theological and technical literature, the author prepared a series of spots targeting youth; coupled with a media mix and face-to-face follow-up, the campaign showed some promise. 229 pages.

[1007] Berckman, Edward M. "'The Old-Time Gospel Hour' and Fundamentalist Paradox." *Christian Century* 95 (March 29, 1978): 333-337.

This examination of the Rev. Jerry Falwell's television ministry and theology concludes that its appeal "lies in its ability to maintain a precarious balance: to communicate the sense of a threatened minority holding on to the true faith in a collapsing world while, at the same time, vigorously presenting an image of success—a thriving, expanding institution using with skill society's most influential medium." 5 pages.

[1008] Bluem, A. William. *Religious Television Programs: A Study of Relevance.* New York: Hastings House, 1969.

Bluem reports a study of religious television programming in the United States for the years 1964-1966, providing descriptions of both national and local productions. He situates his discussion within the need for relevance of religious television to both audiences and broadcasters (given the then-current FCC regulations) and ends with guidelines for production planners. 220 pages.

[1009] Bluem, A. William, John F. Cox, and Gene McPherson. *Television in the Public Interest: Planning, Production, Performance.* New York: Hastings House, 1961.

This rather dated guide to producing public service programming gives a sketch of the basics of television: the structure of the local station, the roles of the production staff, program planning, preparation of materials, using film and videotape, and so forth. The guide's only connection with religious broadcasting comes in terms of the religious broadcaster's need to gain public service time. 192 pages.

[1010] Bromley, David G. and Anson Shupe, eds. *New Christian Politics.* Macon, GA: Mercer University Press, 1984.

One section of this collection of essays on the conservative political groups associated with Christian churches in the United States examines the relationship between the media and the fundamentalist Christian churches. Gary Gaddy reports on his investigation of audience estimates for religious radio and television and suggests new demographic correlations; Razelle Frankl examines the kinds of fund raising appeals made on religious programs while Wesley Miller proposes a model to aid the understanding of how the New Christian Right interacts with the U. S. press. Finally, Jeffrey Hadden analyzes the connections among television evangelists, the news media, and American politics. 300 pages.

[1011] Cardwell, Jerry Delmas. *Mass Media Christianity: Televangelism and the Great Commission.* Lanham, MD: University Press of America, 1984.

An attempt to place the rise of the North American television evangelists in a sociological perspective, this book mixes sociology, personal observation, and Biblical citation to give an uncritical and admiring picture of the group. 215 pages.

[1012] Cardwell, Jerry D. *A Rumor of Trumpets: The Return of God to Secular Society.* Lanham, MD: University Press of America, 1985.

One chapter of this general commentary on religion in America covers religious television. After a brief history of fundamentalist television broadcasting, Cardwell argues that it has led the way to a religious revival in the United States. 109 pages.

[1013] Chappuis, Jean-Marc. "Télévision et présence réelle." *Lumière et vie* 30.155 (octobre-novembre-décembre 1981): 88-100.

Combining cultural analysis with scriptural meditation, Chappuis examines the impact of television on the Church and the Gospel. He looks first at the television viewer to note how television itself has changed our way of regarding images, a development particularly visible through a contrast with classical painting. Next, Chappuis examines the notion of mediated "presence," asking whether a television viewer is a spectator or a participant in events. The Eucharist provides a focus for this latter part of his discussion. 13 pages.

[1014] Chevallier, Bernard. "L'information religieuse à la télévision." *Lumière et Vie* 30.155 (octobre-décembre 1981): 24-27.

From the perspective of a journalist covering religious news, the media now comes between people and their perception of the Church. It is to the reporter, rather than to the priest, that the people turn for information about the Church; the Church itself appears more often in the person of its leaders, as spectacle, as system, as image. The day-to-day experience of the Christian may well differ from this mediated image. 4 pages.

[1015] Diamond, Edwin. "God's Television." *American Film* 5 (1980): 30-35.

This journalistic piece provides a quick introduction to television evangelism in the United States. Diamond argues that two images dominate: the poor boy who made good and a no-apologies materialism. Moreover, the image of the church building has given way to the television studio. 6 pages.

[1016] Ellens, Jay Harold. *Program Format in Religious Television: A History and Analysis of Program Format in Nationally Distributed Denominational Religious Television Broadcasting in the United States of America, 1950-1970.* Diss. Wayne State University, 1970. *Dissertation Abstracts International* 32.1A (1972): 469. Ann Arbor: UMI, 1971. 7117263.

This thorough history of Protestant religious television argues that program formats have chiefly emerged out of economic, technological, and theological grounds. The author traces the changing national religious programs and notes in particular the use of tv spots and drama. While costs and available technology have influenced programming, a few churches make choices based on their theological understanding of the role of the church in society. 487 pages.

[1017] Elvy, Peter. *Buying Time: The Foundations of the Electronic Church.* Mystic, CN: Twenty-Third Publications, 1987; Great Wakering, England: McCrimmon Publishing, 1986.

This history of religious television broadcasting, told from a British perspective, traces the development of all the major issues and people in U. S. religious television. Elvy shows good balance in interviewing broadcasters and their critics and noting the activities of all the churches—mainline as well as evangelical. 160 pages.

[1018] Fishwick, Marshall W. and Ray B. Browne, eds. *The God Pumpers: Religion in the Electronic Age.* Bowling Green, OH: Bowling Green State University Popular Press, 1987.

The essays in this collection—intended as "probes" to stimulate research—present various approaches to the phenomenon of television evangelism in the United States. Some essays are frankly partisan while others show a more neutral attitude to the television evangelists. Topics include examinations of the wealth and the message of success of the preachers, profiles of various individual preachers (especially helpful here is the chapter on "electric sisters"—female evangelists), discussion of Christian rock music, and cartoon images of the evangelists. 196 pages.

[1019] Fore, William F. "The Electronic Church." *Ministry* 1 (January 1979): 4-7.

This essay, based on a presentation to the Seventh Day Adventist Broadcasters Council, acknowledges the role of the mass media and mass mediated religion in North American society, but questions whether the electronic church substitutes a false sense of community for the local church. While the mass media can contribute to evangelization, the local church must also play a central role, not only in religious matters but also in media education. 4 pages.

[1020] Fore, William F. *Television and Religion: The Shaping of Faith, Values, and Culture.* Minneapolis, MN: Augsburg Publishing House, 1987.

In this development of the themes of much of his writing, Fore argues that television "is beginning to usurp a role which until recently has been the role of the church in our society, namely, to shape our system of values, embody our faith, and express our cultural essence." The book examines the world of television, the relationship of the electronic church to the mainline churches, strategies for U. S. and world media, and a theology of communication. By defining communication as a process of establishing relationships, Fore suggests that communication ties in closely to Christianity and that Christianity can uniquely contribute to and criticize communication. 219 pages.

[1021] Fortner, Robert S. "Redeeming the Electronic Church." *The Reformed Journal* 34 (1984): 19-23.

This essay examines the notion of the power of television and the electronic church. Those who hold for a powerful-effects model of television often, consciously or not, follow McLuhan's anthropomorphism and technological determinism. Fortner finds both at odds with the Gospel because the Gospel cannot be less valued than the container (the medium) nor can communication technologies replace human contact. Finally, the power of television stems from its existence as a sales medium which denies personal choice; television evangelism unwittingly accepts both the sales mentality and the loss of choice. 5 pages.

[1022] Frankl, Razelle. *Televangelism: The Marketing of Popular Religion.* Carbondale, IL: Southern Illinois University Press, 1987.

This sociological study of religious broadcasting in the United States traces its origins to the phenomenon of urban revivalism in the nineteenth century (Charles Gandison Finney, Dwight Moody, and Billy Sunday). The modification of this tradition through its encounter with the television industry and its constraints leads to a new socio-religious institution which combines conservative philosophy, sophisticated formats, audience marketing, and revivalism. The book provides a good introduction to the historical and sociological background of the evangelical broadcasters; some (unfortunately dated) content analyses of program formats and fund raising techniques complete its picture of the electric church. 204 pages.

[1023] Gerbner, George, Larry Gross, Stewart Hoover, Michael Morgan, Nancy Signorielli, Harry E. Cotugno, The Gallup Organization, Inc., and Robert Wuthnow. "The Impact of the 'Electronic Church' on the Local Church." *Ministry* 2.4 (Fall 1984): 58-62.

This article reports the findings of a major study of religion and television done by the Annenberg School of Communication at the University of Pennsylvania and the Gallup Organization, at the request of the 1980 Consultation on the Electronic Church. Although the full findings have not been published (released only to the funding organizations), this executive summary indicates that the "audience for religious programs on television is not an essentially new, or young, or varied audience." The study also found no support for the charge that the electronic church takes away from the local church. However, the messages of the evangelical religious programs do conflict with those of the mainline churches. The article also reports other characterizations of program content and audience demographics. 5 pages.

[1024] Girardet, Giorgio. *Il Vangelo che viene dal video: le chiese e la tentazione dei mass-media.* Torino: Claudiana, 1980.

This book, written from an evangelical perspective, offers a critique of church uses of the media—both of the electronic Church in the U. S. and of the Papal use of television. It stresses the centrality of the Word of God and of Christ in any media effort and seeks to develop a religious discourse within the space of the mass media. 94 pages.

[1025] Goethals, Gregor. "Religious Communication and Popular Piety." *Journal of Communication* 35.1 (Winter 1985): 149-156.

Distinguishing denominational religion from civil religion, Goethals argues that the broadcast evangelists fall into the first group, both as heirs of the Reformation and as preachers of personal conversion. Ironically, though, they also serve a secular purpose in "baptizing" television which acts as a sacramental form for the civil religion—not only for religious programs but for cultural and civic events as well. 8 pages.

[1026] Goethals, Gregor. "TV Faith: Rituals of Secular Life." *Christian Century* 103 (April 23, 1986): 414-417.

Following H. Richard Niebhur, Goethals defines religion broadly as "human confidence in a certain conserver of value," and examines the art that helps to support that confidence. After the Reformation's limiting of art in the church, "the need to encounter invisible faith through visible forms" continued outside Protestant Christianity—largely in art. Where the 18th and 19th century artists saw themselves as religious, 20th century secularity has lost sight of this. Instead, we unconsciously re-create the symbols of transcendence in popular media. Television rituals, like the Superbowl and presidential inaugurals, parallel the Catholic sacramental models of art. Presidential press conferences imitate the Protestant evangelical model. 4 pages.

[1027] Graham, Billy. "TV Evangelism: Billy Graham Sees Dangers Ahead." *TV Guide* 31.10 (March 5, 1983): 5-8.

Television does alter its content and it has had a subtle effect on the television evangelists. As costs rise, they ask more often for funds (an abuse of their preaching) instead of examining whether their show should continue as is. Religious news reporting and commentary can give a personal religious perspective but must clearly be labelled as such; the Bible does not address every topic. 4 pages.

[1028] Gritti, Jules. *Télévision et conscience chrétienne.* Toulouse: Edouard Privat, 1963.

This general introduction to television consists of three parts: a survey of the social and economic structures of television in France (contrasted with those of other countries); a look at program types and at the "language" of television; and an examination of issues that touch the audience (family life, education, religious use of television). Gritti relies somewhat on Catholic statements about the arts, but much of the book works just as well as a commentary on the cultural impact of television. It seems almost a "media-education" book several years ahead of its time. 158 pages.

[1029] Hadden, Jeffrey K. "Soul-Saving via Video." *Christian Century* 97.20 (May 28, 1980): 609-613.

This article briefly sets out the history and the major issues raised by the advent of the major television evangelists. Arguing that the technology of television suits the evangelical theological stance towards proselytizing, Hadden points out as well that the cultural climate in the United States of the 1980's also favors this kind of religious outlook. The concerns raised by their critics include the effects of the television ministries on local congregations, their effects on the wider culture and political arena, their methods of fund raising, and the effects of television itself on theology and church. 5 pages.

[1030] Hadden, Jeffrey K. "Televangelism and the New Christian Right." *Religion and Religiosity in America: Studies in Honor of Joseph H. Fichter.* Jeffrey K. Hadden and Theodore E. Long, eds. New York: Crossroad, 1983. 114-127.

This essay sketches the rise to power of the television evangelists. Hadden attributes this rise to three factors: the ability of the television evangelists to exploit discontent in America in the name of Christian virtue; their use of television as a mass communication medium; and their mastery of the ancillary technology of television, particularly the direct mail computer process. 168 pages.

[1031] Hadden, Jeffrey, et al. "Analyses of Religious Television." *Review of Religious Research.* 29.2 (1987).

This special issue features articles which closely examine the Religion and Television Research project in depth. Jeffrey Hadden and Razelle Frankl ("Star Wars of a Different Kind," and "A Critical Review of the Religion and Television Research Report") criticize the report for muddled planning, conflicting interests among its sponsors, poor data interpretation, and poor writing. Robert Wuthnow ("The Social Significance of Religious Television") and Stewart Hoover ("The Religious Television Audience: A Matter of Significance or Size?") offer secondary interpretations of the data from the study. Finally Robert Abelman and Kimberly Neuendorf provide several studies based on independent content analyses of religious television. This collection has great value because the sponsors have not made the original project reports public. 114 pages.

[1032] Haiven, Judith. *Faith, Hope, No Charity: An Inside Look at the Born Again Movement in Canada and the United States.* Vancouver: New Star Books, 1984.

Haiven, a Canadian journalist, examines the world of the television evangelists, alternating between those working in Canada and those working in the United States. While trying to present a balanced picture, many of the anecdotes and testimonies tend to be highly critical of the movement. The material on David Mainse, the host of *100 Huntley Street*, provides a look at the Canadian electronic church and shows its similarities to and differences from its counterparts in the United States. 221 pages.

[1033] Heinze, Peter. *Air-Care: A Feasibility Study in Television Ministry.* London: World Association for Christian Communication, 1982.

This is a report on the possibilities of a televised pastoral ministry for Britain, using a series of centers throughout the country where those in need of counseling and touched by religious broadcasting could phone in or drop in. It envisions a Christian community mediated through television. 45 pages.

[1034] Hilton, Clifford Thomas. *The Influence of Television Worship Services on the Irvington Presbyterian Church, Indianapolis, Indiana.* Diss. Drew University, 1980. *Dissertation Abstracts International* 41.4A (1981): 1648. Ann Arbor: UMI, 1980. 8023785.

Situated within the problematic of the electronic church, this study examines the influence of televised worship services on a particular local congregation; this influence turned out to be much less than the author had expected. The survey and monitoring reports seem somewhat unsophisticated and the reporting style is definitely autobiographical since the study forms part of a D. Min. project. 127 pages.

[1035] Holahan, John C. "Morality for Television." *Ave Maria* 83.17 (April 28, 1956): 12-15, 29.

This interview with Fr. Timothy J. Flynn, communication director for the Archdiocese of New York, addresses questions of rating television shows, much as the Catholic Legion of Decency rated films. Flynn sees that as unrealistic, given the nature of television although he feels that some kind of moral oversight of television is needed. While denying that such work falls to the government, he encourages more active roles for audience members, such as writing to stations. This is very much a piece of the 50's in outlook. 5 pages.

[1036] Hoover, Stuart Mark. *The 700 Club as Religion and as Television: A Study of Reasons and Effects.* Diss. University of Pennsylvania, 1985.

Dissertation Abstracts International 46.5A (1986): 1118. Ann Arbor: UMI, 1985. 8515389.

A detailed study of the audience of one program of the Electronic Church, this dissertation provides an overview of the research into the Electronic Church and examines the components of several research paradigms. Among the findings of this investigation are (1) that the relationship of audience members to the 700 Club is a highly complex one, mediated by previous religious experience, social experience, and current life situation; (2) that watching the program is perceived as different from other television viewing and as an inherently religious activity; and (3) that the 700 Club provides an experience of translocal confirmation for the audience's religious outlook. 428 pages.

[1037] Horsfield, Peter G. "'And Now a Word from our Sponsor': Religious Programs on American Television." *Revue Française d'Études Americaines* 6 (October 1981): 259-274.

After a brief history of religious broadcasting and the relevant FCC policies, this article outlines some factors which account for the popularity of evangelical religious programming (theological, social, technical). It then raises questions regarding the "behavioral effectiveness" of such programming. 16 pages.

[1038] Horsfield, Peter G. *Religious Television: The American Experience.* New York: Longman, 1984.

In this re-working of his dissertation for Boston University, Horsfield presents an excellent introduction to the study of religious television. In his first part he traces the history of the religious broadcasters from the beginning of television service in the United States, noting especially the personalities involved and the controversies spawned within the churches. The second part reviews research in religious television; chapters include the research tradition, the effects of paid-time programming, the size of the audience, audience characteristics, attitude change, relations with the local church, and relations with American culture. The final section extrapolates trends and suggests a strategy for the religious use of television. The book also includes a bibliography. 197 pages.

[1039] Independent Broadcasting Authority. *The Structure and Pattern of Religious Television Now: Report of an IBA Consultation.* London: Independent Broadcasting Authority, 1973.

The report and papers from the 1973 IBA consultation on religious television, this describes the fifth such conference sponsored by the IBA and reviews in some depth religious programming in Britain and possible new approaches, particularly with the end of "reserved" times for religious programs on the BBC and ITV. 127 pages.

[1040] Independent Broadcasting Authority. *The End of a Road: Report of the Seventh IBA Religious Consultation.* London: Independent Broadcasting Authority, 1983.

This IBA consultation examines in detail the U. S. experience of the electronic church with an eye to the British situation, particularly to satellite and cable television. Particularly good is a paper by journalist Clifford Longley which calls for theologians to find a new metaphysical language in order to discuss the mediated reality of broadcasting and its religious implications. To illustrate his point he examines the theology and ecclesiology of the Pope's (mostly televised) visit to Britain. 96 pages.

[1041] Independent Television Authority. *Religion in Television.* London: Independent Television Authority, 1964.

These acts of a meeting between religious television producers and advisers for the British Independent Television foreshadow much later discussion of televising religious programs: what kinds of religious programs should be aired? How can the churches use television? How best communicate with contemporary people? What is the role of myth and symbol? 76 pages.

[1042] Jordan, Noel. "Religion and Television." *Religion in Life* 31.1 (Winter, 1961-62): 108-117.

Mass media promote an "other-direction" in their viewers—a looking to the group for guidance in establishing values and behaviors—and at the same time narcotize the viewers to the world. The church enters this picture when it attempts to broadcast and faces the paradox of trying to free people through the very thing that enslaves them, of trying to communicate when the television professionals would substitute technique. The church should stand opposed to this even in the face of the fear of opposition, offending, and lack of skill. 10 pages.

[1043] Keckley, Paul H., Jr. *A Qualitative Analytic Study of the Image of Organized Religion in Prime Time Television Drama.* Diss. The Ohio State University, 1974. *Dissertation Abstracts International* 35.8A (1975): 5438. Ann Arbor: UMI, 1975. 753111.

Based on a content analysis of 44 prime time shows in a one week sample, this study concludes that religion does indeed appear in television programming, but in either a structural way (in terms of images or buildings) or as an inconsequential aspect of the character's lives. 198 pages.

[1044] Kelly, Francis D., ed. *Media & Catechetics Today: Towards the Year 2000.* [Washington, D.C.]: National Conference of Directors of Religious Education, National Catholic Educational Assocation, n.d.

This collection of five essays or case studies examines the possibilities of television in Catholic religious education. Although the work is dated, the reports of Angela Zukowski (on cable television) and James Hawker (on the moral evaluation of broadcast television) are good. 24 pages.

[1045] Kennedy, Bernard. "The Influence of TV and Videos on the Home." *Australasian Catholic Record* 61 (1984): 219-231.

This is a survey of reports and observations on the influence of television and videos on children by a priest radio talkback host. 13 pages.

[1046] Kieser, Ellwood. "Evangelization Through Electronics." *America* 138 (May 6, 1978): 358-361.

Given that 80 million Americans fall into the unchurched category, the Catholic Church needs to foster missionary outreach and can do this only through a renewed sense of lay evangelization and through the use of the mass media. Television has four advantages here: (1) it is a story-telling medium; (2) it is an experiential medium; (3) it can communicate in the privacy of the home; and (4) it is a mass medium. To use television for evangelization the Church should follow these principles: (1) Preaching the Gospel differs from doing public relations for the Church; (2) all Church activity in the media should reflect an incarnational orientation and be profoundly humanistic; (3) collaborate with those who are committed to the welfare of the human family; (4) be explicit at times and implicit at others; (5) choose different formats to reach different audiences; (6) don't settle for Sunday morning time slots. Funded media strategies should include research, training, pastoral care of communication professionals, collaboration with communicators, television awareness training, advocacy with the FCC, and so forth. 4 pages.

[1047] Krohn, Franklin B. "The Sixty-Minute Commercial: Marketing Salvation." *The Humanist* 40.6 (November/December 1980): 26-31, 60.

This article examines television evangelism in the United States from the perspective of marketing's five functions: market segmentation, product development, pricing, distribution, and sale promotion. Those who criticize the television preachers would do well to look to legislation designed to control commercial businesses, since these laws apply primarily to marketing and might force a re-evaluation of the practices of these preachers. 7 pages.

[1048] Kuhns, William. *The Electronic Gospel: Religion and Media.* New York: Herder and Herder, 1969.

Kuhns sets out to explore parallels between religion and the entertainment media, calling attention to the religious and the entertainment milieux, each of which provides a context for and serves specific functions for human beings. Kuhns provides an excellent cultural analysis of the entertainment media in part two where he examines the functional equivalence of the two milieux in terms of time, hero, presiding over community, moral leadership, ritual, magic, and faith. However, his more specific analysis of the "terrain" of fantasy and its new theological possibilities appears dated, uneven, and overly optimistic, an optimism he derives from Marshall McLuhan. 173 pages.

[1049] Lloyd, Mark Lewis. *A Descriptive Analysis of the Syndicated Religious Television Programs of Jerry Falwell, Rex Humbard, and Oral Roberts.* Diss. The University of Michigan, 1980. *Dissertation Abstracts International* 41.5A (1981): 1822. Ann Arbor: UMI, 1980. 8025718.

This study provides a brief history of each of the evangelists before focusing on its primarily interest: the technical details of program production. The author presents much of the material in tabular form or as primary sources in appendices, with little interpretation, however. Each chapter also contains background on finances, program format, and production personnel and policies. 1038 pages.

[1050] Meyer, Hans Bernhard. "Gottesdienst in audiovisuellen Medien." *Zeitschrift für katholische Theologie* 107 (1985): 415-438.

Meyer seeks a middle position between an uncritical acceptance of media use by the Church and an all-out criticism. He focuses on the case of the televised Mass, beginning with an exploration of the character of the Mass and its possible treatment as an object. He offers next a treatment of the audiovisual means of communication, noting their characteristics and limitations. Finally he argues several theses, including that audiovisuals can give rise to a religious act and can lead to understanding. However, after this discussion, Meyer concludes that he would rather not allow the televising of the Eucharist. 24 pages.

[1051] Morris, Colin. *God in a Box: Christian Strategy in the Television Age.* London: Hodder and Stoughton, 1984.

This delightfully written book sets out to accomplish three things: to introduce the world of television (following the general line of McLuhan); to examine religious television, particularly on the British model; and to explore Christian strategies in the television age. The last section provides a nice synthesis of several approaches to communication and religion (including those of McLuhan, Goethals, Granfield, Dulles, Dillistone, Hamelink, Wilder, and TeSelle); it also provides a sane warning not to lock television into any unidimensional understanding. 238 pages.

[1052] Mylott, Kenneth J. "Unplugging the Electronic 'Church.'" *Lutheran Forum* 20.1 (Lent 1986): 14-15.

Mylott argues that the electronic church does not meet the minimum requirements for a church since it neither teaches nor evangelizes. Its hosts

lack the preparation to teach and possess a suspicion of scholarly or hierarchical authority. They do not evangelize since they preach a gospel of
success and ease. In sum, Mylott argues, they criticize secularism but in
fact are a product of that same secularism. 2 pages.

[1053] Owens, Virginia Stem. *The Total Image: Or Selling Jesus.* Grand
Rapids, MI: Eerdmans, 1980.

Owens argues that Christians today, tempted by the success of the mass
media, project an image of Christ and try to sell Jesus rather than encourage the spirit of Jesus within them. She sets out to free the audience from
the notion that evangelism is an advertising campaign; instead it should
begin with a simple awareness of God's presence and grow from there. 97
pages.

[1054] Parker, Everett C. "Christian Perspective on Mass Communication." *Social Action* 24.8 (April 1958): 3-9.

After sketching the situation of television in the late 1950's, Parker urges
the churches to live up to their responsibilities to help set minimal aesthetic
standards for the media. Rejecting the Catholic approach of the Legion of
Decency as harmful to art, he espouses instead the development of voluntary criteria that bear some recognizable relationship to Christianity;
further, he urges that the churches strongly raise their voices to awaken
consciences to those criteria. 7 pages.

[1055] Parker, Everett C. *Religious Television: What to Do and How.* New
York: Harper & Brothers, 1961.

According to its introduction, "this book is a manual which presents a
theory and practical methods for employing television for a ministry to the
whole public, and for applying the moral principles of the Judeo-Christian
tradition to the secular aspects of television broadcasting." While much
of the book presents basic information about television production, two
chapters cover Christian perspectives on mass communication. The first of
these reviews Protestant strategies for television and suggest some further
reflections for additional planning. The latter chapter encourages people as
individuals and as church bodies to take a more active role in changing or
challenging the way the communication industry affects society. The FCC
provides a case study here. 244 pages.

[1056] Proctor, William Henry. *Herald of Truth: A Study of Religious Television Program Format Changes From 1954-1979.* Diss. The University
of Mississippi, 1980. *Dissertation Abstracts International* 41.11A (1981):
4621. Ann Arbor: UMI, 1981. 8108767.

Based on an historical examination of the "Herald of Truth" television
program produced by the Highland Church of Christ in Abilene, Texas,

this study concludes that the program format has changed over to years in response to the program objectives proposed by church leadership, to shifting audience tastes, to economic factors, and to developments in broadcast technology. The last factor accounts for the greatest amount of change in format. Effectiveness of format change was measured by the number of stations carrying the program and the Arbitron audience ratings for the program. 134 pages.

[1057] Quebedeaux, Richard. *By What Authority: The Rise of Personality Cults in American Christianity.* San Francisco: Harper & Row, 1982.

In this overview of popular religion in the United States, Quebedeaux focuses on the leading members of the electronic church, giving their cultural and personal backgrounds and a sketch of the religious values they represent. The book also includes some more analytic material on religious authority and its varieties in U.S. culture. 204 pages.

[1058] Ryan, Francis J. "Catholic Television Network in the USA." *Multimedia International* 1st ser. 17 (1975).

This short monograph presents a history and overview of the use of the Instructional Television Fixed Service (a microwave television broadcast system for educational uses) by 10 dioceses in the United States. A brief profile of each participating diocesan program is given: size, cost, programming, uses and potential uses. 18 pages.

[1059] Schmid, Gerhard. "Zur rhetorischen Analyse der kirchlichen Fernsehsendungen 'Das Wort zum Sonntag.'" Dissertation: München, 1971.

This dissertation examines the television program "The Word for Sunday" from the perspective of rhetoric. 351 pages.

[1060] Schmid, H. Giles. *Diocesan Learning Networks: Alternatives and Opportunities in Instructional Television.* Washington, D. C.: U. S. Catholic Conference, 1971.

This report suggests ways in which the Catholic Church can use various distribution networks and practices (from bicycling tapes to ITFS systems) to support educational television in its dioceses. While somewhat dated technically, the basic concepts still obtain and the idea checklists still have value. 53 pages.

[1061] Schmitz, Charles H. *Religious Television Program Ideas.* New York: Broadcasting and Film Commission, National Council of the Churches of Christ in the U. S. A., 1953.

Written in the early years of television broadcasting and claiming that "there are no experts in television," this booklet suggests programming ideas for local production. The ideas include shows dealing with counseling, music, demonstrations, news, devotions, panel discussions, dramatic presentations, quizzes, interviews, and general interest. For each idea the booklet lists a title, the purpose of the show, the visual treatment, and the audio treatment. While certainly dated, the booklet may inspire more contemporary ideas or help to start a brainstorming session. 24 pages.

[1062] Schultze, Quentin J. "Vindicating the Electronic Church? An Assessment of the Annenberg-Gallup Study." *Critical Studies in Mass Communication* 2 (1985): 283-290.

In reviewing the Annenberg-Gallup "Religion and Television" research report, Schultze summarizes its history and methods and argues that "the theoretical, methodological, and ideological commitments of Annenberg influenced the research from the beginning." He claims, further, that important questions remain unanswered and that other research methods might be more appropriate to the subject. 8 pages.

[1063] Shayon, Robert Lewis. "The Church and TV—Face to Face." *Social Action* 24.8 (April 1958): 10-15.

Urging the Protestant churches to take a more active role in promoting serious television programs, Shayon suggests that they foster an active audience through the sponsoring of face-to-face discussions about programs. "Attitudes," he writes, "like the Eucharist, need to be shared." 6 pages.

[1064] Sims, Patsy. *Can Somebody Shout Amen!* New York: St. Martin's Press, 1988.

This journalistic exploration of religious revivalism in the United States focuses not so much on the television evangelists as on the travelling revivalists. The one exception is television preacher Ernest Angley. All the figures interviewed and observed fall into the tradition of Dwight L. Moody and Billy Sunday. Sims attempts to present an objective picture, letting characters speak for themselves and the readers decide for themselves. 234 pages.

[1065] Spargur, Ronn. "Can Churches Break the Prime Time Barrier?" *Christianity Today* 14 (January 16, 1970): 339-340.

This brief article advocates a proposal that churches produce prime time programming for television and that the networks treat these offerings in the same way that they treat any pilots: consider them on their merits. Spargur further proposes that spiritual programming be aired at the same time on all channels so viewers can't unfairly compare it to entertainment, that it be financially supported by advertising, and that it follow a dramatic format. 2 pages.

[1066] Stauffer, David D. *Description and Analysis of the Historical Development and Management Practices of the Independent Christian Church Religious Television Program Syndicators.* Diss. Ohio University, 1972. *Dissertation Abstracts International* 33.11A 6386. Ann Arbor: UMI, 1973. 7312652.

Basically a case study of two small syndicators associated with the Independent Christian Church, this dissertation provides a history of the denomination and of the syndicators and then reports questionnaire answers regarding budgeting, production, and distribution practices. The study is limited by its lack of verification and by its lack of detail. 257 pages.

[1067] Steel, William Edward. *A Survey of Religious Television Broadcasting in the Los Angeles Metropolitan Area and Proposals for Change: New Strategies for Mainline Churches.* Diss. School of Theology at Claremont, 1979. *Dissertation Abstracts International* 40.3A (1980): 1138. Ann Arbor: UMI, 1979. 7919930.

This study, somewhat polemic in tone, details the final years of the Religion in Media Association and the attempts of the mainline Protestant churches to recover control of their organization from the more evangelical broadcasters in the Los Angeles area in the late 1970's. The study has added value for its primary historical materials. 198 pages.

[1068] Taylor, James A. "Progeny of Programmers: Evangelical Religion and the Television Age." *The Christian Century* 94 (April 20, 1977): 379-382.

Working from a cultural analysis of the differences between print and television, Taylor argues that the boom in evangelical church membership comes as a result of television—not religious television but ordinary television. Day-to-day television programming emphasizes a caring circle that excludes non-members; it values a conversion experience rather than change by growth; it highlights the individual not society; it offers action rather than reflection. Each of these correlates with an evangelical outlook—an outlook which Taylor claims has grown from its cultivation by television just as Protestantism grew from the development of the printing press. 4 pages.

[1069] Thomas, Sari. "The Route to Redemption: Religion and Social Class." *Journal of Communication* 35.1 (Winter 1985): 111-122.

"A content analysis of religious TV programming shows that Protestant religious teaching varies along class lines of its intended audience and rationalizes respective class positions." The major themes occurring on the programs included redemption, afterlife, acquisition of material goods, money, prayer, and the secular world. Programs directed to higher socio- economic groups appeared more accepting of worldly achievement and material acquisition. 12 pages.

[1070] Trampiets, Frances M. "Religious Television Programming—Can It Work? Communication Research Sheds Some Light on the Question." *Unda-USA White Paper* [Dayton, OH:] Unda-USA, 1986.

This paper is a brief overview, written in a journalistic style, of research findings in the uses and gratifications studies, in the functional approaches to communication, and in persuasion studies. Each area is applied to religious television and the author argues that church communication must attempt to fit into the dominant model of television in the U. S. — entertainment and information. 6 pages.

[1071] Vogt, Gerburg Elisabeth. *Kirche und Fernsehenstalten: Entwicklungen, Konzepte, Programmrealisierungen.* Osnabrück: Verlag A. Fromm, 1978.

This study traces the history of Catholic Church radio and television broadcasting in Germany from its beginnings through its reorganization in the Bundesrepublik. The second part of the study examines the programming of the Church, their production structures, and production techniques. A very exact study of all aspects, it also includes a lengthy bibliography. 349 pages.

[1072] Walsh, Richard J. "Broadcasting and Christian Responsibility: Radio and Television in the United States." *Twentieth Century Catholicism.* Vol. 3. Ed. Lancelot Sheppard. New York: Hawthorn Books, 1966. 58-73.

This article, by a radio and television producer for the National Council of Catholic Men, sketches the major religious programming of the Catholic Church, that is, the programming produced for network broadcast. After this review, Walsh offers a brief defense of the programming policy and notes some developments in the wake of the Second Vatican Council. 16 pages.

[1073] Willaime, Jean-Paul. "Vers les chrétiens électroniques." *Lumière et vie* 30.155 (octobre-novembre-décembre 1981): 56-69.

Asking how the development of the media has influenced the nature of religion, Willaime turns to the historical example of the Reformation and its attendant emphasis on the book. This privatization corresponded with a growth in the social presence of the church. Television causes a similar shift in social practice; research from the electronic church in the United States is added to a survey of French Protestantism in an analysis of the impact of televised religion on the identification of individuals with a church. 14 pages.

[1074] Yancy, Philip. "The Ironies and Impact of PTL." *Christianity Today* 23 (21 January 1979): 1249-1254.

This article describes the ministry of Jim Bakker and the PTL Club, noting its financial difficulties as well as its successes. Overall, though, the tone is negative and questioning of the electronic church on the grounds of bad theology and impersonal Christianity. 6 pages.

Periodicals which run articles on religious television include [9], [22], [27], [31], [38], [42], [50]. Other bibliographic sources for materials on Christian television are [60], [62], [63], [65]. Station and personnel directories may be found in [80], [87], and [89]. Some commentaries on the religious use of television are [274], [301], [302], [311], [319], [323], [324], and [325]. Several books deal with media education for a Christian use of television: [341], [344], [345], and [346]. Finally, some historical references appear in [375], [376], [377], [378], and [417].

Audience Studies

[1075] Abelman, Robert. "Religious Television Uses and Gratifications." *Journal of Broadcasting & Electronic Media* 31.3 (Summer 1987): 293-307.

Reporting a study of heavy viewers of religious television programs, Abelman notes in particular their viewing motives. Not only did this investigation support previous studies, it also noted the ritual use of religious television (to watch the programming as an expression of religiosity) and a reactionary use of religious television (to watch religious television out of dissatisfaction with commercial television). 15 pages.

[1076] Abelman, Robert. "The Impact of the PTL Scandal on Religious Television Viewers." *Journal of Communication and Religion* 11 (1988): 41-51.

Based on earlier research, viewers of the PTL fall into three groups: ritualized (habitual) viewers, instrumental (news- seeking) viewers, and reactionary (curious) viewers. Each group responded to the scandal in the ministry in a different way: the former shows an increase in perceived credibility and importance; the middle group, a decrease in both; and the last group, an increase in perceived personal importance. The research clearly supports the claim that the religious audience seeks a variety of gratifications from their membership in the electronic church. 11 pages.

[1077] Abrams, Michael Elliot. *Religious Broadcasting: A Q-Methodological Study of Elderly Audience.* Diss. University of Missouri, 1981. *Dissertation Abstracts International* 43.1A (1983): 7. Ann Arbor, UMI: 1982. 8213819.

This dissertation combines three approaches to the study of the electronic church: an historical one, a uses-and-gratifications one, and a functional one. While the first two provide a solid look at the phenomenon as it developed, the third gives a different view of the audience. The Q-method allows for audience reactions and their measurement and on this basis suggests a fourfold classification of audience members: the "simple pietic, the moralist, the prophet, and the electrified mystic." 288 pages.

[1078] Armstrong, Ben. "Does the Electric Church Hurt the Local Church?" *Religious Broadcasting* 11.3 (June-July 1979): 19-20, 40-43.

The 1979 Gallup Report, "The Unchurched American," indicates that the unchurched do listen to broadcast religion. Armstrong claims that there is a correlation between evangelical broadcasting and local church growth but cites no specific evidence. 6 pages.

[1079] Bourgault, Louise M. *An Ethnographic Study of the "Praise the Lord Club."* Diss. Ohio University, 1980. *Dissertation Abstracts International* 41.11A (1981): 4530. Ann Arbor: UMI, 1981. 8110489.

In this dissertation the author argues that the "PTL Club" television program works as a socially integrating mechanism to link the religious and social worlds of contemporary U. S. culture. The program accomplishes this linkage through its format and style as well as through the creation of "empathy mechanisms"—content features which promote viewer identification with the program performers and their religious world view. The study includes historical background on religious revivals, sociological analysis of the electronic church, and a content analysis of the program. The value of the study lies not so much in its specific analysis of the "PTL Club" but in its theoretical scope which offers an understanding of the role of religious broadcasting in the lives of its viewers. 378 pages.

[1080] Bourgault, Louis M. "The 'PTL Club' and Protestant Viewers: An Ethnographic Study." *Journal of Communication* 35.1 (Winter 1985): 132-148.

This qualitative study of PTL viewers indicates that religious preference does not always predict viewership nor does viewership always follow socioeconomic or educational status. The more moderate among Fundamentalists form the group which would more likely view the program since some religious groups ban television watching altogether. Finally, many of this group watch the programs as alternative entertainment forms rather than for purely religious content. 17 pages.

[1081] Bourgault, Louise. "The 'Jim Bakker Show': The Program, Its Viewers and Their Churches." *Journal of Communication and Religion* 11 (1988): 32-40.

Based on in-depth interviews with program followers, this study investigates the interaction of the "Jim Bakker Show" with the lives of its viewers and its effects on the religious groups to which they belong. The program combined a fundamentalist tone with a modern lifestyle and provided either religious entertainment or religious inspiration for its viewers. Further, as a bridge program (between fundamentalists and modernity), it promoted tolerance among the fundamentalists and moved some mainline Protestants to a more fundamentalist style. 9 pages.

[1082] Buddenbaum, Judith M. "Characteristics and Media-Related Needs of the Audience for Religious TV." *Journalism Quarterly* 58 (1981): 266-272.

Reporting a 1978 study of the religious television audience in Indianapolis, Buddenbaum finds the same general demographic characteristics as found by other studies: viewers tend to be older, female, less educated, and with lower incomes. She also found weak support for the hypothesis that the religious television audience forms a subset of the general television audience, watching religious television not for entertainment but in order to fulfill the personal needs of self-knowledge and avoidance of loneliness. 7 pages.

[1083] Casmir, Fred L. "A Telephone Survey of Religious Program Preferences Among Listeners and Viewers in Los Angeles." *Central States Speech Journal* 10.3 (Spring 1959): 31-38.

This reports a survey which profiles the typical listener/viewer of religious programs in Los Angeles in the late 1950's. Unfortunately, the sampling seems skewed; however, the data appear typical of other, similar, surveys. Religious program audiences consist mostly of those who attend religious services; thus these programs are not very effective in reaching those people who do not attend church services. 8 pages.

[1084] Chenhwang, Edward Yih-Min. *Thematic Content Analysis as an Approach to Prediction of Audience Receptivity of Religious Radio Programs, With a Demographic Analysis of Program Preference.* Diss. Michigan State University, 1974. *Dissertation Abstracts International* 35.3A (1975): 1683. Ann Arbor: UMI, 1974. 7419794.

This study attempts to correlate themes of religious programming with audience receptivity, based on a study of one station's programming. It found a negative correlation between audience receptivity and evangelical themes (revelation, prophecy, eternity, and last judgment) but a positive one between topics of God-man relations and human relations. The dissertation is stronger on developing a method than on establishing hard data. 492 pages.

[1085] Gaddy, Gary D. "The Power of the Religious Media: Religious Broadcast Use and the Role of Religious Organizations in Public Affairs." *Review of Religious Research* 25 (June 1984): 289-302.

This article reports a study which indicates that "thinking religious organizations should be more active in public affairs leads, to a small degree, to watching or listening to religious broadcasts." However, the effect does not go in the opposite direction: watching religious television does not lead one to hold that the churches should be more active in political affairs. 13 pages.

[1086] Gaddy, Gary D. and David Pritchard. "When Watching Religious TV is Like Attending Church." *Journal of Communication* 35.1 (Winter 1985): 123-131.

Based on a secondary analysis of information gathered in a 1983 nationwide Gallup survey for *Christianity Today* magazine, the authors conclude that the more people watched religious television, the less frequently they attended church. The functional similarity between the two activities accounts for greatest amount of statistical variance in the analysis. 9 pages.

[1087] Independent Broadcasting Authority. *Lonely People and the Media: Report on a Study*. London: Independent Broadcasting Authority, 1978.

An audience study commissioned by Britain's IBA, this research measures the extent to which lonely people use the media and, more specifically, the extent to which they use religious broadcasting. There is empirical support for the use of television by the lonely and for the use of religious television by the already religious. 50 pages.

[1088] Johnson, Stuart P. *Contemporary Communications Theory and the Distribution Patterns of Evangelical Radio Programs*. Diss. Northwestern University, 1978. *Dissertation Abstracts International* 39.10A (1979): 5785. Ann Arbor: UMI, 1978.

This investigation of the audiences for evangelical radio situates a survey of evangelical programs and the stations which carry them within a context of communication theory and the broadcasters' lack of knowledge of both that theory and of the actual demographics of the audience. The survey information itself is rich in detail (about stations, markets, and audience size) and the attitudes toward communication theory among program producers is surprising. 225 pages.

[1089] Johnstone, Ronald L. "Who Listens to Religious Radio Broadcasts Anymore?" *Journal of Broadcasting* 16.1 (Winter 1971-1972): 91-102.

About half the population occasionally listens to religious radio; this audience consists primarily of older, generally Protestant church-goers who did

not complete high school. The farther away from urban centers the respondents were, the more likely they were to listen. Findings for the Lutheran
Hour listeners did not differ greatly from those of the overall sample. Johnstone suggests that religious radio tends to serve as a reinforcement to those
who have religious associations. 12 pages.

[1090] Martin, William. "Television: The Birth of a Media Myth." *Atlantic
Monthly* 247.6 (June 1981): 7-16.

Based on a review of audience data, Martin challenges what he calls the
inflated audience figures of the electric church. Where Armstrong [888]
claims a total audience of 130 million, Martin suggests that 13 million is
more accurate. 9 pages.

[1091] Parker, Everett C., David W. Barry, and Dallas W. Smythe. *The
Television-Radio Audience and Religion*. New York: Harper & Brothers,
Publishers, 1955.

This now classic study of the religious radio and television audience in New
Haven, Connecticut situates the broadcasts within the social history and
demographics of the city. After examining religious programming though
content analysis, the team measures the overall audience for religious broadcasting and then the audiences for specific programs, both in general and
through qualitative methods. After review of their data from interviews
with non-viewers, they conclude with a strategy for religious broadcasting.
Among their recommendations are that the churches should understand
the nature of their real audiences; that the churches should understand
the total role of the mass media in the lives of their constituents; that
the churches should consider a greater variety of audiences and audience
needs in program planning; and that religious agencies should conduct a
continuous and systematic research in this general field. 464 pages.

[1092] Potel, Julien. *Les Mass-media: presse, radio, cinéma, télévision,
publicité ce qu'en pensent prêtres et religieuses, résultats de l'enquête
préparatoire au Congrès de Strasbourg (1969), Moyen de communication
de masse*. Paris: Editions Fleurus, 1969.

This volume reports on a 1968 survey of priests and religious in France
regarding their use of and attitudes towards the media of social communication. Use of media did not differ from the population at large in terms
of time or medium but did differ in terms of type of program or material.
The survey also reported preferences for religious communication content.
Prepared as a background study for the 1969 Congress of Strasbourg, the
report presents mostly raw data, without much analysis. The author notes
that the results would have varied greatly had the survey taken place after
the events of May 1968. 172 pages.

[1093] Ringe, Robert C. *An Analysis of Selected Personality and Behavioral Characteristics which Affect Receptivity to Religious Broadcasting.* Diss. Ohio State University, 1969. *Dissertation Abstracts International* 30.6A (1970): 2655. Ann Arbor: UMI, 1969. 6922197.

This dissertation reports the results of an audience study, focused on personality characteristics, like devotional commitment, degree of orthodoxy, and degree of openmindedness. Little relationship among these variables appeared in the analysis of data from the religious broadcasting audience. 196 pages.

[1094] Robinson, Haddon W. "The Audience for Religious Broadcasts in the United States." *Bibliotheca Sacra* 123 (1966): 67-72.

This report of an audience survey conducted in 1962 indicates that listening to religious radio or television programming correlates positively with age and active church participation and negatively with income and presumably education. In addition Protestants were more likely to listen than were Catholics or Jews. Audience members also showed a preference for nonpreaching program formats (eg, drama, music, and so forth). 6 pages.

[1095] Rockenstein, Walter Harrison. *Children and Religious Television: An Experimental Study of the Reactions of Children in the 5th, 6th, 7th and 8th Grades in Monongalia County, West Virginia, to Children's Religious Television Programming.* Diss. Northwestern University, 1966. *Dissertation Abstracts International* 27.7A (1967): 2217. Ann Arbor: UMI, 1966. 6614054.

This study measured the before-and-after-viewing information and attitudes of children to a specific set of religious programs. Those children who viewed the programs in a school setting (versus a home setting) retained more information, and accepted more attitudes from the programs; similar findings held for churched versus non-churched children and for Protestant versus Catholic children. 629 pages.

[1096] Solt, David C. *A Study of the Audience Profile for Religious Broadcasts in Onondaga County.* Diss. Syracuse University, 1971. *Dissertation Abstracts International* 32.3A (1972): 1544. Ann Arbor, UMI, 1971. 7123470.

This dissertation reports a small audience study, noting that listeners to religious broadcasting tend to be active church members; income, and education are negatively correlated with listening, while age and Protestantism and Bible reading are positively correlated. 103 pages.

[1097] Stacey, William and Anson Shupe. "Correlates of Support for the Electronic Church." *Journal for the Scientific Study of Religion* 21 (1982): 291-303.

Reporting a survey of white homeowners in the Dallas-Fort Worth area, the researchers found that viewers of the electronic church were older, female, blue-collar, long-time Texas residents with less than college education and with young children. Church attendance formed the best predictor of electronic church viewing for fundamentalists; religious orthodoxy, for moderates and conservatives. 13 pages.

[1098] Swartz, Harold L. *A Survey of Attitudes of Methodist Ministers Toward the Use of Television for Religious Purposes.* Diss. Syracuse University, 1967. *Dissertation Abstracts International* 28.4A (1968): 1517. Ann Arbor: UMI, 1967. 6712084.

This survey of Methodist ministers in central and western Pennsylvania indicates that few regularly watch religious television, even though most agree on its value. The group also supported church use of the media, but were hesitant about its funding and showed less enthusiasm for personal involvement in religious mass media. 213 pages.

[1099] Tamney, Joseph B. and Stephen D. Johnson. "Religious Television in Middletown." *Review of Religious Research* 25 (1984): 303-313.

This study tested several reasons for watching religious television against the practices of residents of Muncie, Indiana. Religious preference, age, race, acceptance of Christian Right attitudes, and frequency of prayer all had direct effects on viewing religious broadcasts. Those who watched conservative televangelists scored high on two variables: Christian Right attitudes and religious fundamentalism. 11 pages.

[1100] Wegner, Tobin Vance. *Audience Preference in Los Angeles Religious Program Scheduling.* Thesis. California State University, Fullerton, 1980. *Masters Abstracts* 18.4 (1980): 301. Ann Arbor: UMI, 1980. 1314917.

This study reports that a uses and gratifications based telephone survey in Los Angeles area found that people watch religious television for inspiration, Bible knowledge, and delivery styles. Older viewers differ significantly from younger ones in motivation and preferences, as do church goers from non church goers. Most viewers are already church members. 99 pages.

Cable

[1101] Botein, Michael, David M. Rice, Janel M. Radtke, and Ralph M. Jennings. *Living with Cable Television: A Guide for Catholic Diocesan Directors of Communication.* [Washington, D. C.]: United States Catholic Conference, 1983.

This practical guide provides a general introduction to the cable television business and to the key issues of its franchises. It also gives a step-by-step instruction in negotiating a franchise so that local interested parties (such as a church communication office) can exert maximum influence. Appendices illustrate relevant documentation, give a bibliography on cable television, and list religious organizations to contact for cable information. 157 pages.

[1102] Deskur, André Marie. "Kirche und 'Medienexplosion.'" *Multimedia* 1 (1978): 4.

Deskur, then president of the Papal Commission on Social Communications, analyzes the communication revolution and its implications for the Church. 1 page.

[1103] Jaberg, Gene and Louis G. Warge, Jr. *The Video Pencil: Cable Communications for Church and Community.* Lanham, MD: University Press of America, 1980.

This study provides an optimistic look at cable television's potential for ministry and outreach. Grounded theologically in dialogic communication, multi-media revelation, and a process world view, the study sketches several types of cable ministry (to the consumer, as critique, as communication) and proposes some models for that ministry. While the ideas are good, the cable industry in the United States has unfortunately not developed in the way the authors had hoped. 147 pages.

[1104] Jordan, Joseph R. *The Utilization of Local Cable Television Public Access Programming for the Christian Ministry.* Diss. Drew University, 1984. *Dissertation Abstracts International* 45.11A (1985): 3369. Ann Arbor: UMI, 1985. 8500722.

This D. Min. project outlines the development of a cable television operation for Baptist churches; it includes chapters on preparing the laity, organizing the production staff, developing program topics, and evaluating one's work. An introductory chapter reviews a theological approach to communication: God uses varied means to address humans. Subsequent reflection must focus on the Word and on the method of the communication of Jesus. 122 pages.

[1105] Lau, Ephrem Else. "'Kommunikative Bedürfnisse' erfassen: Die katholische Kirche setzt sich für gründliche Begleitforschung ein." *FUNK-Korrespondenz* 44.4 (November 1982): 1-3.

Reporting on the pilot cable project, "Ludwigshafen," Lau proposes further points of research. 3 pages.

[1106] Leclerc, Roland. "Télévision communautaire et évangélisation." *Cahiers d'études et de recherches* 23 (1978): 1-62.

This monograph reports the results of a study of the uses of cable television by several dioceses in French-speaking Canada. The author specifically examined the ways in which cable might foster a "community television" through local access programming. Several of the dioceses did make use of local access features but few reported any kind of audience study that might indicate the success of their programs; however, all felt that the programming did serve a purpose. Respondents also noted some conflict between the economic interests of cable operators and the community interests of the viewers. Another point of interest had to do with the diversity of the available programming: church groups tended to produce informational, educational, expressive, or entertainment programs. The study includes copies of its instrument and a bibliography. 62 pages.

[1107] Lowe, Herbert F. *Helping an Interreligious Community Relate to Cable Television.* Diss. Drew University, 1983. *Dissertation Abstracts International* 44.11A (1984): 3195. Ann Arbor: UMI, 1984. 8402927.

This project report narrates the creation of the Monmouth County (New Jersey) Interreligious Cable Committee. As a background Lowe sketches a theology of communication based on Fore's work in theology and communication and on Switzer's in pastoral theology and interpersonal communication. He also examines the history of cable television as well as some of the non-program community issues raised by cable television. 134 pages.

[1108] Saint Germain, Barry J. *Cablecast of Worship Services as a Means of Outreach to Shut-ins of Grace United Church.* Diss. Drew University, 1986. *Dissertation Abstracts International* 47.10A (1987): 3781. Ann Arbor: UMI, 1987. 8703149.

This D. Min. project describes the development of a cable ministry in Canada by a local congregation affiliated with the United Church of Canada. Designed to reach shut-ins, the project resembles many similar ones in the United States; however, the Canadian setting provides a look at the cable industry in another country. 182 pages.

[1109] Smith, Roy A., Sr. *Realistic Cablevision Options for a Local Church.* Diss. Lancaster Theological Seminary, 1980. *Dissertation Abstracts International* 41.5A (1981): 1823. Ann Arbor: UMI, 1980. 8024327.

This dissertation combines a qualitative study of 15 church-run cable television operations with a discussion of a theological framework for such services. The author recommends a local church serving a local community through cable and seeks to foster a "spirit-filled" ministry. The survey of church cable operations holds some interest; unfortunately, the theological framework seems weak. 241 pages.

[1110] Smith, Walter Louis. *Exploring with a Congregation Alternative Possibilities of Video Cablecasting as Part of the Church's Ministry.* Diss. Drew University, 1982. *Dissertation Abstracts International* 43.9A (1983): 3022. Ann Arbor: UMI, 1983. 8302420.

This D. Min. project report begins with a simple overview of a theology of Christian communication, pretty much limiting it to a discussion of the source (God), the receiver (humans), and the message (the Gospel). The history of religious broadcasting which follows is distinguished by its attention to non-U. S. religious broadcasting. Cable television provides a realistic alternative for local congregations to enter into the ministry of television communication; the remainder of the thesis describes just such a project in Little Rock, Arkansas. 139 pages.

[1111] UNDA-USA. "Membership Update: VISN." *UNDA-USA Newsletter* special issue (1988).

This supplement to the UNDA-USA newsletter consists of four papers discussing the Vision International Satellite Network (VISN), an inter-faith cable television channel. Still in the planning stages, VISN would allow mainline churches access to the cable market. The papers include statements from Dr. William Fore of the National Council of Churches, Rev. Bernard Bonnot of the Catholic Telecommunications Network of America, Ms. Marynell Ford of the Eternal Word Television Network, and Mr. Richard Hirsch of the U. S. Catholic Conference. Hirsch's paper, the longest, provides a history of the operation and the status of the options for the Catholic Church. 12 pages.

Chapter 8

Intercultural Communication

[1112] Cosmao, Vincent. "Evangélisation et Langage." *Lumière et Vie* 88 (1968): 79-94.

This essays discusses the hermeneutic question of translating the Scriptures into non-Western languages or into the language of the secular West. In either case, there is a need for acculturation before the missionary or translator can begin. 16 pages.

[1113] Cunningham, Milton E., Jr. *New Drums over Africa.* Nashville, TN: Convention Press, 1972.

Christian missionaries ran 90% of all primary schools in East and Central Africa until the Zambian government announced its plans to take on responsibility and control for the schools. After this announcement many of the missionaries turned to radio, television, and audiovisuals as a way to reach the people. Cunningham discusses the changing role of Christian missionaries and the increasing importance of these media in African evangelization. 115 pages.

[1114] Filbeck, David. *Social Context and Proclamation: A Socio-Cognitive Study in Proclaiming the Gospel Cross-Culturally.* Pasadena, CA: William Carey Library, 1985.

This book aims to develop new methods of communicating the Gospel across cultures by integrating materials from communication studies, sociology, linguistics, anthropology, and missiology. After a general introduction to communication, to sociological models of society, and to cultural hermeneutics, the author provides an analysis of tribal society, peasant society, modern society, and developing society, with an eye to communicating the Gospel effectively in each. 180 pages.

[1115] Hein, Charles T., ed. *Communicating Across Cultural Barriers: A Dynamic Equivalent Approach to the Use of Radio and Other Media in Biblical Evangelism.* Nairobi, Kenya: Afrolit Society; Addis Ababa: Radio Voice of the Gospel, 1977.

This volume collects conference papers from a seminar, "Communication of the Biblical Message by Radio and Associated Media," held at RVOG in 1976. The conference participants examined cross- cultural communication and the inculturation of the Biblical message; particular sessions focused on communicating with non-literates and on preparing both broadcast and narrowcast materials. 140 pages.

[1116] Hesselgrave, David J. "Identification—Key to Effective Communication." *Evangelical Missions Quarterly* 9 (Summer 1973): 216-222.

Persuasion requires identification with the audience and so the missionary must strive to understand and be part of the culture to which s/he is sent. 7 pages.

[1117] Hesselgrave, David J. *Communicating Christ Cross-Culturally: An Introduction to Missionary Communication.* Grand Rapids, MI: Zondervan Publishing House, 1978.

This basic (but very thorough) textbook for intercultural communication applies the findings of communication theory to missionary work. Apart from the topics of communication and culture, it deals with language and nonverbal communication, world views (including specific examples from Africa and Asia), cognitive processing, linguistic forms, behavior and social patterns, media, and persuasion. It forms both a good introduction to communication issues and an interesting primer for missionary work. 511 pages.

[1118] Hile, Pat. "Communicating the Gospel in Terms of Felt Needs." *Missiology* 5 (October 1977): 499-506.

Many missionaries look only to universal or ultimate human needs in presenting the Gospel; however, people live in terms of their felt needs. This Churches of Christ anthropologist presents a case study of the Chiquimula-Quiché Indians of Guatemala to illustrate his thesis of situating the Gospel to the needs of the people. 8 pages.

[1119] Jørgensen, Knud. *The Role and Function of the Media in the Mission of the Church (With Particular Reference to Africa).* Diss. Fuller Theological Seminary, 1986. *Dissertation Abstracts International* 47.6A (1987): 2188. Ann Arbor: UMI, 1986. 8621943.

This study examines various sociological and cultural theories of media communication and counterposes to them a theological theory of incarnational communication. From this analysis Jørgensen argues that Christian media communication should "*support* and *improve* the already existing communication within culture, society and Church." This means both a more public communication stance for the Church and a more dialogic communication for the Church. He supports his argument with case studies of Christian communication in Africa where he worked for seven years with Radio Voice of the Gospel. 701 pages.

[1120] Kraft, Charles H. "God's Model for Cross-Cultural Communication—the Incarnation." *Evangelical Missions Quarterly* 9 (1973): 205-216.

In this first part of a two-part article, Kraft suggests that missionaries use the Incarnation as a model for breaking down stereotypes; as God did not enter human history in the way that humans would have expected, so missionaries cannot afford to fulfill the constraining stereotypes of those to whom they are sent. 12 pages.

[1121] Kraft, Charles H. "Ideological Factors in Intercultural Communication." *Missiology* 2 (July 1974): 295-312.

After noting five functions of ideology in society (explanatory, validating, reinforcing, integrating, and adaptive), Kraft proposes a model for the working of an ideological system. Any cross-cultural communication must work within such systems; four principles guide the missionary: choice of frame of reference (one's own or the respondents—what Kraft terms a choice between extractionist and assimilationist positions), achieving credibility, achieving specificity, and allowing the respondent to discover the truth of the message. 18 pages.

[1122] Kraft, Marguerite G. *Worldview and the Communication of the Gospel: A Nigerian Case Study.* South Pasadena, CA: William Carey Library, 1978.

This missiological and anthropological look at the Kamwes people in Nigeria focuses particularly on the communication of the Gospel through inculturation. After describing the culture and some basic intercultural communication theories, the author suggests a strategy to build up the Christian community through an indigenous theology. Much of the material comes from the author's experience as a missionary with the Church of the Brethren. 220 pages.

[1123] Larson, Donald N. "Cultural Static and Religious Communication." *Evangelical Mission Quarterly* 3 (Fall 1966): 48-47.

After noting the coincident components of communication (channel and content, for example), Larson asserts that Christian communication must follow the same rules as all other communication. In intercultural settings, the missionary must learn not only the language but also the thought patterns of the native speakers. The same applies to Christian publishing. 10 pages.

[1124] Loewen, Jacob A. *Culture and Human Values: Christian Intervention in Anthropological Perspective.* South Pasadena, CA: William Carey Library, 1975.

This volume of 29 essays, originally published in *Practical Anthropology* between 1961 and 1970, collects the observations of this Mennonite missionary-anthropologist working with the Indian tribes of South America. Four of the five divisions of the book deal with communication: human values in communication, the cultural setting of communication, communication for stability and change, and healing through communication. The essays in each section combine careful description of a particular tribe or event with an application of observations to missionary methods of communication. Particular topics include reciprocity, self-disclosure, cultural differences, socialization, the Bible, literacy, and self-image, and missionary communication. 443 pages.

[1125] Nida, Eugene A. *Message and Mission: The Communication of the Christian Faith.* New York: Harper & Brothers, Publishers, 1960.

Claiming only "to introduce the reader to principles and procedures of communication and to focus attention on the outworking of such factors in the communication of the Christian faith" (xvi-xvii), this thorough book introduces the topic of Christian intercultural communication (missiology and Biblical translation) by exploring basic topics in communication theory— messages, symbols, structures of communication, social structures, psychological and cultural relationships, and so forth. Many examples from mission work illustrate this very readable text. The last chapter covers the theological bases of communication, noting historical tensions between church and culture, opposing strategies of Christian communication (finding common ground vs. seeking a point of contact), basic principles for communication (equity and love), and a biblical view. The latter section notes that while verbal symbols are of human origin, they still have priority over visual symbols in communicating the truth. Further, in the biblical view, "language symbols reflect a meaningful relationship between symbol and behavior" (p. 224). Biblical communication shows that revelation is dialogic in character and in nature. 253 pages.

[1126] Nida, Eugene A. *Language Structure and Translation.* Ed. Anwar S. Dil. Stanford, CA: Stanford University Press, 1975.

The essays in this volume deal with a basic level of Christian communication: intercultural communication and translation. Many of the essays fall within the purview of specialized linguistics ("Analysis of Meaning and Dictionary Making"; "Semantic Structures") but some deal specifically with missionary work ("Linguistics and Christian Missions"; "Implications of Contemporary Linguistics for Biblical Scholarship"). Throughout Nida remains optimistic about translational equivalence and illustrates this optimism with both linguistic and historical examples. He clearly explains and applies materials from contemporary communication and information theory throughout the work. 300 pages.

[1127] Nida, Eugene A. *Religion Across Cultures: A Study in the Communication of Christian Faith.* New York: Harper & Row, 1968.

This book explores some of the universal psychological and communicative aspects of faith, listing the essential points. Proposing a model of religious communication, it notes cultural needs to use intermediaries between natural and supernatural and illustrates the model through studies of comparative religions. 111 pages.

[1128] Pentecost, Edward C. *Reaching the Unreached: An Introductory Study on Developing an Overall Strategy for World Evangelization.* Pasadena, CA: William Carey Library, 1974.

One chapter in this volume on evangelization strategies deals with communication patterns: it urges an understanding of the culture and an attempt to think in terms of "dynamic equivalences" when translating Christian concepts into another language system. The book, written from an evangelical point of view, also presents material on belief patterns in various countries, anthropological analyses of homogeneous groups, indicators of those ready for evangelization, and suggestions regarding communication channels. 234 pages.

[1129] Reed, Lyman Earl. *Preparing Missionaries for Intercultural Communication: A Bicultural Approach.* Pasadena, CA: Wm. Carey Library, 1985.

In this introductory text for evangelical missionaries, Reed introduces basic intercultural categories, drawn from anthropology: social structure, cultural learning, languages, worldview, and cultural change. He concludes with a scriptural, but very simple, theology of mission. 208 pages.

[1130] Seamands, John T. *Tell it Well: Communicating the Gospel Across Cultures.* Kansas City, MO: Beacon Hill Press, 1981.

This book combines three aspects for evangelistic preaching: material situating the Gospel in terms of other world religions; methods drawn from communication theory to frame messages and overcome barriers; and background materials on Hinduism, Buddhism, Animism, and Islam. The second section offers mostly basic principles for beginners; the third seems more helpful in giving historical and philosophical backgrounds of each religion, points of contact and contrast with Christianity, and theological barriers. 236 pages.

[1131] various authors. "International Seminar on Religious Symbolism and International Communication." *Kerygma* 34, 35 (1980); 36 (1981).

These issues of *Kerygma* publish the papers from a week-long seminar on intercultural communication, held at the Institute of Social Communication, Saint Paul University, Ottawa, in 1980. Papers examine methodological issues as well as presenting case studies from Asia, India, Africa, Latin America, North America, and Europe. Most of the cases address specifically Christian communication efforts. 335 pages.

[1132] Whiteman, Darrell L. "Effective Communication of the Gospel Amid Cultural Diversity." *Missiology* 12.3 (July 1984): 275-285.

Arguing that the "cultural aspects of communicating the Christian Gospel must be taken seriously if communication is to be at all effective," Whiteman suggests a three step process to sort out the essentials of any Christian communication. (1) Discover the original Biblical meanings conveyed in the cultural forms of Hebrew society. (2) Distinguish the original Biblical meanings from the contemporary forms used in our society. (3) Communicate the Biblical meanings in ways that will ensure the maximum transfer of meaning across cultural boundaries. 11 pages.

Chapter 9

Other Media

This chapter presents material about Christian communication which uses a variety of non-mass media. It includes references to Christian art, drama, dance, and music—these form the bulk of the chapter. However, later sections also list materials dealing with sound media (tape recording, phonograph recording, and so forth), comic books, computers, video, and various new communication technologies in the service of the Chrisian churches.

Art

[1133] Alexander, Paul J. *The Patriarch Nicephorus of Constantinople: Ecclesiastical Policy and Image Worship in the Byzantine Empire.* Oxford: The Clarendon Press, 1958.

Within the context of a biography of Nicephorus, Alexander sketches a clear and insightful history of the Iconoclastic Controversy. In addition to the biographical material, chapters deal with the church practice in regards to religious images, the theory and counter-theory of religious images, and Nicephorus's own theory of religious images. 287 pages.

[1134] André-Vincent, Ignace. "Pour une théologie de l'image." *Revue Thomiste* 59 (1959): 320-338.

This article carefully develops a theological and philosophical approach to images. After noting the contributions of the 8th and 9th century iconoclastic debates, it applies more contemporary concepts, including those of the sign and the form. Both sign and form constitute the image; as sign, the image points beyond itself, not as simple representation but as what might be termed a sacramental representation. As a form, the image takes on the symbolic form of a sacred signification. Throughout, the author illustrates his argument with examples drawn from the history of art and religious images. 19 pages.

[1135] Apostolos-Cappadona, Diane, ed. *Art, Creativity, and the Sacred.* New York: Crossroad, 1984.

This anthology in religion and art explores a wide range of attempts to bring the two disciplines together. In part one, several artists share their reflections on the spiritual dimension of art. The second part presents the work of art historians who comment on the religious significance and function of particular artists and works. Notable essays in this section include those by Leo Steinberg (on the hands of Christ in Leonardo's *Last Supper*) and Charles Scribner III (on Caravaggio's London *Supper at Emmaus*). Part three deals with historians of religion; part four, with theologians. This fourth part most explicitly explores the theme of art as a form of Christian communication, with essays by Langdon Gilkey, John Dillenberger, Thomas O'Meara, Paul Tillich, David Tracy, T. R. Martland, and Nicholas Wolterstorff. The fifth part contains essays specifically deemed interdisciplinary. The last part provides two valuable bibliographies: a review essay by John W. Cook on Christianity and the arts, and a more traditional bibliography on special topics in art and religion. 340 pages.

[1136] Athenagoras. "Plea for the Christians. [Supplicatio pro Christianos.]" *Ante-Nicene Christian Library: Translations of the Writings of the Fathers.* Ed. Alexander Roberts and James Donaldson. Vol 2: The Writings of Justin Martyr and Athenagoras. Trans. Marcus Dods, George Reith, and B. P. Pratten. Edinburgh: T. & T. Clark, 1874. 375-421.

This early Christian writing rejects the use of images and art in religion, arguing that these things of earthly origin cannot represent God, because they are created and because they are of earth. 47 pages.

[1137] Bailey, Albert Edward, ed. *The Arts and Religion.* New York: The Macmillan Company, 1944.

These four essays (by Bailey, Kenneth Conant, Henry Smith, and Fred Eastman) constitute the 1943 Ayer Lectures of the Colgate-Rochester Divinity School. Each lecture examines the expression of religion or religious ideas in a particular medium. After Bailey's general introduction to the universality of the arts, individual lectures address painting and sculpture, architecture, music, and drama. By and large historical in orientation and presentation, the lectures give a good overview to their topics. 180 pages.

[1138] Brehier, Louis. *La Querelle des Images (VIIIe – IXe Siécles).* 1904. New York: Burt Franklin [reprint], 1969.

This brief study outlines the history of the iconoclast-iconophile controversy in the 8 th and 9 th centuries. To clarify the issues, Brehier distinguishes among the partisans of the cult of images, those who did not venerate images but who nevertheless defended their existence, and those who opposed the images. The book also gives brief summaries of the theological positions of each group. 64 pages.

[1139] Burckhardt, Titus. *Sacred Art in East and West: Its Principles and Methods.* Trans. Lord Northbourne. London: Perennial Books, 1967.

Arguing that sacred art stems not so much from subject matter as from its form, Burckhardt examines Hindu, Christian, Islamic, and Buddhist art in an attempt to identify its formal characteristics. In the two chapters devoted to Christian art, he notes that "in Christianity the divine image *par excellence* is the human form of Christ; thus it comes about that Christian art has but one purpose: the transfiguration of man, and of the world which depends on man, by their participation in the Christ." Concentrating particularly on architecture and on the historical manifestation of the sacred in art, he illustrates the argument with reference to particular churches and works. The Renaissance, he feels, confused the issue by treating sacred topics in a profane or secular style. 160 pages.

[1140] Cooper, Thomas. "Communicating the Incommunicable: Remarks on the Relation of Theology to Art." *The Clergy Review* 62 (May 1977): 186-193.

Following Thomas Aquinas, Cooper claims that without imagination, theology becomes impossible. Theology must, therefore, come out of the same store as the experience of myth and art. Myth and art mediate the experience of sharing and thus allow a more conscious experience of the holy, an experience which theology can systematize and analyze. "Every true artist and every true theologian seeks to communicate the incommunicable by articulating every man's orientation to the One, the True, and the Good. 8 pages.

[1141] Cram, Ralph Adams. *The Catholic Church and Art.* New York: The Macmillan Company, 1930.

Bemoaning the loss of beauty and aesthetic values in contemporary art, Cram seeks to find in the Catholic faith a tradition which will ground a recovered aesthetic. Much of this work consists of an art history illustrating the alliance between a cultural faith and its art. 121 pages.

[1142] Detweiler, Robert, ed. *Art/Literature/Religion: Life on the Borders.* Vol. 49.2 of *Journal of the American Academy of Religion Studies.* Chico: Scholars Press, 1983.

The essays in this collection explore links between religion and varying kinds of communication, primarily literature but also music and film. At their best, the essays provide theoretical foundations for asking why a given type or instance of communication might be Christian; at their worst, the essays fall into an unhelpful particularism. Noteworthy in the collection are pieces by Huntley Beyer and Rebecca Parker Beyer on the theological implications of contemporary music; Giles Gann on the moral order and criticism; David Helsa on a theology of literary history (an examination of Greek and Christian tragedy); Nathan Scott, Jr. on a critique of narrative theology; and Erasmo Leiva-Merikakis on beauty and theology. The volume contains a bibliography of recent works. 201 pages.

[1143] Dixon, John W., Jr. *Nature and Grace in Art.* Chapel Hill, NC: University of North Carolina Press, 1964.

This book explores the relationship between the work of art and the attitude of the artist toward his/her world, in this case the world of Christianity. "On the one hand is nature (matter) and on the other is grace, and where nature and grace intersect in the work of art, it is religious." The thesis comes to clarity through an examination of works of art in four categories—the art of creation, the art of the image of God, the art of the fall, and the art of redemption. 220 pages.

[1144] Dixon, John W., Jr. *Art and the Theological Imagination.* New York: The Seabury Press, 1978.

This book, a reworking of the 1976 Hale Lectures at Seabury-Western Seminary, poses the question whether words form the best language for theology. Answering that art shows a clearer view of life and of human nature, Dixon illustrates his thesis through art and through art's polyvalent and metaphorical forms. By examining the development of six different styles, Dixon shows various crucial theological aspects of their creators. He looks at the transitions from the ancient world to classical Greece, from late antiquity to early Christianity, from early Christianity to the medieval period, from the early western period to the Renaissance, from the Renaissance to the modern period, and from the modern period to the contemporary period. In each case he suggests that the art can become sacramental to the Holy One. 165 pages.

[1145] Donoso Phillips, José. *Dimensiones cristianas del arte.* Santiago, Chile: Editorial del Pacífico, [1980].

This book is a theological reflection, a meditation, on art. Under the major headings of theology—creation, incarnation, redemption, the Church, grace, the new creation—the author examines the role of Christian art and the Christian artist. 237 pages.

[1146] Dubuisson, Odile. *Children, Crayons and Christ: Understanding the Religious Art of Children.* Trans. M. Angeline Bouchard. Paramus, NJ: Newman Press, 1969.

This study of children's religious art (produced in the course of religious instruction in several Parisian parish schools) examines common themes, the use of color, the distortion of images, and symbols. Beginning with a discussion of particular cases, Dubuisson suggests connections between drawing and Christian behavior and offers suggestions on the use of drawing for teaching children the catechism. 149 pages.

[1147] Ferguson, George. *Signs and Symbols in Christian Art.* New York: Oxford University Press, 1959.

This book, with its 112 reproductions and numerous illustrations, provides a kind of encyclopedia of Christian symbolism. Divided into 16 areas (animals, flowers, earth, the human body, the Old Testament, St. John the Baptist, the Virgin Mary, Jesus, the Trinity, the saints, radiances and colors, religious dress, religious objects, and artifacts), it offers several paragraphs of commentary and explanation of the elements used in Christian art through the centuries. More a reference than a continuous text, the book does answer most questions about specific details in paintings or sculpture. 123 pages.

[1148] Frary, Joseph P. "The Logic of Icons." *Sobornost'* 6th ser. 6 (Winter 1972): 394-404.

After reviewing the traditional claims made about icons (there is a connection between the representation and its prototype; there is a deep and essential connection between the transformation of the fallen world into the redeemed kingdom and icons; and there is a connection between icons and the Incarnation), Frary examines the logic of the icon by looking at three relations: human beings to icons; icons to the Kingdom of God; and human beings to the Kingdom of God. Key to the understanding of these relations is the symbolic nature of icons and the cognitive nature of art. 11 pages.

[1149] Frye, Roland Mushat, et al. "Religion and the Arts." *Theology Today* 34.1 (April 1977).

The theme of this issue deals with religion and the arts. Essays include Roland Mushat Frye, "*Paradise Lost* and the Visual Arts"; Erik Routley, "Theology for Church Musicians"; Elizabeth E. Platt, "The Ministry of Mary of Bethany"; John R. Bodo, "The Arts in the Local Church"; John W. Cook, "Theology and the Arts: Sources and Resources"; Ron Barrett, "Bible Picture Stories"; Douglass Shand Tucci, "The High Mass as Sacred Dance"; and Clifford Elliott, "*Network:* A Film Critique."

[1150] Gilles, René. *Le Symbolisme dans l'art religieux: Architecture, couleurs, costume, peinture.* Paris: La Colombe, 1961.

This book primarily deals with symbolism but searches out its examples within the domain of religious art. Each section follows an historical arrangement, beginning with ancient Egypt and progressing through the Christian era. While the text appears fairly complete, describing and explaining the symbols, few illustrations of the symbols appear in the book. 226 pages.

[1151] Glendenning, Frank, ed. *The Church and the Arts*. London: SCM Press, 1960.

A collection of essays emerging from a three year dialogue on the church and the arts among a pastor, a theologian, a designer, an architect, a writer, a musician, and a dramatist, this book presents both theoretical and practical considerations on the nature of communicating Christianity. E. J. Tinsley presents a good theoretical account of the Incarnation as a method of communication. The other essays tend to be historical in nature, sketching the relationship between the church and design, music, architecture, and so on. They are interesting for the background they provide. 128 pages.

[1152] Grabar, André. *Christian Iconography: A Study of Its Origins*. Bolligen Series 25, number 10. Princeton: Princeton University Press, 1968.

A work of history, this examination of Christian iconography also suggests ways in which the early Church artists expressed Christian dogma through image and juxtaposition of elements in their art. Claiming neither completeness nor systematicity, the author instead seeks to investigate the origins of Christian art from within Greco-Roman society and the purposes which Christian art served for the Church. The book contains 341 illustrations. 224 pages.

[1153] Gutman, Joseph, ed. *The Image and the Word: Confrontations in Judaism, Christianity and Islam*. The American Academy of Religion, Society of Biblical Literature, Religion, and the Arts series 4. Missoula, MT: Scholars Press, 1977.

The essays in this collection include material on Deuteronomy (Gutman); the antecedents of Byzantine iconoclasm (Paul C. Finney); Byzantine iconoclasm (Stephen Gero); epigraphs as icons in Islam (Anthony Welch); art and Christian piety (William R. Jones); patterns of iconoclasm in the early reformation (Carl C. Christensen); and iconoclasm and politics in the Netherlands, 1566. The volume also includes a bibliography. 175 pages.

[1154] Hazelton, Roger. *A Theological Approach to Art*. Nashville, TN: Abingdon Press, 1967.

Art and Christianity meet in the realm of symbol and support one another's enterprise. This theological examination of art looks upon art as disclosure, as embodiment, as vocation, and as celebration. As disclosure, art touches intimately communication since it invites the viewer into a dialogic process that allows one to know the world and the self more completely. As embodiment, art shares in creation—as Christian theology understands that process. Quoting Dorothy Sayers, Hazelton notes that the creative imagination has a threefold aspect which resembles a trinitarian understanding of God. In the image of the Father the creative idea begins; the working out of that idea bears the image of the Son; the dialogue called forth by the work of art forms the image of the indwelling Spirit. As vocation, art resonates with the Christian term since each artist must be engaged, caught up, involved in, responsible for the work of art. Finally, as celebration, art leads the human community to a rejoicing in life itself. 158 pages.

[1155] Jones, Richard M. *Manual for Witness Through the Arts: Guidance for Understanding the Arts and Their Meaning for Witness in the World.* Valley Forge, PA: American Home Baptist Mission Societies, 1961.

This pamphlet sets out a rationale for church involvement in the arts: the arts are part of the world in which Christians live; the arts form a point of contact between church and world; and the arts mold society today. The booklet addresses itself more to church activities for the appreciation of various arts (drama, film, television, literature, painting, photography) than it does to any kind of outreach to artists. To aid in its purpose, it contains procedures, study guides, and bibliographic information. 48 pages.

[1156] Justin Martyr. "First Apology." *Justin Martyr and Athenagoras.* Trans. Marcus Dods, George Reith, and B. P. Pratten. Ed. Alexander Roberts and James Donaldson. Vol. 2 of *Ante-Nicene Christian Library: Translations of the Writings of the Fathers.* Edinburgh: T. & T. Clark, 1874. 7-71.

In chapter 9 of the "First Apology," Justin Martyr condemns religious images as idols, denying that they can reflect the form of God since God has no form. 64 pages.

[1157] Laeuchli, Samuel. *Religion and Art in Conflict: Introduction to a Cross-Disciplinary Task.* Philadelphia: Fortress Press, 1980.

Religion and art exist, closely related and interacting; so too does the study of each. Both fit within a larger culture because both manifest that culture. This volume explores the relationship between the two, calling attention to the ambiguities present in each, the threat which each brings to the other, and the benefits each holds for the other. Important chapters deal with the threat of art, the transmutation of religion, and the analogy between art and religion. 240 pages.

[1158] Lossky, Vladimir. *In the Image and Likeness of God.* Ed. John H. Erickson and Thomas E. Bird. Crestwood, NY: St. Vladimir's Seminary Press, 1985.

This collection of Lossky's essays treats the general theme of the image of God from the perspective of Orthodox theology. The most specifically appropriate essay to the idea of Christian communication is the one devoted to the "Theology of the Image." This provides a balanced view of the Biblical and patristic sources for the concept of the image; accepting Protestant difficulty with the image, Lossky shows its Biblical clarification in terms of the Incarnation. 232 pages.

[1159] Martin, F. David. *Art and the Religious Experience: The "Language" of the Sacred.* Lewisburg: Bucknell University Press, 1972.

This book explores the varieties of art (music, painting, literature, architecture) through the development of an aesthetic which brings Whitehead's and Heidegger's efforts together. Martin situates the discussion in terms of religious experience which, following James, he characterizes by (1) the awareness of limitations, (2) the awe-full awareness of further reality, and (3) the conviction that participation in this reality is important. With this in mind, he turns to art and examines the ways in which it evokes and speaks to religious experience. 288 pages.

[1160] Martland, Thomas R. *Religion as Art: An Interpretation.* Albany, NY: State University of New York Press, 1981.

Martland argues that "what art does, religion does. They both provide directions on how to see and indirectly on what to do." To ask whether there is a Christian art (or a means to determine a Christian art) pushes one back to a prior question—the functions of art and religion. Martland develops his thesis through an historical examination of art and religion, constantly shifting from one to the other to show their functions at particular moments. 221 pages.

[1161] May, Lynn E. Jr., ed. " Communicating Baptist History in Contemporary Media and Art Forms." *Baptist History and Heritage* 12.3 (July 1977).

This issue focuses on "imaginative, creative, non-traditional ways of communicating the Baptist story." J. Gordon Kingsley, Jr., begins with a theme essay that situates topic in terms of several needs: the need to communicate, the need to remember that Baptists traditionally use contemporary media, and the need to understand those media. Erwin M. Hearn, Jr. examines the visual arts; Andrew B. Rawls, audiovisuals; Don Burke, stained glass; Bob Thornton, television and video; and Robert J. Hastings, newspapers. The articles generally feature practical suggestions and illustrations.

[1162] Miles, Margaret R. *Image as Insight: Visual Understanding in Western Christianity and Secular Culture.* Boston: Beacon Press, 1985.

Drawing examples from Christian art and architecture of the 4 th, 14 th and 16th centuries, Miles argues that Western culture and history have been textually oriented and thus implicitly favor "language users" and ignore the majority of the population. She proposes a visual hermeneutic in order to disclose the experience of the average person in the churches and then applies it to 20th century experience. The book is well worth reading. 200 pages.

[1163] Moore, Albert C. *Iconography of Religions: An Introduction.* Philadelphia: Fortress Pres, 1977.

This general study of iconography examines the "types and the meaning of images used in a representative range of the religious traditions of mankind" (page 1). After an introductory section which defines icon, image, religion, and so forth, the book considers primitive religions, Egyptian and ancient near-Eastern religions, Hinduism, Buddhism, Jainism, Shintoism, Judaism, Islam, and Christianity and their uses of and interpretations of images. 337 pages.

[1164] Murray, Sister Charles. "Art and the Early Church." *Journal of Theological Studies* ns 28 (1977): 303-345.

Through a re-examination of the relevant texts from patristic and early church sources, this essay challenges the commonly accepted wisdom that the early church, as a Jewish sect, opposed images. Instead, Murray concludes that only some uses of images (particularly idolatrous ones) faced condemnation by the early church. 43 pages.

[1165] Nichols, Aidan. *The Art of God Incarnate: Theology and Image in Christian Tradition.* London: Darton, Longman, and Todd, 1980.

Sensitive to the role of the visual in contemporary communication, Nichols traces the use of images in Christianity with an eye to the theological underpinnings of such use. Noting various arguments in defense of images, he develops a sketch of a Christology of the image based on the characteristics of the Incarnation. The book proves valuable both for its historical materials and for its attempt to ground a theology of communication in the past practice of the Church. 180 pages.

[1166] Ouspensky, Leonide and Vladimir Lossky. *The Meaning of Icons.* Trans. G. E. H. Palmer and E. Kadloubovsky. 2nd ed. Crestwood, New York: St. Vladimir's Seminary Press, 1982.

This volume, featuring reproductions of and commentaries on over 60 icons, also includes introductory essays on the Tradition of the Orthodox Church and the place of icons within the Church. In one essay, "The Meaning and

Language of Icons," Ouspensky traces the theological basis for iconography, grounding it in the Incarnation (which makes God representable). He then gives an historical sketch of the development and uses of icons in the church, their liturgical function, and the general symbolic values of their elements (subject, background, human body, colors, clothing, architecture, etc.). Other essays describe the technique of iconography and the various types of icons. 222 pages.

[1167] Ouspensky, Leonide. *Theology of the Icon.* Trans. Elizabeth Meyendorff. Crestwood, NY: St. Vladimir's Seminary Press, 1978.

This book presents a "summary of a course on iconology given at the Pastoral Courses of Theology of the Exarchate of the Patriarchate of Moscow in Western Europe, in Paris." After a general introduction to the subject matter, Ouspensky distinguishes the Orthodox teaching from that of the Roman Catholic and Protestant churches. He then begins a generally historical overview of the place and role of art in Christianity. He places particular emphasis on the patristic sources and on the early Church councils through the iconoclastic period. He concludes with a long chapter on "the meaning and content of icons." This book provides valuable information on icons and church art and offers some interesting ideas that might apply as well to other forms of Christian communication. 232 pages.

[1168] Palmer, Michael F. *Paul Tillich's Philosophy of Art.* Berlin: Walter de Gruyter, 1984.

This scholarly study examines Tillich's theology to extract and reconstruct his approach to art, developed in over 40 years of theological reflection. For Tillich, art formed the meeting point of religion and culture; it also provides the key to understanding his own writings on culture and religion. Sections of this book discuss expressionism, Tillich's theology of culture, artistic creation, revelation, and symbols. A lengthy bibliography of Tillich studies introduces the volume. 217 pages.

[1169] Paterson, John Barstow. *Living the Christian Faith in Artistic Creations.* Diss. Lancaster Theological Seminary, 1981. *Dissertation Abstracts International* 42.3A (1982): 1193. Ann Arbor: UMI, 1981. 8119185.

This D. Min. thesis explores the use of art to express the Christian faith. The theological background includes reflection on human beings as created in the image of God, on the role of the Incarnation, and on the ongoing work of the Spirit. In a more explicitly labelled theoretical section, Paterson reduces the theological approach to one dealing with integrity and morality. 178 pages.

[1170] Purdy, William. *Seeing and Believing: Theology and Art.* Butler, WI: Clergy Book Service, 1976.

As a history and commentary on Christian art and its relation to theology and the life of the Church, this book covers some centuries better than others. Particularly good is the discussion of the Gothic period (12th-14th century), the Counter-Reformation and Baroque period, and the contemporary period. In these the attempt to see artistic expression as communicating religious truth succeeds and challenges the reader's concepts of art and expression. 136 pages.

[1171] Ramseyer, Jean-Phillippe. *La parole et l'image: Liturgie, architecture et art sacré.* Neuchâtel, Switzerland: Delachaux et Nestlé, 1963.

This volume proposes a theology of images in dialogue with the Word. Key topics include vision, sign, and Jesus as image of God. Ramseyer uses the Eucharist as *the* image which justifies and measures all other religious images. It points to some essential qualities of any imaging: (1) participation in the Resurrection of Christ and hence in the divinity of Christ; (2) acknowledgment of the humanity of Christ; (3) an eschatological dimension of the Kingdom; and (4) a sign of hope (pages 82-86). These four elements measure the legitimacy and fidelity of all images. 202 pages.

[1172] Réau, Louis. *Iconographie de l'art chrétien.* 3 vols. Paris: Presses Universitaires de France, 1955-1957.

This historical study of Christian iconography examines Christian themes from both the Old and New Testaments and illustrates how artists have embodied them over the years. The first volume contains more general essays on symbolism, liturgical use of art, and historical uses of art. It also includes miscellaneous material on the iconography of the saints. The latter two volumes deal with the Scriptural materials. Volume 1: 480 pages; volume 2: 470 pages; volume 3: 769 pages.

[1173] Ritter, Richard H. *The Arts of the Church.* Boston: The Pilgrim Press, 1947.

Designed to encourage the study of the Christian arts, this book defines them as "the expression of Christianity." After two introductory chapters to situate the discussion, Ritter presents an overview of architecture, furnishings, music, literature, drama, dance, painting and sculpture. Chapters contain historical overviews, descriptions, discussion of the differences among denominations in terms of art, and modern applications. 146 pages.

[1174] Ryken, Leland, ed. *The Christian Imagination: Essays on Literature and the Arts.* Grand Rapids: Baker Book House, 1981.

This collection of essays, many of which come from the American Evangelical tradition, presents a look at the arts and aesthetics from a religious perspective. Two initial sections (on a Christian philosophy of art and a Christian perspective on art) contain essays that explore the theoretical boundaries of Christian art. Later sections focus on literature and writing, visual arts, and music. The essays tend to be short, readable, but not terribly analytic. 448 pages.

[1175] Schönborn, Christoph von. *L'Icône du Christ: Fondements théologiques élaboré entre le Ier et le IIe Concile de Nicée (325-787)*. Fribourg: Éditions Universitaires Fribourg Suisse, 1976.

This historical study examines the concept of the image of Christian patristic and conciliar documents. A first section looks at the dogmatic theory of images, both in trinitarian and in Christological terms. A second part turns explicitly to the image of Christ and under this heading sets forth the arguments of the iconoclastic period. 245 pages.

[1176] Schorsch, Anita and Martin Greif. *The Morning Stars Sang: The Bible in Popular and Folk Art*. New York: Universe Books, 1978.

The communication of Biblical teaching rested greatly on popular art, particularly for illiterate segments of the population. This collection reproduces samples of such biblically-based popular art, much of it American and much of it executed by women in a variety of media (watercolor, oil on canvas, paint on paper, engraving, needlepoint, silk, etc.). 127 pages.

[1177] Seerveld, Calvin. *Rainbows for the Fallen World: Aesthetic Life and Artistic Task*. Toronto: Tuppence Press, 1980.

Written from the Calvinist tradition, this work seeks a Christian aesthetics. The book collects various presentations and essays by the author, examining different aspects of art and artistic appreciation in the lives of Christians. The most valuable essays are those exploring the Biblical charter for aesthetics and the one proposing a more philosophically grounded modal aesthetic theory. 254 pages.

[1178] Trubetskoi, Eugene N. *Icons: Theology in Color*. Trans. Gertrude Vakar. [Crestwood, NY]: St. Vladimir's Seminary Press, 1973.

These essays, originally written in 1915-1917, explore various aspects of Russian iconography. The first, comparing icons with the architecture of Russian churches, states that both contrast two worlds: "the ancient cosmos enslaved by sin and the all embracing church where this slavery is forever abolished." The icon, like the church, subordinates all creatures to a common architectural design in which all gather around Christ and the Virgin. The second essay explicates the meaning of specific icons, noting the ways in which they separate the two worlds of earthly temptation and heavenly reward. The last essay more explicitly connects icons to the history of Russia. 100 pages.

[1179] Van Der Leeuw, Gerardus. *Sacred and Profane Beauty: The Holy in Art*. New York: Holt, Rinehart and Winston, 1963.

This book, written for those Christians and people of art who neither re-
sent art or religion nor enslave it, attempts to "find paths and boundaries
for anyone who says he understands something of the way God speaks
through beauty, anyone who thinks that God's word could never be without the highest beauty." Examining various media in turn (dance, drama,
words, pictorial arts, architecture, and music), van der Leeuw proposes a
theological aesthetics to relate these arts to God. Dance—the movement
of God—and drama (the play of God) image the Father and the work of
creation. Word (the praise of God), image (the image of God) and building
(the house of God) reflect the Son and the work of redemption. Music (the
Spirit of God) reflects the Spirit and the work of eschatology. The book
deserves meditation and suggests how closely the human expression and
religious impulse are connected. 357 pages.

[1180] Veith, Gene Edward, Jr. *The Gift of Art: The Place of the Arts in
Scripture.* Downers Grove, IL: Inter-Varsity Press, 1983.

Written from an Evangelical perspective, this book explores what the Bible
states about art and art's role in the life of a Christian. Commenting on
Exodus 31 (the gifts of the artist, Bezalel who constructed the Ark of the
Covenant), Veith notes that three Biblical principles about art emerge: (1)
art is within God's will; (2) artistic ability is God's gift; and (3) art is a
vocation from God. At the same time, humans can misuse art and turn its
works into idolatry. Therefore, while art itself is not sacred, its meaning
or use can become so. Veith then applies this perspective to religious and
secular art throughout the centuries. 130 pages.

[1181] Waddell, James and F. W. Dillistone, eds. *Art and Religion as Communication.* Atlanta, GA: John Knox Press, 1974.

This collection of essays attempts to "build a bridge" between art and religion by regarding both as specific types of communication. The connection
between the two realms occurs at a higher, theoretical, level where both
utilize similar communication patterns or styles. Essays include "The Way
into Matter," by John W. Dixon, Jr., on sensibility and modern art (arguing that the reason there lacks Christian art is an impoverishment of
Christian sensibility); "The Incarnation, Art, and the Communication of
the Gospel," by E. J. Tinsley; "The Indirect Communication: Kierkegaard
and Beckett," by James D. Whitehill; Waddell's piece on *One Flew over
the Cuckoo's Nest*; and Dillistone's "The Relationship Between Form and
Content/Medium and Message in Christian Communication." 253 pages.

[1182] White, James F. *Protestant Worship and Church Architecture: Theological and Historical Considerations.* New York: Oxford University Press,
1964.

Remarking that Protestant worship has two prevailing attitudes—"worship as centered in the feelings and worship as work done"—White examines how church architecture communicates to the assembled congregation the nature of worship and the nature of the church. Every building, he argues, elicits a particular response from people. With this presupposition, he then examines some principles of liturgical architecture and traces their history from the early Church through the Reformation. The book concludes with a bibliography divided according to Christian worship tradition. 224 pages.

[1183] Whittle, Donald. *Christianity and the Arts.* London: A. R. Mowbray & Co, Ltd.; Philadelphia: Fortress Press, 1966.

"This book sets out to explore the important but intricate relationship between Christianity and the arts" and consists of equal parts exposition and commentary on painting, church architecture, music, fiction, poetry, drama, and cinema. Each chapter provides an historical overview and then a detailed treatment of contemporary examples of the medium. Throughout, "Christian art" refers to those works whose thematic material is overtly Christian, those works which indicate a connection between a Christian vision and the understanding of the world, and those works which see themselves as a re-enactment of creation. The book itself provides a rationale for Christian communication through various media. 157 pages.

[1184] Wilder, Amos N. "The Church's New Concern with the Arts." *Christianity and Crisis* 17.2 (February 18, 1957): 12-14.

The Church's concern with the arts must go beyond the pragmatic or decorative arts, beyond the cultural and professional preparation of the clergy. "More urgent today is the whole question of imaginative vehicles, of symbolization, in religion" (pages 13-14) because society lives by its symbols. "The church itself may proclaim its Christian principles, but Christians may be ruled by sub-Christian imaginations (p. 14). 3 pages.

[1185] Wittkower, Rudolf and Irma B. Jaffe. *Baroque Art: The Jesuit Contribution.* NY: Fordham University Press, 1972.

This collection of papers from a symposium on the subject examines the relationship between the Society of Jesus and the arts of the baroque period, particularly architecture, decorative painting, theater, and music. Wittkower readily admits problems with the theme in that it is difficult to note any specifically Jesuit art since the Jesuits tended to follow local customs and often opted for the pragmatic or available over the beautiful. However, they did have an influence through their spiritual doctrine and educational methods. Other essays treat the Gesù church as a case study for both architectural and artistic influences of the Jesuits. Another essay examines the Jesuit influence on stage design and a final one on music. 139 pages.

Drama

[1186] Alexander, Ryllis Clair and Omar Pancoast Goslin. *Worship Through Drama.* New York: Harper & Brothers, 1930.

"This volume is a collection of twelve services of worship as they have been presented at the Riverside Church, New York City." In addition to the services, which use drama as a center piece, the book contains notes on drama, a brief history of the dramatic element in worship, and staging suggestions. The twelve services include dramatic interpretations of forgiveness, thanksgiving, freedom, love, pride, light, and prayer. Other services are based on the Christmas story, the life of St. Francis, the other wise man, and the life of Abraham Lincoln. 330 pages.

[1187] Bachman, John W. and E. Martin Browne, eds. *Better Plays for Today's Churches.* New York: Association Press, 1964.

This collection presents 12 plays for church performance, dealing with either modern society or Christian themes (the passion, Christmas, and so on.) The plays are *The Case against Eve; Verdict of One; The Circle Beyond Fear; Christ in the Concrete City; A Very Cold Night; Eyes upon the Cross; This Rock; Christmas in the Market Place; The Curate's Play; Emmanuel; Abraham and Isaac;* and *Go Down Moses.* 474 pages.

[1188] Barnard, Floy Merwyn. *Drama in the Churches.* Nashville, TN: Broadman Press, 1950.

This text, designed for adult education by the Baptist Sunday School Board, covers the basics of drama in the church. Chapters include material on a rationale for church drama, the use of church drama, types of church drama, and mechanics of church drama. The book has a clear organization and good style of presentation; it has appended to it a set of examination questions and a brief annotated bibliography. However, the book does seem a bit dated. 132 pages.

[1189] Bates, Katharine Lee. *The English Religious Drama.* New York: Macmillan Company, 1921.

This guide introduces passion plays and saints plays translated into English. Dividing them into miracle plays and morality plays, Bates describes each and notes their dramatic values. 254 pages.

[1190] Baxter, Kay M. *Contemporary Theatre and the Christian Faith.* New York: Abingdon Press, 1957.

The contemporary theatre's concern with exploring the human condition is congruent with many aspects of the Christian faith. Baxter examines how this has come about and discusses various plays pertaining to the human condition, integrity, communication, and the possibility of the resurrection. 112 pages.

[1191] Bennett, Gordon C. *Acting Out Faith: Christian Theatre Today.* St. Louis, MO: CBP Press, 1986.

This book covers the historical, theoretical, technical, and practical aspects of Christian theatre. While Bennett feels that there is a place for comedy in the church, he emphasizes drama "with a spiritual side." Besides his historical overview, Bennett also reviews the contemporary situation, noting specific people, places, and activities. In the theoretical section he defines different play types—miracle plays, morality plays, passion plays, as well as mime and readers' theatre. After some practical comments on staging, he concludes with a resource list of plays, drama collections, and materials; a glossary of terms; and an actor's guide, including exercises and a sample play. 192 pages.

[1192] Browne, E. Martin. "Function of Religious Drama and Its Present Needs." *Christian Drama* 3.2 (Autumn 1955): 5-10.

The welcome address to the First International Conference on Religious Drama, this piece argues that drama can have a special relation to Christianity, that it expresses itself in terms of human relationships, and that drama is primarily religious when human relationships are seen from the Christian point of view. The address continues with an overview of contemporary religious drama in England. 6 pages.

[1193] Burbridge, Paul and Murray Watts. *Lightning Sketches.* London: Hodder and Stoughton, 1981.

This delightful book alternates short essays on drama in the church with scripts of 21 short sketches on topics ranging from David and Goliath to Zacchaeus to the problem of belief in the contemporary world. Helpful hints are given on writing sketches, creating laughter, production, and approaches to the audience. 192 pages.

[1194] Cargill, Oscar. *Drama and Liturgy.* 1930. New York: Octagon Press, 1969.

This study of the origins of drama questions the "liturgical theory" that holds that the mystery plays emerged from liturgical interactions in the medieval period. Cargill argues that the dramas differ significantly enough to postulate a looser relation to the liturgy than commonly thought. The overall study helps to situate the larger question of Christian communication through drama in an historical perspective. 131 pages.

[1195] Carmines, Alvin. "Drama in the Church: An Experiment." *Theology Today* 22 (January 1966): 505-512.

A narrative account of the introduction of drama into the life of the Judson Memorial (Baptist) Church in Greenwich Village, this essay notes that the drama (which was not necessarily "religious" drama) deeply affected and strengthened the life of the church. 8 pages.

[1196] Chapman, Raymond, ed. *Religious Drama: A Handbook for Actors and Producers.* London: SPCK, 1959.

This general handbook covers everything from setting up a parish drama society to writing plays to producing them. Special topics include stage design, lighting, and music. 180 pages.

[1197] Crosse, Gordon. *The Religious Drama.* London: A. R. Mowbray & Co., 1913.

This small volume sketches an introduction to "drama as an art of the Christian Church from its beginnings to the present day." After noting the Church's rejection of Roman drama, Crosse traces the renewal of drama from the 10th century attempts of Hrotsvitha to write plays on the classical model but with themes drawn from the scriptures. Liturgical drama proved more popular and eventually led to religious plays outside of the sanctuary—miracle and morality plays. Focusing mostly on England, Crosse reviews the plays, their plots and their staging, and comments of the loss of religious drama as a result of Puritanism. He also introduces the revival of religious drama in the late 19th century. The book includes illustrations and a bibliography. 182 pages.

[1198] DeAngelis, William. *Acting Out the Gospels with Mimes, Puppets, & Clowns.* Mystic, CT: Twenty-Third Publications, 1982.

This is a collection of 19 scripts for children's Gospel plays, arranged according to the calendar year. The plays follow a Roman Catholic liturgical model. Their quality varies. 95 pages.

[1199] Dyer, Janelle G. *The Australian Christian Play: An Endangered Species.* New York: Vantage Press, 1985.

These 51 modern morality plays from the Lighthouse Christian drama group deal with basic themes ranging from angels to drugs, from grudges to stewardship. This volume provides the script for each short (usually three to four pages) play and indicates the relevant biblical sources. 196 pages.

[1200] Eastman, Fred. "Present Trends in Religious Drama." *The Christian Century* 68.4 (January 24, 1951): 110-112.

This article reports a survey of churches from six denominations across the country regarding their use of drama with their congregations. While the overall incidence of drama fell slightly from 1939, about one in four churches surveyed did use drama; they found biblical drama best suited to their needs which included inspiration and education. 3 pages.

[1201] Eastman, Fred and Louis Wilson. *Drama in the Church: A Manual of Religious Drama Production.* New York: Samuel French, 1933.

The authors define religious drama as that which "has a religious effect upon a congregation ... when it sends the congregation away exalted in spirit and with a deeper sense of fellowship with God and man." Religious drama, then, forms a means of ministering to people. After a brief history of drama in the church, the book walks the novice through the details of play production: choosing the play, directing, acting, stage management, lighting, costumes, etc. 197 pages.

[1202] Ehrensperger, Harold. *Conscience on Stage.* New York: Abingdon-Cokesbury Press, 1947.

This book combines a theoretical look at the religious uses of drama with practical suggestions for the presentation of productions in churches or church halls. "This book presupposes that the dramatic impulse is native, that its nurture is part of the educational responsibility of the church. It insists that there is no separate religious drama, that drama of good quality has religious values, that purposeful, intelligent living is always dramatic, and that episodes from this kind of experience are authentic material for plays." While not intended to form a complete handbook of church drama, the book does in fact address many concrete issues of production and even includes sample scripts. 238 pages.

[1203] Ehrensperger, Harold. *Religious Drama: Ends and Means.* New York: Abingdon Press, 1962.

Combining a general introduction to drama with concrete suggestions for producing church plays, this work is a helpful introductory handbook for everything from the history of drama to the mechanics of stagecraft. Particularly interesting are appendices which sketch developments in religious drama in the United States (in all denominations), suggest plays for church production, and provide a 26 page annotated bibliography on all aspects of church theatrical performance. 287 pages.

[1204] Ellison, Jerome. *God on Broadway.* Richmond, VA: John Knox Press, 1971.

Commenting on the view of God in various commercial plays, this book gives a brief biographical note on the playwrights, a review of the work, an analysis of a particular play (with an eye to the theme of relation to God), and a classification of the playwright according to religious outlook. Playwrights include O'Neill, Wilder, MacLeish, Williams, Miller, Albee, and Chayefsky. 96 pages.

[1205] Ferlita, Ernest. *The Theatre of Pilgrimage.* New York: Sheed and Ward, 1971.

Noting that the theatre of pilgrimage is found only in the Judeo-Christian tradition, Ferlita characterizes it by the questions, "Where do we come from? What are we? Where are we going?" With this general orientation, he then comments on eight plays, each of which illustrate a different dimension of pilgrimage. Plays include *King Lear*, *The Road to Damascus*, *The Cocktail Party*, *Break of Noon*, *Camino Real*, *Hunger and Thirst*, *The Fugitive* and *My Kinsman*, *Major Molineux*. The book has as its subtext the exploration of a Christian theatre. 172 pages.

[1206] Halverson, Marvin, ed. *Religious Drama.* 3 vols. New York: Meridian Books, 1957-1959.

This collection of plays contains the texts of 21 medieval and 13 modern plays with religious themes. Among the modern plays are works by Auden, Fry, Lawrence, Sayers, and Williams. Production notes and commentary by the editor accompany each play's script. volume 1: 410 pages; volume 2: 317 pages; volume 3: 317 pages.

[1207] Houghton, Norris. "Church and Stage Find Common Ground." *Theatre Arts* 42.2 (February 1958): 74-75, 90.

Arguing that drama "that exists to celebrate in theatrical terms the elements of Christian faith; and beyond this, the drama that explores the meaning of life viewed in spiritual terms" constitutes religious drama, Houghton reviews various Broadway and church plays. He also describes different denominational efforts to support religious drama and its study. 3 pages.

[1208] Johnson, Albert. *Church Plays and How to Stage Them.* Philadelphia: United Church Press, 1966.

This practical guide to staging church plays contains three plays written by the author. The opening chapters give a sketchy theoretical introduction to the role of drama in the church (primarily from the Baptist perspective). A chapter on the qualities of a good religious play suggests that the play— beyond the characteristics of good drama– must have an optimistic theme, must not inspire idolatry, must acknowledge the creator, and must show some reverence for human life. 174 pages.

[1209] Jones, Paul D. *Rediscovering Ritual.* New York: Newman Press, 1973.

After a brief introduction which situates modern life in terms of ritual and symbol, Jones blocks out six ritual events that can work with worship or outside of worship. Each communicates a different aspect of the Christian life: birth/rebirth; consolidation; commitment/vocation; reconciliation; departure; and sharing. 81 pages.

[1210] Kelley, Gail with Carol Hershberger. *Come Mime with Me: A Guide to Preparing Scriptural Dramas for Children.* San Jose, CA: Resource Publications, 1987.

After a brief introduction which states that the book's purpose is to make Scripture available to children, this volume presents 10 Biblically-based mimes or dramas for grammar school children. In addition to the script, the text also provides a summary and a follow-up exercise. 90 pages.

[1211] Kendall, Robert D. *A Rhetorical Study of Religious Drama as a Form of Preaching: An Exploration of Drama as a Complement of Monologue Preaching.* Diss. University of Minnesota, 1973. *Dissertation Abstracts International* 34.5A (1974): 2800. Ann Arbor: UMI, 1973. 7325624.

Dramatic presentation forms a valid supplement to preaching for church communication, according to this study. After a brief historical sketch, the author applies Kenneth Burke's method of rhetorical analysis to several plays in order to substantiate the claims that such drama can both proclaim and instruct and that drama is persuasive in religious matters. The bibliography contains a valuable listing of plays for church use. 242 pages.

[1212] Kerr, James S. *The Key to Good Church Drama.* Minneapolis, MN: Augsburg Publishing House, 1964.

Drama offers new possibilities for communicating the Gospel and can be quite effective if done properly. This books guides local congregations through the production of a church drama. It includes everything from setting up a committee and choosing a play to tips for the director and actors to how to build a set. Kerr concludes with a resource list of plays, readings, technical books, and so forth. 71 pages.

[1213] Lewis, Todd V. "Training the Layperson in Religious Dramatic Performance." *The Journal of Communication and Religion* 10.2 (September 1987): 31-41.

This resource guide provides background information for those desiring to promote liturgical or pedagogical drama in churches. It includes guides for directors, information card forms for casting, and an annotated bibliography, mostly listing plays and short sketches. 11 pages.

[1214] Litherland, Janet. *Getting Started in Drama Ministry: A Complete Guide to Christian Drama.* Colorado Springs, CO: Meriwether Publishing, 1988.

This book begins with a sketch of the history of drama and religion, addressing the question, "What makes drama religious?" Then, using specific examples, Litherland reviews situations in which drama can find a place in the church—in worship, in fellowship groups, in dinner theatre, in fund raising, and in publicity programs. She also includes sections on getting started (outlining the facilities needed), on special effects, on directing, on acting, and on drama workshops. The book includes a resource list, bibliography, and index. 134 pages.

[1215] Lynch, William F. "Liturgy and the Theatre." *Liturgical Arts* 12.1 (November 1943): 3-4, 9-10.

This brief historical treatment of early liturgical theatre notes some specifically Christian aspects of the medieval church plays: the merging of symbolism and realism, the theological milestones which influence European art and theatre (the importance of the Passion, the defense of icons, the realistic representation of the Gospels, etc.), and the union of the liturgy and the dramatic. 4 pages.

[1216] McCabe, William H. *An Introduction to the Jesuit Theatre.* Ed. Louis J. Oldani. St. Louis: Institute of Jesuit Sources, 1983.

This volume, a posthumously published revision of the author's reworked dissertation (originally prepared in 1929), examines the history and function of the theatre in Jesuit education across Europe, Asia, and South America from the sixteenth to the eighteenth centuries. For the Jesuits theatrical performance not only provided students with training in oratorical skills; it also served to augment the moral and Christian education they imparted in the classroom and helped them to reach a wider audience in the 620 cities in which they had schools. The book also includes a more detailed treatment of the productions at one school (the English College of St. Omer's) and an examination of the tragedies of Joseph Simons. 346 pages.

[1217] McCleary, John Franklin. "Pulpit and Stage." *The Princeton Seminary Bulletin* 59 (March 1966): 41-47.

After reviewing the situation of drama in the church and noting the strength of the Catholic tradition of such drama, McCleary examines the possibility of a Protestant tradition of religious drama. He suggests both theological and literary perspectives and argues that the commercial stage can well raise serious theological issues. 7 pages.

[1218] McLaughlin, Patrick. "Aims of Religious Drama." *Christian Drama* 3.2 (Autumn 1955): 50-53.

In this reporting of a group discussion, McLaughlin argues that "the only legitimate aim of Religious Drama is to be authentic and complete drama." We behold the full recognition of human life in drama—as created by God, corporeal and spiritual, in space, time and eternity. 4 pages.

[1219] Merchant, W. Moelwyn. *Creed and Drama: An Essay in Religious Drama.* London: S. P. C. K., 1965.

This book, based on a series of lectures at the University of the South, Sewanee, Tennessee, traces a single argument in "the relation between certain beliefs concerning human destiny and the dramatic forms in which they were successively cast." Samplings of drama from several periods illustrate the theme—classical Greece, medieval liturgical drama, Marlowe, Shakespeare, Milton, Byron, Tennyson, Eliot, and Fry. Cautioning the reader to expect an analogical predication of "religious drama" for each age and artist, Merchant develops his theme by following the growing split between religious art and dramatic portrayal. 119 pages.

[1220] Ogden-Malouf, Susan Marie. *American Revivalism and Temperance Drama: Evangelical Protestant Ritual and Theatre in Rochester, New York, 1830-1845*. Diss. Northwestern University, 1981. *Dissertation Abstracts International* 42.5A (1982): 1855. Ann Arbor: UMI, 1981. 8124967.

This study of ritual and drama in the nineteenth century revival movement argues that "although they served dramatically different functions, ritual and theatre were nonetheless significantly interrelated within the Evangelical Protestant community." Where ritual involved actualization, direct efficacy, direct participation, belief, and ecstasy; the theatre involved representation, indirect efficacy, indirect participation (watching an actor), suspension of disbelief, and entertainment. In addition, the study argues that temperance dramas had their origin in revivalism's rituals when clever entrepreneurs set up theatrical performances with the claim that they were religious and would help people change their lives in ways similar to the current revival meetings.

Although the study makes a stronger claim about the origins of American theatre than about any Christian theatre, it does illuminate the connections between Christian worship, revivalism, and drama in ways that help explain the entertainment qualities in present day evangelism. 366 pages.

[1221] Peel, Joyce M. and Darius L. Swann. *Drama for the Church: A Handbook on Religious Drama*. Madras, India: The Christian Literature Society, 1962.

Primarily addressing Christians in India, this collection of essays by the authors argues that drama forms an effective means of communicating the gospel. Individual essays examine drama in its own right, liturgical drama, choral speech, interpreting the psalms in movement, mystery and morality plays, biblical plays, children's plays, shadow plays, and the task of producing a play. 121 pages.

[1222] Prosser, Eleanor. *Drama and Religion in the English Mystery Plays: A Re-Evaluation*. Stanford, CA: Stanford University Press, 1961.

In this study of medieval English drama Prosser proposes that the mystery plays be studied as drama rather than in a purely historical manner and offers a method for accomplishing this by delving into the religious and social world view of the audiences. She argues that the dramatic communication must be seen first as religious before it can be appreciated as good drama. She applies the method to Corpus Christi plays with the theme of repentance: Cain, Joseph, Woman taken in Adultery, Magdalene, and Thomas. 229 pages.

[1223] Rice, Wayne and Mike Yaconelli. *The Greatest Skits on Earth.* Grand Rapids, MI: Zondervan Publishing House, 1986.

This collection of 118 skits is designed for use in Christian education; for the most part, they target a youth or teenage audience. The book has sections on one-act skits, slapstick skits, interviews, classic skits, stunts, audience-participation skits, and one-liners. 237 pages.

[1224] Roberts, Preston. "A Christian Theory of Dramatic Tragedy." *Journal of Religion* 31.1 (January 1951): 1-20.

Arguing that the *Poetics* of Aristotle requires transformation in the light of Protestant theology, Roberts follows Aristotle in addressing the inner content and structure of drama rather than the author or the audience. Illustrating the argument by reference to Christian plays, he claims that a play must possess certain properties to merit the name Christian: (1) the demands upon the audience "are symbolic rather than realistic or allegorical. As a symbol, a Christian play brings together the events and meanings realism and allegory would keep apart." In other words, dualism has no part in a Christian play. (2) Unlike the Greek, a Christian tragic hero has changing qualities and relations. (3) The tragic hero's flaw is the abuse of the radical freedom given by Christ. Like the Christian God, the tragic hero is concrete and involved existentially in the world. (4) The plot of a Christian play is to some extent open. (5) "The effect of a Christian play upon its audience is a sense of judgment and forgiveness rather than a sense of pity and terror." 20 pages.

[1225] Robertson, Roderick. "Toward a Definition of Religious Drama." *Educational Theatre Journal* 9.1 (March 1957): 99-105.

Beginning with a commentary on Graham Greene's *The Living Room,* Robertson argues that the use of ethical or religious materials does not make a drama religious; nor does the effect of the play on the audience. Rather, a religious drama must involve the acceptance of a supernatural order and "present or suggest directly the idea that the ultimate meaning of existence is to be found outside this world and that the proper life for mankind is the search for and finding of a positive relationship with God." In this light, there are three basic types of religious drama: the drama of religious alienation, the drama of religious experience, and the drama of the religious hero. 7 pages.

[1226] Rood, Wayne R. "Religious Drama." *Encounter* 26 (1965): 514-524.

In this review essay, Rood examines six collections of religious drama on the basis of a critical judgment, of a theatrical judgment, and of a theological judgment. He suggests that some of the plays (including those in the collection edited by Bachman and Browne [1187]) make good candidates for production in churches, others provide real possibilities for oral reading and discussion, and still others stand as examples to be avoided. 11 pages.

[1227] Sheehy, Sister Gregory. "Christian Enrichment through the Drama." *Catholic Educational Review* 63 (September 1965): 401-407.

This apologia for drama insists that drama can serve Christian ends since it can lead to "intellectual, aesthetic, philosophical, moral and spiritual advancement." As long as drama leads to holy things, it is good; should it lead away from these, it is bad. 7 pages.

[1228] Spanos, William V. *The Christian Tradition in Modern British Verse Drama: The Poetics of Sacramental Time.* New Brunswick, NJ: Rutgers University Press, 1967.

Through an examination of the dramatic works of T. S. Eliot, Charles Williams, Dorothy Sayers, John Masefield, Christopher Fry, and others, the author argues the thesis that Christian theatre embodies a "sacramental aesthetic" which gives it a unique character and value. This aesthetic, based in the mystery of the Incarnation, "assumes the organic wholeness of the artistic imagination and of the orders of experience that are its objects" (page 26). This sacramental vision sees such a connection between spirit and matter, subject and object, God and nature, that it allows the artist to discover transcendental truths in ordinary human experience. This work's especial value lies in the careful articulation of its thesis which can be applied to works in other media. 400 pages.

[1229] Speaight, Robert. *Christian Theatre.* New York: Hawthorn Books, 1960.

Basically a historical survey of Christian plays or Christian themes in the (mostly English speaking) theatre, this book provides a brief introduction to the liturgical and paraliturgical drama of the middle ages and to the Elizabethan Renaissance and Shakespeare, with looks at the Jesuit theatre in Germany, Calderon in Spain, and Racine and Corneille in France. A final chapter on contemporary religious theatre summarizes the plots of religious drama through the 1950's. Valuable for its ability to situate historically various dramatic movements, the book suffers from the plot-summary approach to religious drama. 140 pages.

[1230] Speaight, Robert. "The Possibilities of a Christian Theatre." *Twentieth Century Catholicism.* Vol. 3. Ed. Lancelot Sheppard. New York: Hawthorn Books, 1966. 101-116.

In this essay Speaight comments on examples of Christian plays, drawing them from the works of Eliot, Fry, Bolt, Sayers, and Hochhuth. He notes that the religious qualities of the plays can come from the subject matter, the treatment, the theme, or the setting; bad writing (as in the case of Hochhuth) has no more a place in religious drama than in any drama. He concludes with a warning that much of the religious quality of plays cannot survive translation into another culture since much of that quality takes meaning from its culture. 16 pages.

[1231] Townsend, Lucy F., Eric Potter, and Kent Lindberg, eds. *Parade of Plays for your Church*. 3 vols. Elgin, IL: David C. Cook Publishing Co., 1986.

Because "drama is one of the best ways to help people capture the reality of the Christian life," the editors of this series have assembled a collection of plays for Christian leaders that have not used drama before. The plays include Christmas plays, Easter plays, Biblical plays, historical sketches, and faith-sharing skits, directed to various age groups.

[1232] Van Zanten, John. *Caught in the Act: Modern Drama as Prelude to the Gospel*. Philadelphia: The Westminster Press, 1971.

Van Zanten contends that "if the Christian faith is to speak to our condition, it must understand that condition." One way of understanding is to look at modern drama as a descriptor of contemporary life. His preparation for Christian communication leads him to analyze several plays, each in the light of a different theme. 201 pages.

[1233] Waddy, Lawrence. *Drama in Worship*. NY: Paulist Press, 1978.

This collection of church drama follows the liturgical year of the Catholic lectionary, providing chancel dramas for each Sunday of the year. A short introduction prepares the reader with comments on staging, music, and so forth. Each play (based on a Biblical reference) has a contemporary setting; the quality of the plays varies. 210 pages.

[1234] Weales, Gerald Clifford. *Religion in Modern English Drama*. 1961. Westport, CN: Greenwood Press, 1976.

This survey of twentieth century British drama examines both commercial drama and church drama for their use of Christian themes, Christian images, or specifically Christian plots—either for religious or purely dramatic purposes. Largely constructed as a series of commentaries and plot summaries, the book reviews the early work of Henry Arthur Jones, J. B. Priestly, and Bernard Shaw, setting the scene for later playwrights, including Laurence Housman, John Masefield, Charles Williams and Dorothy Sayers (in the church drama area) and T. S. Eliot and Christopher Fry (on the commercial stage). The book also includes a look at lesser writers and a 25 page chronology of plays. 317 pages.

[**1235**] Wheeler, Burton M. "Theology and the Theatre." *The Journal of Bible and Religion* 28 (1960): 334-344.

In order to explore the relationship of theatre to theology, Wheeler examines two sets of plays (Eliot's *Murder in the Cathedral* and *The Cocktail Party*, and Fry's *Sleep of Prisoners* and *The Dark is Light Enough*) as well as MacLeish's *J. B.* He argues that while the theologian or the church playwright may assume God and an affinity to that point of view in the audience, the dramatist for the legitimate stage cannot. Both Eliot and Fry observe this as do the two different versions of *J. B.* The different interests of theatre and religious institutions leave their mark on the drama directed to each. 11 pages.

Some other materials on religious drama appear in newsletters or periodicals devoted to church drama, for example [16] and [44]. Historical material for religious drama appears in [369], [380], and [389], while bibliographic references can be found in [67].

Dance

[**1236**] Adams, Doug. *Congregational Dancing in Christian Worship.* Austin: The Sharing Company, 1971.

In an attempt to situate dance within Christian worship, Adams explores the ways dance supports four key themes (community, repentance, rejoicing, and rededication). For each theme, he explores Old and New Testament roots (primarily through linguistic or etymological study), patristic practices, and contemporary examples. The historical theological material, though somewhat sparse, whets one's appetite for more while the examples provide outlines for incorporating dance in worship. 156 pages.

[**1237**] Adams, Doug. it Involving the People in Dancing Worship: Historic and Contemporary Patterns. Austin, TX: The Sharing Company, 1975.

This pamphlet "suggests ways to involve the congregation in dancing worship" by describing historic worship services that could be reenacted by the congregation, and by sketching contemporary worship which makes integral use of dance, particularly in the processions. 22 pages.

[**1238**] Adams, Doug. *Appropriating Australian Folk Dance into Sacred Dance.* Austin, TX: The Sharing Company, 1987.

Following a brief introduction, Adams outlines choreography for a number of Christmas hymns as well as for some traditional Christian hymns. The booklet presents material from a conference on art and worship in Sydney in 1985. 20 pages.

[1239] Backman, E. Louis. *Religious Dances in the Christian Church and in Popular Medicine.* Trans. E. Classen. London: George Allen & Unwin Ltd, 1952. Reprinted, Westport, CT: Greenwood Press, 1976.

This wonderfully complete and scholarly work traces the history of religious dance and documents the uses of dance in Christian worship and life. The book features 133 illustrations, many musical notations, descriptions of each dance and it place of origin, and a large bibliography. The historical description of the gradual falling out of favor of Christian dance holds particular interest. 364 pages.

[1240] Beach, Barbara Kress. *Barefoot in the Chancel.* Boston: Unitarian Universalist Association, n.d.

Primarily a how-to guide to introducing dance in churches and organizing a dance group, this booklet includes some helpful reflections on dance as a means of communication in Christian worship and on choosing subjects for dance. As a nonverbal expression, dance communicates things of the heart and the religious awareness which lies beyond words. 59 pages.

[1241] Blogg, Martin. *Dance and the Christian Faith.* London: Hodder and Stoughton, 1985.

This book has two purposes: to supply an apologetic for dance in Christian worship and faith (particularly to show that dance is biblical) and to teach some basics about dance. The first section deals with dance and scripture, providing commentary on scriptural references to dance and showing what these mean for Christians. A second section gives a brief defense of dance as a way of knowing while the third gives examples of religious dances along with their choreography. 303 pages.

[1242] Daniels, Marilyn. *The Dance in Christianity: A History of Religious Dance Through the Ages.* New York: Paulist Press, 1981.

This book provides a popular history of religious dance from pre- Christian times through the 20th century. The length of the book limits the history to a somewhat sketchy narrative, illuminated by some brief quotations. 88 pages.

[1243] Davies, J. G. *Liturgical Dance: An Historical, Theological and Practical Handbook.* London: SCM Press, 1984.

This book provides a thorough, scholarly, and fairly critical overview of dance within Christianity. The historical section seeks particularly to correct a misreading of patristic sources by Backman [1239] which has had enormous influence. The theological section looks at the meaning of Christian dance and "seeks to break new ground by examining it in relation to the doctrine of human nature, to sacramental theology and to the theology of worship." The last section addresses practical concerns: a common

vocabulary for Christian dance, dance education, and congregational dancing. The book also includes a dense 15 page bibliography, including two
pages of patristic references. 268 pages.

[1244] Davies, J. G., ed. *Worship and Dance*. Birmingham, England: Institute for the Study of Worship and Religious Architecture, University of
Birmingham, 1975.

This collection includes historical, theoretical, and practical essays dealing
with Christianity and dance. The editor presents two particularly good essays: the first, an historical survey of dancing in Church buildings from
the fourth century to the present and the second, an attempt to sketch a
theology of the dance. In the latter he associates dance, play, and ritual;
and examines dance as a way of revealing the sacred through the assertion
of the unity of body and soul. Given the Christian valuation of the flesh
in the Incarnation, dance appears as an expression of salvation through its
unification of body and soul as communication (page 50). Dance, a com-
munal activity, becomes a means of establishing and celebrating Christian
community and worshiping God. Other essays in the collection provide
case studies of dance in worship and scriptural studies of dance in the Old
Testament. 93 pages.

[1245] De Sola, Carla. *The Spirit Moves: Handbook of Dance and Prayer*.
Ed. Doug Adams. Austin, TX: The Sharing Company, 1986.

After an introductory set of reflections on dance and prayer, De Sola provides a series of movements and dances for meditation, for celebrating
the Eucharist, for the church seasons, and for special occasions (baptism,
thanksgiving, retirement, funerals, etc.). A final chapter considers dance as
a ministry in the Christian community. 152 pages.

[1246] Deitering, Carolyn. *The Liturgy as Dance and the Liturgical Dancer*.
New York: Crossroad, 1984.

From the earliest ages people have associated movement and dance with
religious expression. In an attractive presentation, Deitering traces Old and
New Testament roots of liturgical dance through the patristic and medieval
periods to the present day (in the Roman Catholic tradition) and offers
principles of movement, liturgical applications and ideas for dances. 144
pages.

[1247] Fallon, Dennis J. and Mary Jane Wolbers. *Focus on Dance X: Religion and Dance*. Reston, VA: The American Alliance for Health, Physical
Education, Recreation and Dance, 1982.

This collection of essays introduces the religious dimensions and uses of
dance. The first part has four historical essays, tracing the religious uses
of dance from the Greeks, from the Catholic Middle Ages, from the Plains

Indians, and through contemporary conflicts. The second part examines the relationship between dance and organized religion with essays on Mormonism, Southern Baptists, Judaism, and Catholicism. The third part sees dance as spiritual expression. The last part explores dance in places of worship. Photographs or sketches illustrate each essay. 90 pages.

[1248] Fisher, Constance. *Dancing the Old Testament: Christian Celebrations of Israelite Heritage for Worship and Education.* Austin, TX: The Sharing Company, 1980.

This volume presents 12 choreographed dances grouped according to Old Testament themes: the rhythm of life and death, the rhythm of ecstatic response, and the rhythm of nature. The author supplies a brief commentary on each dance, situating it in scriptural and cultural contexts. The book contains guides to sources, recordings, music, and bibliography. 128 pages.

[1249] Fisher, Constance. *Dancing with Early Christians.* Ed. Doug Adams. Austin, TX: The Sharing Company, 1983.

Arranging its material around the themes of the life of Christ, the worship of the early church, mysticism, and the sacraments of the church, this volume reproduces choreographies of 30 dances for church use. Each chapter contains a brief introduction to the theme, the appropriate choreographies (some with illustrations), and, occasionally, musical settings. 176 pages.

[1250] Fisher, Constance. *Dancing Festivals of the Church Year.* Ed. Doug Adams. Austin, TX: The Sharing Company, 1986.

This guide to using dance in the celebration of religious festivals has eight chapters, covering the church year from Lent to Advent and Epiphany. Each chapter begins with a brief discussion of the occasion and outlines the music, choreography, costumes, setting, and participants for each celebration. The book includes photographs illustrating the dances, a bibliography, a resource list, and an index. 119 pages.

[1251] Fisk, Margaret Palmer. *Look Up and Live.* St. Paul, MN: Macalester Park Publishing Company, 1953.

This book presents a series of dances and movements choreographed to various Christian hymns ("There's a Wideness in God's Mercy," "Christ the Lord is Risen Today," etc.) and prayers (The Lord's Prayer) and accompanied by explanations of the material. A presumption is that dance provides a means of worship and healing; the text manages to evoke both. Whether used for worship, private prayer, or retreats, this material invites the reader to experience religious dance in an accessible and prayerful way. 99 pages.

[1252] Foatelli, Renee. *Les Danses Religieuses dans le Christianisme.* Paris: Éditions Spes, 1947.

This volume traces the history of religious dance from biblical times through the early church and the medieval ages to the 20th century. Particularly interesting chapters deal with the pagan influences on Christian dance and with the variety of religious folklore dance in this century, particularly processions, funeral dances, and wedding dances. 111 pages.

[1253] Gagne, Ronald, Thomas Kane, and Robert VerEecke. *Introducing Dance in Christian Worship*. Washington, D.C.: The Pastoral Press, 1984.

Each part of this book deals with a different aspect of dance. Gagne provides an historical overview of dance in the Christian tradition, examining in particular the Fathers of the Church and the medieval period—times which wrestled with a certain ambivalence toward dance. He also gives a very helpful chronology of liturgical dance from 300-1800 A. D. Kane suggests a variety of types of liturgical dance—procession, proclamation, prayer, meditation, celebration, etc.—and gives some choreographical guidelines. VerEecke offers some theological perspectives on dance as communication (drawing on ideas of creation and incarnation) and then specifically examines liturgical dance with its promises and difficulties. A seven page annotated bibliography concludes the book. 184 pages.

[1254] Huff, Joan. *Celebrating Pentecost Through Dance*. Austin, TX: The Sharing Company, 1986.

Huff begins with an overview of the history of Pentecost and then presents choreographic ideas for dances for this feast. Appendices contain summaries of themes, movements, movement qualities, colors and props. 24 pages.

[1255] Kirk, Martha Ann. *Mexican and Native American Dances in Christian Worship and Education*. Ed. Doug Adams. Austin, TX: The Sharing Company, 1981.

After briefly sketching the history of religious dance in the Spanish tradition, Kirk describes eight religious dances found primarily in the Mexico and the American Southwest. 26 pages.

[1256] Krosnicki, Thomas A. "Dance Within the Liturgical Act." *Worship* 61.4 (July 1987): 349-357.

In this piece, based on presentation to the consultors of the Catholic Congregation for Divine Worship, Krosnicki argues that the use of dance in the liturgy should fall under the heading of "gesture and movement" since the term, "dance," has unacceptable connotations in some cultures. Further, he asks for a greater use of gesture and movement, but one that flows from each culture and its understanding of ritualized motion. 9 pages.

[1257] Rock, Judith. "Terpsichore at Louis le Grand: Baroque Dance on a Jesuit Stage in Paris." Diss. Graduate Theological Union, 1988.

This study of the baroque ballets produced in the French Jesuit Colleges between 1660 and 1761 focuses on questions of style and aesthetics, technique, relation to audience, relation to the Jesuits' education goals, and the "feminine" element of the Jesuit education. These highly professional productions formed part of the Parisian communications network and helped both to frame the policies of the king and to shape the outlook of the court in counter-reformation Catholic morality.

The author argues that this tradition has relevance to contemporary Church relations to the performing arts since it supports alternative directions—to focus on art in non-liturgical settings and contexts and "to find revelation in form as well as in content." 546 pages.

[1258] Sautter, Cynthia D. *Irish Dance & Spirituality: Relating Folkdance & Faith.* Ed. Doug Adams. Austin, TX: The Sharing Company, 1986.

Adams introduces this booklet with a discussion of the communicative aspects of Celtic dances. Sautter outlines the uses of Celtic dance which leads her into a theological discussion of Irish dance and its sacred quality. She includes basic Irish dance steps and a demonstration of using Irish dance in the sanctuary. 32 pages.

[1259] Taylor, Margaret Fisk. *A Time to Dance: Symbolic Movement in Worship.* Philadelphia: United Church Press, 1967.

Symbolic choral dance—"interpret[ing] through symbolic movement"—is an art that can be used to assist Christians in their worship. Taylor traces the use of symbolic choral dance throughout the history of the church and offers suggestions for its implementation and use in local churches. 180 pages.

[1260] Taylor, Margaret. *Hymns in Actions for Everyone: People 9 to 90 Dancing Today.* Ed. Doug Adams. Austin, TX: The Sharing Company, 1985.

This booklet presents symbolic movements and prayer gestures for 25 common Christian hymns in order to deepen the experience of worship and to foster spiritual growth of congregational members. 90 pages.

[1261] Tucci, Douglass Shand. "The High Mass as Sacred Dance." *Theology Today* 34.1 (April 1977): 58-72.

The art-form of the liturgy unites architecture and action and becomes a sacred dance. Following Underhill, Tucci considers each of these aspects of the high Mass (in both the Roman and Anglican rites), noting that it continually struggles for the incarnation in itself of the supernatural, attempting to balance voice, music, space, movement, decoration, and design. 15 pages.

Additional materials on sacred dance appear in specialized journals (for example, [45]) or in bibliographies ([52], [76], and [78]).

Music

[1262] Blanchard, John, Peter Anderson, and Derek Cleave. *Pop Goes the Gospel*. Welwyn, Hertfordshire, England: Evangelical Press, 1983.

Within the context of a evangelically-based condemnation of rock music as sexually oriented, satanic, and occult, this book treats the possibility of Christian rock and rejects it. 160 pages.

[1263] Desrosiers, Yvon. "Réflexion chrétienne sur la chanson d'aujourd'hui." *Cahiers d'études et de recherches* 5 (1965): 1-23.

After giving a general history of recent French popular music, Desrosiers notes that its theological significance lies in the role it plays in contemporary life. Music allows relaxation and both inserts an individual into the wider community and gives the individual some privacy from that community. Moreover, different music (particularly poetic music) promotes reflection on significant life themes. 23 pages.

[1264] Hunter, Stanley Armstrong, ed. *The Music of the Gospel*. New York: Abingdon Press, 1932.

This book consists of 26 essays, each dealing with a specific Christian hymn. The essays describe the hymn, its composer, and the context of its composition. A combination of devotional reflection and historical background make this volume a reference, at least for older Protestant hymns. 344 pages.

[1265] Jasper, Tony. *Jesus and the Christian in a Pop Culture*. London: Robert Royce Limited, 1984.

This book takes a look at the pop music culture from a Christian point of view. It is valuable as a resource book since it reprints various church reports on popular music, lists Christian rock stars, songs, and musicals, and provides a reference to religious music and publishing in the U. K. and in the U. S. A. 227 pages.

[1266] McCann, Forrest Mason. *The Development of the Hymn in Old and Middle English Literature*. Diss. Texas Tech University, 1980. *Dissertation Abstracts International* 41.4A (1981): 1613. Ann Arbor: UMI, 1980. 8022623.

Primarily a work of music history, this study demonstrates the existence of an English hymnody tradition before the Reformation through a consideration of religious verse and song from Caedmon to the Reformation. 198 pages.

[**1267**] Mendl, R. W. S. *The Divine Quest in Music.* London: Rockliff, 1957.

Though it contains a good deal of music history, this book ambitions more: to be "an essay on the relationship between music and God." To illustrate the theme, Mendl examines works of Bach, Handel, Mozart, Beethoven, Schubert, Berlioz, Mendelssohn, Chopin, Schumann, Liszt, Verdi, Franck, Bruckner, and Brahms. He chooses to pass over more well- known liturgical or religious composers, preferring to establish his thesis with more controversial figures. 252 pages.

[**1268**] Pugsley, Richard John. *The Development of the Music Program in the Community of Jesus.* Diss. Columbia University, 1983. *Dissertation Abstracts International* 44.12A (1984): 3623. Ann Arbor: UMI, 1984. 8403279.

This study uses the example of an ecumenical Christian community as the basis for an exploration in music education. However, the context of the study leads to an investigation into the role of music in the wider Christian community. Historical materials include discussion of the place of music among the Moravians, Shakers, and members of the Ephrata Cloister. For each, as well as for the Community of Jesus, Pugsley asks how the music program is based on and expresses the underlying philosophy and way of life of the group. 276 pages.

[**1269**] Winter, Miriam Therese. *Vatican II in the Development of Criteria for the Use of Music in the Liturgy of the Roman Catholic Church in the United States and Their Theological Bases.* Diss. Princeton Theological Seminary, 1983. *Dissertation Abstracts International* 44.5A (1984): 1495. Ann Arbor: UMI, 1983. 8320294.

This dissertation provides a detailed examination of church music in the Roman Catholic tradition. Winter presents the conciliar material in the context of a wider liturgical movement and notes the shifts in theological outlook which made it possible. The third, historical, section traces the Catholic use and legislation of music to the middle ages; from this Winter deduces the criteria for music and its theological base. 436 pages.

[**1270**] Winter, Miriam Therese. *Why Sing? Toward a Theology of Catholic Liturgical Music.* Washington, D. C.: The Pastoral Press, 1984.

Intended as an overview of music in the Catholic liturgy, this study presents historical, conciliar, and papal sources for current practice and examines the shifting theological background for church music in the last five centuries. Based on the author's dissertation, the book includes an excellent bibliography on church music that runs to over 100 pages. 346 pages.

Sound Media

[1271] Hack, John. *How to Operate a Cassette Tape Ministry*. Nashville, TN: Broadman Press, 1981.

"Simply stated, a cassette tape ministry in a church is a program for making available for wide distribution sermons and other recorded material of interest to people inside and outside of a church." This book—a text for the Southern Baptist Church Study course—provides a lot of practical information about tape recording and equipment as well as much down-home advice based on the experiences of many churches. Truly thorough (from recording an original, preparing the master, to financing to storage), the book also has a good chapter on copyrights and permissions. 128 pages.

[1272] Søgaard, Viggo B. *Everything You Need to Know for a Cassette Ministry: Cassettes in the Context of a Total Christian Communication Program*. Minneapolis, MN: Bethany Fellowship, Inc., 1975.

Cassette players open up a new dimension for missionaries who can leave tapes of sermons, instructions, hymns, etc. for people to listen to and learn from at their own pace. This book covers every aspect of working with cassettes from the technical and financial to the content and production. The author's emphasis on research to better meet the needs of the audience forms an important framework of the book; examples, while helpful, do seem limited since they come exclusively from the author's own evangelical missionary work in Thailand. 221 pages.

[1273] Thompson, Phyllis. *Faith by Hearing: The Story of Gospel Records*. Los Angeles: Gospel Recordings, Inc., 1960.

This small book tells the story of Gospel Records, a recording company that seeks to produce records of Gospel texts and songs in native languages for use in missionary work. Narrating the biography of the work's foundress, Joy Ridderhof, the book traces her work from the first Spanish-language record in 1938 to over 3000 dialect recordings in 1960. The work's "complete dependence on the Lord for wisdom, strength and supply of every need" shows through in its history and in the narration of that history. 64 pages.

Comic Books

[1274] Francart, Roland. *Tresors de la B.D. [Bande Dessinée] religieuse de 1941 a 1985.* Brussels: CRIABD [Centre religieux d'information et d'analyse de la bande dessinée], 1985.

An exhibition guide to a collection of religious comic strips, this fine booklet situates religious comics within the larger French tradition of cartoons and gives a brief introduction to each artist and his or her work, showing samples of each. The booklet also contains a bibliography. 56 pages.

[1275] Horstmann, Johannes, ed. *Religiose Comics: Aum pastoralen Einsatz von "Bibel-Comics" und von "allgemeinen religiosen Comics."* Schwerte: Katholische Akademie Schwerte, 1981.

This collection of papers given at a 1980 conference on religious comics contains studies on the varieties of religious comics, on narrative theology in comics, on the pastoral use of the comics, on illustrated Bible stories, and so forth. It provides a good introduction to the uses of religious comics. 243 pages.

[1276] Knockaert, André and Chantal van der Plancke. "La bande dessinée saisie par la religion." *Lumière et vie* 30.155 (octobre-novembre-décembre 1981): 35-44.

This article describes the impact of comic books on religious education in France. Noting first the various artists and their approaches (usually independent of any ecclesiastical direction), it also examines the world of the readers. A final section reviews the types of comic books and the different ways in which they can serve catechetical roles. 10 pages.

[1277] Knockaert, André and Chantal van der Plancke. *Bible Comics and Catechesis.* Trans. Lumen Vitae. Brussels: Editions Lumen Vitae, 1979.

This detailed study of Bible comics places these comics in a context of contemporary culture and of contemporary religious education. Primarily based on French-language comics, the study examines the overall phenomenon and then provides a close reading of two episodes portrayed in the texts: the Annunciation and the Temptation. This analysis follows the structuralism of de Saussure and its adaptation by Propp (in his study of the folk tale). The authors' introduction notes the anxiety with which many religious educators and pastors regard the comics, fearing that Jesus will become simply another super-hero; however, they hold out more promise for this medium. In addition, the study gives a chronological bibliography of Bible comics from 1945 to 1979 and a scholarly bibliography of other studies on the same subject. 171 pages.

Computers

[1278] Bedell, Kenneth B. *The Role of Computers in Religious Education.*
Nashville: Abingdon Press, 1986.

This general introduction to computers in education applies a variety of
principles to religious education: selecting software, setting up a classroom, home uses of religious software, and administrative uses of computers. Thorough in its material, the book's purpose is to help in the evaluation
of computers for religious education on the local level. An appendix lists
available software. 143 pages.

[1279] Beer, Stafford. "Cybernetics and the Knowledge of God." *The Month*
34 (1965): 291-303.

Starting with the cybernetic explanation of control systems, constraints,
and information, Beers examines human knowledge as inherently limited.
He then applies this material to religious language and religious inference
attempting to reach beyond the constraints and explains the process in
terms of systems theory and frames of reference. 13 pages.

[1280] Brown, Ronald. "Information Technology and the Christian." *Cru-
cible* January-March 1983: 4-13

After introducing the microelectronics revolution and computers, Brown
suggests that the appropriate Christian response is to insure that information leads to communication, knowledge, and wisdom. 10 pages.

[1281] Clemens, E. V. *Using Computers in Religious Education.* Nashville:
Abingdon Press, 1986.

This basic introduction covers a range of topics including theological perspectives on technology, using computers in religious education, evaluating
software for religious purposes, and suggestions for teaching activities. A
helpful appendix lists software for religious education. 79 pages.

[1282] David, Austin amd Michael P. Ball. "The Video Game: A Model for
Teacher-Student Collaboration." *Momentum* 17.1 (February 1986): 24-26.

This article describes a video game used in religious education. Modelled on
several popular commercial games, this one, called "The Healer," teaches
the benefits of using power for good and holds out the value of healing
one's enemy and the environment. 3 pages.

[1283] Foltz, Jerrold Lee. *The Use of Personal Computers in Local Congregations: A Study and Critique.* Diss. Eastern Baptist Theological Seminary,
1985. *Dissertation Abstracts International* 46.10A (1986): 3061. Ann Arbor: UMI, 1985. 8528621.

"This thesis-project investigates the current use of personal computers by clergy of various denominations in their ministry." Word processing and office tasks dominate most present use; the author suggests greater educational uses for church computers. He also suggests the need for theological reflection on several aspects of computers: "impersonalization," glorification of technology, privacy, and secularism. 130 pages.

[1284] Granfield, Patrick. *Ecclesial Cybernetics: A Study of Democracy in the Church.* New York: The Macmillan Company, 1973.

This study applies the tools of cybernetics with its focus on "information transmission for the purpose of communication and control" to Roman Catholic Church governance. While the book formally falls under the heading of ecclesiology, its use of a communicative method of analysis marks it as an important step in looking at intra-church communication. 280 pages.

[1285] Granfield, Patrick. "The Local Church as a Center of Communication and Control." *Proceedings of the Catholic Theological Society of America* 35 (1980): 256-263.

Applying a cybernetic theory of communication to the local church (which he tends to cautiously identify with the diocese), Granfield argues that the local church is a subsystem within the universal church and that therefore three cybernetic principles have theological significance. First, the principle of legitimate diversity allows a variety of thought patterns, ecclesial structures, and liturgical practices to exist within a community. Next, the principle of collegiality provides for wide participation in church life. Finally, the principle of subsidiarity encourages local churches to govern themselves. 8 pages.

[1286] Levasseur, Jean-Marie. "L'Ordinateur en pastorale." *Communication humaine aujourd'hui* 143 (février 1987): 1-10.

A general commentary on the religious uses of the computer, this article suggests that information processing systems can provide the religious worker with resources in word processing, documentary research, database searching (various examples include the corpus on religious events in France, the Bible, the works of Aquinas, the documents of Vatican II, etc.), and pastoral planning. The article also provides some basic guidelines to setting up databases for maximum compatibility. 10 pages.

[1287] Orna, Mary Virginia. *Cybernetics, Society and the Church.* Dayton, OH: Pflaum Press, 1969.

An attempt to examine human life and religious responses in the vocabulary of information theory and cybernetics, this book suggests a creative re-reading of several areas of Christian living: communication, education, and theology. On more solid ground in its treatment of cybernetics and optimistic in its view of computer technology, the book is not quite convincing in its theological arguments. 177 pages.

[1288] Parsons, Michael W. S. "Information, Technology and Theology." *Modern Churchman* 28.2 (1986): 42-48.

While Christian theology does not explicitly deal with computers, it certainly does deal with information and has often reflected on power and the exercise thereof. This gives it warrant to speak to a society in the midst of the computer revolution. The churches must remind people of the information source's responsibility (to honesty, for example) and of the information receiver's responsibility (to correctly use that information). Beyond this, the churches can also point out the benefits of this new technology— particularly its interactive quality. 7 pages.

[1289] Stratman, Bernard. "Church and Media Environments in the 1980s: An Integrated Approach to Communication and Information Management." *Catholic Library World* July-August 1978: 20-26.

This paper attempts to set an information management data base system within the context of a "futurology" and ministry. Apparently the system should better supply ministerial and adult education needs. 7 pages.

Video

[1290] Diehl, Erhard and Kurt Sprenger, eds. *Mehr Evangelium in den Medien: Die Herausforderung der neuen Medien.* Witten: Bundes-Verlag, 1982.

This collection reprints papers and presentations from the "first evangelical media congress." Topics include "Christ in the mass media"; the history of broadcasting in West Germany since 1945; evangelical publishing; an overview of the new media (video recorders, videodisc players, videotex, cable television, and direct broadcast satellites); and the electronic church. The volume also has a glossary, a guide to evangelistic publishing houses, and a guide to further reading. 104 pages.

[1291] Emswiler, Tom Neufer. *A Complete Guide to Making the Most of Video in Religious Settings.* Normal, IL: Wesley Foundation Books, 1985.

A guide to videotape resources for churches in the United States, this book provides good chapters on library development, copyright issues, and study guides. Chapters on theology, equipment, local production, and funding are elementary at best. However, the chapter listing video distributors in the United States is alone well worth the price of the book. 133 pages.

[1292] Holland, Daniel W., J. Ashton Nickerson, and Terry Vaughn. *Using Nonbroadcast Video in the Church.* Valley Forge, PA: Judson Press, 1980.

A beginner's handbook on using video in local churches, this guide discusses possible uses for television, its advantages (particularly its intimacy), and some very elementary concepts of how videotape recording works. It also includes some case studies and some references to video sources. 126 pages.

[1293] Huntley, David Anthony. *Video and Missions: A Consideration of the Missiological Use of Video with Special Reference to the Thailand Hospital Video Venture, Together with a Study of the Likely Impact of Video and Teletext in Missiological Applications in Developing Countries.* Thesis: Fuller Theological Seminary, 1981. *Masters Abstracts* 19.4 (1981): 352. Ann Arbor: UMI, 1981. 1316473.

Video provides the possibility of narrowcasting within a missionary effort, adapting the message to the particular audience and culture. This thesis uses a case study approach to missionary video in a hospital setting in Thailand; within this study, it introduces key aspects of video. There is, however, little theological consideration beyond a concern for inculturation. "The thesis concludes with a favorable assessment of the usefulness of the video medium, provided that the programming and production is firmly rooted in the relevant cultural context." 106 pages.

[1294] Jaissle, Jürgen, ed. *Kirche und elektronischer Text.* Frankfurt am Main: Gemeinschaftswerk der Evangelischen Publizistik, 1983.

This set of papers and reference materials was prepared for a conference on videotex and the church, sponsored by the Evangelical Church in Germany. It contains articles on the church videotex project, consequences of cable technologies for the church, religious perspectives on the new technologies, as well as basic information about videotex and a bibliography. 135 pages.

[1295] Kabler, Ciel Dunne. *Telecommunications and the Church.* Virginia Beach, VA: Multi Media Publishing, 1979.

This book gives a simplified introduction to the use of video in and by churches. The writing style tends towards lists of items or interviews and so limits the book's practical value. However, the brainstorming-type lists of ways to utilize video in the church and in Bible study do suggest lots of interesting projects, particularly for non-broadcast or non-cablecast situations. 166 pages.

[1296] O'Sullivan, Jeremiah Ryan. *Video y pastoral: Diagnóstico de centros de producción y uso pastoral del videocassette en América Latina.* Caracas, Venezuela: OCIC-AL [Organización Católica Internacional del Cine y Audiovisual—América Latina], 1985.

Brief introductory chapters treat communication and the church in Latin America, the complementary uses of the mass media and the group media, and the technology of the videocassette. This volume also reports a survey of the actual uses of videocassettes in the Catholic churches of Latin America, by country and by use. An appendix provides a directory to organizations and people involved in this work and a partial listing of productions available. 152 pages.

[1297] Ouellet, Bertrand, ed. "Le vidéotex et l'Église." *Cahiers d'études et de recherches* 33 (1984): 1-35.

This number of the *Cahiers d'études et de recherches* consists of some of the papers delivered at an international conference on videotex and the Church, held in Durham, England in July 1984. Ouellet introduces the papers by providing a history of this conference and its predecessors, by noting the participants, and by giving an overview of the uses of videotex by the churches in Europe and North America. In the papers themselves, R. - F. Poswick inquires as to the extent which this new medium might shape the message; John Orme Mills offers a theological critique of videotex; and Hans-Wolfgang Hessler sketches the social impact of this new technology. 35 pages.

[1298] Ouellet, Bertrand. "Le vidéotex: Un nouvel outil pour la pastorale." *Cahiers d'études et de recherches* 32 (1984).

In this monograph Ouellet introduces the notion of videotex as a potential new technology for Christian communication. Videotex (or videotext or teletext or viewdata) couples computer technology with either broadcast or telephone line transmission to provide information, one screen at a time, to subscribers. Materials, consisting of texts and illustrations, are arranged by topic, available by successive menus. Churches, mostly in Europe, make use of these services to provide information about religious topics and programs. A service is planned for French-speaking Canada and will have a Catholic participation through the Office of Social Communication in Montreal.

[1299] Parsons, Michael W. S. *Viewdata and the Churches.* Durham, England: North of England Institute for Christian Education, 1985.

This report on the Christian Viewdata project (on England's PRESTEL network) includes a general introduction to church use of videotex, its costs, benefits and limits, a survey of its users, and a review of religious viewdata internationally. It concludes with a brief theological discussion and reproductions of the Prestel pages created for the project. 91 pages.

[1300] Sykes, S. W. "What's It All For? Christian Education and the Media." *Religious Teletext Workshop.* Durham, England: DAIS, 1981. 1-5.

Christian education is education for worship, thus acting as a corrective to purely instrumental, cognitive, evocative or moral definitions of Christianity. This approach also integrates the media into Christian education. Teletext must occur in this context if it can serve a purpose in Christian education. (Other material in this booklet gives a technical overview of teletext.) 5 pages.

[1301] Turner, R. Chip. *The Church Video Answerbook: A Nontechnical Guide for Ministers and Laypersons.* Nashville, TN: Broadman Press, 1986.

This short guide presents an elementary look at video; the non-technical presentation will help some readers but may well put off those with a basic knowledge of television and video technology. More helpful are the chapters which brainstorm ideas for using video in religious education, in ministry and in local community outreach. The book contains literally hundreds of ideas that seem workable. Appendices provide information on equipment maintenance, production, copyright law, and sources of programming and equipment. (Many of the program ideas are geared to the Southern Baptist Convention and to using the Baptist Telecommunication Network.) 127 pages.

[1302] Van Eck, Arthur Orville. *The Description of Three Exploratory Uses of the Video Tape Recorder in Christian Education.* Diss. Columbia University, 1969. *Dissertation Abstracts International* 30.9A (1970): 3812. Ann Arbor: UMI, 1970. 7004524.

This investigation of the videotape recorder as an educational tool explored the VTR as a program delay device, as a means of producing local educational materials, and as a means for teacher self-evaluation. Citing 48 potential assets and 29 potential liabilities, the study concludes that church educators need to weigh these factors in each situation in determining the usefulness of video equipment. 263 pages.

New Media

[1303] Funiok, Rüdiger. "Die neuen Medien als Chancen der Verkündigung." *Lebendige Seelsorge* (1987): 258-261.

Taking a positive approach to the "new media," Funiok argues that they present creative possibilities for ministry and proclamation of the Gospel. 4 pages.

[1304] Gjelsten, Gudm., ed. *Satellite Communications and Christian Mission.* Kristiansand, Norway: International Mass Media Institute, 1979.

This collection of papers from an international seminar includes more technical presentations on the nature of satellite broadcasting as well as theological reflections on the role of the Church in satellite communication.

Generally evangelical in tone, the reflections stress the urgency of preaching the Gospel and the cooperation of human agents with the divine initiative. Authors include Erich Kraemer, Sigurd Aske, and Edwin H. Robertson. 96 pages.

[1305] Lutheran World Federation Commission on Communication. "The Churches and New Communications Technologies." *LWF Documentation* 17 (March 1984): 11-20.

This 1982 statement on the new technologies (electronic communication, computerized combinations, video recording, etc.) reviews positive and negative aspects and lists several guiding principles. These include (1) the new technologies should serve the needs of all people; (2) churches should encourage and assist research into their social effects; (3) churches should lobby governments to insure a fair distribution of satellite placements; and (4) churches should utilize these means insofar as they can in their ministries. The statement concludes with six action steps deduced from the guiding principles. 10 pages.

[1306] Moser, Georg. "Was will die Kirche mit den neuen Medien?" *FUNK-Korrespondenz* 32-33 (1980): 1-5.

Moser, a leading Catholic bishop in terms of communication policy, offers some pastoral reflections on the religious possibilities of the new media. 5 pages.

[1307] Nientiedt, Klaus. "Geht die Kirche den Medien auf den Leim?" *Herder-Korrespondenz* (1985): 445-447.

This essay warns the Catholic Church not to get involved blindly in activities dealing with the new media of communication. 3 pages.

[1308] Reynolds, J. P. "Being Church in the Information Age." Thesis: Jesuit School of Theology at Berkeley, 1984.

The thesis explores various aspects of the information era and applies some of concepts drawn from its study to the Church, arguing that the Church must take advantage of the new technologies. There is a lot of summary information, but little of it is developed. Material on liturgy and feminist theology is also included. 107 pages.

[1309] Schätzler, Willi. "Die Kirchen in der BRD angesichts der Neuen Medien: Die Vorstellungen und Projekte der katholischen Kirche." *Die Neuen Medien und die Kirchen in der BRD und in Frankreich.* Ed. Josef Listl. Rhein: Kehl, 1983. 119-133.

This essay gives a survey of the churches in the Federal Republic of Germany and in France regarding activities with the new media. 15 pages.

[**1310**] Vogt, Gerburg Elisabeth. "Die Kirche vor dem Problemkomplex der neuen Medien." *Communicatio Socialis* 13 (1980): 214-224.

Vogt investigates the position of the Catholic Church regarding the new media. 11 pages.

[**1311**] Zukowski, Angela Ann and Rita V. Bowen, eds. *Religious Education and Telecommunications.* Dayton, OH: Center for Religious Telecommunications, 1985.

This booklet presents the papers from a symposium whose panelists are Catholic educators and communications personnel. The papers range in topic from the history of media use by Christianity to possible religious uses of television; the papers also vary in quality. Of special interest are the papers of Thomas Martin ("Content of Religious Television") and Angela Ann Zukowski ("Television as an Educational Medium"). 50 pages.

Name Index

All numbers refer to bibliographic entries.

Abbey, Merrill R., 94, 575
Abelman, Robert, 921, 999, 1000,
    1001, 1031, 1075, 1076
Abrams, Michael Elliot, 1077
Achtemeier, Elizabeth, 51
Adams, Doug, 52, 1236, 1237, 1238,
    1258
Adams, Henry Babcock, 95
Adams, Jay E., 96
Administrative Board of the U.S.
    Catholic Conference, 221
Aikman, Duncan, 419
Aitken, Douglas, 436
Albrecht, Gerd, 857
Albrecht, Horst, 1002
Alexander, Danny Lee, 1003
Alexander, James E., 125
Alexander, Paul J., 1133
Alexander, Ryllis Clair, 1186
Allen, Mary E., 788
Allen, Robert J., 350
Allen, Robert L., 1004
Allen, Ronald J., 560
Alley, Robert S., 274
Allmen, J. J. von, 97
Allworthy, A. W., 351
Alonso-Schökel, Luis, 460
Altizer, Thomas J. J., 461
Amalorpavadass, D. S., 787
Amani, Leo Masawe, 53
American Lutheran Church, Com-
    mission on Public Com-

munication, 789
Ames, Charlotte, 54
Amgwerd, Michael, 330
Anderson, Margaret J., 566
Anderson, Peter, 1262
Anderson, Robert, 79
Anderson, Ruth D., 352
Andre-Vincent, Ignace, 1134
Andrew, Agnellus, 353
Ansah, Paul, 286
Antoncich, Ricardo, 158
Apostolos-Cappadona, Diane,
    1135
Argamentería García, Rodolfo,
    291
Armstrong, Ben, 80, 664, 887,
    888, 1078
Arn, Win, 576, 657
Arndt, Georg, 354
Arnett, Ronald C., 577
Ashman, Chuck, 420
Aske, Sigurd, 159, 937, 938, 1304
Assmann, Hugo, 889
Associated Church Press, 81
Athenagoras, 1136
Atienza, Max, 912
Atkinson, John, 98
Augustine, 355
Austin, Charles M., 790
Aycock, Martha, 51
Ayers, R. H., 356
Ayfre, Amédée, 833, 834, 845

Baacke, Dieter, 662

Title Index

All index entries refer to bibliographic item numbers.

Subject Index

About the Compiler

PAUL A. SOUKUP, S.J., a member of the Communication Department of Santa Clara University, has explored ways of integrating theology and communication study for the past few years. He is a research associate of the Jesuit-sponsored Centre for the Study of Communication and Culture in London and has worked with the World Association for Christian Communication and the Communication Committee of the U.S. Catholic Conference. A graduate of The University of Texas at Austin (Ph.D., communication), Father Soukup also holds the M.Div. and S.T.M. from the Jesuit School of Theology at Berkeley. He is the author of *Theology and Communication: An Introduction and Review of the Literature* (London: WACC, 1983) as well as several articles on the topic.